Leading literary historian and eighteenth-century specialist Pat Rogers has long been recognized as an authority on the poet Alexander Pope. This volume addresses the many facets of Pope's world and work, and represents Rogers' important contribution over the years to Pope studies. A substantial new essay on 'Pope and the antiquarians' is presented alongside considerably revised versions of essays published in scholarly journals, which together cover most of Pope's major work, including the *Pastorals*, *Windsor-Forest*, *Rape of the Lock*, *Epistle to Arbuthnot*, and *The Dunciad*. There are general essays on form and style, Pope's social context, his dealings with the Burlington circle, and his battles with the publishing trade.

Essays on Pope gathers for the first time the best writing on this celebrated author by one of our foremost critics, and is an indispensable resource for scholars of eighteenth-century literature.

ESSAYS ON POPE

ESSAYS ON POPE

PAT ROGERS

DeBartolo Professor in the Liberal Arts, University of South Florida

CAMBRIDGE
UNIVERSITY PRESS

Published by the Press Syndicate of the University of Cambridge
The Pitt Building, Trumpington Street, Cambridge CB2 1RP
40 West 20th Street, New York, NY 10011–4211, USA
10 Stamford Road, Oakleigh, Melbourne 3166, Australia

First published 1993

Printed in Great Britain at the University Press, Cambridge

A catalogue record for this book is available from the British Library

Library of Congress cataloguing in publication data

Rogers, Pat.
Essays on Pope/Pat Rogers.
p.   cm.
'The essays in this volume have been selected from those written over the past
twenty-five years' – Pref.
Includes index.
ISBN 0 521 41869 0
1.   Pope, Alexander, 1688–1744 – Criticism and interpretation.
1.   Title
PR3634.R53   1993
821'.5 – dc20   92-297850   CIP

ISBN 0 521 41869 0 hardback

UP

for Richard and Kate Wilson
two more Beverlonians

Contents

Preface

The essays in this volume have been selected from those written over the past twenty-five years, and they represent about a third of the items published in that stretch of time. One item, Chapter 14, has not previously appeared in print. The others have been published in various places, some in relatively inaccessible locations including books which have been out of print for some time. Essays which were reprinted in *Eighteenth-Century Encounters* and *Literature and Popular Culture in Eighteenth-Century England* (both 1985) have generally been excluded. There is one exception: Chapter 10, which came out for the first time in the former volume, has been reproduced here as the issues underlying its argument remain matters of strong contention in current historiography. Not more than one essay on any given poem has been included. Whilst no attempt has been made to cover every aspect of Pope's career, the selection is designed to embrace the work of every phase and the broad range of the poet's interests.

For the most part I have confined revision to small acts of refurbishment, by way of an attempt to regularize forms of reference and to correct any mistakes. The main argument has been left undisturbed in every single essay. It would be possible to swell the footnotes by incorporating the findings of recent scholarship, but to do this in any thoroughgoing way would distort the shape of the original. In those cases where the argument of an earlier essay would be called into doubt by subsequent research, I have naturally omitted the essay from this selection. Pope scholarship moves ahead at a steady rate, and important books by critics such as Maynard Mack, Howard Weinbrot and Howard Erskine-Hill continue to affect the way in which we read the poetry. But in only one area, that of feminist scholarship, does the picture seem to have been transformed in a really significant way. As a result I have made some adjustments in passages of the essays which deal with Pope's relations with women and with sexual politics, drawing on the work of such critics as Carole Fabricant, Ellen Pollak and Valerie Rumbold. In addition, references have been supplied in the notes to a few significant recent works which bear on issues touched on in my argument without, I hope, subverting it.

It may be appropriate to say something briefly on method. In fact, the method adopted varies in accordance with the subject-matter of the essay. There would be something wrong if this were not the case, since doctrinaire method should properly bend before the primacy of the text. The aim is not to test a critical theory, but to explore particular poems and to illuminate aspects of Pope's world – his career, his contacts, his intellectual setting and his imaginative bearings. Certain essays relate Pope to the literature of the preceding century, on the grounds that he seems to me the last great poet of the English Renaissance. But other essays show him firmly rooted in his own time, for example as part of the extended Burlington circle (backward-looking as that group was in some respects).

Pope's work embodies a peculiarly fruitful dialogue between a remarkable individual talent and a highly developed sense of the traditions available to him. It follows that any enquiry into his achievement must be ready to move freely between the personal and the public – between local stylistic concerns and large historical issues. Though the essays I have selected are loosely grouped into sections on text and on context, the division is arbitrary. Robert Darnton has written, 'I confess that I do not see a clear way of distinguishing idiom from individuality. I can only testify to the importance of working back and forth between texts and contexts. That may not be much of a methodology, but it has its advantages' (*The Great Cat Massacre*, 1984, p. 262). That was said in an effort to describe the methods of cultural history, but it applies equally to literary scholarship where a writer such as Pope is involved. If I had sought a fancy title for this selection, 'idiom and individuality' would just about have done it. I hope that putting the essays together will show that what is idiomatic in Pope is both individual and general. His work was acutely conditioned by his private history – his invalidism, his religion, his inner drive to establish a great *œuvre* – but it was also marked by the impress of external matters – his friendships; his contact with the world of booksellers, professional authors and critics; and his involvement with art, architecture and gardening. Finally, it is worth recalling that Pope's supreme talent lay in satire. Satirists need plenty of friends, for support in their insecure vocation; and they need plenty of enemies for stimulus and for copy. (The sixth essay attempts to illustrate this point, with reference to the *Epistle to Arbuthnot.*)

Every year fresh work continues to pour out on Pope, testifying to his enduring interest for new generations of readers. Each shift in critical ideology confirms his central place in the life and mentality of his age. Most recently, a collection entitled *Pope: New Contexts*, edited by David Fairer (1990), has been assembled entirely by younger scholars, a heartening sign that Pope will go on being read well into the twenty-first century. This emboldens me to think that the material presented in the following fourteen essays may engage the interest of those who have come lately to Pope, and who may in turn move on to examine further aspects of this endlessly fascinating poet. It is a curious fact that the writer who might have seemed most representative of the outdated 'old' eighteenth century of belletrism should prove to be the one whose work yields most to the more advanced probings of contemporary criticism. Pope has somehow earned admission to the 'new' eighteenth century; whatever the ideological slant we give to the notion, Pope refuses to be edged out of the picture.

A revisionist Pope has some attractions, and it might be felt that a credible Pope for the 1990s must be subject to a process of destabilization and disruption. There is indeed apparent potential for such a critical strategy in the work of Maynard Mack and David Foxon especially. In his examination of the poetic manuscripts, *The Last and Greatest Art* (1984), Mack explores evidence to show how we can occasionally glimpse 'some hint of the creative chaos from which ... Pope could eventually cause a poem to "rise".' Equally, in his important survey, of *Pope and the Early Eighteenth-Century Book Trade* (1991), Foxon demonstrates that Pope adapted his poetic plans to the requirements of his publishing programme, and tailored his current work to the bespoke needs of *Works* in the press.

On the surface these findings may suggest an author radically unstable in this methods and constantly prone to changes in creative mind. But they should not be pressed too far. Mack's examination is confined to a minority of the poems, and even amongst these there are more cases where the manuscript reveals a steady progress from original conception to final version. Pope's habitual care in revision naturally produces alterations in detail and occasional shifts in emphasis; but in the majority of instances there is no dramatic reordering of the material, and there is not a shred of evidence in the poems where no manuscript survives that there was any greater degree of reconsideration. (I exclude from account here the famous process of rewriting which yielded the altered versions of *The Rape of the Lock* and *The Dunciad*: we have no manuscript evidence for the former and rather little for the latter.) Only in the case of the *Epistle to Arbuthnot*, which we now see to have emerged from an earlier poem which Pope had intended to address to William Cleland, can one speak of wholesale reorganization. In general, the evidence is negative as regards a disintegration of Pope's canon. When I remark below (p. 25) that Pope's poetry 'always knows where it is going', I mean as it ultimately appears on the page. This is not to deny that the text often had been arrived at after a laborious series of trials and errors, as is true of so many great works of literature. The point is that Pope does finally achieve a clearcut and unambiguous sense; the earlier struggles have had to be unearthed, like the lower levels of Troy, and are invisible to a reader without access to the buried manuscript drafts. It would be perverse to suggest that the published text has no stability simply because we happen to be able to disinter the hidden foundations.

The findings in Foxon's book provide stronger signs of an habitual tendency on Pope's part to change his mind on large creative issues. It is clear from this study that in the 1730s Pope sometimes started or suspended a poem partly in response to external factors, such as the availability of a given work for a forthcoming collection (depending on the copyright situation), and seems to have written items to fill gaps of a given size. Foxon takes us beyond what we already knew from such books as Miriam Leranbaum's study of *Alexander Pope's Opus Magnum 1729–1744* (1977). Leranbaum had followed the twists and turns of Pope's irresolute schemes with regard to his planned series of philosophical poems branching out from the *Essay on Man*. It is fully apparent now that the standard layout of Pope's canon, as exemplified in Warburton's edition of 1751 and almost all subsequent editions, relates to a late reconceptualization of the *œuvre* by Pope and Warburton. There are inescapable consequences for an editor here; and indeed in my volume of Pope for the Oxford Authors (1993) I have departed from precedent by printing the *Moral Essays* and *Imitations of Horace* as they appeared, spaced out chronologically, not recombined in their familiar groupings. But editing is one thing, and criticism another, and I am not convinced that this rearrangement either obliges or empowers us to read the individual poems as peculiarly tentative, provisional or unstable. That Pope was uncertain about where he might put the *Epistle to Burlington* in his *Works* does not prove that he was uncertain about what he was saying in the midst of the poem.

Recent scholarship has certainly enhanced our understanding of the context in which Pope worked, and there are some important debates under way as to where precisely he stood in relation to contemporary issues. (One thinks of essays on his politics by scholars including Howard Erskine-Hill, H. T. Dickinson and J. A. Downie.) However, apart from the fact we have generally reached no consensus on these matters, it remains the case that the main sense of the poetry is commonly not at issue in these enquiries. Much of the scholarship turns on isolated passages, on remarks in the correspondence or in Spence's anecdotes, or in the external testimony of contemporaries and subsequent biographers. It is seldom that the material reviewed would promote a wholesale recasting of one's reading of the poem, from the ground upwards. It is for this reason that the analysis of Pope's poetic response to the social world of his time (reprinted pp. 129–67 below) seems to me to preserve whatever validity it may have had on its first appearance, disregarding a few details where I have made small adjustments. If one were to write such an essay today, one might well select a few different instances, and lay slightly more emphasis on this or that aspect of the subject, in the light of twenty years' ongoing scholarship: John Cannon's study of the peerage, *Aristocratic Century* (1984), supplies a new synthesis of the facts, and several historians have filled out our understanding of the country gentry. But, as indicated, only in respect of the position of women have we come to a new recognition of phenomenological and existential realities which offer a totally fresh vista on the subject.

As has also been indicated, essays have not been reprinted where the progress of scholarship leads me to lose any degree of faith in the argument originally proposed. In other words, this selection incorporates only those essays where I stand by the original assertions. Later work might be adduced which would refine or qualify details, but in no case has the march of Popian criticism superseded the findings. One has constantly to rethink one's earlier opinions, but one does not always have to revise them. Three hundred years have now passed since the birth of Pope: we need to go on exploring his mind and art, but we should not expect to find him dissolving into a new entity every decade. These essays may help to show that the poet who was available for inspection a quarter of a century ago still remains within our gaze and still challenges us, as he did then, to confront his energy, imagination and wit. He always manages to stay ahead of efforts to limit him or relegate him to a marginal role; the more we learn of the essential history of his time the less we can afford to patronize him. Any sustained attempt to come to terms with his work is likely to end up as a mode of celebration for his astonishing achievement, and the selection of essays offered here may have the slender merit of showing cause for that celebration, whatever defects they may individually display.

Acknowledgements

I am grateful for permission to reprint essays which have previously appeared in print, in a slightly different form, as follows:

1 *Literary English since Shakespeare*, ed. G. Watson (New York, 1970), pp. 236–65.
2 *An Introduction to Pope* (London, 1976), pp. 9–19.
3 *Eighteenth-Century Studies*, XIV (1980), 1–17.
4 *Studies in Philology*, LXXVII (1980), 282–99.
5 *Review of English Studies*, XXV (1974), 25–38.
6 *British Journal for Eighteenth-Century Studies*, II (1979), 63–5.
7 *The Use of English*, (1973), 142–6.
8 *Anglia*, XCII (1974), 79–112.
9 *Writers and their Background: Alexander Pope*, ed. P. Dixon (London, 1972), pp. 101–42.
10 *Eighteenth-Century Encounters* (Brighton, 1985), pp. 75–91.
11 *The Library*, XXVII (1972), 326–31.
12 *Publishing History*, III (1978), 7–36.
13 *Durham University Journal*, XXXVI (1975), 219–26.

Item no. 14 has not previously been published; an earlier version was given as a lecture at the Pope bicentenary conference at the Yale Center for British Art in 1988.

Abbreviations

Corr	*The Correspondence of Alexander Pope*, ed. George Sherburn, 5 vols. (Oxford, 1956)
EC	*The Works of Alexander Pope*, ed. W. Elwin and W. J. Courthope, 10 vols. (London, 1871–90)
Mack, *Garden and City*	Maynard Mack, *The Garden and the City: Retirement and Politics in the Later Poetry of Pope 1731–1743* (Toronto, 1969)
Mack, *Life*	Maynard Mack, *Alexander Pope: A Life* (New Haven and London, 1985)
Prose Works	*The Prose Works of Alexander Pope*, vol. 1, ed. Norman Ault (Oxford, 1936); vol. 2, ed. Rosemary Cowler (Oxford, 1986)
Spence	Joseph Spence, *Observations, Anecdotes, and Characters of Books and Men*, ed. J. M. Osborn, 2 vols. (Oxford, 1966)
TE	*The Twickenham Edition of the Poems of Alexander Pope*, ed. J. Butt *et al.*, 11 vols. (London, 1939–69)

The Dunciad is quoted, unless otherwise indicated, from the 'B' text, that is the four-book version of 1743.

The following abbreviations are used for journal titles:

ECS	*Eighteenth-Century Studies*
JEGP	*Journal of English and Germanic Philology*
MLQ	*Modern Language Quarterly*
N&Q	*Notes & Queries*

PBA	*Proceedings of the British Academy*
PLL	*Papers on Language & Literature*
PQ	*Philological Quarterly*
RES	*Review of English Studies*
SEL	*Studies in English Literature 1500–1900*
SP	*Studies in Philology*
YES	*Yearbook of English Studies*

CHAPTER I

Pope and the syntax of satire

Spence is always invaluable. It is a shame, though, that we should have to rely on him so heavily. Anecdotes can possess charm as well as graphic immediacy, but there is a limit to the amount of serious enlightenment which they can provide. Pope must have tangled with the grammarians in his earliest youth, long before the last book of *The Dunciad* was set down. Unhappily we know very little of this stage in his development. Spence cites a remark to the effect that it was the family priest (one Banister, alias Taverner) who 'taught [him] the figures, accidence and first part of grammar'. Such nuncupatory testimony is proverbially suspect; and it would be better for this essay – which constitutes, roughly, the first part of a poetic grammar of Pope's work – if we had fuller evidence.[1] It would be nice even to have as much to go on as in the case of Martinus Scriblerus.

Martinus, it may be recalled, sampled parts of both the trivium and the quadrivium, not to mention metaphysics and gymnastics. But in Chapter VII, where one might have expected a formal analysis of the Scriblerian trivium, rhetoric and logic are joined by metaphysics. This is a pointed substitution, and we may guess at Martinus' deficiencies from the parallel information that rhetoric, too, is passed over briefly – it has already been covered in *Peri Bathous*. That Martinus did learn some grammar, doubtless of a pedantic kind, we know from his association with Conradus Crambe. This was the schoolfellow carefully chosen for him by his deluded father: a word-chopper by hereditary right. Chapter IX of the treatise, which describes 'How *Martin* became a great Critic', thus

---

[1] Spence, I, 8–10, §14–17. Spence quotes Pope's remark, 'I did not follow the grammar [in the earliest reading of the classics he attempted], but rather hunted in the authors for a syntax of my own,' (I. 11, §22). See also George Sherburn, *The Early Career of Alexander Pope* (Oxford, 1934), pp. 38–41.

describes the influence of 'the puns of Crambe...on the Mind and Studies of Martinus':

> He conceiv'd, that somewhat of a like Talent to this of Crambe, of *assembling parallel sounds*, either *syllables*, or *words*, might conduce to the Emendation and Correction of *Ancient Authors*, if applied to their Works, with the same *diligence*, and the same liberty...

Here is the hint for *Virgilius Restauratus* and the various attacks on Bentley.[2] But something more than the over-niceties of classical scholarship is at issue. This is the satiric tip of an iceberg: for Pope throughout his life was vitally concerned with words, their inter-actions, their bumps and jars, their contrast or alignment, their phonetic weight, semantic range, and structural role. For Pope, as for any other practising poet, 'the Dance of Numbers, and the Change of Rime' (Savage's phrase) came down ultimately to questions of verbal shape.

There are surprisingly few commentators on the structure of Pope's language. Geoffrey Tillotson has invoked a Euclidean image to describe what might be called the geometry of syntax.[3] That phrase recalls certain others used by Donald Davie in his absorbing book, *Articulate Energy*. Indeed, Davie speaks at one point of 'a diagram of forces' in a line of Pope's prolonging the same metaphor.[4] However, he has little to say directly on Pope; and in addition, as Christine Brooke-Rose has pointed out, the book is finally about conceptual processes rather than syntax in the narrow sense. Brooke-Rose, in her turn, confines herself to metaphor, somewhat stringently defined, and her analytic method comes uncomfortably close in places to downright parsing; besides producing statements like 'He [Shake-speare] is very good indeed on Intransitive Verbs...'[5] These are, needless to say, gaps which are prescribed by the declared scope of each book. Much more disappointing is Rebecca Price Parkin's study of Pope's 'workmanship'. Her chapter on 'Parallelism, Antithesis,

---

[2] *Memoirs of Martinus Scriblerus*, ed. C. Kerby-Miller (New Haven, Conn., 1950), pp. 118–24, 129: see also notes, pp. 243–71. 'Crambe' was defined by Nathaniel Bailey as 'a Repetition of Words, or saying the same Thing over again'. A cognate form was 'Crambo', a rhyming game; Kerby-Miller, p. 247.

[3] Geoffrey Tillotson, *Augustan Poetic Diction* (London, 1964), pp. 14, 124.

[4] Donald Davie, *Articulate Energy* (London, 1955), p. 82. Cf. 'Syntax like Mathematics', pp. 91–5. Davie's phrase 'the path of an energy through the mind' (p. 157) is a peculiarly apt one, for Pope just as much as for Wordsworth, whose poetry calls forth the expression.

[5] Christine Brooke-Rose, *A Grammar of Metaphor* (London, 1958), pp. 21, 296. Pp. 303–5 are devoted to a summary of Pope's practice, based on the rather limited sample afforded by *Eloisa to Abelard*.

and Paradox' could hardly be further from linguistic concerns. The antithesis is that of subject-matter or intention, not syntax; and in any case antithesis is a deliquescent thing for Parkin, always on the point of melting into paradox. We are indeed told that 'good poems may and do exist in which paradox is lacking or negligible' – a concession hardly wrung from the author – but paradox has itself softened into something larger and hazier than a rhetorical figure. As with the modern use of 'irony', we are dealing with psychological rather than lexical effects – paradox has become a state of mind. There are some interesting observations at the outset: 'Antithesis is a special kind of parallelism, and paradox may be defined as a special case of antithesis in which both halves of the antithesis are stated to be true.' But soon the hunt for 'tension' begins, as unending and as self-enclosed as the quest for the grail.

According to Parkin, the predominance of antithesis and parallelism 'in neoclassical English poetry, and particularly in the poetry of Pope, has long been acknowledged and commented on'.[6] That would have been my own impression until recently. But as far as Pope goes, the truth seems to be that the detailed applications of these resources have seldom been considered. Pope's imagery, his diction, his versification, even his rhyming, have found able analysts. But on his poetry as a verbal structure we have little: linguistics, not an over-modest science in general, has kept unusually silent, and criticism at large has exhibited less valour than discretion. To be blunt, W. K. Wimsatt is the only guide offering his services on this expedition, apart from those who promise an easy day for a lady.

I

Wimsatt distinguishes between 'verse, where patterns of form do not…support parallels of stated meaning, but run counter to meaning': and prose, where symmetrical syntax 'comes fairly to the aid of logic'. In his view, it is rare to find 'equalities of verse' coinciding with 'parallels of meaning'.[7] On this showing, it is rhyme

---

[6] Rebecca Price Parkin, *The Poetic Workmanship of Alexander Pope* (Minneapolis, Minn., 1955), pp. 66–84.
[7] See for example W. K. Wimsatt, 'One Relation of Rhyme to Reason', in *The Verbal Icon* (Lexington, Ky., 1967), pp. 154ff. Wimsatt's other valuable contributions to this broad field of study include *The Prose Style of Samuel Johnson* (New Haven, Conn., 1941), especially Chs. I, II, on parallelism and antithesis, as well as Ch. IV, 'The Consistency of Johnson's Style'; and his edition of *Alexander Pope: Selected Poetry and Prose* (New York, 1951), especially pp. xxii–xxxiii.

especially which dislocates the potential logic of the verse form by means of its irrational and irrelevant congruence. My own view is that a distinction has indeed to be drawn between the two modes of discourse, but that it should be drawn on different grounds. The basic fact is that in prose syntax any degree of parallelism is willed and therefore noticeable. It is a patterning imposed on recalcitrant material, or at least on neutral material. By contrast poetry is ductile, its inherent structure being hospitable to repetitive statements of any kind. To put this in concrete historical terms, we may distinguish (1) the typical symmetries of Renaissance prose, whether Ciceronian, Senecan, Euphuistic, 'baroque' or however labelled; and (2) the equivalences, positive or negative, achieved by Pope and others in the heroic couplet. In the first case, even where there is a deliberate attempt 'to avert an impending symmetry, to sabotage in advance what threatens to evolve into too fussy a balance',[8] there is a more or less regular effect attained by setting one member of a sentence against another. The sentence carves out its own channel, and it is within the control of the writer to fix its external bounds, as the ideas conveyed seem to demand. But Pope is working with another independent variable, the couplet itself. And even if we disregard rhyme for the moment, it is plain that many syntactical parallels will be swimming with the tide of the verse. The line unit in its own form asserts an identity and a balance. It follows that symmetry, either of sound, of meaning or of construction, is less immediately apparent: the congruence may be put down to the pressure of the verse rhythm, or may even go unobserved insofar as it is a separate entity from that rhythm.

An example will help. In his dialogue with Fortescue (Horace, *Satires*, II.i)[9] the satirist replies to his friend's hint that excessive boldness will call out physical assault in retaliation:

> *P*. What? arm'd for *Virtue* when I point the Pen,
> Brand the bold Front of shameless, guilty Men,
> Dash the proud Gamester in his gilded Car,

---

[8] Jonas A. Barish, *Ben Jonson and the Language of Prose Comedy* (Cambridge, Mass., 1960), p. 71. Much of Barish's excellent discussion is germane to the present essay: see for instance his comments on the 'slight sense of *offness*' favoured by baroque writers (p. 73), which tallies with many of Tillotson's observations on the fondness in Pope for 'unequal balance' – *On the Poetry of Pope* (Oxford, 2nd edn, 1950), pp. 127–8. For the Renaissance background, see also Brian Vickers, *Francis Bacon and Renaissance Prose* (Cambridge, 1968), Ch. IV, 'Syntactical Symmetry'.

[9] Quotations and line-references follow *TE*. For *The Dunciad*, see pp. 98–128 below.

Bare the mean Heart that lurks beneath a Star;
Can there be wanting to defend Her Cause,
Lights of the Church, or Guardians of the Laws?
Could pension'd *Boileau* lash in honest Strain
Flatt'rers and Bigots ev'n in *Louis*' Reign?
Could Laureate *Dryden* Pimp and Fry'r engage,
Yet neither *Charles* nor *James* be in a Rage?
And I not strip the Gilding off a Knave,
Un-plac'd, un-pension'd, no Man's Heir, or Slave?
I will, or perish in the gen'rous Cause.   (105–17)

An attentive reader will be alive to the successive questions incorporated within the third, fourth, fifth and sixth couplets here. The effect Pope seeks is to imply that his desire to speak out is as well justified as that of earlier satirists, and that his situation is broadly equivalent. The parallelism in the construction asserts the social and moral identity which Pope is claiming. And, of course, the sudden shift to a blunt affirmative style ('I will...') carries all the more impact because of the successive queries – rhetorical as they are – which have preceded this line. What might easily escape observation is an earlier series of equivalent statements. From the second line to the fourth Pope places a strong stress on the first syllable of each verse. Again, every one of these stresses falls on an active transitive verb, occupying the first part of a trochaic (i.e. inverted) foot. Following this verb we get a direct object in the formula 'the + moral adjective (monosyllabic) + noun', and then a phrase qualifying that object. The total effect is to distract attention from the line unit as such. The parallelism runs across the couplet form; the rhymes are in any case rather flat and unassertive; and the emphasis on the initial verb also contributes to this process. It might be said that Pope achieves an eloquent syntactical form by modifying and even impairing his basic metrical scheme.

This passage gives us, in fact, a disguised parison, as the rhetoricians would say: that is, a series of clauses using the same parts of speech in the same order. Analysts of Renaissance prose often set down the structure of a sentence in a kind of visual lay-out.[10] There is some point in doing that, since the diagram enacts the reader's response; its contours are a fact additional to the plain prose utterance. But the verse parison just looked at already contains its own diagrammatic statement: indeed, arguably, it offers a formal

[10] See for instance Vickers, pp. 115–40. For the rhetorical figures alluded to in the text, see Vickers, p. 97, and Wimsatt, *Verbal Icon*, pp. 176–7.

tautology. Pope's use of the standard symmetrical forms which Puttenham and others catalogue allows for that fact. Generally he avoids simple repetitive formulae, since the ineluctable repetition of the verses themselves provides a mode of continuity – any naked parallelism superadded can only appear jejune. So we find him indulging in what Tillotson calls 'significant variation'; that is, bending versification or sentence-structure so as to produce some uncovenanted or even discordant effect.

Another subdued version of the parisonic device (this time involving a train of direct objects) is found in the *Epistle to Arbuthnot*. It occurs during Pope's celebrated vindication of his own career – immediately after the couplet describing his conversion from 'Fancy's Maze' to 'moraliz'd…song':

> That not for Fame, but Virtue's better end,
> He stood the furious Foe, the timid Friend,
> The damning Critic, half-approving Wit,
> The Coxcomb hit, or fearing to be hit;
> Laugh'd at the loss of Friends he never had,
> The dull, the proud, the wicked, and the mad;
> The distant Threats of Vengeance on his head,
> The Blow unfelt, the Tear he never shed;
> The Tale reviv'd, the Lye so oft o'erthrown;
> Th' imputed Trash, and Dulness not his own;
> The Morals blacken'd when the Writings scape;
> The libel'd Person, and the pictur'd Shape;
> Abuse on all he lov'd, or lov'd him, spread,
> A Friend in Exile, or a Father, dead;
> The Whisper that to Greatness still too near,
> Perhaps, yet vibrates on his SOVEREIGN's Ear –
> Welcome for thee, fair Virtue! all the past:
> For thee, fair Virtue! welcome ev'n the *last*!   (342–59)

Commentators have been so busy explaining the allusions that they have scarcely had time to remark the subtle technique or the ends it serves. The long catalogue of nouns may be regarded as in apposition to the initial object 'Foe'. That places a huge emphasis on the verb 'stood', which has to carry all the rest of this swollen predicate on its back. I take the meaning to be 'withstood', with a hint of the modern sense, 'put up with' – the nobly suffering satirist's Christ-like capacity to forbear every ill done to him thus indicated. All these can be endured for the sake of virtue.

In moving from grammar to rhetoric, however, it is noteworthy that the passage involves a sort of anaphoric construction. That is to say, the repeated phrases almost all start with the word 'the'. Now this is of course the greyest-looking word in English, though recent analysts have shown that the definite article is neither as definite nor as innocent as that. The result is to be scarcely aware of the parallelism set up by its use; when the passage is abstracted from its context, as I have just abstracted it, the repetition may be obvious, but in normal reading I doubt if many are conscious other than in the dimmest way of its anaphoric basis. And that is as Pope would wish it. Iterative constructions generally carry a hectoring air with them. Here the poet is seeking a more muted kind of symmetry. His employment of phrase introduced by 'the' performs several functions. (1) It lends a certain impersonality to the catalogue of outrages; 'the Writings' are those of 'one Poet' (line 336) rather than those simply of the actual Alexander Pope. This not only deflects the charge of egotism: it serves wider imaginative purposes, by suggesting that others might have been in Pope's situation and might not have behaved as stoically as he did. This effect is strengthened by the participle phrases, of which more in a moment. (2) It implies a factuality, an agreed historicity, in the events to which it refers. A grammarian has written that '*the* assumes familiarity or previous knowledge'. Pope exploits the article to suggest that there is no argument about the threats, say, having been offered; he insinuates the idea that the only debate is about what exactly they constituted or why they were offered. (3) At the same time the formula conveys a measure of generalization; *the* tale is one of many, *the* lie 'often' encountered. (The article comes to the aid of the adverb; it is almost as if a continuous tense of the verb, such as the imperfect, were used.) The coxcomb is any coxcomb, not worth identifying more closely. An entire line is built up of these emblematic forms ('The dull, the proud...'), making it sound almost like a modern movie title. These are representative men, and women: Pope's syntax asserts that there are many more where they came from. (4) In this context any noun without an article, or with a different form of the article, will stand out. With line 346, 'the Friends' would suggest that they really were friends if only for a moment: the omission of 'the' indicates 'the loss of such so-called friends...' 'Dulness' is a sprawling mass unable to bear the definition even of a simple article; the chiasmic line allows 'Dulness' to be qualified not merely by the symmetrically placed 'not his own', but also by the original epithet 'imputed' – which would not be possible if 'the' were repeated before the second noun. Abuse is scattered casually, piecemeal. And finally there is the sudden shift to 'a Friend', the special case of Atterbury, and 'a Father', the unique parental role. In a manner both economical and moving, Pope has switched from the general or public case to the intimate: grammar directs the change.

Nor is this the only interesting feature of the syntax. A cursory reading will disclose the fondness for participles: more especially, for past participles serving as predicative adjectives. Or rather, the strict grammatical form is predicative, the implied sense is perhaps equivalent to that of an absolute construction. So 'imputed Trash' has the force of a passive verb; trash has been and is still being imputed to the poet. So too with 'hit', 'unfelt', 'reviv'd', 'o'er-thrown', 'blacken'd', 'libell'd', 'pictur'd', and so on. Each of these words could be expanded into a full predication. The pattern would be: 'I do not feel these blows', and 'They continue to libel my person and to depict my physical appearance.' But Pope's refusal to commit himself to such a positive assertion is deliberate; the poetry gains because it leaves the reader with an agentless process of denunciation and terrorism. A sinister third-person anonymity attaches to the oppressors of Pope – they are everywhere. If the satirist had come straight out and named his enemies, the impression would be so much the less threatening. Speaking of the passive voice in a different context, Christine Brooke-Rose has well said: 'The very helplessness of the subject, even in metaphoric relation to the verb, emphasises the instrumental ... force of the indirect object which is really responsible for the metaphoric change.'[11] Similarly, Pope uses an implied passive, built into the actual syntactical function of the participle, to convey his own open, though not vulnerable, position before the onslaughts of his detractors. Once more, grammar enacts a complete human situation. If not quite 'a little tragic plot', the repetitive construction does much in its own structural identity to make Pope's imaginative point.

This kind of pseudo-parallelism is among the commonest effects of Pope's verse. There is likewise a pseudo-antithesis, an opposition which turns out to be less and less complete the longer it is sustained.

---

[11] Brooke-Rose, pp. 229–30. The same writer comments, 'Pope ... really lets himself go with verbs. He uses proportionately more intransitive verb metaphors than any other poet' (p. 235). Even where the strict grammatical form is not that of a verb, Pope often manages to get an active propulsive force into other parts of speech.

In a short form this trick can be seen when Pope unleashes his famous couplet on Lady Mary Wortley Montagu:

> From furious *Sappho* scarce a milder Fate,
> P-x'd by her Love, or libell'd by her Hate...[12]

Here the grammar supplies a suggestion of alternatives, but the sense is clearly 'it's all the same either way'. Pope is fond of such spurious adversative constructions: in the epistle *To Augustus* we get

> But those who cannot write, and those who can,
> All ryme, and scrawl, and scribble, to a man.   (187–8)

There *ought* to be a difference between the two groups, Pope is saying, but in practice they both contribute to the flood of unwanted book-making. Similarly, at the end of that harsh yet beautiful vision of the condition of woman, which Pope inserts in his *Epistle to a Lady*:

> See how the World its Veterans rewards!
> A Youth of frolicks, an old Age of Cards,
> Fair to no purpose, artful to no end,
> Young without Lovers, old without a Friend,
> A Fop their Passion, but their Prize a Sot,
> Alive, ridiculous, and dead, forgot!   (243–8)

Pope employs what is generally called the antithetical style, yes. But he does so assert an equivalence rather than an antimony. The alternatives set out on either side of the caesura ought to be contradictory: the sad reality is that they are not contradictory at all. As a result the perversity and mutability of this world stand forth all the more plainly. Life, in belying the expectations of the heroic verse form,[13] exposes the shallow optimism of those who look to find human felicity wherever they go. The last line but one, with its beautiful

---

[12] Hor. *Sat.* II.i.84–5. There is a kind of alliterative chiasmus here, very common in Pope: cf. '*R*iches that *v*ex, and *v*anities that ti*r*e.' The only reference to such a device I have seen is that of F. W. Hilles, 'Johnson's Poetic Fire', *From Sensibility to Romanticism*, ed. F. W. Hilles and H. Bloom (New York, 1965), p. 72.

[13] Tillotson writes that the Augustans 'saw man as an oxymoron, a cross-hatching, a contradiction in terms...To say what they saw inevitably required the couplet' (*Augustan Poetic Diction*, p. 15). Arguably the last sentence overstates the matter. But in any case it is clear that the couplet is capable of expressing both massive certainties and prim compromise. According to W. H. Auden ('Pope', *From Anne to Victoria*, ed. B. Dobrée (London, 1937), p. 100), 'no form will express everything, as each form is particularly good at expressing something. Forms are chosen by poets because the most important part of what they have to say seems to go better with that form than any other; there is generally a margin which remains unsaid...' In my view Pope often gains effects by playing off what the couplet *seems* to assert against what reality proclaims. For brief but excellent comments on the passage from the *Epistle to a Lady* quoted in the text, see Allan Rodway, 'By Algebra to Augustanism', *Essays on Style and Language*, ed. R. Fowler (London, 1966), pp. 63–9.

phonetic architecture, carries within its own grammar the clue to the entire technique. Really the word 'but' is a fraudulent usage. The genuine link to connect such indistinguishable fates would be 'and'. In the final line, however, there is an authentic choice offered. Such an old age of tedium and dishonour may be a living death. But presumably most women would prefer to be alive and ridiculous than dead and forgotten. The conjunction we might have anticipated in this case is 'but'. That the connotations of such basic linguistic particles has been blurred is no accident. This is the grammar of paradox, these are the language-games played by satire.[14]

In Chapter X of *Peri Bathous*, Pope indulged himself in a little fun at the expense of Lee, Ambrose Philips, Blackmore, and others, with a section called 'The Antithesis, or Seesaw'. The trope was defined as the figure 'whereby Contraries and Oppositions are balanced in such a way, as to cause a reader to remain suspended between them, to his exceeding delight and recreation'.[15] The examples cited show that Pope had in mind a sort of mechanical oxymoron – 'The Gods look pale to see us look so red.' Pope himself never fell victim to this functionless mode of opposing things, any more than he did to the mindless parallelism which lesser writers exacted from the couplet form; except that, as Peter Dixon has neatly illustrated, he can employ 'deliberately mechanical balance and repetition' for a special purpose.[16] We rarely see Pope 'cultivating expressive forms for their own sake'.[17] He resists the easier, more automatic effects of the heroic couplet in favour of a more inward method. Once more the *Epistle to Arbuthnot* will provide an instance:

> Yet then did *Gildon* draw his venal quill;
> I wish'd the man a dinner, and sate still:
> Yet then did *Dennis* rave in furious fret;
> I never answer'd, I was not in debt:
> If want provok'd, or madness made them print,
> I wag'd no war with *Bedlam* or the *Mint*.   (151–6)

---

[14] For interesting comment on the use of these conjunctions, cf. Barish, p. 17; Brooke-Rose, pp. 80–7, 303. John Dennis senses in an obscure way Pope's fondness for pseudo-linkage, whereby 'he seems to take pains to bring *something* into a Conjunction Copulative with *nothing*, in order to beget *nothing*'. See his *Remarks on the Rape of the Lock* (1728), extracted by J. D. Hunt (ed.), *Pope: The Rape of the Lock A Casebook* (London, 1968), p. 64. On Pope's deceptive use of the word 'but', see A. L. Binns, '"Linguistic" Reading', in Fowler, p. 125.
[15] Quoted from Wimsatt, *Pope*, p. 334.
[16] Peter Dixon, *The World of Pope's Satires* (London, 1968), p. 88. See also p. 96, on the 'persistent balancing of the half-lines' in an imitation of Donne, so as to mime 'the minuet-like progression of...court ritual'.   [17] Wimsatt, *Johnson*, p. 49.

Initially one supposes that Gildon represents poverty, Dennis madness. Yet in the second line quoted, Pope emphasizes his own passivity – which in turn suggests the fury of Gildon, not of Dennis. Similarly the fourth line constitutes in effect an answer to the first: Pope's freedom from poverty allows him to escape the 'raving' of Dennis. In the last couplet appears a typical chiasmic sequence, want/madness/Bedlam/Mint. Moreover want 'provokes', that is, stirs up and excites – the postponement of the composite object 'them' means that the verb attains an absolute or intransitive force. This last is a common device in Pope. The total effect of this degree of interplay is to indicate that madness and poverty are very near allied. In Pope's world of Dunces, the Bedlamite and the pauper are of imagination all compact. By the time we reach line 155, the word 'or' has become little more than a sign of equation. Behind the superficial antithesis lies an inescapable identity. Behind the conscious iteration used to mark Pope's own position ('I wish'd ... I never answer'd ... I wag'd') lies a complex series of adjustments which go to illustrate the *unlikeness* of Pope from his oppressors.[18]

II

If, then, Pope is not confined to the cruder mechanisms of Augustan verse, there is much in the satiric tradition that he does exploit. He was not one to reject valuable effects simply because they were obvious or close at hand. The inheritance he enjoyed was one descending primarily from Waller, Dryden, and perhaps Prior.[19] Now, 'The facility provided by the couplet is that it requires the

---

[18] Pope habitually breaks up lists by one means or another. A fair example would be the beginning of *Sober Advice from Horace*, where the transition from common to proper nouns serves to fix the roster in the here and now (i.e. to resolve it), and yet paradoxically to disrupt the previous smooth sequence:

> The Tribe of Templars, Play'rs, Apothecaries,
> Pimps, Poets, Wits, Lord *Fanny's*, Lady *Mary's*.   (1–2)

A double response is called for. Actually Hervey and Lady Mary are unmistakable, unique; but there is a subliminal idea of 'et hoc genus omne', so that the fearsome couple both belong to the list and subvert its reality. The repeated heavy stresses aid the process. 'Lord' is actually in a weak position, metrically, but like 'Pimps' it receives a fairly strong emphasis. We are drawn to feel that it is the lordship and ladyship of the couple (as well as their peculiar demerits) which align them with the rest of the tribe. For the use of the plural number, see p. 109 below.

[19] It is often forgotten that Prior's use of octosyllables in *Alma* by no means represents an invariable choice. *Solomon* antedates the greater part of Pope's major work, excluding the *Rape* and the *Iliad*.

deployment of specific meanings, moment by moment: every shot has to count.'[20] In other words, the couplet – unlike, say, the Pindaric ode as then understood and practised – tends to deal with one thing at a time. Its structure imposes a type of serial form on the material.[21] Hence the readiness with which it accommodates itself to itemization: one thinks of the 'receipt' or recipe pattern which Pope used more than once. But yet again Pope's inclination is to turn the inventory into something else. His lists, which at first appear to follow passively the sequence of the line-units, generally prove to have more autonomy, more life of their own. One might instance the description of Narcissa ('Now deep in Taylor... Now drinking citron... Now Conscience chills her...').[22] Or take this passage from the *Epistle to Cobham*:

> See the same man, in vigour, in the gout;
> Alone, in company; in place, or out;
> Early at Business, and at Hazard late;
> Mad at a Fox-chace, wise at a Debate;
> Drunk at a Borough, civil at a Ball,
> Friendly at Hackney, faithless at Whitehall.   (130–5)

The alternatives start off mildly enough, with each side capable of an innocent interpretation – gout did not necessarily imply dissolute living. As we move on, the more aggressive meanings force their way to the surface. But at least, if it is unworthy always to be gaming late into night, there is the corresponding virtue of being 'early at Business'. At this point, the stress is on the 'puzzling Contraries' which Pope has been anatomizing. By the last couplet, our reaction has grown more suspicious. If the man is drunk at his constituency, then doubtless that is because he has been spending his time (to quote Bubb Dodington's immortal phrase) 'in the infamous and disagreeable compliance with the low habits of venal wretches'.[23] That

---

[20] Denis Donoghue, 'Swift as Poet', in *Swift Revisited*, ed. Denis Donoghue (Cork, 1968), p. 81.

[21] Atterbury characteristically deplored the fact that there was 'no distinction of parts' in English writers before Waller: see Geoffrey Tillotson, *Pope and Human Nature* (Oxford, 1959), p. 186. One recalls, too, Johnson's complaint that Prior's glorified Spenserian stanza became 'unnecessarily tedious' – 'an uniform mass of ten lines thirty-five times repeated, inconsequential and slightly connected, must weary both the ear and the understanding' (*Life of Prior*). The 'want of method' which is the 'great defect' of *The Seasons* (*Life of Thomson*) may likewise have been produced by the inconsequentiality of blank verse, as opposed to the 'connectedly various' couplet – a misappropriation of Tillotson's phrase for Pope himself (*On the Poetry of Pope*, p. 159).

[22] *Epistle to a Lady*, 63–8: cf. Horace, *Ep.* II.i.156–60.

[23] *The Political Journal of George Bubb Dodington*, ed. J. Carswell and L. A. Dralle (Oxford, 1965), p. 264.

he is civil at the mayoral ball, then, suggests no very honourable motive. This impression is confirmed in the last verse quoted. The members for Middlesex were nominated at Hackney, so the sense is patent: the man is ready with promises before the election, faithless afterwards. Both the alternatives offered are ignoble. Under cover of suggesting the variety of human character, Pope has insinuated one of his miniature *exempla* to reveal the present state of political morality.

The duplicity of his technique rests on a simple psychological fact. Augustan heroic verse is constructed around near-recurrences, elements which seem to resemble their predecessors but do not quite. In reality the poem is moving on, but the almost-congruous members (rhyme, metric pattern, often syntax) lull us into believing that no advance has been made. As Denis Donoghue says, the ode delights in postponement.[24] The couplet, whatever its putative delays, entails constant progression. This is promoted partly by internal workings. With the line, 'Poxed by her Love, or libell'd by her Hate', much of the impetus derives from the placing of the two crucial words at either end of the verse. The whole metrical scheme springs shut, with the hinge after the fourth syllable. Pope uses all kinds of means to give his lines this self-enclosed energy. Other poetic techniques, in other historical circumstances, have been designed to blur the divisions between separate units, to allow free movement back and forth among the constituent parts of the poem. But the entire aesthetic of Augustan England was ranged against such a practice – its entire ethic, too, one might almost say. The strength of eighteenth-century poetry at its best is that it is good at knowing the syntactic moment to leave. Pope's verse, above all, gains momentum and life from its refusal to merge one statement into another. Typically he achieves continuity by linguistic signals, by partial repetition or by some kind of verbal gesture ('Now...now/Hence.../Hear this! and...'). What he does *not* do is dislocate the structure of his language so that the sequence of ideas fluctuates or turns back on itself.[25]

---

[24] Donoghue, p. 79.

[25] One of the most misleading passages in Pope occurs in the *Epistle to Burlington*. We need, it may be, a new Laokoon in Pope criticism. Certainly the poet has the skill 'decently to hide': but he pleasingly confounds us by quite other methods than varying and concealing the bounds of his verse. Or at least: if the limits of the couplets resemble a ha-ha, they do so all the more because you cannot after all get rid of a boundary, or move it, just by concealing it from the curious gaze.

Pope's description of Stanton Harcourt, in a letter to Lady Mary Wortley Montagu (dated 1718 by George Sherburn in *Corr*, I, 505) illustrates very clearly the *puzzled* reaction

The phrase 'verbal gesture' perhaps calls for explanation. At its simplest, this takes the form of mimetic construction, where the connectives act out grammatically the relationship described. Sometimes this is done with prepositions, as with this passage from a satiric prose work of Pope, *A Further Account of the most Deplorable Condition of Mr Edmund Curll* (1716). A porter is sent to find Curll's authors at various addresses, including 'At the Laundresses, at the Hole in the Wall in *Cursitors* Alley, up three Pairs of Stairs, the Author of my *Church History* – if his Flux be over – you may also speak to the Gentleman who lyes by him in the Flock Bed, my *Index-maker*.' Or again: 'At a Tallow-chandlers in *Petty France*, half way under the blind Arch...' or 'At the Bedsted and Bolster, a Musick House in *Morefields*, two Translators in a Bed together.'[26] Now what Pope does with physical locations here, by means of prepositions and adverbs mainly, he does with moral relations elsewhere. And not necessarily in a context of satire: a straightforward case is the celebrated opening to *Windsor-Forest*:

> The Groves of Eden, vanish'd now so long,
> Live in Description, and look green in Song:
> *These*, were my Breast inspir'd with equal Flame,
> Like them in Beauty, should be like in Fame.
> Here Hills and Vales, the Woodland and the Plain,
> Here Earth and Water seem to strive again,
> Not *Chaos*-like together crush'd and bruis'd,
> But as the World, harmoniously confus'd:
> Where Order in Variety we see,
> And where, tho' all things differ, all agree.
> Here waving Groves a chequer'd Scene display,
> And part admit and part exclude the Day;
> As some coy Nymph her Lover's warm Address
> Nor quite indulges, nor can quite repress.   (7–20)

And so on. Obviously the controlling fact in this passage is the care with which the integrity of the line-unit is preserved. The major syntactical divisions all coincide with line-endings; minor breaks in the sense fall at the caesural pause. More remarkable, however, is something which does not necessarily follow from that state of affairs. In every case the beginning of the verse (after the very first,

---

which men of the time display when 'the whole is so disjointed, & the parts so detacht from one another, & yet so joining again one can't tell how'. To this degree a house, like a poem, ought to be an organized arrangement, a configuration whose parts should relate to one another in an intelligible fashion. But by quoting this instance I am no doubt breaking the self-denying ordinance I have just set.   [26] *Prose Works*, I, 278–9.

announcing the subject) conveys the relation of the ideas presented to those which have gone before. On occasions the relationship is spatial (*here/where*, and so on); sometimes it is one of analogy (*like/as*); sometimes the link is negative or restricted (*not/and part*). Throughout, the connectives provide us with a conducted tour not merely of the literal forest but also of its imaginative significance for Pope – its historical and mythopoeic identity. And these verbal signals emphasize the discrete nature of the units, structural or metrical, by the very act of describing their mutual relationship.

A more complex instance occurs in the delightful poem to Teresa Blount, on her banishment to the country after the coronation in 1714. The theme of the girl exiled from the pleasures of the town was a stock satiric occasion: *Rambler*, numbers 42 and 46, take it up. In Pope's version, fair Zephalinda is wafted away from gay sparks to 'old-fashion'd halls, dull aunts, and croaking rooks':

> She went from Op'ra, park, assembly, play,
> To morning walks, and pray'rs three hours a day;
> To pass her time 'twixt reading and Bohea,
> To muse, and spill her solitary Tea,
> Or o'er cold coffee trifle with the spoon,
> Count the slow clock, and dine exact at noon;
> Divert her eyes with pictures in the fire,
> Hum half a tune, tell stories to the squire;
> Up to her godly garret after sev'n,
> There starve and pray, for that's the way to heav'n.   (13–22)

Pope begins by reiterating the change enacted in Zephalinda's journey: she went 'to plain-work, and to purling brooks...' Having accustomed us to this transition, he shifts from the prepositional 'to' and drifts, inconsequentially as it seems, into the infinitive. A series of verbs, strictly in this same form, is now employed in the succeeding lines: *muse/spill/trifle/count/dine/divert/hum/tell*. There frequency answers to the tedious routine of life: the absence of a subject robs them of the activity we associate with a verb. They are things going on without Zephalinda's conscious agency, almost without her connivance. Three of these truncated infinitives mark the opening of three lines in a row; then the miserable article 'up' – again a verbless directive, appropriate to trance-like states such as sleepwalking. Then two more grey non-activities, as Zephalinda sees them: starve and pray. The fulcral point occurs at the strange cacophonous juncture 'Or o'er cold coffee...' In the light of what has already been said, it should be no surprise that this grammatical alternative turns out to be for Zephalinda no human alternative at all.

Geoffrey Tillotson has written of Pope's poems that 'they assemble the least fluid parts of speech and yet escape congestion either of meaning of metre' – an observation recalling Owen Barfield's similar description of 'architectural' poetry, where 'the poet is working in solid masses, not in something fluid'.[27] The fact is that Pope was not after fluidity, insofar as that represents a poetic virtue to us today. He wanted poetry, just as Samuel Johnson did, to render the existing categories of reality, and not to blur those essential differences in nature or in magnitude which were present in every sphere of life – moral, social, physical, or metaphysical. The duty of language was to overcome the inarticulate energy of mere flux.

III

It is possible to distinguish broadly between two methods of organization in poetry: I will call these closed and open syntax. The extreme form of open syntax is found in such modes of verse as imagism, where prose logic has been abandoned and the only continuum is one of figurative association. But the method is found in a good deal of older poetry, and it does not necessarily imply a breakdown of *all* 'logical' sequence. The differentia lies in the fact that, where the syntax is open, there may be more than one separate – indeed competing – manner of linking the units of sense, each of which is logically feasible and poetically convincing.

One index of this state of affairs is the employment of light punctuation. Of Puttenham's three 'intermissions of sound', open syntax characteristically utilizes the comma as against the colon or the period.[28] The reason is obvious. The comma is a fluid stop; it *may* mark a break in thought, but it may not. And whereas a full stop firmly closes one segment and introduces another, the comma vacillates – its effect may, so to speak, stretch forward or back. The words it governs (I do not think that is too strong a term) may be affected in quite different ways. To this extent, it offers one more type of ambiguity: but an ambiguity dependent not on the semantic role of the words in question so much as on their structural role.

[27] Tillotson, *On the Poetry of Pope*, p. 104; Owen Barfield, *Poetic Diction* (London, 2nd edn, 1952), p. 96.
[28] There are some useful remarks on this topic in Ian A. Gordon, *The Movement of English Prose* (London, 1966), pp. 20–2.

To speak again in general terms, I would regard open syntax as the preferred mode of what might be styled the poetry of contemplation. By this I mean poetry which is absorbed by the sheer grandeur or beauty or multiplicity of things as they are. It belongs to the literature of *rapture*, more than anything else. In short, open syntax is appropriate to a verse where relationships are in doubt, where the simple quiddity or mere existence of things is more important than the way in which they interact. The presence or immanence of any object or idea can be rendered by nouns, even if the connectives are in doubt or removed. To express a *state* requires no propositions or verbs. As with the project in the Laputan Academy, the poet need carry round with him only names for *things* – provided we take that word to cover abstractions too. The poetry of contemplation tends to move in a series of jerks from one object or essence to another; it operates like one of those guidebooks which dilates impressively on the merits of each tourist attraction, but never explains how the traveller can get from one to the next. It is a poetry of localized celebration, not one of direction-finding.

To put the matter in this way is to invite the suspicion that a hostile judgement is intended. In order to eliminate that impression, I will cite briefly three outstanding examples of the style I have attempted to describe. Firstly, the eleventh stanza of Milton's *Nativity Hymn*:

> At last surrounds their sight
> A Globe of circular light,
>   That with long beams the shame-fac't night array'd,
> The helmed Cherubim
> And sworded Seraphim
>   Are seen in glittering ranks with wings displaid,
> Harping in loud and solemn quire,
> With unexpressive notes to Heav'ns new-born Heir.

Writing of such sustained elevation and majesty needs no routine critical commendation, which can only usurp the function of a formal vote of thanks. It is noteworthy, however, that nouns and adjectives dominate the stanza. The main verbs are few and rather colourless: *surrounds, array'd* (in subordinate clause), *are seen*. All the glitter and all the dignity proceed from the evocative or surprising epithets (*shame-fac't, unexpressive*), as well as the clear ringing nouns, usually rhyme-words. It is generally dangerous to place too much reliance on punctuation in early texts, but we know enough of Milton's own intentions to be sure that his best effects were not achieved through the drunken invention of apprentice compositor X or Y. It is interesting, then, to note the total absence of heavier stops. The stanza was not, of course, chosen at random. But it is not untypical. Stanzas xiv and xv also restrict themselves to commas as far as intermediate punctuation goes: and so do the second and third stanzas.

Not altogether dissimilar is the technique of this portion of Blake's *Jerusalem* (c. 4, lxxxix). Here there are three colons, but they divide off parts of a list, rather than serving their habitual grammatical end of marking syntactically discrete statements.

> Tho' divided by the Cross & Nails & Thorns & Spear
> In cruelties of Rahab & Tirzan, permanent endure
> A terrible indefinite Hermaphroditic form,
> A Wine-press of Love & Wrath, double, Hermaphroditic,
> Twelvefold in Allegoric pomp, in selfish holiness:
> The Pharisaion, the Grammateis, the Presbiterion,
> The Archiereus, the Iereus, the Saddusaion: double
> Each withoutside of the other, covering eastern heaven.
> Thus was the Covering Cherub reveal'd, majestic image
> Of Selfhood, Body put off, the Antichrist accursed,
> Covern'd with precious stones: a Human Dragon terrible
> And bright stretch'd over Europe & Asia gorgeous.
> In three nights be devour'd the rejected corse of death.

The very real power this stanza develops is generated by a sort of galvanic running, jumping, and standing still – on the spot. There is throughout a marked preference for heaping up and simply presenting: and so lists of nouns, avoidance of main verbs, particularly active, transitive forms, and repeated appositional devices. Open syntax often figures itself as a search for covert methods of achieving the force, if not the reality, of apposition. Until the last line, Blake confines himself to indicating and naming.

Finally, a familiar instance from Hopkins: the fourth stanza of *The Wreck of the Deutschland*:

> I am soft sift
> In an hourglass – at the wall
> Fast, but mined with a motion, a drift,
> And it crowds and it combs to the fall;
> I steady as a water in a well, to a poise, to a pane,
> But roped with, always, all the way down from the tall
> Fells or flanks, of the voel, a vein
> Of the gospel proffer, a pressure, a principle, Christ's gift.

The peculiar lurching motion of this verse is aided by a number of technical features, notably the stanza-form (an impeded expansive movement) and the alliteration. There is a slightly garbled style of repetition, as though produced by a speech defect – the strange locution '*a* water in a well' has something of the effect of an involuntary reiteration, found in a Spoonerism or a tongue-twister: just as people will say, after a number of rapid attempts, 'The Poleith police dismisseth uth'. The net result is a series of parallel forays, a crab-wise advancement towards the final two words, where the spluttering alliteration is at length resisted. In Hopkins's case, the syntax is at once more complex, more interesting and more important than in either Milton or Blake. Nevertheless, it is evident that key moments of transition are marked by a comma; that, apart from line four, verbs play virtually no part in the organization; and that the line-unit has little to do with the developing sense of the stanza.

Hopkins, to take another famous example, is interested in the windhover for what the bird is in itself. The falcon may represent the glory of God as mediated to us in 'Brute beauty and valour and act': but the poet is not concerned with its position in the scale of things, earthly or divine. Augustan poetry, on the other hand, is very often about social intercourse, 'conversation', ideas of hierarchy and subordination, of reciprocity – trade is the great image of moralists, poets and dramatists alike, as in Lillo's *London Merchant*. These mutual dealings can be on an abstract level: there is the interplay of private vice and public virtue in Mandeville's morality, which at times reads strangely like an algebraic sum. The poets of this age needed a form which could do more than assert that things are, or are not, the verse of rapt contemplation or wonder. They sought an idiom that could define and illustrate *connections*, which might be causal or temporal or anything else. It was with this aim in view that they developed a style placing strong emphasis on connective particles and repetitive signals. The language is gestural; it conducts the reader along an intelligible itinerary, like a good cicerone, instead of simply showing him or her the sights.

One side effect of this elective affinity for sequentiality is that eighteenth-century poetry makes full use of the verse-form as given. The style allows the ideas of expressive units to flow with the tide. Now the fact is that any series of lines in themselves impose a chain of subsequence, which naturally hovers on the edge of a consequence by a *post hoc ergo propter hoc* trick in the reader's mind. The Augustan poets

capitalized on this fact. It is an ineluctable feature of all poetry set out
in consecutive lines – even freaks of the 'Easter Wings' kind – that
one verse follows another in a repeated wave-like motion. Even some
forms of concrete poetry fall in with this pattern. A good many writers
ignore this fact of aesthetic life as a tiresome contingency; others go
so far as to make a positive effort to counteract its malign presence.
The characteristic energy of Augustan verse is devoted to accepting
and gratifying the need as one native to the condition of poetry. The
couplet form, primarily, is a machine in which to live consecutively.

I say advisedly 'couplet', without specifying the closed variety.
Quite a high proportion of eighteenth-century poetry handles the
couplet with some degree of licence. But the pentameter line and the
emphatic rhyming normally found make for regularity, even where
the sense floods over from one couplet to the next. Syntax, too, makes
its contribution when parallel sentence-shapes are used – with a
similar proviso, that semantically the parallelism may be a spurious
one. Paul Fussell has said that 'Pope customarily endstops tightly,
and his endstopping helps enact his customary analytic view of his
materials.'[29] This is true; but the same one-thing-at-a-time manner
of discourse can be achieved even where enjambement is rather free.
The epistle to Bolingbroke will furnish an example:

> But when no Prelate's Lawn with Hair-shirt lin'd,
> Is half so incoherent as my Mind,
> When (each Opinion with the next at strife,
> One ebb and flow of all follies all my Life)
> I plant, root up, I build, and then confound,
> Turn round to square, and square again to round;
> You never change one muscle of your face,
> You think this Madness but a common case,
> Nor once to Chanc'ry, nor to Hales apply;
> Yet hang your lip, to see a Seam awry!   (165–74)

This passage beautifully renders the comic indecision Pope is, with
studied mock-modesty, attributing to himself. The ideas play deftly
in and out of the couplet. The sentence is organized around two long
subsidiary clauses (concessive in effect, though introduced by 'when'
– the force is almost that of 'quand même...'), followed by a series of
verbs describing Bolingbroke's reaction. The main statement is
delayed by the generalizing parenthesis, which brings Pope's whole

---

[29] Paul Fussell, *Poetic Meter and Poetic Form* (New York, 1967), p. 117.

biography into account. The 'ebb and flow of follies' are exemplified in two casually analogical lines. In line 169, the repetition of the personal pronoun before 'build', as against its omission before the surrounding verbs, adds to the impression of feckless vacillation. With the next line, Pope reverts to a rocking-horse measure which acts out a pointless turnabout:

> Turn round to square, and square to round again.

After this long catalogue of aimless meandering, Pope presents Bolingbroke's attitude as firm and straightforward: the syntax correspondingly abjures the finicky adjustments of parenthesis and antithetical phrasing. This is a beautiful piece of poetic work-manship; but it has little to do with those engines of tension which Rebecca Parkin describes so enthusiastically.

On most occasions, however, Pope does take advantage of the 'facility' provided by the couplet: Donoghue's word is suggestive, is conveying the idea (along with that of capacity) of a trading management, an understanding by which certain benefits can be obtained on agreed terms. An instance of the more usual method is the splendid peroration on Vice in the *Epilogue to the Satires*, I. Suddenly, with the ejaculation 'Lo!', the calm prose logic is disrupted, and the tight endstopping is momentarily overset:

> *Virtue* may chuse the high or low Degree,
> 'Tis just alike to Virtue, and to me;
> Dwell in a Monk, or light upon a King,
> She's still the same belov'd, contented thing.
> *Vice* is undone, if she forgets her Birth,
> And stoops from Angels to the Dregs of Earth:
> But 'tis the *Fall* degrades her to a Whore;
> Let *Greatness* own her, and she's mean no more;
> Her Birth, her Beauty, Crowds and Courts confess,
> Chaste Matrons praise her, and grave Bishops bless:
> In golden Chains the willing World she draws,
> And hers the Gospel is, and hers the Laws:
> Mounts the Tribunal, lifts her scarlet head,
> And sees pale Virtue carted in her stead!
> Lo! at the Wheels of her Triumphal Car,
> Old *England's* Genius, rough with many a Scar,
> Dragg'd in the Dust! his Arms hang idly round,
> Our Youth, all liv'ry o'er with foreign Gold,
> Before her dance; behind her crawl the Old!
> See throning Millions to the Pagod run,

> And offer Country, Parent, Wife, or Son!
> Hear her black Trumpet thro' the Land proclaim,
> That 'Not to be corrupted is the Shame.'   (137–60)

With verse of such astonishing resource, one scarcely knows where to begin commentary. Confining attention to linguistic issues, however, one could point to the couplet,

> Her Birth, her Beauty, Crowds and Courts confess,
> Chaste Matrons praise her, and grave Bishops bless...

The inversion in the first line, with the mention first of the qualities, then the response, gives the reaction a sense of inevitability; phonetic likenesses in the second half of the verse subtly reinforce the impression of an automatic and mindless falling into line. When we come to the next line, the heavy assonance goes to produce a prim, tight-lipped air. Moreover, the omission of 'her' at the end of the statement, where it would appear in prose, adds to the feeling that the bishops do not really know what it is they are blessing. This trick is used, incidentally, in the *Epistle to a Lady*, where we are told of Atossa:

> So much the Fury still out-ran the Wit,
> The Pleasure miss'd her, and the Scandal hit.   (128–9)

where the identical notion of random and uncontrolled effect attaches to the second verb.

Even more interesting are lines 155–6 of the Epilogue, which run:

> Our Youth, all liv'ry'd o'er with foreign Gold,
> Before her dance; behind her crawl the Old!

Youth and age are isolated at the extreme edges of the couplet. They strain towards one another like jousting knights about to tilt; the remaining ideas are forced inwards and receive a new stress. This placing also sharpens the contrast between the antithetical verbs 'dance' and 'crawl'. It thrusts attention on the rhyme word 'Gold', which Pope wishes to get in the centre of our mind, as carrying the real moral urgency. Youth and age are examples of the subject of Vice; they emphasize the range of humanity affected. Their banishment to the extreme limits of the couplet is symbolically appropriate.

IV

I have argued that closed syntax was peculiarly suited to the ends which eighteenth-century poets set themselves. It ministers to that coherence they habitually sought – that variety of precision which takes the form of knowing too in what direction that move takes you.[30] This aptness could be explained by a number of factors. There is, for example, the continuing prestige of formal logic. The study of logic may not have occupied such an important place in education around 1700 as a century or more earlier. Yet one has only to recall R. S. Crane's persuasive argument that 'old-fashioned textbooks in logic' still penetrated Swift's imagination sufficiently to set up the first vague stirrings of Book IV of *Gulliver* – the first distant prospect of Houyhnhnmland.[31] And apart from logic, there was the master-science of the seventeenth century, geometry. Descartes, Hobbes, Leibniz and others had converted men to the view that the human condition could best be explained, literally or morally, in spatial terms. It is with Locke, however, that psychology becomes openly a *relational* subject; and this is where the Augustans got not merely an idiom but a way of disposing that idiom.

A glance at the contents page of the *Essay Concerning Human Understanding* immediately shows Locke's mind as operating across antimonies, as so many eighteenth-century poems do. Ideas 'of Sensation' are contrasted with those 'of Reflection'. There are ideas of pleasure and pain, of duration and of expansion; ideas of cause and effect, identity and diversity. There are clear and obscure ideas, real and fantastical, distinct and confused, true and false. There are abstract and concrete terms, and much else. As well as the antithetical habit of mind, the schematization illustrates a trick of thinking of

---

[30] One might adapt a passage from *Rambler* no. 137 to the poetic context: 'The chief art of learning...is to attempt but little at a time. The widest excursions of the mind are made by short flights frequently repeated; the most lofty fabricks of science are formed by the continued accumulation of single propositions.' The phrase omitted and replaced by dots was 'as Locke has observed'.

It is because he fails to appreciate this aggregative intention, I think, that Francis Berry presents so unfavourable a view of Pope's linguistic effects. In Pope, he writes, 'the Verbs have only local application. Though they perform their logical and syntactical purpose with a marvellous efficiency, having served that immediate purpose they do not act on the Verbs of other passages, or on passages as a whole, whether adjacent or distant. Having served their immediate purpose their energy expires' – *Poets' Grammar* (London, 1957), p. 122. Quite so: but this is precisely the aim of analytic poetry and of closed syntax.

[31] R. S. Crane, 'The Houyhnhnms, the Yahoos and the History of Ideas', *Reason and the Imagination*, ed. J. A. Mazzeo (London, 1962), pp. 243ff.

ideas as combinations or dispersals of simpler essences.[32] The alignment of moral and mathematical here is highly suggestive; this is one version of the ethical calculus. But more to the point is the stress Locke lays on that form of interaction which can be expressed as a *dependency*.

Later on in his *Essay*, Locke comes to write of 'Relation'. The understanding, he says, is not confined, in the consideration of anything, to that precise object: 'it can carry any idea as it were beyond itself, or at least look beyond it, to see how it stands in conformity to any other'.[33] He goes on to show how many words directly express a 'reciprocal intimation', such as husband and wife; and further, that certain words, apparently absolute, 'do conceal a tacit, though less observable, relation'. *Old* and *imperfect* are cited as cases in point.[34] Later still, Locke in his chapter 'Of other Relations' describes various modes of comparison. These include 'ideas of proportional relations' (simple comparison, in effect); 'natural relation', arising out of 'the circumstances of... origin or beginning' (blood ties and the like); 'moral relations'; and 'instituted or voluntary relations'. The last are especially interesting. These have to do with 'a moral right, power, or obligation to do something'. Examples are a general's right to command an army, a citizen's right to certain privileges. Locke defines this class of relation in his normal contractual terms, as 'depending upon men's wills, or agreement in society'. Then follows the significant passage:

Now, though these are all reciprocal, as well as the rest, and contain in them a reference of two things one to the other; yet, because one of the two things often wants a relative name, importing that reference, men usually take no notice of it, and the relation is commonly overlooked: e.g. a patron and client are easily allowed to be relations, but a constable or dictator are not so readily at first hearing considered as such. Because there is no peculiar name for those who are under the command of a dictator or constable, expressing a relation to either of them; though it be certain that either of them hath a certain power over some others, and so is so far related to them, as well as a patron is to his client, or general to his army.[35]

There could be no more representative expenditure of energy, in the age, than an effort of this kind. Locke is attempting to uncover

---

[32] 'Essences' is used in the non-technical sense. It is of course a slippery term, as Locke himself recognized (III.iii.12).

[33] *Essay*, II.xii.4. In fact all three sorts of idea seem to involve relations; but I am concerned simply with what Locke himself says.

[34] *Essay*, II.xxv.1–3.   [35] *Essay*, II.xxviii.1–4.

relationships of mutual obligation, based on patterns of dominance and submission. And Pope too was a child of his age. He could only make sense of things if he could see them in some sort of vertical, generally hierarchical, scheme. To understand how one man or one act 'stands in conformity to any other' is to seize the moral, psychological, and social significance of those compared – i.e., both terms of the comparison.

An important rider follows from this. If a poetry of relational statements is one specially fitted for a particular historical context, it is also uniquely suitable for one literary form. Recently the phrase 'situational satire' has gained some currency. But it is a redundant expression. All satire is a placing activity; it rests on the writer's being sure how one thing stands in relation to the next. The basic stance of the satirist is of one who knows a hawk from a handsaw. More pertinently, Augustan satire was built on a long tradition of *laus et vituperatio*: it dealt out praise or blame in accordance with standards which might be personal or public. Moreover, it commonly utilized devices such as mock-heroic, burlesque, parody, imitation – all of which imply a *dependency* of one thing upon another, all of which involve a locational activity by which one thing (the 'parasite') is set against another (the 'host').[36] Satire, in short, is inalienably comparative as regards both intent and method. Its style and literature structure reflect the fact.

Pope's poetry is one of sharply defined transitions, and its central merit is that it always knows where it is going. To put it in a slightly different way, ideas in Pope never hang about on the doorstep; if they are leaving, they leave. Some of the credit for this cleanness of outline may go to the heroic couplet, with its Miesian economy of design. A larger factor, I would contend, was the poet's unrelaxing vigilance in the matter of grammatical links and copulatives. The nature of his syntax – unambiguous, transparent, compact – was an essential precondition of his critique of the world: for satire, in describing how

---

[36] Johnson characteristically defines burlesque in terms of disproportion (*Life of Butler*). It is instructive to contemplate, too, the distortions of scale which underlie so much satire, notably *Gulliver's Travels*. As a final observation, one may adduce the fact that within Pope's lifetime Johnson was busy composing parliamentary debates. The closest student of this undertaking has noted that 'Johnson tends to treat each speech as a unit, to give each...a carefully turned beginning and an end'. Again, 'Johnson, when he writes a succession of short speeches, tends to treat it as a series'. In fact the real debates contained more forensic interplay and cross-cut exchange. Johnson's speeches depart from reality under this very aspect; they 'have little relation to one another'. See B. B. Hoover, *Samuel Johnson's Parliamentary Reporting* (Berkeley and Los Angeles, Cal., 1953), pp. 61, 135–6.

things stand in relation to one another, demands a language which
likewise connects and locates.[37]

Yet I would not wish to end by merely adapting Lytton Strachey,
and seeming to assert that closed syntax is Pope's criticism of life.
Deft, shapely and high-pressured as his language is, it is only because
of the higher imaginative ends it serves that we notice it at all.
Bethel's sermon on temperance (*Sat.* II.ii) is astonishingly concise
('You know my Laconic Style', wrote Pope in a cable-ese letter to Dr
Cheselden).[38] But it is not the language poets use which confers
immortality: in the end, it is ripeness of judgement which is all, in
satire as in every sort of literature.

> How pale, each Worshipful and rev'rend Guest
> Rise from a Clergy, or a City, feast!
> What life in all that ample Body say,
> What heav'nly Particle inspires the clay?
> The Soul subsides; and wickedly inclines
> To seem but mortal, ev'n in sound Divines.
> On morning wings how active springs the Mind,
> That leaves the load of yesterday behind?
> How easy ev'ry labour it pursues?
> How coming to the Poet ev'ry Muse?
> Not but we may exceed, some Holy time,
> Or tir'd in search of Truth, or search of Rhyme.
> Ill Health some just indulgence may engage,
> And more, the Sickness of long Life, Old-age:
> For fainting Age what cordial drop remains,
> If our intemp'rate Youth the Vessel drains?   (75–90)

---

[37] As regards the larger organizational units in the poem, one may set alongside this account
Earl Wasserman's description of the 'disjunctive blocks' which make up Pope's 'Ode for
Musick': quoted in Maynard Mack (ed.), *Essential Articles for the Study of Alexander Pope*
(London, 1964), p. 167. If the Jacobean nightmare was that things would fall apart, the
primal Augustan terror was that everything would *merge*. A contrast might also be drawn
with Milton. Ronald D. Emma has this to say of *Milton's Grammar* (The Hague, 1964), 'He
was seldom in a hurry to leave an idea ... Where we would now require periods Milton often
uses colons, semicolons, or commas, perhaps with a rhetorical rather than a strictly logical
objective. It is a patience-trying task to determine where one sentence ends and another
begins according to our conventions' (p. 142). Emma calls Milton 'a poet of qualification
more than of predication' (p. 142). This recalls Josephine Miles' distinction between
phrasal and clausal poetry: see *Eras and Modes in English Poetry* (Berkeley and Los Angeles,
1957). In Professor Miles' scheme, Pope emerges as a 'balanced' poet, along with Hopkins,
as against the 'phrasal' Milton and Blake (pp. 8–9). There is not space to argue out my
disagreements with Professor Miles, which spring chiefly from the method she has chosen to
adopt. But my own view is that a less crude apparatus than the simple count of the
adjective–verb ratio would show Pope to be a highly predicative poet. Finally his
imaginative technique is one of assertion rather than description.

[38] *Corr*, IV, 372.

CHAPTER 2

The politics of style

I

From his earliest years Pope set himself to introduce a new 'correctness' to English poetry. It seems an odd ambition to us; and not merely because it implies a censorious attitude towards the 'irregular' beauties of Shakespeare and Milton. Beyond all this, we are ill at ease with an aesthetic which places such a high value on what seem to us aridly technical skills. But for the Augustans it was different. The new polish they looked for in art was a matter of glamour, pride, self-confidence. 'Correct' poetry was part of a swelling nationalism and a swaggering modernism; it came ready equipped with a justification in cultural history:

> ...Britain to soft refinements less a foe,
> Wit grew polite, and Numbers learn'd to flow.
> Waller was smooth; but Dryden taught to join
> The varying verse, the full resounding line,
> The long majestic march, and energy divine.
> Tho' still some traces of our rustic vein
> And splay-foot verse, remain'd, and will remain.
> Late, very late, correctness grew our care,
> When the tir'd nation breath'd from civil war.
> Exact Racine, and Corneille's noble fire
> Show'd us that France had something to admire.
> Not but the Tragic spirit was our own,
> And full in Shakespear, fair in Otway shone:
> But Otway fail'd to polish or refine,
> And fluent Shakespear scarce effac'd a line.
> Ev'n copious Dryden, wanted or forgot,
> The last and greatest Art, the Art to blot.
> (Horace, *Ep.* II. i. 265–81)

Note the precise distinctions drawn between Waller and Dryden, Racine and Corneille, Shakespeare and Otway. Always Pope is busy *discriminating*.

It is worth looking with some attention at the key words in this passage, especially the honorific epithets. Wit must be 'polite' – that is, civilized, courtly, free from affectation. 'Refinements' may involve the gentler qualities but can also accommodate the 'energy' of a vigorous master such as Dryden. The effects to be shunned are 'rustic', what Matthew Arnold was to characterize by his phrase 'the note of provinciality'. Instead, literature should be urbane and agreeable. The 'exact' language of the great French dramatists is commended for its classical precision and bite. One can see in all this a conscious programme, a manifesto for contemporary poets, as well as a reductive account of the sloppiness of preceding generations. There are similarities with the Imagist declaration at the start of this century, notably in the attitude of T. E. Hulme and Ezra Pound to decadent Romanticism.

This then is anything but a timid defence of arbitrary rules. It is a call to action; Pope belonged to an age-group which believed itself at an important watershed in taste. In fact, some heavy demands are laid on poetry in the high Augustan era. It is permitted to relinquish the quest for false sublimity; the pressure on a major writer to produce an authentic English epic was never again to reach its Renaissance dimensions. But by way of compensation poetry was asked to mirror a social revolution. More than that, it was asked to foster and indeed guide this process. The English nation was to throw off its insularity and attain a new cosmopolitan ease. This meant that society needed a thorough course of education, and poets were to be among the principal instructors. It was no longer acceptable for writing to be crabbed, rough, ill-proportioned. But nor were the dilettante Restoration coterie-poets much help, that 'Mob of Gentlemen who wrote with Ease' (Horace, *Ep*. II. i. 108). A distinct professional competence was required – a solid control masked beneath the suave insouciance of the verse.

It is easy to see how in this situation the heroic couplet acquired its overwhelming attraction. It is a shapely mode of writing, firmly structured but pleasant in appearance. It solicits a clean organization of thought; the poet must know what he wants to say first, and what second, and how he is going to get from one to the other.[1] Yet the couplet has its own aesthetic appeal, deriving from its underlying symmetry. As everyone observes, figures like parallelism and antithesis flourish strongly in the Augustan climate; somehow the ideas seem to fall into such pairings without any effort on the part of the poet. In addition, there was a definite social component in the preference for this form. Blank verse had become associated with high Miltonic aspirations. This was a view which events in Pope's lifetime did little to change. Both good poets like James Thomson in his *Seasons* (1726–30) and bad poets like Thomas Newcomb in his *Last Judgement* (1723) helped to preserve the vaunting claims of blank verse. But couplets were quite another thing. They were well bred, gentlemanly, elegant.

Let us be more concrete. Pope devoted his whole career to mastering the couplet, and we should be clear on the advantages he derived.

(1) The heroic couplet was perspicuous; it invited a lucid approach, in that the formal demands make for sequentiality.

> On this Foundation *Fame*'s high Temple stands;
> Stupendous Pile! not rear'd by mortal Hands.
> Whate'er proud *Rome*, or artful *Greece* beheld,
> Or elder *Babylon*, its Frame excell'd.
> Four Faces had the Dome, and ev'ry Face
> Of various Structure, but of equal Grace:
> Four brazen Gates, on Columns lifted high,
> Salute the diff'rent Quarters of the Sky.
> Here fabled Chiefs in darker Ages born,
> Or Worthys old, whom Arms or Arts adorn,
> Who Cities rais'd, or tam'd a monstrous Race;
> The Walls in venerable Order grace:
> Heroes in animated Marble frown,
> And Legislators seem to think in Stone. (*Temple of Fame*, 61–74)

Here the ideas seem to be forming a regular queue to gain admittance to the poem. It is very different from Milton, say, where the struggle to articulate engenders a titanic struggle between thought and expression, registered in the convoluted syntax. Pope moves steadily on, like an experienced rock-climber; he does not make a move until he knows where he is going after *that*.

---

[1] See pp. 1–26 above; and more generally, J. A. Jones, *Pope's Couplet Art* (Athens, Ohio, 1969).

(2) The couplet was flexible. It was in touch with conversational rhythms – indeed, Pope's later work shows an increasing tendency to adopt colloquial airs:

> *P.* How Sir! not damn the Sharper, but the Dice?
> Come on then Satire! gen'ral, unconfin'd,
> Spread thy broad wing, and sowze on all the Kind.
> Ye Statesmen, Priests, of one Religion all!
> Ye Tradesmen vile, in Army, Court or Hall!
> Ye Rev'rend Atheists! – *F*[riend]. Scandal! name them, Who?
> *P.* Why that's the thing you bid me not to do.
> Who starv'd a Sister, who forswore a Debt,
> I never nam'd – the Town's enquiring yet.
> The pois'ning Dame – *Fr.* You mean – *P.* I don't. – *Fr.* You do.
> *P.* See! now I keep the Secret, and not you.
> The bribing Statesman – *Fr.* Hold! too high you go.
> *P.* The brib'd Elector – *Fr.* There you stoop too low.
> *P.* I fain wou'd please you, if I knew with what:
> Tell me, which Knave is lawful Game, which not?
>
> (*Epilogue to Satires*, II, 13–27)

But such cross-talk acts are only one of innumerable effects available to Pope. He can be high and sententious, obscene, skittish, tender, or whatever he pleases.

(3) The form was, as it were, poetically neutral. It could carry sustained narrative or the most delicately chiselled epitaph. Pope was able to modulate in and out of the set genres without elaborate formal preparations – thus, *Windsor-Forest* incorporates a topographical poem, a political panegyric, an economic prophecy, a lyrical interlude, an Ovidian set-piece, and much else. The poet can change gear as smoothly as he does only because of the unassuming, inconspicuous amenity afforded by the couplet.

(4) The couplet is particularly well adapted to a number of rhetorical devices which suited Pope's ends. Among these are paradox, contrived anti-climax, zeugma, syllepsis and parison. Some of these are noticeable only to the reader, a rare one nowadays, who is trained to spot particular 'turns'. Others, though, are very obvious – like punning. And in any case W. K. Wimsatt has written so well on the subject that detailed treatment is not in order here. In summary, Wimsatt shows how in Pope 'the abstract logic of parallel and antithesis is complicated and offset' by these other rhetorical

figures, and above all by rhyme.[2] This can be illustrated by a simple example:

> Then flash'd the living Lightning from her Eyes,
> And Screams of Horror rend th' affrighted Skies.
> Not louder Shrieks to pitying Heav'n are cast,
> When Husbands or when Lap-dogs breathe their last,   158
> Or when rich China Vessels, fall'n from high,
> In glittring Dust and painted Fragments lie!
>
> (*Rape of the Lock*, III, 155–60)

Obviously the main satiric impact here comes in the second couplet, with its delicious zeugma in line 158. But the rhyme words enact the same confusion of levels and play the same arch mock-heroic game. In appearance the couplet is a little prim, which is just what the ironist asks of it.

(5) The form obliges the reader to attend carefully. There is none of the open-ended garrulity of free verse; an analytic hold is placed on the material even as it is enunciated. Pope employs the heroic couplet as a placing and discriminating device. In contemporary aesthetics, deriving from Locke and Addison, it was usual to split the creative act between *invention* (fancy: the synthetic power of the imagination) and *judgement* (the operation of a critical intelligence). Particular stress was laid on the latter, though the sturdy critic John Dennis for one felt the emphasis was sometimes misplaced. But for Pope, as for the Renaissance writers, concern for ordonnance was a moral issue as well as a technical one. The poet placed his words with minute care, rather as one would set precious stones in a piece of fine jewellery. Precision not merely prettifies, it embodies all the intellectual commitment bestowed on the work. The couplet, indeed, is a machine for thinking in; but it is at the same time a jewel box, to display craftsmanship and to lend allure to finely textured ideas:

> The lucid Squadrons round the Sails repair:
> Soft o'er the Shrouds Aerial Whispers breathe,
> That seem'd but *Zephyrs* to the Train beneath.
> Some to the Sun their Insect-Wings unfold,
> Waft on the Breeze, or sink in Clouds of Gold.
> Transparent Forms, too fine for mortal Sight,
> Their fluid Bodies half dissolv'd in Light.

[2] W. K. Wimsatt, *The Verbal Icon* (London, 1970), p. 180.

> Loose to the Wind their airy Garments flew,
> Thin glitt'ring Textures of the filmy Dew;
> Dipt in the richest Tincture of the Skies,
> Where Light disports in every-mingling Dies,
> While ev'ry Beam new transient Colours flings,
> Colours that change whene'er they wave their Wings.
>
> (*Rape of the Lock*, II, 56–68)

This would be exquisite writing in any context. But it is the finicky precision of the language and the minute delicacy of the verse movement that give the passage its note of intimacy. Such an impression is hard to attain with any looser-knit metrical scheme. The couplet lets us explore the tiniest detail.

Of course, not all Pope appears within the confines of a single couplet. He learnt to compose in sweeping verse paragraphs, directing the argument with measured authority. As his career went on, he became particularly adept at the larger structural devices – e.g. the resolution of a satiric poem by means of a contrasting block of compliment or celebration (often turned towards the dedicatee, as in the *Epistle to a Lady*). But it remains true that the fundamental architectural unit is not the paragraph but the couplet. Within these twenty syllables Pope deployed an extraordinary range of artifice. By ceaseless variations he defeats our expectations and avoids monotony. By small shadings of rhythm, tone or syntax he creates surprise and delight:

> He look'd, and saw a sable Sorc'rer rise,
> Swift to whose hand a winged volume flies:
> All sudden, Gorgons hiss, and Dragons glare,
> And ten-horn'd fiends and Giants rush to war.
> Hell rises, Heav'n descends, and dance on Earth,
> Gods, imps and monsters, music, rage and mirth,   234
> A fire, a jig, a battle, and a ball,   235
> Till one wide Conflagration swallows all.
>
> (*Dunciad*, A, III, 229–36)

The pace quickens or slows at the poet's will (line 234 here has six stresses, line 235 only four) and there is a constant interplay between the strict metrical pattern and the free-flowing syntax, with its catalogues, suspensions, alliterative echoes and so on. For a long time, Pope was bogged down in a sterile debate concerning the relations of 'sound' and 'sense' in poetry, much of it tediously annexed to the more jejune sort of onomatopoeia. But when he devoted himself to composing, instead of theorizing, everything fell into place. Pope made the couplet into a marvellously supple piece of phonetic engineering.[3]

II

It would equally be wrong to give the idea that his expressive power derives solely from the vehicle he employed. The twentieth century has been able to find in Pope almost every poetic beauty which has successively arrogated critical notice. There is plangency and lyrical grace, as in *Eloisa to Abelard*; there is vibrant metaphysical wit, as in *The Dunciad*; there is arcane symbolism, as in *The Temple of Fame*; there is myth, virtually everywhere. At present Pope is most admired for a kind of prophetic urgency, evident principally in his later works. But if teasing social badinage ever comes into fashion again, he will satisfy that demand just as easily – and much the same could be said of high moral and discursive writing. There is scarcely any aesthetic canon which would exclude Pope from literary distinction, unless it is the cult of the ill-made poem.

The wider implications of Pope's technique have never been exposed in a wholly convincing manner. In my view, his poetic style is beautifully calculated to express what might be termed (simply for convenience) the Augustan outlook on life. In the first place, it shuns obscurity, as Georgian churches sought to dissipate the gloom of Gothic structures. Second, his style operates in a consecutive manner; it nurtures logic and connection. Other poetic techniques, in other ages, have been designed to blur distinctions – to allow free movement back and forward among the constituent parts of the poem. Milton, Blake and Hopkins can all be shown to favour his mode of working. But the strength of eighteenth-century poetry was that it knew the syntactic moment to leave. Pope's verse gains momentum and verse precisely from its refusal to merge one statement into another:

> Turn then from Wits; and look on Simo's Mate,
> No Ass so meek, no Ass so obstinate;
> Or her, that owns her Faults, but never mends,
> Because she's honest, and the best of Friends:
> Or her, whose Life the Church and Scandal share,

[3] See I. Ehrenpreis, 'The Style of Sound: The Literary Value of Pope's Versification', *The Augustan Milieu*, ed. H. K. Miller, E. Rothstein and G. S. Rousseau (Oxford, 1970), pp. 232–46, especially pp. 244–5.

For ever in a Passion, or a Prayer: 106
Or her, who laughs at Hell, but (like her Grace)
Cries, 'Ah! how charming if there's no such place!'
Or who in sweet vicissitude appears,
Of Mirth and Opium, Ratafie and Tears,
The daily Anodyne, and nightly Draught,
To kill those foes to Fair ones, Time and Thought.
Woman and Fool are two hard things to hit,
For true No-meaning puzzles more than Wit.

(*Epistle to a Lady*, 101–14)

The successive antitheses make their point because they arrive in a prepared environment. Line 106 is full of rhetorical charge. It involves antithesis and zeugma, with a hint of paradox. The small reservation 'or a Prayer' would easily get lost in the thrashing syntax of (say) Gerard Manley Hopkins. But it springs straight out at us here, so orderly is the grammatical context.

Third, Pope's style asserts the intelligibility and connectedness of things in a genteel, elegant idiom. It manages to avoid dislocation and disruption, as the work of Pope's friend Swift did not. Again the poetic vocabulary chimes in with the prejudices of the age. As Geoffrey Tillotson, a brilliantly observant analyst of linguistic effect, once noted, 'Correctness elicits and does not abuse the reader's confidence...His alertness is intensified, his curiosity, his trust increased.'[4] Many of Pope's greatest achievements rely on this delicate negotiation with the reader; and it is crucial that Pope should get the audience on his side. Other writers in other situations can afford to alienate or insult the people whom they are addressing. Shock tactics are a common feature in modern literature. But Pope needs first to enlist our sympathy. He makes writing seem a civilized business, a polite form of communication as unthreatening as (to take extreme examples) a wine list or a bus timetable. Of course, there are really the most powerful undercurrents of feeling ready to surface within the poem. But, like most of his contemporaries, Pope found a posture of innocence, a demure manner, a placid front, useful to his purposes. If his style had been less witty, polished and agreeable, he would not have been able to do many of the things he did.

Finally, Pope's style is adapted not just to contemplating or celebrating – it compares, contrasts, judges. Where other writers, before and since, have evolved a use of language which would

---

[4] G. Tillotson, *On the Poetry of Pope* (Oxford, 2nd edn, 1950), p. 116.

maximize other attributes of experience, Pope was chiefly occupied
by sorting and ranking functions. A comparison is needed here, in
fact, to make this plain. Here is Milton's Eden:

> Thus was this place,
> A happy rural seat of various view:
> Groves whose rich Trees wept odorous Gumms and Balme,
> Others whose fruit burnisht with Gold Rinde
> Hung amiable, *Hesperian* Fables true,
> If true, here onely, and of delicious taste:
> Betwixt them Lawns, or level Downs and Flocks
> Grasing the tender herb, were interpos'd,
> Of palmie hilloc, or the flourie lap
> Of some irriguous Valley spread her store,
> Flours of all hue, and without Thorn the Rose:
> Another side, umbrageous Grots and Caves
> Of coole recess, o're which the mantling Vine
> Layes forth her purple Grape, and gently creeps
> Luxuriant; mean while murmuring waters fall
> Down the slope hills, disperst, or in a Lake,
> That to the fringed Bank with Myrtle crownd,
> Her chrystall mirror holds, unite their streams.
> The Birds thir quire apply; aires, vernal aires,
> Breathing the smell of field and grove, attune
> The trembling leaves, while Universal *Pan*
> Knit with the *Graces* and the *Hours* in dance
> Led on th' Eternal Spring   (*Paradise Lost*, IV, 246–68)

Now Pope's 'Groves of Eden', transported to England, and embodying a conscious Miltonic recollection: we join the passage a few lines
later than in the previous essay (p. 14 above):

> Here waving Groves a chequer'd Scene display,
> And part admit and part exclude the Day;
> As some coy Nymph her lover's warm Address
> Not quite indulges, nor can quite repress.
> There, interspers'd in Lawns and opening Glades,
> Thin Trees arise that shun each others Shades.
> Here in full Light the russet Plains extend;
> There wrapt in Clouds the blueish Hills ascend;
> Ev'n the wild Heath displays her Purple Dies,
> And 'midst the Desart fruitful Fields arise,
> That crown'd with tufted Trees and springing Corn,
> Like verdant Isles the sable Waste adorn.
> Let *India* boast her Plants, nor envy we
> The weeping Amber or the balmy Tree,

> While by our Oaks the precious Loads are born,
> And Realms commanded which those Trees adorn.
> Not proud *Olympus* yields a nobler Sight,
> Tho' Gods assembled grace his tow'ring Height,
> Than what more humble Mountains offer here,
> Where, in their Blessings, all those Gods appear.
> See *Pan* with Flocks, with Fruits *Pomona* crown'd,
> Here blushing *Flora* paints the enamel'd Ground,
> Here *Ceres'* Gifts in waving Prospect stand,
> And nodding tempt the joyful Reaper's Hand,
> Rich Industry sits smiling on the Plains,
> And Peace and Plenty tell, a STUART reigns.
>
> (*Windsor-Forest*, 17–42)

Milton shows us a scene; Pope takes us on a guided tour. His landscape is composed, planned, resonant with meanings. Milton is taken up with the sheer sensuous wonder of Eden; Pope maps out his groves with fastidious care. He starts with a contrast on the accented '*These*' (line 9) and proceeds through a whole series of antitheses, explicit or implicit. Milton's 'here' is a vague locative: Pope's is set directly against a clear cut 'there'. Milton alludes for a moment to classical myth, but simply to compass his atmospheric ends – to enrich the awe and mystery. Pope applies directly to the classics, as a touchstone and contrast. His style is always quick to detect rivalries:

> While by *our* Oaks the precious Loads are born,
> And Realms commanded which *those* Trees adorn.

Pope's language is full of small direction signs, which control the relationship of one thing to another – *not/but*, *part/part*, *nor/nor*, *not/than*. In short, Milton presents experience, Pope arranges it. He has been shown to import into his Homer a strong emphasis on perspectives, not present in the original; and we have the same organizing process at work in *Windsor-Forest*. Pope needed a poetic language of location and comparison: and the couplet – sharp and sequential – was a key part of this language.

CHAPTER 3

Form and pattern in the Pastorals

I start with a bare computation. In Alexander Pope's *Pastorals*, as published with minor revisions throughout his lifetime, there are 386 lines. The verse count is 'Spring', 102; 'Summer', 92; 'Autumn', 100; 'Winter', 92. However, each of the first three poems is addressed to a named dedicatee, and each has as its second paragraph an invocation to this patron. ('Winter' is inscribed to the memory of 'A Fair Young Lady', later identified as Mrs Tempest, and has no corresponding paragraph.) These passages run to 10, 4, and 6 lines. If they are excluded the whole work contains 366 verses, a leap-year total which is as exact an approximation to the calendar as a poem in the strictest couplet form can attain. I am aware that this is the sort of arithmetic which gives number symbolism a bad name, and perhaps justly. ('So they have reached Pope', some readers may feel.) However, a critic who discovers such a fact ought, I think, to report it; particularly where the implied symbolism resides not in some arcane or deeply submerged correspondence, but in the very nature of the poem's subject matter. Pope's theme is imaged in the bowl described by Daphnis in the opening pastoral:

> Four Figures rising from the Work appear,
> The various Seasons of the rowling Year.   ('Spring' 37–8)

I do not wish to press any further on the facts at this stage; merely to observe that Pope never added or deleted lines, as he did in the course of most revisions he undertook.[1]

Most commentators are frankly bored with the *Pastorals*, and if they have anything good to say it is often by way of suggesting that

---

[1] Alastair Fowler, *Triumphal Forms: Structural Patterns in Elizabethan Poetry* (New York, 1970), pp. 85–6, finds certain patterned forms in Pope's work, but observes a 'less precise symmetry' than his model requires, with features that are 'inexact numerically'. He does, however, detect recessed symmetry in the two-canto *Rape of the Lock*, promptly obliterated in the revision.

Pope somehow transcends mere beautiful lyricism. The end result is generally in one way or another to belittle that lyricism. An interesting case in point is supplied by R. A. Brower's discussion. Brower observes that

> like Theocritus, Pope uses many of the traditional devices of song; refrain-like repetition, euphonious alliteration...and the blend of assonance and alliteration with faintly sensuous imagery...There is also the immediate impression, continuously renewed, of musical intricacy.

He then analyses the rhythmic shape of three couplets from the 'Where-e'er you walk' passage in 'Summer'. These lines, we are told, 'are the poetry of picturesque song that Pope later dismissed with an indulgent smile. But are they nothing more?' The question is rhetorical, of course; Brower is able to show that 'pure song' is overlaid by Pope's 'power of dramatizing'. Moreover, in his later work, Pope 'continued to exploit' his pastoral vein – usually, it seems, by way of parody – and takes advantage of its 'absurdity'. Later in his book, Brower states that in *Windsor-Forest* 'in contrast with the *Pastorals*, there are some ideas worthy of the name'. The chapter from which I have been quoting is called 'The Shepherd's Song', but its author can descry only a very thin charm in song as such.[2]

Perhaps Brower said openly what other critics feel and keep quiet about. If so, there is surely very little hope of retaining the *Pastorals* as any sort of live poetry. For they are lyric utterances before all; quite apart from the explicit passages where the shepherds are caught in the act of song, the basic impulse pervading the entire sequence is that of sonorous, melodious, or plangent expression. The mood shifts from joyous to melancholy to elegiac; the narrative mode alternates in and out of dialogue; but the song quality is always there. What Brower calls 'the traditional devices of song' are there for a good reason – not just to supply a decorative musicality, but to allow the theme fully to convey itself. Pope's aim is to re-enact the natural cycle: the 'rowling Year', chiefly, but also the course of human life and the progress of the day. The elaborate symmetries and echoes he employs, in my view, are a way of rendering cyclical events; the

[2] R. A. Brower, *Alexander Pope: The Poetry of Allusion* (Oxford, 1959), pp. 23–24, 60. A more directly hostile critic is James Reeves, who deplores the frequency of literary 'echoes' (a significant word): see *The Reputation and Writings of Alexander Pope* (London, 1976), pp. 118–24. Other important discussions of the work are Martin Battestin, 'The Transforming Power: Nature and Art in Pope's Pastorals,' *ECS*, II (1969), 183–204; and David S. Durant, 'Man and Nature in Alexander Pope's Pastorals', *SEL*, XI (1971), 469–85.

surges and diminuendos in the expressive medium relate to troughs and crests of human life as we experience it as a temporal process. No one seems to have explored these rhythms in any detail, though Geoffrey Tillotson wrote a short analysis of the verse technique as it is manifested within the structure of single lines (or, in two cases, couplets).[3] My aims here are to outline some of the repetitive effects used in the *Pastorals* and to indicate what they seem to me to be doing.

I

Pope's closest source for individual poems is normally an eclogue by Theocritus or Virgil; but his overall plan has more to do with *The Shepheardes Calender*. As Pope saw it in the prefatory *Discourse* published in 1717, Spenser 'has one peculiar to himself; he compares human Life to the several Seasons, and at once exposes to his readers a view of the great and little worlds, in their various changes and aspects' (this last an astrologically weighted term). But the design of a month-by-month calendar involves repetition, 'because the year has not that variety in it to furnish every month with a particular description, as it may every season'. Pope accordingly went back to a seasonal scheme:

> Of the following Eclogues I shall only say ... That they have as much variety of description, in respect of the several seasons, as *Spenser*'s: That in order to add to this variety, the several times of day are observ'd, the rural employments in each season or time of day, and the rural scenes or places proper to such employments; not without some regard to the several ages of man, and the different passions proper to each age.[4]

In the event Pope pays comparatively little regard to the last issue, beyond a general progression from the courting rituals of 'Spring' to the musing upon last things in 'Winter'. However, the poet is abundantly justified in claiming an obvious sequentiality in his design that Spenser could not match. The movement of time through the day supplies a clear alternative to the seasonal rhythm, not by way of active disruption or syncopation, but rather as it charts a separate (if parallel) course. Moreover, the mention of the Thames at an early point in three poems ('Spring' 3, 'Summer' 2, 'Winter' 13–14) cements the structure; it also brings in a recollection of Spenser, and underlines both local and national patriotism.

---

[3] Geoffrey Tillotson, *On the Poetry of Pope* (Oxford, 2nd edn, 1950), pp. 124–30.
[4] *TE*, I, 32–3.

That Pope was the first pastoral poet to use the times of day in this fashion (as his phrasing allows us to suppose) seems highly unlikely. He was certainly not the first artist in any medium to splice these time-scales together. It had been done by Nicolas Poussin, the very painter most conspicuous in discussions of Pope's work.[5] The series, *Four Seasons* (now in the Louvre), date from a later stage in the career of Poussin; they were executed between 1660 and 1664 for the Duke de Richelieu, and had then passed into the collection of Louis XIV. However, many engravings and copies were made: two paintings sold in London in 1712 appear to have been copies of the Spring and Winter pieces.[6] Pope's friend Jonathan Richardson knew of them, though he misattributes them to Albani in his *Account* (1722); Horace Walpole also refers to them, in a letter to Conway of 29 October 1774. According to Anthony Blunt, 'In antiquity the seasons had usually been represented by allegorical heads of figures, sometimes accompanied by scenes with human beings or putti performing the actions appropriate to each part of the year... In the Middle Ages artists represented the seasons by episodes taken from everyday life, usually from country life.'[7] Poussin's innovation was to treat the subject through four biblical episodes, each drawn from the Old Testament; he thus could be said to have added to the pagan iconography a historical and prophetic dimension. To one long-familiar not only with Virgil, but also with the commentators and scholiasts upon classical epic – as Pope was – this would have made

---

[5] See Giorgio Melchiori, 'Pope in Arcady: The Theme of *Et in Arcadia Ego* in his Pastorals', *English Miscellany*, XIV (1963), 83–93, reprinted in *Essential Articles for the Study of Alexander Pope*, ed. Maynard Mack (Hamden, Conn., 2nd edn, 1968), pp. 149–58. Morris R. Brownell, *Alexander Pope and the Arts of Georgian England* (Oxford, 1978), pp. 34–5, draws attention to the interest in Poussin's heroic pictures shared by Pope and Jonathan Richardson the elder.

[6] Anthony Blunt, *The Paintings of Nicolas Poussin* (London, 1966), pp. 9–10. The auctioneer Pelletier regularly advertised in the *Spectator*. Jeffry B. Spencer, *Heroic Nature: Ideal Landscape in English Poetry from Marvell to Thomson* (Evanston, Ill., 1973), p. 206n., remarks, 'Pope probably knew the Seasons pictures; they were highly admired and often engraved.' Professor Spencer provides by far the best account of the landscape element in Pope's *Pastorals* (see *Heroic Nature* pp. 198–208), but her concern is with the content and meaning of particular scenes, rather than with the overriding image of the year. My contention is not that individual scenes in Poussin and Pope are in all respects closely comparable, but that both artists use a symbolic 'progress' based on temporal sequence.

[7] Anthony Blunt, *Nicolas Poussin: The A. W. Mellon Lectures in Fine Art* (New York, 1967), p. 333. Blunt also detects a link with an equally admired painter, Claude Lorrain: 'Claude dedicated his etching, *The Dance of the Four Seasons*, to [Michel] Passart, who had commissioned the *Orion* from Poussin. The figures are shown dancing to the music of Time, and it is likely that Claude also had in mind the idea of the seasons as a symbol of the regular movement of the universe' (p. 334n).

good artistic sense. The 'sacred eclogue' *Messiah* is a generic expression of his urge to link classical and Christian tradition. The *Pastorals* largely avoid sacred concerns, but like Poussin's series they comprise a cyclical sequence rather than a block of four static allegories.[8]

Poussin certainly used the motif of four seasons elsewhere, for example in *Phaeton before Helios* (Blunt § 173), where there is also a circle of the zodiac and a figure representing Time. More debatably, there is the painting now in the Wallace Collection, *Ballo della Vita Humana* (Blunt § 121), which has acquired fortuitous renown as the basis of Anthony Powell's *roman fleuve* entitled *A Dance to the Music of Time*. Erwin Panofsky interprets the four dancers depicted as allegorical figures of Poverty, Labour, Riches and Luxury.[9] However, in 1713 the picture was catalogued in the Palazzo Rospigliosi at Rome, where it was kept, as a representation of the four seasons, and that is the way connoisseurs apparently knew it until Panofsky reinterpreted the allegory. As is well known, the picture shows four female figures in a circle, with their hands linked, dancing to an air played by Time on his lyre. In the sky Apollo can be seen driving his chariot through the circle of the zodiac. Similarly on the bowl which Daphnis stakes, in Pope's 'Spring', the zodiacal signs are depicted along with the seasons (39-40). Panofsky discusses what he calls a 'cosmic rhythm' in Poussin, and this is appropriate to literary as well as graphic representations of the subject.

Again Pope could not have known the original of the *Ballo*, but he could easily have seen one of the numerous copies. A collector, James Graham, apparently related to the connoisseur Richard Graham (with whom Pope was acquainted by 1716), brought back many such items – including Poussins – from France and Italy; they were offered for sale in the *Spectator* in 1711. Although Pope did not himself take up painting seriously until 1713, he had been keenly interested

---

[8] Blunt cites an article by W. Sauerländer in *Münchner Jahrbuch der bildenen Kunst* (1956), associating Poussin's series with Mosaic and prophetic history. The thesis involves a certain awkwardness, as it requires logically the removal of autumn to a position between spring and summer; but Sauerländer's identification of summer with the Christian era and winter with the last judgement casts some light on Pope's poems. See Blunt, *Poussin: The Mellon Lectures*, p. 334.

[9] Erwin Panofsky, '*Et Ego in Arcadia*', *Philosophy and History: Essays Presented to Ernst Cassirer*, ed. R. Klibansky and H. J. Paton (Oxford, 1936), pp. 223-54. It would not of course be impossible for two separate allegories to be present: in that case, Panofsky's four terms might correspond respectively to winter, spring, summer and autumn, or more likely to winter, autumn, spring and summer.

in the visual arts since childhood. The evidence is insufficient to show that any painting by Poussin could have served as a direct model for the *Pastorals*, but it could be said with total prudence that the habits of mind exemplified in Poussin were still available to the poet. (Claude had also produced an etching on *The Dance of the Four Seasons*, and as Blunt says he probably 'also had in mind the idea of the seasons as a symbol of the regular movement of the universe'. It is in the survival of such symbolic and mythological associations that the 'habits of mind' persist.)[10] In particular there was a tendency to envisage the passage of time as a measured and rhythmic progression, rather than a chaotic flux, something aesthetically pleasing for all its inevitability. The imaginative impulse in both Poussin and Pope is to reproduce this rhythm in the very texture and proportions of their art.

It would be possible, but perhaps over-ingenious, to see older pagan correspondence caught up in Pope's scheme. According to one body of tradition the seasons were associated respectively with Apollo, Ceres, Bacchus and Pluto – Pope has a reference to Phoebus at 'Spring' 45, and to Ceres at 'Summer' 66, but the pattern breaks down (and anyway a rival goddess for Spring was Flora, as in Botticelli's *Primavera*). More to the point is the inclusion of heavenly bodies appropriate to each season, and believed to affect the climate: *Phosphor* at 'Spring' 26, *Sirius* at 'Summer' 21, *Arcturus* at 'Autumn' 72, and *Orion* at 'Winter' 85. These are more than chance astronomical observations; they form part of the characterization of each season according to its mood or internal weather. Likewise the vista opens and closes in a significant fashion. *Spring*, the morning scene which Poussin had set in paradise, is located by Pope's note (to 17) in a valley, with view of drawn breaking 'on the Mountain's Side' (21). There is dense foliage, with flowers and birds much in evidence among the 'plains' of Windsor. *Summer* had been represented by Poussin as a rich open landscape, drawing the eye back from reapers in the cornfield to distant hills and buildings. Pope similarly evokes a more extensive scene 'by the River's side' for his

[10] For other possible pagan symbols, see Blunt, *Poussin: The Mellon Lectures*, p. 334. For Pope and Richard Graham, see *Corr*, I, 157. This obscure figure has a notably sketchy entry in the *DNB*. For James Graham, see Elizabeth Wheeler Manwaring, *Italian Landscape in Eighteenth-Century England* (New York, 1925), p. 64; *Spectator* no. 67 (17 May 1711); and *Lover* no. 12 (23 March 1714), where Poussin is again represented in Graham's stock. Robert Walpole was one contemporary British collector who was soon to acquire Poussins from Italy; Pope visited his London home in later years, but probably not by the date of the *Pastorals*.

noonday episode, until at its close the shepherds bring their flocks into the shade (85–87). Poussin's evening scene had pictured Joshua and Caleb, who had spied out the promised land of Canaan for forty days, returning with the grapes which were the fruit of this land (Numbers 13: 21–6). Pope's subject is admittedly remote from this but his setting of hills, cliffs, rocks and caves does correspond to the sharp and rugged peaks in Poussin. *Winter* represents the deluge, hardly a pastoral theme, and again it has a more closed-in appearance. Set in a grove, with rains, springs, floods, 'dropping Trees' and streams. Pope's moonlight episode is certainly his most watery; but I do not intend to force any connection between Poussin's deluge and the flood that 'o'erflows with Tears' in Pope (66). I wish to indicate a broader but still suggestive mode of congruity: each artist has used differentiation by landscape setting as part of his means to give each season a particular atmospheric colouring. Part of the meaning of each work inheres in these contrasts between the constituent parts.

Whether or not Pope knew any of the older models to which I have referred, he was certainly familiar with one transcendent image of human life viewed as a perfect circle. This was the shield of Achilles in Book XVIII of the *Iliad*. Pope began his full-scale translation of the poem within four years of the publication of the *Pastorals*, but he had already in 1708 attempted sample sections of Homer at the instigation of Sir William Trumbull.[11] His own version ultimately contained an extended note on the shield, which expressed the orthodox view that this image was consciously design as 'a representation of the universe'. Vleughel's drawing of the shield was engraved by Gribelin for Pope's edition. It shows twelve symmetrical divisions, forming four groups of three. One group is allotted to agriculture (tillage, harvest, vintage) and one group to pastoral life (lions and herds of cattle, sheep, and a rustic dance). It is possible to interpret in a variety of ways not merely the shield as it is in Homer, but also the later interpretations of the passage themselves: in broad terms the two groups mentioned correspond respectively to the *Georgics* and the *Eclogues*, or, if you will, *Windsor-Forest* and the *Pastorals*.[12] The immediate point is that such symmetrical schemes – what might be called 'circular allegory' – were abundantly familiar to educated

[11] For the genesis of the *Iliad*, see *TE*, VIII, xxxv–xlvi.
[12] See *TE*, VIII, 358–66; and Brownell, pp. 40–2. Pope suggests that the shield may be regarded as 'a sketch for…an *universal Picture*' (*TE*, VIII, 363).

readers, and Pope could count on instant recognition of his seasonal design as it expressed a cyclical ordering of recurrent phenomena. The bowl described by Daphnis is a reduced version of Achilles' shield, under its aspect as a metaphor of time.

II

The regular succession of natural events, seasonal or diurnal, served as 'a common symbol for the harmony of the universe' in pagan art.[13] Pope's technique is to emphasize repetitive, cyclical and echoic effects both through his diction and through symmetries in syntax and rhythm. This is most apparent in 'Autumn', least in 'Summer'; but it applies throughout.

Most commentators have stressed the visual data of the *Pastorals* – Brower says that 'behind the painter's eye and the choreographic eye is the mythological eye that sees life in trees and mountains and streams', while Norman Ault draws attention to 'Pope's unusual love of colour'.[14] In my estimate the total composition is affected equally by *aural* phenomena. 'Spring' opens with a regular alternation of the senses:

> First in these Fields I try the Sylvan Strains,
> Nor blush to sport on *Windsor's* blissful Plains:
> Fair *Thames* flow gently from thy sacred Spring,
> While on thy Banks *Sicilian* Muses sing;
> Let Vernal Airs thro' trembling Osiers play,
> And *Albion's* Cliffs resound the Rural Lay.   (1–6)

Gently, perhaps because it replaces Spenser's *softly*, suggests quietness of sound as well as movement; *Airs* are literally breezes, but the subsidiary idea of a musical air is difficult to suppress altogether. The dedication stanza (7–16) calls up the muse and her 'slender Reed', the lyre, the thrush and nightingale considered as songsters, silence and 'all th'Aerial Audience'. The song contest which forms the centre of 'Spring' begins with a quatrain (23–6) invoking parallel ideas that associate 'joyous Musick' with the efflorescence and progenitive power of the season. Other conceits (e.g. Strephon's quatrain at 69–72) link natural sound with growth, love, and well-

---

[13] Blunt, *Poussin: The Mellon Lectures*, p. 332. For a similar exploitation of Renaissance seasonal schemes by an eighteenth-century poet, see Pat Rogers, 'James Thomson and the Correspondence of the Seasons', *Revue des Langues Vivantes*, XLII (1976), 64–81.

[14] Brower, p. 24; Norman Ault, *New Light on Pope* (London, 1949), p. 86.

being throughout creation. And the opening image of cliffs that 'resound' is taken up by Damon's line, 'Begin, the Vales shall ev'ry Note rebound' (44).

The same elements are present in 'Summer', with an additional reference to the 'pipe' or flute handed on by Colin Clout to Alexis (39–42). This time Pope allots more emphasis to the theme of resounding noises; the complaint of Alexis is conveyed to us as it floats across the air, sonorously beating the bounds of this pastoral landscape:

> Ye shady Beeches, and ye cooling Streams
> Defence from *Phoebus'*, not from *Cupid's* Beams;
> To you I mourn; nor to the Deaf I sing,
> The Woods shall answer, and their Echo ring.
> The Hills and Rocks attend my doleful Lay,
> Why art thou prouder and more hard than they?   (13–18)

Again at a climatic moment, the imagery turns from cool gales and glades to an aural celebration of the beloved:

> Oh! how I long with you to pass my Days,
> Invoke the Muses, and resound your Praise;
> Your Praise the Birds shall chant in ev'ry Grove,
> And Winds shall waft it to the Pow'rs above.
> But wou'd you sing, and rival *Orpheus'* Strain,
> The wondring Forests soon shou'd dance again,
> The moving Mountains hear the pow'rful Call,
> And headlong Streams hang list'ning in their Fall!   (77–84)

Nature characteristically witnesses the concerns of mankind in the *Pastorals* by 'listening'.

'Autumn' is the most symmetrically patterned composition in the set, and the densest in aural suggestion. In its hundred lines there are more than forty words with an import of sound. Again both suspiration and reverberation are strongly in evidence. The first refrain, used in the song of Hylas, evokes a soft whispering effect: 'Go gentle Gales, and bear my Sighs along!' Ægon's song employs more resonant tones: 'Resound ye Hills, resound my mournful Lay!' The impression of echo is enacted by syntax and metrics:

> Thro' Rocks and Caves the Name of *Delia* sounds,
> *Delia*, each Cave and echoing Rock rebounds.   (49–50)

Here the chiasmus is able to convey the impression of a cry falling away into the distance; the echoes in phrasing mimic a precise acoustic phenomenon. And throughout 'Autumn' the phonetic properties of verse are supported by heavy repetition of ringing sounds in the diction.

'Winter' avoids any approach to tintinnabulation, and emphasizes quieter sounds – whispers, murmurs, sighs, warbling streams: though *remurmur* (64) does convey a gentle resonance. Aural expressions are introduced to suggest the absence of an accustomed sound:

> The silver Swans her hapless Fate bemoan,
> In Notes more sad than when they sing their own.
> In hollow Caves sweet *Echo* silent lies,
> Silent, or only to her Name replies,
> Her Name with Pleasure once she taught the Shore,
> Now *Daphne*'s dead, and Pleasure is no more!   (39–44)

Or alternatively the substitution of gentle sound for silence:

> No more the Streams their Murmurs shall forbear,
> A sweeter Musick than their own to hear,
> But tell the Reeds, and tell the vocal Shore,
> Fair *Daphne*'s dead, and Musick is no more!   (57–60)

Thyris' lament occupies the largest portion of 'Winter', and once more a refrain is used to produce a softly lapping quality, as of water splashing quietly against a sandy shore. Incidentally, the words *sing/song*, with the inflected forms, occur seven times in 'Winter'; this compares with totals elsewhere in the *Pastorals* – 'Spring' seven, 'Summer' five, 'Autumn' eight, and *Windsor-Forest* (434 lines) twelve. This represents a frequency for a single lexical grouping very close to the count for *all* colour words, whose intensity of usage so struck Norman Ault.[15] In fact sound effects are present more densely here than in any subsequent work by Pope, excluding only the *Ode for Musick*, written at about the same period. The 'Rural Lay' works first of all through auditory suggestion.

Direct reference, through imagery, diction, or allusion, is only one side of the technique. At a deeper level of construction the *Pastorals* are shaped to express in their own poetic identity the flux and reflux of the natural world. Their significant form is that of *song* – with refrains, antiphonal stanzas, choric exchanges, and many other patterned features. Within each poem there are structural symmetries, e.g. the cyclical design of 'Spring', from the flocks going out and spreading over the valley (17–20) to their return for shelter

---

[15] Ault, pp. 82–100.

(101–2). At the local level a wide range of balanced figures re-enact these symmetries in grammatical terms. All these features – whether structural, strophic, metrical or rhetorical – have a single artistic function: to set up a regular alternation of rhythmical members. The 'rowling Year' is presented as though nature held it on a tight spring; the renewal of each season comes with the force of a sudden recoil ('Autumn', 31–8). The underlying figure is echo, that is, repetition generally with minute variation; the resulting impression is of an ordered universe, intelligible even in its harshest moments (as in 'Winter') and predictable even in its mutations. The intervals of nature in the countryside around Windsor are articulated by the carefully wrought units of poetic statement.

'Spring' is the longest section, with 102 lines, owing to its ten-line compliment to Sir William Trumbull. Without this dedicatory paragraph the total would be 92, that is (exactly as these things can be) the number of days between the vernal equinox and the summer solstice.[16] The remaining structure consists of six lines announcing the theme (1–6); six more setting the scene (17–22); introductory paragraphs by Daphnis, Strephon and Daphnis again in six-line stanzas (23–40); a four-line interjection by Damon followed by twelve successive stanzas alternately by Daphnis and Strephon (41–92); and finally ten lines spoken by Damon. The thirteen central four-line stanzas match, coincidentally or otherwise, the number of weeks in a quarter. 'Summer' is 92 lines long, and the omission of four lines addressed to the patron Garth would in this case disturb the diurnal count, running from midsummer to autumnal equinox – a fact which may or may not indicate the absurdity of making this connection. There are eight introductory lines before the dedication and the song of Alexis: the verse paragraphs may be diagrammatically stated as 8, 10, 12, 14, 10, 26, and then 8 again. The gradual movement of unfolding visible up to this stage in the poem leads to the famous paragraph analysed by Brower; this is constructed

---

[16] The figures are not affected by the fact that in the Julian calendar, still used in Britain, the vernal equinox had slipped back as early as 11 March by 1582; at that date Pope Gregory XIII introduced the reformed calendar, standard in Europe henceforward. The displacement between the two calendars, notwithstanding the eleven-day gap in Pope's time, arose from the attempt to correct a discrepancy of less than a day in a century. As Alastair Fowler points out, the day count for the quarters was not arrived at simply by arithmetic, but was given conventionally in works on astronomy. (The calculation might be by astrological signs, by calendar months, by quarter-days, etc.) Pope could have consulted tables in the standard authorities, or copied Renaissance pastorals (Fowler, *Triumphal Forms*, p. 139, quotes one such poem employing a scheme of 365 lines).

almost entirely in four-line units (often corresponding with the sentence-structure) with an extra couplet (71–2) breaking the scheme at its centre:

> Oh deign to visit our forsaken Seats,
> The mossie Fountains, and the Green Retreats!   (71–2)

The paragraph is thus organized in three fours (59–62, 63–6, 67–70), a lone couplet (71–2), and three more fours (73–6, 77–80, 81–4). The hinge couplet makes sense with either preceding or succeeding verses: the invitation to the nymph can be read as a culmination of previous entreaties ('Come lovely Nymph', 63), or as introducing the description of her appearance in the 'sylvan scenes', which occupies the following lines. In other words, the entire passage works perfectly well as two interlocking couplet 'sonnets', 59–72 and 71–84. Brower calls this paragraph 'Pope's poetic best', that is, of course, as far as the *Pastorals* go. It should be a corrective to easy dismissal of formal balance to realize that these celebrated lines are complex figures in an ornate carpet, structurally appropriate as well as poetically evocative.[17]

'Autumn', as remarked, is exactly 100 lines in length; a little more conveniently this time, omission of the six verses dedicated to Wycherley would take us to within two of the days in this quarter. It is even more elaborately patterned than 'Spring', with 6 introductory lines, 42 devoted to Hylas' song, 42 to that of Ægon, and 4 by way of conclusion. However, the verse paragraphs are differently assembled for the two participants in the song contest. For Hylas it is 4, 6, 8, 8, 8, 8; for Ægon, 2, 8, 6, 6, 8, 8, 4. Hylas is the more even-toned and even languorous competitor; Ægon's more abrupt and impassioned utterance is slightly less rounded in formal shaping. As for 'Winter', this is cast as a dialogue with the leading role taken by Thyrsis; the exchange is largely conducted in eight-line units. The pattern is Lycidas, 8; Thyrsis, 6; Lycidas, 6; Thyrsis, 6, 2 (an inscribed epitaph), 8, 8, 8, 8, 8, 8; Lycidas, 8; Thyrsis, 8. This is clearly very near to a regular strophic ode, with Thyrsis responsible for 64 lines in all, a nicely square Pythagorean number once more. The total of 92

---

[17] The paragraph is made up of thirteen couplets, again corresponding to the weeks in the quarter. Alastair Fowler suggests to me that the potential anomaly regarding the diurnal count may be explained by the phrase 'the Streams forgot to flow' (5). This alludes to the passage in *Æneid*,VIII, 86–9, where the flow of the Tiber (and of time) is suspended. Spenser's use of this passage in *Prothalamion* is discussed by Fowler, *Conceitful Thought: The Interpretation of English Renaissance Poems* (Edinburgh, 1975), pp. 73–4.

lines, one may gratefully add, precisely corresponds with the days in
the quarter during a leap year.[18]

Such nakedly mathematical assemblages express only a limited
amount in themselves. But Pope does a good deal more with his
constructs than leave them as idle symmetries for the attention of
time-killing numerologists. In 'Spring', for example, the regular
alternation of Daphnis and Strephon is used to develop a complicated
eddying movement, with each snatch of song responding to the last
and phrase answering phrase:

STREPHON

In Spring the Fields, in Autumn Hills, I love,
At Morn the Plains, at Noon the shady Grove;
But *Delia* always; absent from her Sight,
Nor Plains at Morn, nor Groves at Noon delight.

DAPHNIS

Sylvia's like Autumn ripe, yet mild as *May*,
More bright than Noon, yet fresh as early Day,
Ev'n Spring displeases, when she shines not here,
But blest with her, 'tis Spring throughout the Year.   (77–84)

The ideas introduced in Strephon's first couplet are reversed in two
different ways, first by his own concluding line in this quatrain and
then by Daphnis' reply. If lines 77–8 are represented schematically as
follows:

$$\text{In }\overset{a^1}{\text{Spring}}\text{ the }\overset{b^1}{\text{Fields}}\text{, in }\overset{a^2}{\text{Autumn}}\text{ Hills I }\overset{b^2}{\text{love}},$$
$$\text{At }\overset{c^1}{\text{Morn}}\text{ the }\overset{d^1}{\text{Plains}}\text{, at }\overset{c^2}{\text{Noon}}\text{ the shady }\overset{d^2}{\text{Grove}}$$

then the first reversal (line 80) takes the form $d^1c^1d^2c^2$, with *delight*
matching *I love* in line 77. The second reversal (81–2) adopts the
pattern a^2a^1/c^2c^1. A series of antithetical constructions stands in
direct parallelism to an earlier series, with the result that a contrast
in meaning goes along with an identity in syntax and music.
Throughout 'Spring' the amoebean stanzas are used with remarkable ingenuity, their elements dovetailing in a variety of ways. There
is widespread use of what classical scholarship terms 'recessed
symmetry', i.e. the sequence *abccba*, which again provides a sense of
recoil – a movement outward and then back inward. The favourite

---

[18] The song contest in 'Autumn' occupies thirteen stanzas; the dialogue in 'Winter' (which
uniquely has no introduction or dedication, and begins with the poem's first line) takes
thirteen verse-paragraphs also. There are of course thirteen weeks in a quarter.

expressions recur in metrically conspicuous positions: rhyme words include *day, year, spring, field, grove, shade, plain, lay, strain, air*, defining the parameters of time and space within which the song contest is located. We cannot be required to enjoy this sustained effect of chimes, but it is pointless to deny its existence.

'Autumn' employs less straightforward parallelism than 'Spring'; instead of antiphonal stanzas we have 42 lines devoted in turn to each of the two singers. Nevertheless the poem is if anything even more cunningly wrought, with its concluding phrase harking back to its opening words, and an insistent use of refrain. There are notable differences, too, as between the performances we witness. Hylas employs a number of three-line parallelisms (24–6, 27–9, 32–4, 36–8, 40–3, 43–5). These triplets, absent from Ægon's song, are counterpointed against the regular rhyming couplets; the effect is in some degree that of the time-signature 6/8 in music. A single example, from the first such patterned stanza, should be enough to illustrate the device:

> Go gentle Gales, and bear my Sighs along!
> For her, the feather'd Quires neglect their Song;
> For her, the Lymes their pleasing Shades deny;
> For her, the Lillies hang their heads and dye.
> Ye Flow'rs that droop, forsaken by the Spring,
> Ye Birds, that left by Summer, cease to sing,
> Ye Trees that fade when Autumn-Heats remove,
> Say, is not Absence Death to those who love?   (23–30)

Note the characteristic cross-reference to other seasons, which is one of Pope's principal ways of defining the home key of a particular pastoral. All three central stanzas organized in this way have a marked strophic quality, as though they were clearly separate units such as those found in ottava rima: the patterning enhances a sense of formalized song, rather than mere discursive speech. Added to this is the refrain which opens each stanza; a tiny variation is introduced by the alternation of the words *away* and *along*. The first, third, and fifth stanzas read

> Go gentle Gales, and bear my Sighs away!

whereas the second and fourth have

> Go gentle Gales, and bear my Sighs along!

The final line repeats the *away* variant, and thus echoes the opening lines.

Similar small adjustments are found in the order of ideas and constructions within individual stanzas. Thus the first triplet-based paragraph has birds/trees/flowers as the subject of its opening segment; in the second half these are repeated in the order flowers/birds/trees. Recessed symmetry appears once more (as in lines 49–50), quoted above, p. 45. Following this comes the song of Ægon, where the sense is tied much more closely to the couplet structure, and where a more urgent note is achieved by the shorter units of organization. Again the refrain has alternative forms; the first, third and fifth paragraphs begin

> Resound ye Hills, resound my mournful Strain!

while the second, fourth and sixth substitute

> Resound ye Hills, resound my mournful Lay!

The two forms are brought together in a final quatrain, which has the resumptive function of the envoi in a ballade or the concluding stanza in a sestina:

> Resound ye Hills, resound my mournful Lay!
> Farewell ye Woods! adieu the Light of Day!
> One Leap from yonder Cliff shall end my Pains.
> No more ye Hills, no more resound my Strains!   (93–6)

Both songs have the long *a* sound as one rhyme variant, and this quatrain links Ægon's lament to the introductory lines where the same rhymes are found. In fact long vowel sounds characterize the rhyming of the entire poem. Out of the fifty couplets sixteen rhyme on a long *a* (including the first and last pairs); other typical rhymes involve long *o*, (as in *mourn/forlorn*) long *i*, *ee* (*seen/green*). The plangent note is sustained by a careful restriction of phonetic range; Pope shuffles these few sounds into different combinations – *pain* against *swain*, then against *strain*, which is itself set against *plain*, and so on. This is a different kind of virtuosity from the exuberant rhyming found in *Don Juan*, and perhaps a harder effect to appreciate nowadays, but it is crucial to Pope's strategy of echo and reverberance, in sound and meaning.

A few of these patterns have been touched on by Geoffrey Tillotson and Jacob H. Adler (though most have not) and of course the

relations of rhyme and reason in Pope have been finely discussed by
W. K. Wimsatt.[19] But the broader structural significance of these
techniques in the *Pastorals* has never been examined. In my
submission, Pope was interested in something more than local
decorative values, although that was certainly a consideration. His
use of such a device as the varied refrain – there is another in
'Winter' – suggests a debt to Renaissance poetic practice, not just
inert awareness of the older rhetoric.[20] The poems were his diploma
piece, copied out as an elaborate calligraphic feat,[21] and they display
what was already an antiquated regard for structural symmetry. In
form, the *Pastorals* more often recall Wyatt than the typical works of
Prior or Swift; it is as though Pope has gone beyond Denham, Waller
and Cowley, the acknowledged masters of versification, diction and
imagery, to find an older principle of formal ordonnance. If I am
right, it would be easily explicable that the *Pastorals* should reveal
Pope in closer contact with the doctrines of the Renaissance (as well
as the techniques) than we generally find him later. I am not
attempting to enlist Pope as a fully paid-up member of the
Pythagorean brotherhood, or to turn him into an out-and-out
numerologist. The suggestion is merely that the *Pastorals* have some
traces of the older views about correspondences in the universe, as
they clearly have remnants of the patterned structure which
expressed such beliefs.

Symmetry is not the same thing as art, and even in a Renaissance
context the fulfilment of an arithmetic scheme is less than a sufficient
condition for artistic success. None the less, Pope could reasonably
develop a poem on the seasons according to a stricter formal pattern
than was customary in Augustan poetry. He announces early on the
theme of 'the rowling Year' and the zodiac, 'Where twelve fair Signs
in beauteous Order lye' ('Spring', 40), as they are depicted on the
bowl of Daphnis. He could still count on at least some awareness in
his readership of what A. Kent Hieatt calls 'the elaborate, mytho-
logizing association of the movements of the heavens with the life of

---

[19] Tillotson, pp. 124–30; Jacob H. Adler, *The Reach of Art: A Study in the Prosody of Pope*
(Gainesville, Fla., 1964), pp. 34–44; W. K. Wimsatt, 'One Relation of Rhyme to Reason:
Alexander Pope', *MLQ*, V (1944), 323–8, reprinted in Mack, *Essential Articles*, pp. 63–84.

[20] A characteristic rhetorical figure, not isolated by Tillotson or Adler, is the repetition of a
word or phrase at the conclusion of one line at the start of the next: see 'Autumn' 86–7,
'Winter' 61–8. Technically this is *anadiplosis*, or (in its extended forms) *gradatio*.

[21] For a description of the manuscript, see John Butt, 'Pope's Poetical Manuscripts', *PBA*, XL
(1957), 23–39, reprinted in Mack, *Essential Articles*, pp. 545–64.

man.'[22] Through their echoes of sound and sense, their tessellation of seasonal and astral references, Pope's *Pastorals* eloquently reanimate the dead conceit of the music of time. I am not sure if this will be found an adequate defence in the 1990s for the poetry as we have it, but it is better than shirking the formal implications and moralizing the song.

---

[22] A. Kent Hieatt, *Short Time's Endless Monument: The Symbolism of the Numbers in Edmund Spenser's Epithalamion* (New York, 1960), p. 75. For the Renaissance background to temporal symbolism, see Fowler, *Triumphal Forms*, pp. 133–61, where the use of the calendar to serve as a model of cosmic harmony is described. One basic structural device used by Pope and largely ignored by the commentators is his allocation of the four closing lines of the work ('Winter', 89–92) to 'the several *Subjects* of the four Pastorals, and to the several *Scenes* of them, particularized before in each'. This reinforces the scheme of four-in-one, in a way which Renaissance theorists would have found entirely comprehensible.

CHAPTER 4

Windsor-Forest, Britannia *and river poetry*

I

Until very recently there were few more jumbled areas of Renaissance scholarship than that surrounding river poetry. It was widely known that Spenser had planned by 1580 to write an *Epithalamion Thamesis*, and that Camden's *Britannia* included some oddly dispersed fragments of an anonymous poem *De Connubio Tamae et Isis*. But the authorship and bibliographical history of the latter work were by no means firmly established: whilst the relation of Spenser's projected epithalamion to the marriage pageant of the Thames and Medway in the *Faerie Queene* (IV.xi) had not been properly explored. Finally, the mythological treatment of British rivers which occurs in poets as diverse as Drayton, William Browne and Milton had been left without any defined genealogy or coherent background. These omissions have been remedied, first by Jack B. Oruch in a study of the contribution made by Spenser and Camden to river-marriage poetry, and second by George Burke Johnston in his timely edition of Camden's poetry.[1] Quite apart from the localized merit of these contributions, they serve to open up wider scholarly vistas by delimiting a frame of reference in which later poems can be read with increased precision and point. I wish to suggest that as late a work as Pope's *Windsor-Forest* (1713) falls into this category. I do not say that it is *tout court* a 'river-poem', or that all its central strategies are related to this form of writing; but I do seek to show that appropriate generic features are prominent in the workings of this rich and complex utterance.[2]

---

[1] Jack B. Oruch, 'Spenser, Camden, and the Poetic Marriage of Rivers', *SP*, LXIV (1967), 606–24; 'Poems by William Camden', ed. George Burke Johnston, *SP*, LXXII (1975), xi, 1–143.

[2] All references to *Windsor-Forest* follow *TE*, I. Line numbers are preceded by the form *WF*.

On a factual level, it is certain that Pope knew *Britannia* when he completed *Windsor-Forest* – indeed that it was in his head at the time of writing. Line 65 is adapted from a line in 'an old monkish writer, I forget who', as the note has it: the source is Camden's account of the New Forest under the Normans, in his chapter on Hampshire. As the Twickenham editors of Pope remark, 'Pope had almost certainly read' this account, and one might add read with full attentiveness. It need hardly be emphasized that the picture of England under the Norman yoke, 'To Savage Beasts and Savage Laws a Prey' (*WF*, 45), is an important component of the moral and political statement of *Windsor-Forest*. That Pope's conception of the first two Williams should appear to derive from Camden's narrative is therefore a clue to the imaginative genetics of the poem. Another possible borrowing, though far less significant, occurs at line 348, where Pope may be recalling Camden's linkage of the River Darent with the battle of Otford. The Twickenham editors also indicate a few analogues in Pope's text to Drayton's *Poly-Olbion*, most of them naturally enough in the context of rivers. A more sustained parallel, with the section on Arden in Song XIII, is not mentioned.

Taken individually, most of these comparisons are suggestive rather than intensely striking, and they would not seem wholly to bear out the Twickenham editors' claim:

The Bible, Spenser, Drayton, Denham, Waller, Milton, along with Camden and the Anglo-Saxon chronicler, are used to impart to the poem suggestions not only of English landscape and history, but also those of Christian tradition and prophecy.[3]

However, Pope's antiquarian sources are both more extensive and more artistically cohesive than the edition permits us to see. Pope liked to make fun of the antiquaries, particularly men like Humfrey Wanley, whom he encountered in the entourage of the Earl of Oxford; and his only recorded comments on Drayton are disparaging.[4] Nevertheless, a careful examination of the text will show that *Windsor-Forest* makes pervasive use of British topographical

---

[3] *TE*, I, 132. The editors rightly speak of a 'rich and various background of both classical and native materials', but few of the native sources have been explored in detail.

[4] See *Corr*, II, 304; IV, 428. Pope writes that 'a very mediocre poet, one Drayton, is yet taken some notice of because Selden writ a very few Notes on one of his Poems'. Selden's notes to Song XVII of *Poly-Olbion* cover such matters as the course of the River Mole and the death of William Rufus, but there is no clear evidence that Pope made use of this or any other section of the notes. See *Poly-Olbion*, ed. J. William Hebel (*Michael Drayton Tercentenary Edition*, Vol. IV) (Oxford, 1933), pp. 341–62.

writers. And since, as Oruch makes clear, river poems constituted a recognizable genre, with well-marked themes and conventions (mostly associated with marriage as an emblem of concord)[5] the density of reference to crucial examples has the effect of welding the poem into this tradition. As a loco-descriptive work, *Windsor-Forest* at first fixes its main symbolic weight on the forest as such, though the river makes increasingly frequent entries (the 'plenteous streams' in the fishing episode, 134–46, for instance, or the culmination of Lodona's myth, 204–18). But after a direct apostrophe to the Thames (219–34), the poetic logic seems to require a gradual movement downstream from Windsor through London to the open sea.[6] Sylvan imagery is swallowed up within this irresistible current:

> Thy Trees, fair *Windsor*! now shall leave their Woods,
> And half thy Forests rush into my Floods.   (*WF*, 385–6)

This comes from the sustained and impassioned declamation by Father Thames, which forms a climax in thought and feeling to the poem. If it is agreed that the river lies at the heart of the poem's meaning, then we can reasonably enquire whether any of the earlier river poetry to which it alludes serves to underpin this meaning.

De Connubia Tamae et Isis is, of course, in Latin; and we can now be reasonably sure that it was written by William Camden himself.[7] The overwhelming probability is that Pope encountered the poem in Edmund Gibson's translation of 1695, where the Latin is printed followed by an English verse translation. Gibson's preface tells us that 'the Verses which occur in Mr. Camden's Text, were all translated by Mr. [Basil] Kennet of Corpus Christi College in Oxford'.[8] The 1695 edition of *Britannia*, it has been said, 'seems to have lain on the parlour tables of most well-to-do people'.[9] Pope's bent towards 'rambling', as well as orthodox antiquarian interests, might have led

---

[5] Oruch, pp. 616–18.

[6] A fuller consideration of this point will be found in my essay, 'Time and Space in *Windsor-Forest*,' in *The Art of Alexander Pope*, ed. H. Erskine-Hill and A. Smith (London, 1979), pp. 40–51.

[7] Oruch, pp. 609–11, and Johnston, pp. 36–40, agree on this conclusion.

[8] *Camden's Britannia, Newly Translated into English*, ed. Edmund Gibson (London, 1695), sig. a2ʳ. (References are to the column, as the pages are not numbered in the main text.) It is of course possible that Pope read one of the early editions in Latin, or else the translation by Philemon Holland (1610); but in view of the huge currency of the Gibson version during Pope's formative years, this is a far less likely supposition.

[9] *The Journeys of Celia Fiennes*, ed. Christopher Morris (London, 1947), p. xxv. See also Stuart Piggott, *William Stukeley: An Eighteenth-Century Antiquary* (London, 1985), pp. 18–21. For the importance of this edition to Defoe, see my article 'Defoe as Plagiarist,' *PQ*, LII (1973), 771–4.

him in the direction of the book.[10] He could not, in any case, have been oblivious to the great surge of interest in local history, topography and archaeology which occurred in his lifetime. Building on Camden, Dugdale and (in a different branch) Ogilby, an impressive body of scholars combined in what has been termed 'a new discovery of Britain'. Men like Gibson, Thoresby, Nathaniel Salmon, Browne Willis, Roger Gale, Stukeley, Thomas Cox and White Kennett (brother of Basil) produced important work in the first quarter of the eighteenth century. Several of these had links with the Saxon scholars and literary historians, headed by Hickes, Hearne and the Elstobs, who revolutionized the study of Old and Middle English.[11] Pope had close personal dealings with Wanley alone, but he had casual contacts with others. For example, William Stukeley was an early friend of Warburton, retailed gossip about Pope in his private diary, and even owned a copy of Kneller's profile of Pope.[12] Stukeley was a close friend of Maurice Johnson, the antiquarian through whose offices Pope and Gay were elected to the Gentlemen's Society of Spalding in 1728. Further, Pope helped Aaron Thompson with his edition of Geoffrey of Monmouth (1718). None of this proves beyond doubt that Pope was ever himself a full-blooded antiquarian; but it shows that he was familiar with the 'matter of Britain', and provides a valid context in which to set the indisputable references to Camden.

II

The first sustained allusion occurs, as already indicated, in the passage on the Norman oppression of forest inhabitants, which draws on Camden's description of the New Forest.[13] But there is in addition a marked similarity, not previously observed, with Camden's section on Windsor Forest, which immediately follows a long excerpt from *De Connubio*. If Pope read any part of *Britannia* attentively, we can be sure he would do so in respect of the chapter dealing with Berkshire, and specifically those paragraphs concerning his boyhood home in the Forest. The more direct parallels (disregarding a broad thematic congruence) are these:

[10] See my essay 'Pope's Rambles', in *Eighteenth-Century Encounters* (Brighton, 1985), pp. 41–55.
[11] The best account is that of David C. Douglas, *English Scholars 1660–1730* (London, rev. edn, 1961): as well as (for local historians) Piggott, pp. 13–25.
[12] *The Family Memoirs of the Reverend William Stukeley, M.D.* [ed. W. C. Lukis] (Durham, 1882), pp. 94, 121, 127–30, 403. See below, pp. 253–7.
[13] It is possible that Pope also had in mind *Poly-Olbion*, XVII, 111–29, but apart from a single line (*WF*, 83) the parallelism is somewhat vague.

Windsor-Forest (43–92)	*Britannia* (1695 edn)
Not thus the Land appear'd in Ages past, A dreary Desart and a gloomy Waste, To Savage Beasts and Savage Laws a Prey, And Kings more furious and severe then they: Who claim'd the Skies, dispeopled Air and Floods, The lonely Lords of empty Wilds and Woods. Cities laid waste, they storm'd the Dens and Caves, (For wiser Brutes were backward to be Slaves).	And it is incredible how much ground the Kings of England have suffer'd every where to lie wast, and have set apart for the shutting up of Deer...Neither can I believe that any thing was the cause, but too great delight in hunting (tho' some attribute it to want of people); for since the Danish times, they have continually afforested more and more places, and for their preservation have imposed very strict laws, and appointed a *Chief-Ranger* or *Forester*, who is to take cognizance of all causes relating to the Forests, and may punish with loss of life or limb any one that shall kill the Deer in any Chase or Forest. (col. 149)
What could be free, when lawless Beasts obey'd, And ev'n the Elements a Tyrant sway'd? In vain kind Seasons swell'd the teeming Grain, Soft Show'rs distill'd, and Suns grew Warm in vain; The Swain with Tears his frustrate Labour yields, And famish'd dies amid his ripen'd Fields. What wonder then, a Beast or Subject slain Were equal Crimes in a Despotick Reign; Both doom'd alike for sportive Tyrants bled, But while the Subject starv'd, the Beast was fed.	[Quoting John of Salisbury:] You have heard that the fowls of the air and fishes of the sea are common. But these are the King's, and are claimed by the Forest-Law wherever they fly. With-hold thy hand, and forbear, lest thou fall into the Huntsman's hands, and be punish'd for Treason. The Husbandmen are debarr'd their Fallows, whilst the Deer have liberty to stay abroad; and that their feedings may be enlarg'd, the Farmer is cut short of the use of his own grounds. What is sown or planted they keep from the Countryman, pasturage from the Graziers, and throw the Beehives out of the Flowry

Plots; nay, even the Bees themselves are scarce suffer'd to use their natural liberty. (149–50).

Proud *Nimrod* first the bloody Chace
    began,
A mighty Hunter, and his Prey was
    Man.
Our haughty *Norman* boasts that
    barb'rous Name,
And makes his trembling Slaves the
    Royal Game.
The Fields are ravish'd from th'
    industrious Swains,
From men their Cities, and from Gods
    their Fanes:
The levell'd Towns with Weeds lie
    cover'd o'er,
The hollow Winds thro' naked
    Temples roar;
Round broken Columns clasping Ivy
    twin'd;
O'er Heaps of Ruin stalk'd the stately
    Hind;
The Fox obscene to gaping Tombs
    retires,
And savage Howlings fill the sacred
    Quires.

William the Conquerer destroy'd all the towns, villages, and churches; and turning out the poor inhabitants, made a forest for wild beasts of more than thirty miles in circuit... This he did either to make a more easie access for his Normans into England... or to indulge himself in hunting; or to raise money by methods tho' never so unjust. For he, more merciful to beasts than to mankind, appointed a most grievous pecuniary mulct, and other severe penalties, to be inflicted on those who should trespass on his game. (115)

Aw'd by his Nobles, by his Commons
    curst,
Th' Oppressor rul'd Tyrannick where
    he *durst*,
Stretch'd o'er the Poor, and Church,
    his Iron Rod,
And serv'd alike his Vassals and his
    God.
Whom ev'n the *Saxon* spar'd, and
    bloody *Dane*,
The wanton Victims of his *Sport*
    remain.
But see the Man who spacious Regions
    gave
A waste for Beasts, himself deny'd a
    Grave!

But divine vengeance was not long wanting to this impious project of the King's; for Richard his second son, and William Rufus King of England another of his sons, both lost their lives in this forest; the latter being casually shot by an arrow by *Walter Tirrel*.

[*Quotes verses by Bishop White*:]
Towns, Fields, and Churches,
    took from God and
    Men,

Stretch'd on the lawn his second
    Hope survey,
At once the Chaser and at once the
    Prey.
Lo *Rufus*, tugging at the deadly Dart,
Bleeds in the Forest, like a wounded
    Hart.

Succeeding Monarchs heard the
    Subjects Cries,
Nor saw displeas'd the peaceful
    Cottage rise.
Then gath'ring Flocks on unknown
    Mountains fed,
O'er sandy Wilds were yellow
    Harvests spread,
The Forests wonder'd at the unusual
    Grain,
And secret Transport touch'd the
    conscious Swain.
Fair *Liberty*, *Britannia's* Goddess, rears
Her chearful Head, and leads the
    golden Years.

A spatious forest made in
    Beaulieu-plain:
The King a Hart, Vengeance
    the King pursu'd,
And *Tirrel's* arrow drunk his
    guilty blood. (115)

...By the Barons revolt, the
Charta de Foresta was extorted
from Henry 3, wherein, having
abrogated those rigorous laws,
he granted others more
equitable, to which those that
live within the limits of the
Forests are at this day bound
to be comfortable. (150)

It will be apparent that the essential movement of the rhetoric here, charting the course of tyranny, nemesis and rebirth, is incomplete without the general passage on forest law and the statement of reform in Plantaganet times. In both cases the analogue comes, not in the New Forest passage, but in Camden's chapter on Berkshire.

The relevance of this fact is that it shows the interfusion of Camden and Pope at a juncture embodying the deepest concerns of *Windsor-Forest*.[14] The two to three pages which the antiquary devotes to Windsor and its surroundings supply more than a vivid backcloth to the poem: they are woven into the fabric of the verse. Camden describes the history of the castle and its royal associations (and, as Paul Fussell has memorably observed, 'the whole poem is dignified by [the castle's] proximity').[15] He gives an account of the Order of the Garter and lists the original knights under Edward III a factual rendition of the themes poetically embellished in *Windsor-Forest* (*WF*,

---

[14] See the classic account of Earl R. Wasserman, in *The Subtler Language* (Baltimore, Md., 1959), pp. 113–28.

[15] Paul Fussell, *The Rhetorical World of Augustan Humanism* (Oxford, 1965), p. 207. The Twickenham editors suggest that Pope may have recalled at *WF* 400 Camden's remarks on the supposed etymology of the name Windsor (151).

299–310). Camden evokes in his busy, literal-minded way the same sense of locality which Pope exploits in the opening sections of his poem:

Scarce any Royal Seat can certainly have a more pleasant situation. For from an high hill rising with a gentle ascent, it hath an admirable prospect round about. Its front overlooks a long and wide valley, chequer'd with corn-fields and green meadows, clothed on each side with groves, and water'd with the calm and gentle Thames. Behind it arise hills every where, neither craggy nor over-high, adorn'd with woods, and, as it were, consecrated by nature it self to *Hunting*. (145)

It would be absurd to suggest that this passage and others comparable 'explain' Pope's work – he had eyes to take in the real landscape, quite apart from any literary descriptions. But, some way short of nakedly conceived 'influence', there is an unmistakable congruence of idiom – the groves, the chequered landscape, wooded fields which 'adorn' the scene, the 'gentle' Thames, and noble 'prospect' of corn and pasture-land – all terms employed in the poem.

But the two texts attain their most inward similarity at the point where Camden quotes fifty-four lines from *De Connubio*, the fragment first included in the 1600 edition of *Britannia*, and identified by Johnston as Kennett's excerpt No. 2. The poem is introduced as containing material 'in which Father *Thames* endeavours to celebrate the dignity of the place, and the Majesty of Queen Elizabeth then keeping her court there'. It is not so much as mentioned in the Twickenham edition, and accordingly I cite Kennett's translation of the entire fragment:

> Now on the bank fam'd Windsor's towers appear,
> Mount their high tops, and pierce the utmost air.
> At this (but first does Eaton's walls salute,
> Where stern *Orbilius* governs absolute,
> And in proud state his birchen scepter shakes)
> Thames lifts it's azure head, and thus he speaks:
> *Windsor*, no more thy ancient glories tell,
> No more relate the wonders of thy hill;
> Thy Forts, thy Fenns, thy Chapel's stately pile:
> Thy Spires, thy smiling Fields, thy happy Springs;   10
> Thy Cradles, Marriage-beds, or Tombs of Kings.
> Forget the Knights thy noble stalls adorn,
> The Garter too by them in honour worn:
> Tho' that great Order found the first in fame,
> And swells so high with mighty *George*'s name,

That *Burgundy* contemns her golden Fleece,
And the light French their scallop'd chains despise.
Rhodes, *Alcala* and *Elbe* with shame disown
The painted crosses on their mantles shown.
These glories now are all eclips'd by one,   20
One honour vies with all thy old renown.
When on thy courts, and on my bank we see
Elizabeth (then *Thames* with bended knee
Stoops low to pay obeysance to her name;
And thus goes on, pleas'd with his mighty theme.)
Elizabeth, whom we with wonder stile
The Queen, the Saint, the Goddess of our Isle:
Whose praise should I endeavor to rehearse
Within the narrow bounds of feeble verse;
As soon huge *Athos* might on *Atlas* stand   30
Rais'd by my strength; as soon my weary hand
Might count the endless globules of my sand.
If any grace on purpose I'd conceal,
What I pass by will prove the greatest still.
If her past deeds inspire my joyful tongue,
Her present actions stop th' imperfect song.
Should her strict justice fill my rising thought,
Her mercy comes between and drives it out.
Or was my subject her triumphant Arms,
Alas! more trophies grace her conqu'ring charms.   40
That virtues flourish, and the peaceful gown;
That all to laws are subject, laws to none:
That *Scotland* hath refus'd the *Gallick* yoak,
And *Ireland* all her savage arts forsook:
That *Ulster*'s sons at last reform'd appear;
To her they owe, the fame belongs to her.
Virtues, that single make us thro'ly blest,
United, all adorn her princely breast.
To heaven her Godlike mind Religion bears,
Justice to profit honesty preferrs.   50
Deliberate prudence cautious thoughts inspires,
And temp'rance guides her innocent desires.
Her settled constancy's unshaken frame
Deserves the noble motto, STILL THE SAME.
But ah! my numbers all are spent in vain,
And grasp at what they never can contain.
Should some wild fancy all th' encomiums joyn
That worth could e're deserve, or post feign,
The panegyrick would be still too mean.

O may her years increase with her renown, 60
May constant joys attend her peaceful Crown,
While I may streams or banks may call her own!
And when she dies (if Goddesses can die)
May I straight fail, and be for ever dry! (148)

This is more overtly panegyrical than anything in *Windsor-Forest*, and Kennett's bathetic style takes us into a lower realm of literary experience. But, quite apart from the numerous verbal parallels (compare lines 1–2 with *WF*, 287–8; line 6 with *WF*, 330, 351; lines 22–3 with *WF*, 384), there is a striking identity of purpose. In each case the poet uses the conceit of Father Thames lifting his head to praise a British queen, whose peaceful reign unifies the people and causes envy among foreign nations. The past glories connected with Windsor, such as the foundation of a great chivalric order and the burial of kings, will be eclipsed by the new gold age inaugurated by the queen. Naturally Pope's vision is a richer one; his language is far more resourceful, he moves from mere gestures of panegyric to an eloquent prophecy of events on a world scale. Nevertheless, both poets focus their nationalistic and patriotic themes in a *local* image, that of the river which 'visits *Windsor*'s fam'd Abodes, / To grace the Mansion of our earthly Gods' (*WF*, 229–30).

From the moment that Father Thames enters the text of *Windsor-Forest* (329), a natural impulsion carries the poem downstream; and the generic motifs of river-poetry become more prominent. *De Connubio* had begun with a marriage in the upper Thames, but it too progresses along the river past Windsor, Runnymede, Hampton Court and Richmond to the capital. At the start of his catalogue of tributaries, Pope mentions the traditional 'parent' streams:

First the fam'd Authors of his ancient Name,
The winding *Isis*, and the fruitful *Tame*. (*WF*, 339–40)

This of course is the subject of Camden's poem, announced in the Oxfordshire chapter: 'Near this place [Dorchester] Tame and Isis with mutual consent joyn as it were in wedlock, and mix their names as well as their waters' (264).[16] A separate excerpt is given in the Gloucestershire chapter, and Pope's description of Father Thames is itself indebted to the account of the Isis here:

---

[16] Compare also *Poly-Olbion*, XV, 103–4, 282, for the Thames as child of this marriage.

> *Isis*, whom British streams their monarch own.
> His never-wearied hands a spatious urn
> Down on his azure bosom gravely turn,
> And flaggs and reeds his unpoll'd locks adorn.
> Each waving horn the subject stream supplies,
> And grateful light darts from his shining eyes.
> His grizzly beard all wet hands dropping down,
> And gushing veins in wat'ry chanels run.   (241–2)

As for the tributaries, the 'several pleasant Islands' in the Cole (279) reappear in *WF* 342; the 'small and clear river *Vandal*' (158) figures as 'the blue, transparent *Vandalis*' (*WF*, 345); the sluggish course of the 'very gentle stream' of the Lea is described by Camden (294–5) and by Pope, 'The gulfy *Lee* his sedgy Tresses rears' (*WF*, 346); the 'sullen *Mole* that hides his diving Flood' (*WF*, 347) is fully covered in *Britannia* (155–6), where the same verb *hide* is used; and the line concerning the Darent (*WF*, 348), as already observed, is probably based on Pope's reading of Camden (190) – the 'gentle chanel' becoming 'silent' in the reworking. There are other river-poems lying behind this section: the marriage of Thames and Isis (which is the basis of Song XV in *Poly-Olbion*), the Mole, and the Wandal 'so wondrous cleer' all accompany the progress downstream from Windsor to London in Drayton (XVII, 1–104), while one stanza of Spenser's pageant (*Faerie Queene*, IV.xi.29) is particularly close to Pope's rendition.[17] However, it is only in *Britannia* that we can trace the single, as it were unilinear, movement borrowed by Pope at the climax of his design:

> Strait the joyful stream
> Proud of the late addition to it's name
> Flows briskly on, ambitious now to pay
> A larger tribute to the sovereign sea.   (266)

For Drayton and Spenser, the Thames is one among a large number of rivers celebrated, important certainly, but seen as a contributor to a broader action.[18] For Camden and Pope, the swelling flood of the Thames as it flows towards the sea is an emblem of national well-being.

---

[17] Curiously Camden omits the Loddon (*WF*, 342); there is a bare reference in *Poly-Olbion*, XV, 293, but Pope no doubt included this river as it flowed within a mile or two of his boyhood home at Binfield. It might be added that Camden refers to 'the winding, but pleasant and gentle streams of the Isis' (137), which equates with *WF*, 340.

[18] A comparable notion is briefly raised by Drayton in *Poly-Olbion*, XV, 103–12, but it is never developed or made into an organizing theme of this song.

This becomes explicit in the London sections. Spenser's Troynovant (*Faerie Queene*, IV.xi.28) is picturesque, mythological, heraldic. Drayton's capital is busy but curiously vague in outline, the treatment perfunctory and stiff (*Poly-Olbion*, XVII, 89–104). *De Connubio* is much more full-blooded:

> Stretch'd on a rising hill betwixt the strands,
> *London*, her mother *Troy's* great rival stands.
> Where heaven and earth their choicest gifts bestow,
> And tides of men the spatious streets o'reflow.
> *London*! the mighty image of our Isle,
> That we great *Britain* of it self may stile.
> Where *Chryse, Paris, Rome* and *Ormus* yield,
> In metals, learning, people, wealth excell'd.   (324)

Likewise Pope's vision of the 'two fair Cities' of London and Westminster (*WF*, 375–84) harnesses the accumulated energies of the poem in order to assert the fulfilment of a noble national destiny. The capital gathers up the themes as the lower Thames collects the confluent waters. Its material riches exemplify 'the beauteous Works of Peace' (*WF*, 378). This is a point Pope is able to make more cogently because he can present London as the natural centre of more leadership, situated at the headwater of naval and commercial traffic:

> Thy Trees, fair *Windsor*! now shall leave their Woods,
> And half the Forests rush into my Floods,
> Bear *Britain's* Thunder, and her Cross display,
> To the bright Regions of the rising Day.   (*WF*, 385–8)

What had been, earlier in its course – and in the poem – a relatively placid and domestic current, with 'hush'd Waves' and mourning willows, fed by 'lingring Streams', has now become a waterway to empire, an avenue towards the great oceans of the world.[19]

For the image to open out in this way, it is essential for Pope to mute the overtly militaristic and aggressive overtones of the language. A standard motif of river poetry was the challenge to foreign waters

---

[19] This aspect of the poem is treated more fully in my essay 'Trade and Empire: *Annus Mirabilis* and *Windsor-Forest*', *Durham University Journal*, LXIX (1976), 14–20. For Pope's development of the Troynovant theme, see Donald T. Torchiana, 'Brutus: Pope's last Hero', *JEGP*, LXI (1962), 853–67, and Miriam Leranbaum, *Alexander Pope's 'Opus Magnum'* 1729–1744 (Oxford, 1977), pp. 155–74.

to provide an equal.[20] *De Connubio* offers a concise example in the Richmond section:

> While the proud river thus his worth proclaims;
> 'Great you that Europe boasts her noblest streams,
> 'Yield all to me: for such an ebb and flow
> 'No rival flood but *Scheld* and *Elb* can show.'   (158)

Windsor-Forest enlists this spirit of emulation for an unexpected purpose; the Tyber, Hermes, Nile and the rest are outdone by the Thames as it ministers to 'the Blessings of a peaceful Reign' (*WF*, 355–74).[21] Formally this verse-paragraph alludes to the Treaty of Utrecht; in the context of river poetry, it substitutes for the customary marriage device (as in Camden and Spenser) an alternative image of concord – that is, the suspension of national hostilities and the advent of a new era of co-operation. Pope went out of his way to emphasize the theme of peace, rather than patriotism pure and simple. In a note he indicated his 'opposition to the horrors and devastations of war' and his 'hostility to the name of *Marlborough*'. The river remains the controlling symbol, as in *De Connubio*, but instead of a marital union we are given a vision of international brotherhood:

> Oh stretch thy Reign, fair *Peace*! from Shore to Shore,
> Till Conquest cease, and Slav'ry be no more:
> Till the freed *Indians* in their native Groves
> Reap their own Fruits, and woo their sable Loves,
> *Peru* once more a Race of Kings behold,
> And other *Mexico*'s be roof'd with Gold.
> Exil'd by Thee from Earth to deepest Hell,
> In Brazen Bonds shall barb'rous *Discord* dwell.   (*WF*, 407–14)

According to Oruch, the most thorough investigator in this area, Camden himself is solely responsible for the 'remarkable innovation' of using 'a myth centered in the marriage of two rivers'.[22] The purest expression of the myth comes in *De Connubio*, where 'Faith and Concord speak them [Thames and Isis] into one (265)'. The notion lingered on, in a more and more desultory fashion, through the eighteenth century, with 'a trickle of river marriages conceived by minor poets whose gurgling songs no longer are remembered'.[23]

---

[20] *Poly-Olbion*, XV, 263–80, has a passage on great rivers in fact and legend, but handled philosophically and spiritually rather than historically or politically. Drayton's lines 264–5 may have influenced 'Spring' 61 in Pope's *Pastorals*.

[21] *WF*, 367 echoes a line from *De Connubio* in *Britannia* (266). The Ganges, Nile, Rhine and 'Ister' (*WF*, 359–68) all figure in Camden (241).

[22] Oruch, p. 613.   [23] Oruch, p. 624.

If my apprehension of the poetic strategies of *Windsor-Forest* is in any degree justified, then we should see this as an important adaptation of river-poem conventions to a broader literary purpose. This is not to say that the poem has no other sources, models, or operative conventions; it is simply to indicate one substantial tradition underpinning the topographic metaphors employed by Pope.

III

I have left aside a particular issue raised by any possible link between *De Connubio* and *Windsor-Forest*. It will be recalled that the Windsor fragment contained a celebration of the Garter:[24]

> Tho' that great Order found the first in fame,
> And swells so high with mighty *George*'s name,
> That *Burgundy* contemns her gold Fleece,
> And the light French their scallop'd chains despise.
> *Rhodes*, *Alcala* and *Elbe* with shame disown
> The painted Crosses on their mantles shown.   (148)

St George's Chapel, Windsor, is of course the home of the order, and it is apt that a reference to the emblem of St George occurs in Pope's poem:

> Bear *Britain's* Thunder, and her Cross display,
> To the bright Regions of the rising Day.   (*WF*, 387–8)

The lines as originally drafted read more strikingly:

> Now shall our fleets the bloody Cross display
> To the rich regions of the rising day.

The editors tell us that the cross is that of St George, on the Union Jack; but the joint English and Scottish flag, though it had existed since the previous century, was not in 1713 a powerful popular symbol. 'The bloody Cross' suggests unambiguously the red cross of St George considered in isolation. The use of this image cements the poetic symbolism, in that British endeavour is traced back to the home of chivalry in Windsor; at a subliminal level we are perhaps invited to conceive of the new empire-builders as crusaders and defenders of the faith.

Behind the reference in *De Connubio*, and indeed behind the whole Windsor section of *Britannia*, lies an important area of buried history.

---

[24] See also *Poly-Olbion*, XV, 313–18.

As Frances Yates has pointed out, 'There had been a great revival of the Order [of the Garter], its ceremonies, processions, and ethos, during the reign of Elizabeth, who had used it as a means of drawing the noblemen together in a common service to the Crown.' In 1612, five years after the fullest text of *De Connubio* was assembled in *Britannia*, the Elector Palatine was invested with the order at Windsor. He had come to England for his wedding to Princess Elizabeth, the daughter of King James I. This important dynastic marriage, which had far-reaching implications for almost all European monarchies, took place on 14 February 1613 at Whitehall Palace. Entertainments to celebrate the event had included a fireworks display on 11 February, acting out the story of St George and the dragon. On 14 and 15 February two masques were presented at court. The latter, for which Francis Bacon was possibly responsible, is of less direct interest. The earlier of the two performed was written by Thomas Campion and designed by Inigo Jones. The union of Germany and Britain was symbolized by a scene linking 'Rhenus' and Thames; a prophecy in verse foretold the appearance of a great race of kings (compare *WF*, 411); and other emblems of union were presented in elaborate spectacle. It is perhaps worth adding that the Elector was himself a member of the Order of the Golden Fleece, to which Camden refers.[25]

Here we have several of the motifs of river poetry converted to a theatrical and political setting: marriage, concord, prophecy, and specifically the union of the Rhine with the Thames. It is as though *De Connubio* had been dramatized for a royal command performance. Whether or not we should attach special significance to the Red Cross symbolism in either Camden or Pope, I do not know. It is certain that *Windsor-Forest* is a strongly royalist poem, and it was dedicated to a man recently admitted to the order of the peerage – Lansdowne, whom Pope suggests as a suitable recipient for the Garter (*WF*, 289–90).[26] Writing in the wake of the notorious twelve new peerages

[25] This paragraph is based on Frances Yates, *The Rosicrucian Enlightenment* (London, 1975), pp. 27–42 and *passim*.

[26] See Frances M. Clements, 'Lansdowne, Pope, and the Unity of *Windsor-Forest*', *MLQ*, XXXIII (1972), 44–53; and my article, 'The Enamelled Ground: The Language of Heraldry and Natural Description in *Windsor-Forest*', *Studia Neophilologica*, XLV (1973), 356–71. The Earl of Oxford, the close friend whom Pope first met in 1713, had been admitted to the Garter in the previous year. Swift, who was regularly at Windsor during the period of the Harley administration, took an interest in the installation ceremonies (e.g. *Journal to Stella*, 22 December 1710). He had hopes of becoming Dean of Windsor, which might have involved (as it did for the fortunate incumbent of this office in 1714) the post of Registrar to the order.

created to force the Utrecht provisions through, Pope might reasonably have seen a need to 'draw...noblemen together in a common service to the Crown'. On the evidence available, it cannot be definitely established that Pope intends any arcane political meaning with his allusion to the Red Cross.[27] What the events of 1612–13 do show is that the common devices of river poetry could be turned to wider public and propagandist ends. (Some motifs, such as personified rivers, survived in the pageantry of the Lord Mayor's Show, an occasion celebrated in *The Dunciad*.[28]) Many such emblematic techniques of the Renaissance were available in Pope's day, as modern scholarship has amply illustrated; and so sophisticated a poet as Pope knew how to take such opportunities. We shall, in my view, understand *Windsor-Forest* better if we recognize that its courtly, masque-like, richly embroidered mode has roots in the Renaissance river poem. In particular its resonant concluding prophecy, uttered by the Thames, goes back to the progenitor and defining example of this genre, *De Connubio Tamae et Isis*, which lies scattered in fragments about that master-work of national piety, *Britannia*.

[27] It is interesting to observe the many connections between the Order of the Garter and Rosicrucian ideology, indicated by Frances Yates. A single representative instance is provided by the studies in Rosicrucian lore made by Elias Ashmole, the distinguished antiquarian whose history of the Garter (1672) was republished with additions in 1715. I do not claim that Pope was deeply versed in Rosicrucian philosophy, though he knew enough of it by the end of 1713 to fill out the revised *Rape of the Lock* with the mythology of *Le Comte de Gabalis*. He seems also to have been a freemason, and of course early masonry was heavily imbued with Rosicrucian associations (Yates, pp. 249–60). Ashmole had also been a freemason; so, amongst others mentioned in this essay, was William Stukeley. Finally we might observe that Pope, unlike Camden and Drayton, makes no mention of St George by name – possibly because the appellation was tactless with the Elector of Hanover waiting in the wings to end the era when 'Peace and Plenty tell, a *STUART* reigns' (*WF*, 42). See also Douglas Brooks-Davies, 'Messianic Alchemy in *Windsor-Forest*', *YES*, XVIII (1988), 125–42.

[28] Robert Withington, *English Pageantry: An Historical Outline* (Cambridge, Mass., 1920), II, 3–145, describes allegorical and mythical elements in civic pageantry which survived until the decline of the Lord Mayor's Show early in the eighteenth century. The 'triumphs of London' devised by Elkanah Settle included an apparition of Neptune. For Pope's use of the Show, see Aubrey Williams, *Pope's Dunciad* (London, 1955).

CHAPTER 5

Faery lore and The Rape of the Lock

Everyone knows that Pope added the machinery of sylphs and gnomes when he revised *The Rape of the Lock* in 1714. And most people – aside from John Dennis – think it was a valuable addition. However, the precise imaginative territory opened up by this means has never been charted in any detail.[1] The declared Rosicrucian origins of the machinery appear to have disabled criticism in a puzzling way. I wish to offer a threefold argument. First, that the gnomes are as important as the sylphs in the design. Second, that Pope writes in a tradition of rustic 'faery' lore, involving Shakespeare, Spenser, Drayton and others. And third, a relatively minor point, that the work of William Diaper – notably *Dryades*, published in December 1712 – has a perceptible relevance to the additions Pope made.

On July 1712, in the *Spectator* no. 419, Addison supplied the classic definition of the 'fairy way of writing'. In this species of composition, he tells us,

the poet quite loses sight of nature, and entertains his reader's imagination with the characters and actions of such persons as have many of them no existence, but what he bestows on them. Such are fairies, witches, magicians, demons, and departed spirits.

Addison then goes on to specify the qualities required of a poet attempting this mode:

It is impossible for a poet to succeed in it, who has not a particular cast of fancy, and an imagination naturally fruitful and superstitious. Besides this, he ought to be well versed in legends and fables, antiquated romances, and

---

[1] The most extended discussion of the sylphs is Appendix B in *TE*, II, 378–83. This is the edition followed throughout. On the Cave of Spleen, see the article by Lawrence Babb, *RES*, XII (1936), 165–76. K. M. Briggs (*The Fairies in Tradition and Literature* (London, 1967), pp. 156–8) is concerned with the status of the elementals from the point of view of folk history, rather than their imaginative function.

the traditions of nurses and old women, that he may fall in with our natural prejudices, and humour those notions which we have imbibed in our infancy. For, otherwise, he will be apt to make his fairies talk like people of his own species, and not like other sets of beings, who converse with different objects, and think in a different manner from that of mankind...These descriptions raise a pleasing kind of horror in the mind of the reader, and amuse his imagination with the strangeness and novelty of the persons who are represented in them. They bring up into our memory the stories we heard in our childhood, and favour those secret terrors and apprehensions to which the mind of man is naturally subject.[2]

Now Addison, of course, advised against the expansion of the *Rape* from two cantos to five. Perhaps he felt that Pope's imaginative endowments were not 'naturally superstitious'. But in the event Pope chose to fill out his cast-list with 'persons as have many of them no existence'. Moreover, the Cave of Spleen is enough to remind us that 'strangeness and novelty' are among the effects of the poem, and that 'terrors and apprehensions' are not always kept at bay even in the gracious world of Belinda.

In his discussion of the sylphs Geoffrey Tillotson rightly pointed out that Pope grafts the Rosicrucian mythology on to 'all the Nurse and Priest have taught' (I, 30), and remarked that by this stroke Pope 'connects the machinery with the beliefs of his own country, a connection required of an epic poet'.[3] Quite so: but Pope goes further. He makes pagan folklore act as a mock-heroic prop and a handmaiden of the social satire. But it also operates as a kind of poetic amplifier, enlarging the fantastic and surrealistic capacities of the work. The true proportions of the *Rape* are not defined by the habitual decorum of comic epic; they enclose the heathen psychology of 'spleen' and the dreamlike visions scattered throughout. The *Rape* is like Virgil, but it is also (designedly) like *A Midsummer Night's Dream*. Its dominant mood is one of a rapt and enchanted wonder.

This note is struck as soon as Ariel, who had caught 'The Morning-Dream that hover'd o'er her Head', wakens Belinda:

> Fairest of Mortals, thou distinguish'd Care
> Of thousand bright Inhabitants of Air!
> If e'er one Vision touch'd thy infant Thought,
> Of all the Nurse and all the Priest have taught,
> Of airy Elves by Moonlight Shadows seen,

---

[2] *The Spectator*, ed. D. F. Bond (Oxford, 1965), III, 570–1.   [3] *TE*, II, 380n.

> The silver Token, and the circled Green,
> Or Virgins visited by Angel-Pow'rs,
> With Golden Crowns and Wreaths of heav'nly Flow'rs,
> Hear and believe!   (I, 27–35)

One does not have to seek far for an exactly contemporary evocation
of 'the circled Green' and elves by moonlight. This comes from
Dryades: or, The Nymphs Prophecy, which Swift found 'very good' on its
appearance in December 1712:[4]

> The Moon, with doubtful Rays, deceiv'd the Sight,
> And waving Boughs gave an uncertain Light.
> When my chill'd Spirits sunk with sudden Fear,
> And trembling Horror bid the Search forbear;
> My heedless Steps had touch'd the hallow'd Ground,
> Where airy Daemons dance the wanton Round;
> Where fairy Elves, and Midnight *Dryads* meet,
> And to the smiling Moon the Sylvan-Song repeat.
> Tall rifted Oaks, and circling Elms had made
> A central void amid surrounding Shade...   (40–9)

I am not here concerned with 'influence' – the argument is that
Belinda was familiar with such verses, not Pope – but it is interesting
to observe how Pope's lines 31–2 echo Diaper's 45–8 (*airy*, *elves*,
moonlight/*midnight* – each in the identical metric position – *circled*/
circling, *shadows*/*shade*, even the chime of *silver*/*sylvan*).

   Ariel goes on to refer to 'Some secret Truths from learned Pride
conceal'd, / To Maids alone and Children are reveal'd.' Similarly
Addison had continued his *Spectator* paper with a caveat against
scepticism: 'Men of cold fancies, and philosophical dispositions,
object to this kind of poetry, that it has not probability enough to
affect the imagination.' In Pope's terms,

> What tho' no Credit doubting Wits may give?
> The Fair and Innocent shall still believe.   (I, 39–40)

The gloss from Addison comes pat, and supplies an ironic edge to
Ariel's persuasives:

Nay, many are prepossessed with such false opinions, as dispose them to
believe these particular delusions; at least, we have all heard so many
pleasing relations in favour of them, that we do not care for seeing through
the falsehood, and willingly give ourselves up to so agreeable an imposture.[5]

---

[4] The text followed is that of *The Complete Works of William Diaper*, ed. Dorothy Broughton
(London, 1951), pp. 57–81.   [5] *Spectator*, ed. Bond, III, 571–2.

This is an excellent account of Belinda's approach to life. And it steadily dawns on us that the sylphs represent a kind of pretext for her. Their role in the plot is to be as a non-conscience, endorsing every impulse towards coquetry and vanity.

Soon afterwards, indeed, Ariel explains the cosmic transformation which underlies the fairy state:

> For when the Fair in all their Pride expire,
> To their first Elements their Souls retire:
> The Sprights of fiery Termagants in Flame
> Mount up, and take a *Salamander's* Name.
> Soft yielding Minds to Water glide away,
> And sip with *Nymphs*, their Elemental Tea.
> The graver Prude sinks downwards to a *Gnome*,
> In search of Mischief still on Earth to roam.
> The light Coquettes in *Sylphs* aloft repair,
> And sport and flutter in the Fields of Air.   (I, 57–66)

This, shorn of its vibrant metaphysical wit, is what Pope found in *Le Comte de Gabalis*. But there are many riders to the passage. It is the first mention of the gnomes. That they should be made the avatars of prudish womanhood is significant – for Clarissa, the nearest voice to sanity we hear, is to be deemed a 'prude' by Thalestris (V, 36). According to *Gabalis*, the gnomes were 'the Guardians of Treasures', and also of precious stones (such as the sparkling cross, the easily lost necklace, the ear-rings).[6] In the source, as Tillotson remarks, all the faery creatures were friendly; it is Pope who makes the gnomes sinister. As for Diaper, he leaves them neutral:

> The earthy *Gnomes*, and fairy Elves are seen,
> Digging in lowest Mines with busy Men;
> There labour on the fruitless Work intent,
> While deeper Snows the wonted Dance prevent.   (157–60)

The preceding lines themselves recall the next section of Ariel's speech:

> The Elfin Pow'rs (who can at Pleasure leave
> Aerial Bodies, and new Forms receive)
> Cast off their Vehicles and freed from Sense...   (153–5)

Compare Pope:

> For Spirits, freed from mortal Laws, with ease
> Assume what Sexes and what Shapes they please.   (I, 69–70)

---

[6] Cited by Tillotson, *TE*, II, 380.

Again it is not a question of 'borrowing' (there is a closer Miltonic analogue for Pope's lines),[7] but of an affinity in mode and phrasing.

Ariel passes on to describe the role of the sylphs in guarding the 'Purity of melting Maids... When Musick softens, and when Dancing fires'. Then, more specifically:

> Oft when the World imagine Women stray,
> The *Sylphs* thro' mystick Mazes guide their Way,
> Thro' all the giddy Circle they pursue,
> And old Impertinence expel by new.
> What tender Maid but must a Victim fall
> To one Man's Treat, but for another's Ball?
> When *Florio* speaks, what Virgin could withstand,
> If gentle *Damon* did not squeeze her Hand?...
> This erring Mortals Levity may call,
> Oh blind to Truth! the *Sylphs* contrive it all.
>   Of these am I, who thy Protection claim,
> A watchful Sprite, and *Ariel* is my Name.   (I, 91–8, 103–6)

This is a feminization and domestication of the nymph's speech in *Dryades*:

> Unbody'd Pow'rs are not confin'd to Floods,
> To purling Riv'lets, or to shady Woods.
> Kind Daemons on ungrateful Man attend,
> Observe their Steps, and watch the hated Fiend.
> The same good *Genii* guard the harmless Sheep,
> When weary'd *Damon* lies in thoughtless Sleep;
> The same, whose Influence aids th' unsettled State,
> And gladly hastens on the Work of Fate...
> Inferior Orders, have a meaner Home,
> And here in Wilds, and woody Mazes roam,
> To learned *Magi* we strange Spells impart,
> Myst'ries disclose, and tell the *secret* Art.
> With Sacred *Miselto* the *Druids* crown'd
> Sung with the Nymphs, and danc'd the pleasing Round...
> Mortals to Earth, and mean Delights inclin'd,
> No Pleasure in abstracted Notions find...
> Tho' to good Daemons they their Safety owe,
> Few are the Happy those, who their bless'd Guardians know.
>   (318–49)

---

[7] Tillotson (*TE*, II, 381) appositely quotes Burton in a related context. Puck, of course, was famous for Protean disguises.

The comic ineptitude of the sylphs as guardians refers to a mock-pastoral, rather than a mock-heroic, framework. We are less with Ovid or the Rosicrucian philosophy than with druids and genii.

The next important addition of material in 1714 occurs in the second canto, with the famous description of the sylphs in their gossamer beauty.[8] It is unnecessary to quote this at length; but it is worth observing a fleeting Spenserian quality in the writing, closest perhaps to the description of the butterfly's wings in *Muiopotmos*, stanza 12 ('his shinie wings as silver bright...').[9] There follows another speech by Ariel addressed to 'Sylphs and Sylphids', styled by way of apposition.

> Fays, Fairies, Genii, Elves, and Daemons...   (II, 74)

It is worth remarking that the term *elf*, by origin simply the Saxon word for a spirit, came to have a specialized sense – Sir Walter Scott, in his *Demonology and Witchcraft*, describes elves as 'Sprites of a coarser sort, more laborious vocation and more malignant temper, and in all respects less propitious to humanity than the Fairies'.[10] As the *Rape* progresses, we see more and more of these malignant capabilities.

The various tasks performed by the aerial spirits are then presented in verse of self-conscious, almost parodic dignity and port. The special function of the sylphs, of course, is 'to tend the Fair'. Pope then itemizes the cosmetic arts in which these spirits excel. The joke is that 'in other poets [and, one might add, folklore generally] fairies are country creatures'.[11] What Pope does is to allot the routine of dress and make-up in the sophisticated society world to creatures traditionally identified with nature. He makes pastoral machinery serve not merely urban purposes (as the currently popular 'town

---

[8] Brief but valuable comments on the sylphs are found in the following: Cleanth Brooks, *The Well-Wrought Urn* (London, 1968), pp. 71–3; G. Wilson Knight, *The Poetry of Alexander Pope: Laureate of Peace* (London, 1955), p. 26; I. Jack, *Augustan Satire* (Oxford, 1952), pp. 80–4; W. K. Wimsatt (ed.), *Alexander Pope: Selected Poetry & Prose* (New York, 1951), pp. xxxvi–xxxvii; J. S. Cunningham, *Pope: The Rape of the Lock* (London, 1961), pp. 38–9; R. A. Brower, *Alexander Pope: The Poetry of Allusion* (Oxford, 1959), pp. 151, 155–6; Martin Price, *To the Palace of Wisdom* (Garden City, NY, 1965), pp. 151–4; Robin Grove, 'Uniting Airy Substance: *The Rape of the Lock*', *The Art of Alexander Pope*, ed. H. Erskine-Hill and A. Smith (London, 1979), pp. 52–88.

[9] Pope cites the description of the butterfly's wings from *Muiopotmos* in a note to *The Dunciad*, IV, 421. The section there quoted, from the second stanza of Spenser's poem, seems equally applicable to the sylphs ('the Empire of the Air'). The pervasive debt of Pope to Spenser remains to be fully investigated.

[10] See K. M. Briggs, *The Anatomy of Puck* (London, 1959), pp. 189–9. Pope added elves to the spirits in *Gabalis*: see *TE*, II, 164n.   [11] *TE*, II, 383.

eclogue', like Swift's *City Shower*, did) but *courtly* ends. The sylphs are woodland fairies conscripted to boudoir duties.

After this comes one of the passages everyone remembers, in which Ariel foretells that certain 'black Omens' will be fulfilled – Belinda will 'stain her Honour or her new Brocade...'. A note of bossiness apparent in his presentation from the start emerges more clearly in the series of orders Ariel issues to the other sylphs. And dire physical torments are promised to those who neglect their post: they will

> Be stopt in *Vials*, or transfixt with *Pins*;
> Or plung'd in Lakes of bitter *Washes* lie,
> Or wedg'd whole Ages in a *Bodkin's* Eye...   (II, 126–8)

Here we are close to the fate of another Ariel, at the hands of 'the foul witch Sycorax'. But the electric atmosphere and genuine threat present in *The Tempest* are missing here; there is something reminiscent of Lilliputian bluster in the torments devised by the microscopic commander:

> Gums and Pomatums shall his Flight restrain,
> While clog'd he beats his silken Wings in vain;
> Or Alom-*Stypticks* with contracting Power
> Shrink his thin Essence like a rivell'd Flower.
> Or as *Ixion* fix'd, the Wretch shall feel
> The giddy Motion of the whirling Mill,
> In Fumes of burning Chocolate shall glow,
> And tremble at the Sea that froths below!   (II, 129–36)

Even these punishments fall in with the pint-sized drawing-room scale of the drama. One consequence is that Ariel's speech takes on an air of petulance and spite – qualities which had long been associated with the figure of Robin Goodfellow and the hobgoblin. 'Useful as they are', writes K. M. Briggs, '[the hobglobins] are easily offended and are often mischievous'. Amongst other things, they 'do domestic chores, work about farms, guard treasure, keep an eye on the servants, and generally act as guardian spirits of the home'.[12] The sylphs would not have been seen dead on a farm, but otherwise they incorporate a sophisticated version of this way of life.

In Canto iii Pope added little except the game of ombre and the attempted intervention of a sylph to forestall the rape itself. But in the

---

[12] Briggs, *Anatomy of Puck*, p. 15.

next canto some eighty crucial lines were introduced. The Cave of Spleen is a deeply imaginative section in its own right, but its full contribution to the poem has generally been missed. The best comment I know is that of J. S. Cunningham:

> The whole episode of the Cave is partly a hilarious romp among well-to-do hypochondriacs, the devotees of 'sweet vicissitude', and partly a nightmare tour through the landscape of *ennui*, repression and distorted impulse which lies so close to the scene of Belinda's perilous gaiety. These are the bogeys behind Thalestris' fear of scandal and its aftermath, and behind Clarissa's warning to the maid who scorns a man.[13]

All this is well said; but it is not, I think, the whole story. One wonders how carefully Cunningham has selected the word 'bogey', for the passage does indeed give us something very close to a literal portrayal of demonic spirits. The sylphs had shown us the benign side of faery lore – nothing worse than the pranks of Puck. But the gnomes are clearly related to the various forms of 'bogy beast', malignant creatures whose role is to haunt, or to ravish, or to presage death.[14] Besides this, the gnomes have a much more effectual leader in Umbriel.

The episode of the Cave fulfils many functions beyond the parody of a journey to the underworld, its official reason for being in the mock-heroic scheme. Substantively, it enlarges the tonal range of the poem. It brings in a more sinister colouring, as Cunningham's remarks suggest. But it also imports an element of fantasy and grotesque invention. Just as Timon's villa outgrows its original moral identity as an exemplum of (bad) 'taste', and takes off into a lunatic and almost independent existence, so the Cave moves from satire into surrealism. And just as *The Dunciad* works through strange epiphanies and contorted visions of unnatural grandeur, so the *Rape of the Lock* enlists a quality of deliberate freakishness, wild prodigies, sudden transformations.[15] The underlying feeling is hallucinatory:

---

[13] Cunningham, pp. 50–1.

[14] Briggs, *Anatomy of Puck*, p. 186 and *passim*. Pope in his dedication calls the gnomes 'Daemons of the Earth' (*TE*, II, 143).

[15] It is interesting that the description of the Cave involves a reference to contemporary theatrical spectacles (IV, 43–6). This was to become an important feature of *The Dunciad*; and indeed there are numerous concrete parallels between the Cave of Spleen and that of 'Poverty and Poetry' in the later poem. Compare *Rape*, IV, 17–54, with *The Dunciad*, 'B' text, I, 33–84. Both 'domes' are chill, windswept places; the tutelary goddess on her throne is surrounded in each case by allegorical handmaidens; monstrous and abortive forms populate either cave alike; both locations are dark and inaccessible; both are filled by strange vapours, and so on.

> A constant *Vapour* o'er the Palace flies;
> Strange Phantoms rising as the Mists arise;
> Dreadful, as Hermit's Dreams in haunted Shades,
> Or bright as Visions of expiring Maids.
> Now glaring Fiends, and Snakes on rolling Spires,
> Pale Spectres, gaping Tombs, and Purple Fires... (IV, 39–44)

The garish imagery perfectly expresses the hyper-intense effects reported by users of mescalin and similar drugs.

But there is more than tone and texture involved. The section includes a whole miniature psychomachia – a dramatization of conflicting forces within the poem at large. The sylphs have embodied frivolity, heedlessness, the 'lighter' impulses of women. The gnomes, on the other hand, represent what might be briefly termed biology:

> Here, in a Grotto sheltered close from Air,
> And screen'd in Shades from Day's detested Glare,
> She sighs for ever on her pensive Bed,
> *Pain* at her Side, and *Megrim* at her Head. (IV, 21–4)

Newspaper advertisements of the day, puffing some 'physick' to cure women's spleen, obviously have the effects of menstruation in mind.

Now all this can be directly related to the traditional beliefs relating to the fairy kingdom. In particular, where sylphs were ethereal spirits, gnomes were made from the terrestrial element itself. They were, in every sense, *earthy*. The contrast is well expressed by a seventeenth-century disciple of Boehme:

The Mole lives in his Hill, and the industrious Ant hath her little Cottage higher than the Surface of the Earth, and the bigger Mountains... are the dwellings of other Creatures, some lodg'd there by confinement or their own choice, others born and bred in the Earth, who delight in places abounding with strong Metalline and Mineral Vapours, both as suitable to their natures, and where the casual lying of the Rocky Ore makes handsome Caverns and Chambers for these darksome Guests... Nor is the Aery Region disfurnisht of its inhabitant Spirits; Some of the *Jewish* Rabbins say, that by the creation of the Fowls of Heaven mentioned in *Genesis*, is understood not only those whose Bodies we see, and catch, and feed upon, but that far more numerous Progeny of Aerial Spirits, lodg'd in Vehicles of a thinner-spun thred than is (otherwise than by condensation) visible to our dim sight.[16]

If one points out that Pope's diction associates the haunt of the gnomes with confinement, caverns, vapours and darkness; or that it

---

[16] Cited by Briggs, *Anatomy of Puck*, pp. 170–1.

links the sylphs with fine threads, invisibility, the sky, vehicles, it is not in order to suggest anything resembling a 'source'. A more accessible analogue, besides, would be Burton's *Anatomy of Melancholy*, the standard authority on spleen. Burton actually recognizes six classes of 'sublunary Devils'; Gabalis and presumably Pope follow the commoner practice of amalgamating terrestrial and subterranean sprites. The former in Burton include fauns, satyrs, and Robin Goodfellow. The latter

are conversant about the center of the earth to torture the souls of damned men to the Day of Judgment, their egress and regress some suppose to be about Ætna, Lipari, Mons Hecla in Iceland, Vesuvius, Terra del Fuego, &c., because many shrieks and fearfull cries are continually heard thereabouts, and familiar apparitions of dead men, Ghosts and Goblins.[17]

Pope is content to peer under the volcano of feelings long enough to detect 'Sighs, Sobs, and the War of Tongues'. But tortured souls are everywhere.

One need not appeal to Freud or Frazer in order to maintain that Umbriel's descent is crucial to the imaginative logic of the poem. It is surely apt that a study of female manners (social as well as sexual) should allude to the physiological at some point. The older doctrine, gravely accepted by Pope, located the seat of affection in the spleen. But perhaps by 1714 this was a genteel euphemism for the womb – we know that Pope studiously adopted a 'rather fastidious' attitude towards spleen[18] – though he is smiling behind his prim words. In terms of 'amorous Causes' what matters is that the gnomes are much better at protecting treasures (as was their traditional role) than were the sylphs – mere domestic pets masquerading as guard-dogs. And there is a penetrating psychological accuracy in making gnomes the fairy equivalents of prudes, likewise trained to look after deep secrets and buried treasure. It is ironical that Belinda should trust her 'inestimable Prize' to the care of light-minded sylphs.

[17] *The Anatomy of Melancholy*, I, 11, I, ii; ed. Floyd Dell and Paul Jordan-Smith (New York, 1938), p. 171. See also K. M. Briggs, *Pale Hecate's Team* (London, 1962), pp. 48–54. As Briggs observes, 'It is difficult to know where to start quoting from Burton, and where to stop': Babb and Tillotson have established many direct parallels in the text of the *Rape*. It is interesting that Burton cites Olaus Magnus as an authority on terrestrial devils (p. 168). The Swedish writer is used by Tillotson to gloss the almost contemporary *Temple of Fame* – see *TE*, II, 263, 264, 411.

[18] Babb, p. 173. One notes that the onset of Belinda's 'grief' is produced by rending 'the swelling Bag' (IV, 91) 'and all the Furies issue at the Vent'. See also IV, 142.

There is a further point about the Cave. Its visions and dreams bring to a head a whole current of allusion to such matters. Ariel himself had appeared to Belinda through this agency. Now fairies were in general regarded as the bringers of dreams. In its purest form the belief relates to one particular demon, the *mara*, whose name survives in 'nightmare' and 'mare's nest'. But it became attached to other creatures, notably Shakespeare's highly idiosyncratic Queen Mab.[19] Moreover, as 'ghosts appear and disappear among fairies, devils and angels',[20] it is natural that the task of inducing bad dreams should become overlaid with the function of the incubus (as Umbriel seems to act, IV, 71-2) and with the fulfilling of omens. On one level the *Rape* enacts a contest between the sylphs and the gnomes; Ariel can merely read the presages, but 'triumphant *Umbriel*' helps with his kind to bring about the climax (V, 83-6). Aptly, it is prudes not coquettes who aid Belinda's revenge.

The addition of the machinery, then, enabled Pope to reinforce a dialectic already visible in the action. If Patricia Meyer Spacks is correct in identifying two states of mind in Belinda – 'the serene self-absorption of the period before the 'rape', the hysterical self-indulgence afterward' – then the fairy characters have much to do with this shift.[21] Sylphs generate self-absorption; gnomes breed hysteria. Like the element he inhabits, Ariel proves insubstantial; his charm is vacuous, his moral identity negligible outside the 'purest *Aether*'. Umbriel's 'proper Scene', the underworld, is all too physical. In the first case we have 'Bodies half dissolv'd in Light', in the second 'Bodies chang'd to various Forms by *Spleen*'. One connotes the world of mooning adolescence and the other an atmosphere of neurotic repression. In both cases a degree of sexual hypocrisy is involved, and Belinda is equally liable to either affliction. Her 'secret Passions' owe as much to the gnomes as to the sylphs.

What is most striking, however, in the total satiric strategy is not the nature of this dialectic in itself. Rather, it is the way in which Pope seems drawn to import native faery lore to dramatize the conflict of elements. He adds 'Elves' to the spirits found in *Gabalis*; he borrows traditional items such as the nightmare; and he makes explicit allusions to Shakespeare. More generally, he constantly recalls the mood and feeling of earlier faery writers. For instance, the stress Pope

[19] Briggs, *Anatomy of Puck*, pp. 21, 47.   [20] Briggs, *Pale Hecate's Team*, p. 222.
[21] P. M. Spacks, *An Argument of Images* (Cambridge, Mass., 1971), p. 233.

lays on the miniature size of the sylphs (appropriate to his mock-heroic task) derives directly from *A Midsummer Night's Dream*, where 'the innovation that strikes us most is the fairy smallness, not new to folklore, but nearly new in literature.'[22] Shakespeare's tiny beings, at once pert, delicate and palpable, are as far removed from *Gabalis* as they are from Ovid. In fact Shakespeare drew on romance traditions (accorded only lightly mocking references by Pope), but he made much heavier use of indigenous folklore. With the small size and mischievous pranks of Puck comes a certain imaginative density, eagerly seized by Pope in creating the sylphs. Like Puck, the sylphs 'have none of that flimsy quality which strikes one in later fairy stories'.[23] Equally, Titania's famous description of 'contagious fogs', floods, and frosts overlooked by the moon, 'pale in her anger' (*MND*, II.i.88–117), has several links with *The Rape*, notably Ariel's speech at ii.73–90. But again, it is not so much precise echoes that one notes, as an overall sense of delight and wonder, as though Pope's text had received a poetic infusion from the *Dream*.[24] Both works concern bickering love-affairs, titillating fairies, potent philtres, sinister transformations. But what chiefly unites them is not narrowly fictive, but imaginative: an indulgence in weird and even apparently silly effects, combined with a strong moral awareness:

> But all the story of the night told over,
> And all their minds transfigur'd so together,
> More witnesseth than fancy's images,
> And grows to something of great constancy,
> But, howsoever, strange and admirable.   (*MND*, v.i.23–7)

After Shakespeare came what has been termed 'the fashion for the miniature', embracing Drayton, William Browne and Herrick, amongst others.[25] Pope certainly knew some work by all three, though he thought Drayton 'a very mediocre Poet'.[26] Yet, as with

---

[22] Briggs, *Anatomy of Puck*, p. 45. For a glancing comparison between the sylphs and Shakespeare's fairies (Pope's are of an 'inferior race') see *EC*, II, 136.

[23] Briggs, *Anatomy of Puck*, p. 47.

[24] For the imaginative uses of folklore in *A Midsummer Night's Dream*, see D. P. Young, *Something of Great Constancy* (New Haven, Conn., 1966), pp. 16–32. Many of Young's comments regarding 'the blending of folklore and myth' could be applied with little adjustment to *The Rape of the Lock. See also pp.* 155–66, on metamorphosis and dramatic metaphor. There is a recollection of Titania's speech in *The Dunciad* (A) i, 69–76 (*TE*, V, 68).

[25] See Briggs, *Anatomy of Puck*, pp. 56–70.

[26] *Corr*, IV, 428. A mock-archaic 'Fairy Tale, in the Ancient English Style' was printed by Pope in his edition of Parnell's poems in 1722, containing reference to 'Midnight Faeries daunc[ing] the maze'. The date of this work is uncertain (Parnell died in 1718). For Pope's

the Spenser of *Muiopotmos* and the Milton of *Comus*, there is fitfully a
coarser burlesque vein in Pope's *Rape*, not at all remote from
Nymphidia – compare the parenthesis on Belinda's bodkin (V.89–96),
and its breezy garrulous chat, with Drayton's knowing description of
Queen Mab's chariot (129–52). Of course, Drayton is arch and
archaic where Pope is prosily explicit: but the *area* of parody is very
closely analogous.

More speculative is the impression left by Diaper when Pope came
to rework the poem. But, bearing in mind the timing of the revision
(late 1713) and the fast-developing friendship of Pope and Swift
during this year, it is likely that Diaper's name came up at some time
during their meetings. When *Nereides* appeared in March 1712, Swift
had written to Stella of Diaper:

> I think to recommend him to our Society tomorrow … P—on him, I must do
> something for him. & get him out of the Way. I hate to have any new Witts
> arise; but when they do rise I would encourage them. but they tred on our
> Heels, & thrust us off the Stage.

Swift's society did not yet include that other new wit, Pope. But it
may well have done by the following December, when Swift in his
best officious style presented Diaper to Lord Bolingbroke, 'with a
new Poem, which is a very good one'.[27] Moreover, *Dryades*, the work
in question, was designed to celebrate the Tory peace, and to laud
Oxford and Bolingbroke. Since Pope was even then preparing for
publication *Windsor-Forest* (he mentions its progress in a letter of 5
December 1712),[28] it is in the highest degree improbable that he
would have overlooked the appearance of such a poem. As for Swift,
he kept in contact with Diaper for several more months, visiting him
in 'a nasty Garret' in February[29] and writing on 30 April with
renewed promises to aid the other man's career.[30] Direct association
dwindled after this (Diaper lived only until 1717), but it has even
been surmised that Swift persuaded Pope to drop a couplet in the
1728 *Dunciad* out of respect for Diaper's memory.[31]

That conjecture seems implausible. But another supposition of the
Twickenham editor, that Pope was well aware of Diaper during the

---

other relations with Drayton, see my essay 'Drayton's Arden and *Windsor-Forest*', *PLL*
XVII (1981), 284–91, as well as the previous essay in this book.
[27] *Journal to Stella*, ed. H. Williams (Oxford, 1948), II, 512, 586.   [28] *Corr*, I, 162.
[29] *Journal*, II, 619 (wrongly indexed as 519).
[30] For a history of the dealings of Swift and Diaper, see Broughton, pp. xvi–xx.
[31] *TE*, V, 173n.

latter's active period, is altogether convincing. If so, Pope would have encountered in *Dryades* much in this vein:

> Men led by Sense, and partial to themselves,
> Nor roving Daemons own, nor wandring Elves.
> But who can know th'intelligible Race,
> Or guess the Pow'rs that fill th'aerial Space!
> Oft the tir'd Horse is forc'd to scour the Plain,
> When *Fairies* ride fix'd in his twisted Mane.
> And I, ye Gods, have wondrous Circles seen,
> Where wanton Sprites in Mid-night Dance have been,
> And press'd their rounding Steps on ev'ry new-mow'd Green.
>
> (74–82)

When Pope comes to imagine the powers 'that fill th'aerial Space', he will inevitably clothe this diction of elves, sprites and demons with a fresh perception. Thus, Diaper's 'Circles' become 'the giddy Circle' (I, 93), suggestive of the social round; 'aerial Space' is subtly amplified as 'Fields of Air' (I, 66) or 'Crystal Wilds of Air' (I, 106), pseudo-pastoral variants that make their own point. Equally, Diaper's description of the woodland genii as

> Bless'd Beings, whom no earthy Fetters bind,
> Nor to the pressing Weight of Clay confin'd!
> Of un-mixt *Aether* form'd ...
>
> (89–91)

appears curiously metaphysical beside Pope's exact vision of the sylphs' condition.

Yet, if the detailed treatment is different (that is partly a difference in talent, partly a question of genre), there remains a bedrock of shared allusion and parallel diction. Diaper is full of delicate imagery, drawn from insect life or fibrous growth. He even dilates upon the microscopic visions made possible by 'wondrous Opticks', though Marjorie Hope Nicolson left him out of her famous study of Newton and the eighteenth-century poets. So we have 'Strange puny Shapes, unknown to vulgar Eyes. / So shadowy Forms, and sportive Daemons fly / Wafted on Winds, and not perceiv'd when nigh' (547–9). Or again:

> Th' indulgent Pow'rs have giv'n a second Sight,
> That kens the airy Silph, and wand'ring Sprite.
> No flitting Elf the subtle Eye escapes,
> When wanton *Genii* sport in antick Shapes.
>
> (554–7)

This is too near Irish blarney to resemble what Pope does with his faery machinery; but the material is similar. Diaper even sets the Great Chain of Being briefly rattling in an evocative passage:

> If to the finish'd Whole so little goes,
> How small the Parts, that must the whole compose!
> Matter is infinite, and still descends:
> Men cannot know where lessening Nature ends.   (564–7)

This is cited less to establish a connection with the first epistle of *An Essay on Man* than to illustrate Diaper's ability to work on a tiny scale without the waggish air of Drayton.

Let me reassert that the aptness of *Dryades* in this context has little to do with sources or analogues. It is more a matter of finding out what kind of poem *The Rape of the Lock* is. The revised work, as it seems to me, is a fantasy of enchantment as well as a social satire. It is about sprites and goblins, visions and nightmares, and not just beaux and belles – still less judges and jurymen. To this end Pope has gone far beyond the Rosicrucian scheme, and indeed far beyond 'machinery' in its habitual inert embodiment. He has constructed a psychodrama within Belinda and her circle.[32] But the real colliding forces are supernatural. The *Rape* provides a battle of the pigmies in which spleen and coquetry compete for Belinda's soul. Despite the ironic pseudo-compliment at the end, her reputation *is* lost (note the gossiping speculations, V, 113ff.) and 'Airs, and Flights, and Screams, and Scolding' are all that Belinda can summon. The central fact is that the sylphs are unheeded, the gnomes triumphant. And these were creatures that Pope could never have taken straight out of the Rosicrucian manuals. He found them in some deep recess of the poetic imagination, among the rural hobgoblins where Shakespeare discovered *his* fairy beings.

---

[32] Here my views have been partly anticipated by Brower, who writes, 'By deftly linking his invented deities with popular country beliefs, and with the "Heathen Mythology" of Fate and Jove, Pope makes us feel the presence of forces greater than Belinda and the Baron and their friends' (p. 156). Brower and Jack are among the few critics to indicate the 'marvellous' as opposed to the 'social' component in the poem; but neither draws out at all fully the native faery element.

CHAPTER 6

Timon's Villa and Chatsworth

One of the most contentious, as well as poetically impressive, passages in Pope's work occurs in the description of Timon's villa, which occupies lines 99 to 172 in the *Epistle to Burlington*. From the start this section has given rise to extensive discussion: at first, as to the identity of Timon, and more recently on the basis of the architectural and gardening satire – where, in fact, is Timon's villa? There is now a considerable literature attempting to establish an 'original' for the house and garden which figure in Pope's lines. To the claims of Cannons and Houghton have been added those of Blenheim, advocated by Morris R. Brownell. It might be felt that enough is enough, since the number of appropriate locations must be finite.[1]

Before deliberating the claims of one more candidate it is worth looking once again at the lines in question. First the general description:

> At Timon's Villa let us pass a day,
> Where all cry out, 'What sums are thrown away!'
> So proud, so grand, of that stupendous air,
> Soft and Agreeable come never there.
> Greatness, with Timon, dwells in such a draught
> As brings all Brobdignag before your thought.
> To compass this, his building is a Town,
> His pond an Ocean, his parterre a Down:
> Who but must laugh, the Master when he sees,
> A puny insect, shiv'ring at a breeze!
> Lo, what huge heaps of littleness around!
> The whole, a labour'd Quarry above ground.
> Two Cupids squirt before: a Lake behind

---

[1] The starting point for all discussion is F. W. Bateson's edition of the *Epistle to Burlington* in *TE*, III.ii, especially Appendix B, 'Timon and the Duke of Chandos', pp. 170–4. For Houghton, see *Garden and City*, pp. 272–80; for Blenheim, see Morris R. Brownell, *Alexander Pope and the Arts of Georgian England* (Oxford, 1978), pp. 309–17, 381–3.

> Improves the keenness of the Northern wind.
> His Gardens next your admiration call,
> On ev'ry side you look, behold the Wall!
> No pleasing Intricacies intervene,
> No artful wildness to perplex the scene;
> Grove nods at grove, each Alley has a brother,
> And half the platform just reflects the other.
> The suff'ring eye inverted Nature sees,
> Trees cut to Statues, Statues thick as trees,
> With here a Fountain, never to be play'd,
> And there a Summer-house, that knows no shade.
> Here Amphitrite sails thro' myrtle bow'rs;
> There Gladiators fight, or die, in flow'rs;
> Unwater'd see the drooping sea-horse mourn,
> And swallows roost in Niulus' dusty Urn.   (*TE*, III.ii.146–9)

Then some more particular features:

> And now the Chapel's silver bell you hear,
> That summons you to all the Pride of Pray'r:
> Light quirks of Music, broken and uneven,
> Make the soul dance upon a Jig to Heav'n.
> On painted Cielings you devoutly stare,
> Where sprawl the Saints of Verrio or Laguerre,
> On gilded clouds in fair expansion lie,
> And bring all Paradise before your eye.
> To rest, the Cushion and soft Dean invite,
> Who never mentions Hell to ears polite.
>   But hark! the chiming Clocks to dinner call;
> A hundred footsteps scrape the marble Hall:
> The rich Buffet well-colour'd Serpents grace,
> And gaping Tritons spew to wash your face. (*TE*, III.ii.151–2)

The picture is complicated by the fact that some of the details by an odd freak fit most snugly the gardens at Chatsworth, where a daughter of the addressee Burlington was to settle years later as wife of its owner, and where Pope's own *Master Key to Popery* – alluding to the identification of Timon – lay unpublished until this century. The oddity seems less if we remember that the mannerist layout of the gardens had been the work of the first Duke of Devonshire, a Whig grandee who had died in 1707. The design had been carried out in the 1690s, before the time of the Earl (b. 1695) or the Countess of Burlington (b. 1699). By the 1730s the style seemed distinctly old-fashioned, and many including Horace Walpole thought it ripe for the reconstruction performed by the fourth Duke, Burlington's son-in-law, in the 1760s. The gardens were severely criticized in 1725, for instance, by George Vertue, a satellite of the Earl of Oxford known to Pope.

From the start, observers had drawn attention to a vein of splendour not too far from vulgarity in the adornment of Chatsworth. Celia Fiennes, who made her visit in 1697 during the major phase of refurbishment, was kinder than some, but she too was amazed by the scale of things and the abundance of elaborate work performed by Verrio, Laguerre and Cibber. Laguerre was actually at work on the ceilings when she came to the house, lying on a scaffolding board like Michelangelo in the Sistine Chapel. She commented on the large stone pillars forming the piazza, and spent some time on the plumbing – 'There is a fine grotto all stone pavement roof and sides. This is designed to supply all the house with water besides several fancies to make diversion... You went down steps into a bath big enough for two people.'[2] Almost a century later Arthur Young was far more critical. It would have taken the gothic taste of an earlier age to find anything to admire in the garden furniture, including 'Nilus's leaky body, dolphins, sea-nymphs and dragons vomiting water, trees spirting it from their branches, and temples pouring down showers from their roofs'. Four handsome lions were 'spouting' water. This was in 1770 (the *Farmer's Tour* was published a year later), so it is possible that Young was seeing the place partly through the eyes of Pope's poem.[3] But it is further evidence that Chatsworth was widely regarded as comically over-ornate, as neither Blenheim nor Houghton was.[4] (Blenheim, of course, had been redesigned by Capability Brown before Young's time, and Cannons had quickly fallen into decay.) Whilst Pope had no especial reason for animus against the Duke of Devonshire, a solid Whig and Kit-Cat without great political influence, that would not have stopped him utilizing the house for his own purposes. And one fact needs to be stated, which

---

[2] Quoted from *The Journeys of Celia Fiennes* by Richard Trench, *Travellers in Britain: Three Centuries of Discovery* (London, 1990), p. 85. The very fact that Pope's note to line 146 specifies decorative work by Laguerre and Verrio at Blenheim, but *not* the famous Chatsworth ceilings, may be regarded as significant – so oblique Pope generally is.

[3] Quoted from Young's *Farmer's Tour* by John G. Gazley, *The Life of Arthur Young 1741–1820* (Philadelphia, 1973), p. 66. (An inaccurate version of parts of the description is given by Trench, p. 159.) Note the specific mention of the Nilus statue.

[4] Brownell argues, pp. 310–11, that Blenheim suits the case better than Houghton, because its garden was more French and formal initially (that is before Brown laid out the grounds). But the gardens at Chatsworth were more formal than Blenheim's had ever been; they derive from the late seventeenth century and the high baroque moment.

has often been forgotten: Timon may or may not be based on a real person, the Duke of Chandos or someone else; it does not follow that the villa is necessarily based in any detail on that figure's own house. What we need to know for the present purpose is less the exact standing of the Duke of Devonshire in Pope's mind than the impression he had received of Chatsworth, as it had been rebuilt by William Talman and expensively refitted throughout.

Most strikingly, the scene was depicted in 1724 by William Stukeley, the famous antiquarian who was also among Pope's acquaintances.[5] Stukeley makes much of the 'very large sizes' and 'dimensions' of the house in his account of Chatsworth (*Itineranium Curiosum*, 1724: my quotations are from the second edition of 1770). There is reference to the 'curious fabric and ornaments'; as well as 'prodigious architraves'. We are told that 'the cieling and walls of all the apartments [are] charged with rare paintings of Varrio and other famous hands'. In addition, Stukeley notes, 'the chapel is a most ravishing place', an epithet curiously appropriate to Pope's satiric description of Timon's chapel: on both the last two descriptions, compare *Epistle to Burlington* (141–50).

When Stukeley moves out of doors, the correspondences are even more striking:

The gardens abound with green-houses, summer-houses, walks, wildernesses and orangeries, with all the furniture of statues, urns, greens, etc. with canals, basons, and water-works of various forms and contrivance, sea-horses, drakes, dolphins and other fountains that throw up the water: an artificial willow-tree of copper spouts and drops water from every leaf: a wonderful cascade, where, from a neat house of stone like a temple, out of the mouths of beasts, pipes, urns etc. a whole river descends the slope of a hill, a quarter of a mile in length, over steps, with a terrible noise and broken appearance, till it is lost under ground.

The modern historian of Chatsworth supplied additional information: there was a Triton fountain (compare Pope, line 154), a Sea Horse fountain (compare line 125), and a Neptune fountain (compare the reference to his wife Amphitrite in line 123). The cascades and waterworks were of course famous in their time.[6]

There is an added factor. The sculptor principally engaged in the carving of these statues (after which each fountain was named) was

[5] For Stukeley's connection with John Gay, see Clive T. Probyn in *British Journal for Eighteenth-Century Studies*, I (1978), 108–10.

[6] See Francis Thompson, *A History of Chatsworth* (London, 1949), pp. 86–8.

none other than Caius Gabriel Cibber, father of Colley. In the later version of *The Dunciad*, when the nerve-centre of Dulness was transferred to the neighbourhood of Bedlam, Pope alluded in both text and note to the work of Cibber senior on the gates of the hospital. (See *Dunciad*, B text, I, 31.) The Sea Horse fountain was especially prominent at Chatsworth; it was sited near the grand parterre on the south side of the house. A view by Kniff, engraved by Kip for *Britannia Illustrata*, made this aspect of the gardens familiar to a wide circle of readers.

These are much more specific and individual touches than the parallels noted for some of the rival sites, which relate to such general features as the presence of a lake or 'bason'. The word 'down' (106) fits the Derbyshire scenery better than that of the other estates, whilst the 'keenness of the Northern wind' (112) takes on added significance.

I would not claim that Pope had only Chatsworth in mind, and would accept the view that Timon is a composite portrait. None of the proposed sites possessed all the attributes of Timon's villa: Houghton had no lake, Blenheim had no Verrios. But the facts quoted here surely prompt a strong suspicion that Chatsworth was one of the models.[7] It is possible that Pope had never been to the house, but he had first-hand witnesses such as Vertue, as well as the celebrated description in Defoe's *Tour*, vol. 3 (1726): Defoe actually calls the ornamental lake a 'pond' (compare line 106). But above all there was Stukeley's account, which suggests the *unnaturalness* of the design so innocently; and for Pope such a hint was enough.

More generally it may be felt otiose to go on pursuing these 'originals' for Pope's imaginative flights. One answer to this is that contemporaries evidently read poetic texts in a distinctly literal manner, and were constantly on the look-out for allusions to real life. Such a degree of referentiality was the normal reader-response of the time. Pope must have designed his works with such a mode of reading in his mind, even if (what is unlikely and certainly unproved) he wishes to discourage such an approach. His tortuous disavowals regarding the identification of Timon with the Duke of Chandos

---

[7] Chatsworth perhaps had more features, and some of the most striking, among those pertinent to the issue. For example, the 'keen Northern wind' (112) was certainly more in evidence in the neighbourhood of the Peak District than in gentler southern climes. The scenery comprehends what might be termed 'downs', unlike the flat surroundings of Houghton, Blenheim and Cannons.

nowhere indicate that he thought such things could not be found in his poetry. In essence he says that Timon was not meant to be Chandos, and that the picture took the form of a general satire.[8] Nobody who has read his private letters will easily be convinced that Pope was averse to satirizing individuals, even where the ultimate imaginative import of the passage might run beyond the lineaments of that individual. Sporus clearly starts from Hervey, even if the depiction takes us beyond the characteristics of a given historical personage. The same argument would seem to work for places as well as persons. Timon's villa is assuredly not 'just' Chatsworth, but a good deal of the Chatsworth landscape may have gone into its *mise-en-scène*.

ADDENDUM

New information which came to light as recently as 1989 supplies further support for the case outlined here. It relates to the previously unpublished travel diary of Sir John Percival (1683–1748), later first Earl of Egmont. The tour he made round England in 1701, together with the Virginian writer and colonial official William Byrd II of Westover, has now been edited by Mark R. Wenger as *The English Travels of Sir John Percival and William Byrd II* (Columbia, Mo., 1989). Percival, best known for his later political diary, was only six years senior to Pope, and bred in a similar intellectual climate. The impressions he gained of the places he visited with Byrd are likely to reflect attitudes current in Pope's formative years.

It is therefore significant that Percival devotes an especially long entry to Chatsworth, just as its remodelling was in the course of completion. It seems to have made more impact on him than almost any other site visited on an extensive trip. Percival, of course, was awed and impressed where Pope would be appalled; but the objects of attention are closely parallel. As with the journal of Celia Fiennes, Pope cannot have seen the manuscript account, which lay in the family archives until 1950, since when it has been in the British Library collection.

Percival was particularly impressed with the Brobdignagian scale of the estate, and keeps citing its dimensions. He pays particular

---

[8] See *TE*, III.ii.xxvi–xxix. Bateson rightly observes that 'It is important to recognize that the basis of Pope's satire is fact' (p. xliii). What this means is not that the satire clings to fact so tenaciously that its merit is dependent upon literal accuracy, but that the truth-claim can be sustained, *inter alia*, by an appeal to recorded examples as evidence of the phenomena undergoing satiric treatment.

attention to the decorative work of Verrio and Laguerre, specifying individual items such as the latter's ceiling in the great hall and the former's allegory of virtue and vice in the dining room. He was even more struck by the chapel, where Laguerre's Ascension with the four evangelists took his eye: the ornamented pulpit and altar seemed equally beautiful to his taste. The 'pretty Studdy of books' earns a mention after this. Bemused by the opulence of the interior ('The carv'd work of wood about this house cost 2600^11', he notes gushingly), Percival turns to the outdoor scene. The great canal with its fountain elicited his admiration, as did 'an artificiall tree of leather out of evry leaf of which comes a Stream of water'. (The editor suggests the tree was made of copper, not leather.) He then turns to the waterworks proper and singles out the usual objects of wonder, such as two nereids with urns at the end of the cascade. The huge canal had as a set piece near the house 'two large Statues of Flora & Aphritite'. 'In the gardine are 5 descents' – the 'platform' style Pope alludes to. A summer house had its roof painted with a design of Castor and Pollux; nearby there was another fountain 'that plays 30 or 40 pipes. Tis an oval bason wth a Neptune in the middle and on each side of his a sea Nymphs [*sic*].' Percival goes on to quote further huge dimensions, massive outlay of money, profusion of ornament in every department (whether fishponds, outhouses, stables, ironwork or anything else). 'Ile attempt no further to describe this Pallace least I do it injustice' (pp. 151–7).

Percival's is the response of a very young man, and his naïveté can be forgiven. Broadly speaking he was reflecting a general sense of awe at the scale and magnificence of this 'palace'. Even today, Chatsworth remains an extraordinary edifice, sumptuously appointed and located in a superb setting. We need not impute to Pope a special contempt for the architecture, gardening or ornamental styles used by the Duke – there was, incidentally, 'a grotto where the water runs continually on each side of which you goe up Stairs into the House' (on the west front). But the poet needed an emblem of profuse expense, and houses such as Blenheim, Cannons and Chatsworth fitted his purposes, whatever the merits of particular features in each house. He had plenty of informants, men such as the second Earl of Oxford, in addition to published accounts such as those of Stukeley and Defoe, quite apart from his own firsthand knowledge of country houses built up on his 'rambles' around England. The interest of Percival's extra-long entry for Chatsworth lies in its demonstration that many of the main aspects of Timon's villa were in place at Chatsworth from the start of the century, and were observed by the kind of man Pope frequently ran across.

However, Pope's links with this potential informant were closer than that. The two men knew each other by 1715 (when Percival was subscribing to the *Iliad*) and may have been introduced by the latter's close friend George Berkeley, who refers admiringly to Pope in a letter to Percival on 7 March 1713.[9] Correspondence between Pope and Percival, in both directions, survives from the period 1722–4. It is thus conceivable that Percival shared with Pope his recollections of Chatsworth; but that is not a necessary part of the case argued here.

[9] *The Works of George Berkeley*, ed. A. A. Luce and T. E. Jessop (London, 1956), VIII, 62.

CHAPTER 7

A drama of mixed feelings: the Epistle to Arbuthnot

One of the words critics use most frequently in discussing the *Epistle to Arbuthnot* is 'anxiety'. It is certain that this complex poem, so elaborately pieced together out of shreds and patches of verse, caused Pope much trouble in the writing, and possibly in the recollection of painful experiences it called up.[1] At the very outset, jagged cadences suggest indecision as well as weariness:

> Shut, shut the door, good *John*! fatigu'd I said,
> Tye up the knocker, say I'm sick, I'm dead... (1–2)

What follows is partly a comedy of indecision, where alternating energies are permitted to drive through the verse, and competing attitudes are allowed to surface at different points. In a sense, Pope has made a virtue out of the disorder of his feelings, and also of the haphazard manner in which the poem was put together.

The *Epistle to Arbuthnot* survives as one of the few eighteenth-century texts regularly studied in schools and colleges. It would be cynical to ascribe this power of endurance to academic inertia; but my experience suggests that the poem continues to be taught along rather predictable lines. It does not seem to have benefited directly from the great upsurge of scholarly interest in Pope over the last few decades. Unlike many critical revaluations, the new estimate of Pope has been much more than a palace revolution within academic court circles. Many readers who would not claim to be Pope 'specialists' have learnt to appreciate the daring mythopoeic invention of *The*

---

[1] It is now clear from extant manuscript drafts that the poem as we have it evolved from one planned around 1732 and addressed to William Cleland. The manuscripts have been edited by Maynard Mack, *The Last and Greatest Art* (Newark, Del., 1984), pp. 410–54. An important reading of the poem as embodying contrariety and contradiction, commending at once 'the contrary values of forbearance and anger', is Ian Donaldson, 'Concealing and Revealing: Pope's *Epistle to Arbuthnot*', *YES*, XVIII (1988), 181–99.

Rape of the Lock, or the surrealist fantasy in *The Dunciad*. Yet the poem
which young people most frequently encounter is still, I would guess,
Arbuthnot. It would be a great shame if they were left to suppose that
this work, unlike the rest of Pope, is immune to a fresh approach. In
fact the old literary history did as badly by *Arbuthnot* as ever it did by
the mock-heroic poems.

What Pope gives us, as I have indicated, is a comedy of irresolution.
The official meaning of the *Epistle*, and the one enshrined in our
manuals, draws attention to Pope's impatience with his persecutors
– whether they be libellers or importunate friends. The ideal way of
life is embodied at the end in Pope's father, 'inheriting no Strife'
(392). We are, seemingly, invited to commiserate with Pope on his
own troubled existence.

Now it is true that the work is described as 'a Sort of Bill of
Complaint' – the technical term used of a plea in Chancery, that
form of real-life protest in which Pope became increasingly involved
towards the end of his career.[2] But it is not self-evident against what
or whom the complaint is made. Partly, no doubt, the string of
sycophants and calumniators mentioned in the text. But on a deeper
level the discontent seems to be as it were reflexive: it is Pope's
personal inability to forge a mode of living as harmonious as that of
his father which provokes the uneasy tone. After all, the *Epistle*
incorporates some measure of rage and impatience (how much
precisely, we need not calculate here). These are obviously qualities
foreign to the Stoic pose which Pope adopts at several points in the
text (151–8; 173–4; 215–30; 334–59). It is as though the poetry
denies what the sentiments assert. Pope supplies a content of sweetness
and light, but the verse bristles with an abrasive independence.

Not that the poetic texture is uniformly sour – far from it. Much of
the writing is jocular and amused. But even here one feels that Pope
is preoccupied by the world around him, rather than stoically
detached. Somehow he appears to take a curious pleasure in
cataloguing the annoyances to which he is exposed. The petitioners
and bores have become necessary to him. All satirists need enemies,
but Pope was unique in the close study he made of his adversaries.
(Who else would have Grub Street attacks bound up in a special
volume, like a museum of torture-appliances?) He fed on the assaults
of others: his artistic constitution took on its rudest health in a climate

---

[2] See below, pp. 184–9.

of opposition. To an unusual extent Pope's creative faculties needed the whetstone of contention.

So the delicious portrait of his insults and injuries takes on a new aspect. The difficulties and distractions arouse irritation (comically built into the verse-utterance), but it is out of this that the poetry is born and Pope, *qua* writer, defined:

> What Walls can guard me, or what Shades can hide?
> They pierce my Thickets, thro' my Grot they glide,
> By land, by water, they renew the charge,
> They stop the Chariot, and they board the Barge.
> No place is sacred, not the Church is free,
> Ev'n *Sunday* shines no *Sabbath-day* to me:
> Then from the Mint walks forth the Man of Ryme,
> Happy! to catch me, just at Dinner-time.   (7–14)

In the widest sense, the *Epistle* is concerned with the place of the artist in society – the need for withdrawal combined with the equally urgent necessity to engage in a wide range of human activities. Pope dramatizes a common twentieth-century uncertainty. Like many modern writers, he feels that he requires existential breathing-space, yet at the same time hungers for relationships, experience, commitment. And the satirist, above all, must dodge his guards and come out of hiding some time.

Pope's talkative, humorous style ought not to blind us to his serious implications. His catalogue of persons from Porlock is achieved through hyperbole and cod-melodrama, but it strikes home:

> Is there a Parson, much be-mus'd in Beer,
> A maudlin Poetess, a ryming Peer,
> A Clerk, foredoom'd his Father's soul to cross,
> Who pens a Stanza when he should engross?
> Is there, who lock'd from Ink and Paper, scrawls
> With desp'rate Charcoal round his darken'd walls?
> All fly to *Twit'nam* ...   (15–21)

Behind the puns and the easy manner lies an ominous fact. Twickenham was not just Pope's 'retreat', the suburban fastness from which he could observe the city. It was also the chosen domicile of one whose parents (always lurking near the surface in this poem) had been forced to leave London by the Ten-Mile Act. Thus the locality emphasizes Pope's heritage as a Catholic.[3] More and more we see that he truly *was* one who had been bequeathed strife.

---

[3] See below, pp. 129–41.

Ironically, his isolation and exposure are emphasized by a stream of unwelcome visitors. The one day of freedom for the debtor means another day of bondage for the hapless, homekeeping Pope.

These undercurrents are not confined to the autobiographic sections or to the formal artistic credo. They emerge, typically, when Pope is writing of others. Thus the famous portrait of Addison:

> Shou'd such a man, too fond to rule alone,
> Bear, like the *Turk*, no brother near the throne,
> View him with scornful, yet with jealous eyes,
> And hate for Arts that caus'd himself to rise;
> Damn with faint praise, assent with civil leer,
> And without sneering, teach the rest to sneer;
> Willing to wound, and yet afraid to strike,
> Just a hint a fault, and hesitate dislike;
> Alike reserv'd to blame, or to commend,
> A tim'rous foe, and a suspicious friend,
> Dreading e'en fools, by Flatterers besieg'd,
> And so obliging that he ne'er oblig'd;
> Like *Cato*, give his little Senate laws,
> And sit attentive to his own applause;
> While Wits and Templers ev'ry sentence raise,
> And wonder with a foolish face of praise.　　　　(197–212)

I have left out the concluding couplet, beautifully though Pope prepares for it. The lineaments are highly individual, yet a general indictment is also present. The passage describes a culture of feeble other-directed trendsters, anxious to learn the right thing to say and yet fearful of committing itself. The lines, one might say, enact a literary politics of consensus. One sees how the overtones of 'obliging' just before the cesura in line 208, are trapped and diverted in an unexpected direction by the end of the verse. Pope is striving to establish a satiric rhetoric of plainspeaking, bold assertion, exactly the opposite of the timorous Atticus manner. Such an intent hardly consorts with the quietude which Pope is ostensibly seeking. The satirist's freedom to speak out carries with it the loss of personal inviolacy; public themes are bound to erode the writer's privacy.

Thus, although Pope proclaims a modest classic ambition, to 'maintain a Poet's Dignity and Ease' (263), his poem belies the pretence. *Otium cum dignitate* is a reward for superannuated courtiers, not active satirists. Much nearer the truth is a phrase that crops up earlier on – 'Glad of a quarrel' (67). As the Horatian imitations regularly show, a quiet life would be death to the true poet. Indeed,

Satire II.i ironically allows Pope to opt for tame conformity, harmless 'grave Epistles...Such as a King might read, a Bishop write...' (151–2). The overall drift of the poem is to present the satirist as radically alienated from the current power structure, and directly challenging legal authority. Equally, the first *Epilogue to the Satires* shows virtue as intact so long as it settles for the 'beloved, contented' world of quiet impotence. In this light it is surely implausible that the *Epistle to Arbuthnot*, designated the prologue to these imitations, should seriously endorse a life of supine acquiescence. Pope is well aware of the attractions of graceful inutility. But his artistic mission was to fight in the thick of the battle, and the vehement energies of his style always disclose that.

In short, the reading of the *Epistle* as a weary personal protest misses its fundamental meaning. The work is more than private apologia or petulant retort. It is a defence of satiric poetry and a study of artistic vocation. Pope's impatient query, 'Heavens! was I born for nothing but to write?' (272) proves embarrassingly near the mark. Through the vitality of its comedy, the vigour of its language and the immediacy of its presentation, the *Epistle* embodies an intense moral vision totally at odds with any quietist creed. Throughout we see the 'militant attitude towards experience' which Northrop Frye discerns in all satire. However much Pope claims to have achieved detachment,

> I pay my Debts, believe, and say my Pray'rs,
> Can sleep without a Poem in my head,
> Nor know, if *Dennis* be alive or dead...   (268–70)

the poem signals to us behind his back that he is protesting too much. The life of cultivated ease proves to be a daydream Pope can only fitfully indulge. The conflicting drives within him nourish a superbly comic self-dramatization, but they also illuminate the condition of the artist at large. Like Yeats, Pope confronted his own poetic destiny in his work; and like Yeats he created an art that richly transcended its autobiographic occasion.[4]

---

[4] Mack's discussion in *Garden and City* remains the fullest exploration of Pope's self-fashioning and his creation of a poetic identity. The Twickenham estate is seen as crucial to that process: and it may therefore be no accident that the poem which incorporates Twickenham most directly is the *Epistle to Arbuthnot*, the work which exemplifies the process, as it were, in the poetic act. Besides, Twickenham was itself a kind of vector of the public and private (see my Introduction to The Oxford Authors *Alexander Pope* (Oxford, 1993), pp. viii–ix.

CHAPTER 8

The name and nature of Dulness: proper nouns in
The Dunciad

That Pope has a special way with proper names has been observed
before now.[1] And indeed a usage as idiosyncratic as '*Sternhold* himself
he *out-Sternholded*' cries aloud for comment. One does not have to be
a grammarian to discern the interest of a line like

And call her Angel! Goddess! Montague!

Nor to respond with delight and quickened attention to a number of
parallel constructions ('...nine such Poets made a Tate'). However,
such observations have never been enlisted in the service of any
account of Pope's wider aims. I shall seek to show that Pope
characteristically exploits a penumbra of doubt which surrounds
proper nouns used in this way. He deliberately blurs the status of such
nouns in order to reinforce certain thematic and satiric motifs. Above
all, *The Dunciad* can be seen to derive much of its imaginative density
from this trick.

In this one instance we do have a pointer from previous criticism.
Aubrey Williams has demonstrated how Pope employs the word
'Heidegger' (spelt in fact with the last two letters reversed, I, 290) to
convey the sense of a mythical beast rather than that of the actual
showman. 'Never again, inside the poem, can the name refer solely
and strictly to the historical Heidegger.' With Theobald the case is
much the same, but it is more intensively worked by Pope. In
Williams' terms, 'The important thing is that a "Tibbald" has never
been defined...The Tibbald of the *Dunciad* is not quite the Theobald

---

[1] A brief but penetrating consideration of this point is by M. Mack, '"Wit and Poetry and
Pope": Some Observations on his Imagery', *Pope and his Contemporaries*, ed. J. L. Clifford
and L. A. Landa (Oxford, 1949), pp. 20–40. Mack speaks of a 'peculiarly suggestive kind
of metaphorical play between concrete and abstract', and notices how personified figures
are 'suddenly brought into incongruous union with a judge named Page'. These figures
include Dulness.

of history.' *A* Tibbald, indeed, comes to suggest 'a *species* of dull writer' [my italics].[2] At this point the critic moves on to separate conjectures which need not detain us here, though his mention of the magical properties which were felt to inhere in names is relevant to much of my own account. Besides, the discussion occupies a very few pages, and is largely confined to the two names already considered. In my view there is a similar process at work throughout the entire poem – and just as much so in the revised *Dunciad*, where Tibbald of course figures hardly at all.[3]

I

Eighteenth-century grammarians appear to have been uneasy about the distinction between common and proper nouns. They make it all right, but they are never very happy about describing its basis. A typical attempt, no less so for being almost certainly derivative, is that of James Greenwood in his manual of 1711: Chapter IV deals with '*Substantives*, Proper and Common'.

* *Nouns* are either *proper or common.*
* *A Noun Substantive proper*, is a word that belongs to some (*individual*) Particular one of that kind; as *Ann, James, Peter, Mary,* &c.
* *A Noun Substantive common*, is a Word which belongs to all of that kind; as *Man, Woman, Horse, Tree,* &c.
Besides Persons, Countries also, Cities, Rivers, Mountains and other Distinctions of Place, have usually found peculiar Names, they being such words as Men have often Occasion to mark particularly. And it is not to be doubted, but if we had reason to mention particular *Horses,* as often as we have to mention particular *Men,* we should have proper Names for the one, as familiar as for the other; and *Bucephalus* would be a Word as much in use, as *Alexander.*

Jockeys, he continues, do apply a system of personal naming to the horses under their charge. All this is, I suppose, accurate; but it is

---

[2] *Pope's Dunciad: A Study of its Meaning* (London, 1955), pp. 65–76, contains a splendid analysis of the way in which the Dunces are assigned a 'realm of half-truth'. The quotations are from pp. 66–8. On Tibbald, see also W. K. Wimsatt, 'Rhetoric and Poetry: Alexander Pope', *The Verbal Icon* (Lexington, Ky., 1967), p. 181.

[3] In this essay I have confined my attention to *The Dunciad*; aspects of Pope's poetic grammar in other works are discussed on pp. 1–26 above. Quotations and line references follow *TE*, V. Unless otherwise indicated, the source is the revised (B) text.

crude and empirical, and displays little sense of the true nature of the
distinction. As usual with Greenwood, the writing is most inelegant,
too. After this passage (in which we might notice the reference to
Persons, Countries, Cities, Rivers and Mountains – *The Dunciad* is
chockful of allusions to each), Greenwood moves on to his normal
question-and-answer session, an early form of programmed learning:

Q.   Is the word *Anne*, a proper or common Noun?
A.   It is a proper Noun...

So with 'woman', the answer providing the explanation, 'for every
Woman is called a Woman, but every Woman is not called *Anne*'.
The near-tautology is betraying. Nor is Greenwood much more
convincing when he gets on to the origin of names. 'Names were first
imposed on Men for Distinction sake.' He discussed briskly the
derivation, either biblical or Saxon/Norman (the two seem to be
much the same to Greenwood), of common English names.[4]

A better-known grammar is that sometime attributed to Richard
Steele, or to the Dunce, Charles Gildon, but today generally called
Brightland's grammar from its publisher. The topic is treated rather
less confusingly here, but its Lockean flavour leaves it still some way
short of complete ludicity.

There are two sorts of *Ideas*, one Represents to us a single Thing, as the *Idea*
of one's *Father*, *Mother*, a Friend, his own Horse, his own Dogg, &*c*. The other
Idea presents to me several things together, but of the same Kind, as the *Idea*
of a Man in General, Horses in General, &*c*. [Brightland instances Plato and
London, then gives examples of common or 'appellative' nouns.]...Yet the
proper Name often belongs to several at the same time, as *Peter*, *John*, *Robert*,
&c., but this is only by Accident, by Reason that many have taken the Same
Name...

This last formulation does not appear to solve very much. And when
Brightland seeks for an instance to show how distinctions are
preserved, he lights on the case of adding 'the Second' to Charles,
which again seems an unrepresentative case.[5]

---

[4] *An Essay towards a Practical English Grammar* (London, 1711), pp. 42–6. The distinction
between individual and general is found in similar terms in James Shirley, *An Essay towards
an Universal and Rational Grammar*, ed. J. T. Philipps (1726), pp. iv–v.

[5] *A Grammar of the English Tongue* (1711), ed. R. C. Alston (Menston, 1967), p. 75. On the
authorship of this work, see R. C. Alston, *Bibliography of the English Language*, Vol. I (Leeds,
1965).

More impressive than either of these is a work by the historian of typography and classical scholar, Michael Maittaire. This dates from a year later than the manuals of Greenwood and Brightland, yet its approach strikes one today as far more enlightened. His taxonomy lists substantives as either 'Appellative and common, whose signification, appellation and name belongs to many... Or Proper, belonging to one only; as *Peter, London*. Those Adjectives are Proper which are derived from a Substantive Proper...' (Nestorian is the example given). Most significantly for Pope, Maittaire realizes that 'an appellative noun can be used sometimes as Proper; and a Proper, as an Appellative'. Thus we speak of 'the Philosopher', meaning Cicero – not a very good instance – and can say 'Cowley was the English Pindar', or 'the Cicero of the Age'.[6] Now Pope's only contact with Maittaire involved an act of rare clemency – almost one of spoiling the poem to please the friend. At the request of the Earl of Oxford, he left out Maittaire from *The Dunciad*.[7] This was in the first version of the poem. Where the classic would have come in is not clear (perhaps in the Scriblerian apparatus?), since his natural place would be with Bentley, Freind and Alsop in the new Book IV. Maittaire was a master at Westminster School, which made him a guardian not only of sound linguistic training but also of the infant Harleys. 'Westminster's bold race' (IV, 145) included, indeed, several members of the Earl's family; and if a thrust such as 'Words we teach alone' (IV, 150) could well be applied to a scholar of Maittaire's persuasion, he was no more a pedant entire than was Busby. Pope would be aware of the endeavours of Westminster alumni in English as well as classical philology. Of course he still may not have thought much of the result.

There are other signs of an imperfect ability to sever proper nouns from common at this period. Many dictionaries included a good number of what were really encyclopaedia entries. There were some specialized dictionaries of proper names, but very often the most

[6] *The English Grammar* (1712), ed. R. C. Alston (Menston, 1967), pp. 36–7. One may also observe that Christopher Cooper's influential *English Teacher* (1687) contained a list of common and proper nouns that have the same or near sound (e.g. Bede and bead), a further indication of the ways in which contemporaries were liable to confusion. See the edition by B. Sundby (Lund, 1953), p. 97. Scripture proper names are listed, with their pronunciation, on pp. 107–9.

[7] See *Corr*, II, 496. The Earl had procured a book from Swift for Maittaire's use a number of years earlier – *The Correspondence of Jonathan Swift*, ed. H. Williams (Oxford, 1963, 5), III, 155.

heterogeneous terms lie cheek by jowl. Macaulay complained that Sir William Temple, through carelessness or ignorance, aligned the historical and the fabulous, as would a compendium of phrase and legend. In the same way we might say that the Augustans often tended to align the unique with the commonplace. They do not seem always to have been very sure when they were using a proper noun. To this indecision, the practice of capitalizing nouns on rhetorical principles, or on no ground at all, must have contributed. Greenwood, surprisingly, has enough *nous* to see this, and recommends that the practice should be confined to the initial letter of proper nouns and of 'every word of special Note', such as God, Queen, Sir. The grammatical status of these latter words must have been even cloudier than it is today.[8]

Pope's own consciousness of the part which names play in his fiction is acknowledged in several places. Among the appendices to the poem itself, we can find a number of references to that habit of supplying exact nomenclature which has exercised critics ever since. For instance in the preface from 'The Publisher to the Reader', there is this:

There may arise some obscurity in Chronology from the *Names* in the Poem, by the inevitable removal of some Authors, and insertion of others, in their Niches. For whoever will consider the Unity of the whole design, will be sensible, that the *Poem was not made for these Authors, but these Authors for the Poem*...

I would not have the reader too much troubled or anxious, if he cannot decypher them; since when he shall have found them out, he will probably know no more of the Persons than before.

Yet we judg'd it better to preserve them as they are, than to change them for *fictitious names*, by which the Satyr would only be multiplied, and applied to many instead of one. Had the Hero, for instance, been called *Codrus*, how many would have affirm'd him to be Mr. *W* – Mr. *D* – Sir R – *B* – &c. but now, all that unjust scandal is saved, by calling him *Theobald*, which by good luck happens to be the name of a real person.[9]

The note here is one of defensive irony, with a pose of serendipity at the end: when a major replacement was made, fifteen years later, Pope adopted a more defiant attitude. At this juncture he is content to emphasize the obscurity of the Dunces by suggesting that their names are as good as arbitrary anyway – nobody will recognize them

[8] Greenwood, p. 257.   [9] *TE*, V, 205–6.

even if they are identified. They have, indeed, no real identity except as Dunces; they possess names, one feels, by grace or dispensation. The same rhetorical aim is apparent when Pope explains his inclusion of notes in the Variorum edition of 1729 ('Advertisement'): since 'it is only in this monument that [the Dunce] must expect to survive', he deserves to be specified 'just to tell what he was'.[10] Behind this offhand remark lies, of course, a good deal of literary shoptalk in Pope's correspondence, notably with Swift.

Whether or not Pope was really concerned that Gildon might live in fame as long as the satirist himself (as Swift contended had been the case with Maevius and Virgil),[11] we may take leave to doubt. Yet the poet was exercised by the issue of *names*, not only in the sense of literary reputation, but also inasmuch as the dunces' anonymity was a source of strength to their cause. If Pope or Swift published a satire, even if they withheld their name, it was not long as a rule before the work was fathered on to them – talent is the biggest give-away. But a nameless hack could snipe away with impunity, confident that no one could come up with *his* name on internal evidence. Hence the anxiety revealed in the 'Letter to the Publisher', attributed to William Cleland:

But when his moral character was attack'd, and in a manner from which neither Truth nor Virtue can secure the most Innocent, in a manner which though it annihilates the credit of the accusation with the just and impartial, yet aggravates very much the guilt of the accuser; (I mean by authors without Names:)...[12]

The whole convention of anonymous publication deserves fuller attention. For instance, it is evident that the bookseller occupied a much more important role in the literary world, actually and symbolically, when his was the only name which stood on the title page. It would scarcely be an exaggeration to say that in these circumstances the author might appear a second-order, derivative figure – a mere employee; whilst the true agent was the bookseller.[13]

---

[10] *TE*, V, 8.   [11] See *Corr*, II, 343–4; for Pope's reply, p. 349.   [12] *TE*, V, 13.
[13] There is an interesting paragraph, in this context, on what is called the 'Title-Page Man', i.e. bookseller, in a letter which was contributed in all probability by Defoe to *Mist's Weekly Journal* on 12 April 1719. The writer exempts booksellers from the charge of uttering obscenities, on the grounds that the author is the true begetter of such bawdy books. But that he should have to argue such a case is significant. See W. Lee, *Daniel Defoe: His Life and Recently Discovered Writings* (London, 1869), II, 34–5.

If that is so, it helps to explain the importance men such as Curll and Lintot acquire in satire, especially in *The Dunciad*.

Pope utilizes all these suggestions of 'anonymity', i.e. the literal withholding of one's name, to bring out the virtual anonymity, i.e. obscurity, of the Dunces. In Martinus Scriblerus' essay 'Of the Poem', the random collocation of names conveys the idea that any Dunce is as good as another, that Pope had better things to do than make a careful selection of particular individuals:

And the third [*read* second] book, if well consider'd seemeth to embrace the whole world. Each of the Games relateth to some or other vile class of writers. The first concerneth the Plagiary, to whom he giveth the name of More; the second the libellous Novellist, whom he styleth Eliza; the third the flattering Dedicator; the fourth the bawling Critick or noisy Poet; the fifth the dark and dirty Party-writer; and so of the rest, assigning to each some proper name or other, such as he cou'd find.[14]

Of course, the direct aim here is to hit at specific men and women such as Moore-Smythe and Eliza Haywood. But the passage also draws on the cumulated energies of the poem; its archaic, solemnly itemized style works on us to produce an impression of generic description. The labels are arbitrary because they appertain to classes rather than to monads. On the other hand, the phrasing may suggest that Pope's choice in not quite as arbitrary as all that – More is '*the* Plagiary', on one level any literary pilferer, on another *the* representative case in point. Similarly Eliza stands both as surrogate for a wider body of low-class fiction, and as *the* (authentic, quintessential) libellous novelist.

David Lodge has written that the novelist 'can never reproduce the naturality, the "givenness" of names in the real world'. If there is a correspondence between a fictional name and the character of its bearer (as with Heartfree or Quiverful), we feel according to Lodge that 'art has trespassed into life'.[15] In the light of this comment, it may be of interest that the phrase 'given name' now means, in American usage especially, a first or Christian name. Such appellations are within human choice, 'given' in the sense of having been voluntarily accorded – not in the sense of being ineluctable *données* of the situation. For Pope, the point is this: he can choose which authors out of the whole contemporary gallimaufry to put into his book. Thus

---

[14] *TE*, V, 51–2.   [15] *The Language of Fiction* (London, 1966), p. 45.

he has the freedom of the parents at a christening ceremony; yet at the same time these men did actually exist before the poem was written, so that they remain surnames, *ungiven*, arrived at by the blind operations of chance. Quiverful is a naked piece of invention, and hence perhaps a supererogatory nudge from the author. The name More was not, precisely, invented by Pope: so that its accreted overtones of excessive production, bare wastes or unattractive expanses seem to us to be parts of its meaning which we can legitimately take into account.[16] 'More', in fact, has some of the 'discreet appropriateness' which has been discovered in the character names used by Defoe and Richardson. It also has the inevitability of a name quite indifferently chosen, such as the one Mr Bumble gave to the orphan Oliver in his care. Even here, the selection is perhaps not *absolutely* random: a little earlier or later on the list, and the parish boy would have been called Oliver Swubble or Oliver Vilkins. So would the novel: and, for that purpose, neither seems somehow to do quite as well.

II

Satirists generally take one of two courses. They may decide to make a bold, frontal approach. In that case they will proceed as Byron does, and write openly of Bob Southey or the simple Wordsworth. Alternatively, they may choose to hide behind a screen of fictive nomenclature. They will then write of Labeo, of Maevius or of Sir Balaam.[17] It is true that in the second case a recognizable individual

---

[16] A modern grammarian writes, 'Proper names differ from appellatives in having no conceptual content. They merely indicate an object without implying a description of it... Proper names represent a direct way of naming things' – P. Christopher, *The Articles* (Copenhagen and London, 1939) pp. 59–62. For Pope the trick is to find names which suggest rather than describe, His duncely appellations do not describe a function (as *Fletcher* or *Brewer* originally did), or physical appearance (as *Redhead* once did): they indicate the status of the object. Either by the phonetic content of a word, or by some kind of lexical association (pun, rhyme, alliteration) with other appellatives, the name becomes momentarily a common noun.

[17] At one point in *The Dunciad*, Pope hints at what Mack calls the 'allusive' method of naming habitual in his *Moral Essays*. This is the reference to 'Sir Gilbert' (II, 251). Undoubtedly this means Sir Gilbert Heathcote, the wealthy financier; in the A text, II, 241, the name had been left as 'Sir G**'. At the same time, the phrase carried with it something of the flavour of Sir Balaam, a semi-allegorical quality permitted by the omission of the individualizing surname. To denude a baronet or a knight of his family name is also to rob him of pretensions towards nobility – the peerage are peers, as it were, by right of surname, so that we have Chesterfield, Lyttelton, Cobham set off more than once against Sir Robert, the upstart

is easily discerned peeping out from behind a screen; no great
penetration is needed to pick out well-known eighteenth-century
figures imperfectly concealed in the robes of a Latinate sobriquet in
more than one satire. But I am talking about a different issue – not
whether the writer has particular persons in mind, but whether he
actually refers to them by their own name. Under this aspect,
Edward Young's highly generalized Lavinia stands on the same
footing as Dryden's unmistakable Achitophel.

Now the Augustan satirists developed an intermediate form of
reference; and in Pope especially this semi-direct method of allusion
is of great significance for the wider imaginative ends of the poem.
The trick is observable in Dryden. There was a real Flecknoe, of
course, and a real Thomas Shadwell. But all we get within the poem
itself is Mac Flecknoe and *Sh—*. In a context where other names are
spelt out in full, the truncated form suggests a truncated existence:
the style of nomenclature conveys a kind of belittlement or insult.
Obviously, it was common enough to refer to figures by their initials
in a tract on state affairs. But there it was a matter of caution: the
writer dare not offend the laws against seditious literature, and feared
the consequences of too direct a statement of identity. The joke is that
no one would fear Shadwell's rage. To reduce his name to the
somewhat contemptuous formula '*sh—*' is thus to make a grotesque
feint, as a speaker might pretend to duck from the ill-directed missile
of a heckler. However, it is the eponym which really counts.
MacFlecknoe is and is not Shadwell, just as Tibbald is and is not
Theobald. As soon as the title is bestowed, Shadwell's identity is in
some degree compromised. He occupies a sort of shadow world, living
out a half-life which is not exactly fiction and not exactly reality. The
title is *bestowed*, for Shadwell's name is also a statement of his
hereditary function. As with a Highland chieftain, his name
proclaims his responsibility: as with a royal style, such as Pippin
XIV, his name announces the basis of his succession. It is of the
highest importance in both *Mac Flecknoe* and *The Dunciad* that the
events narrated centre on the coronation of a new chieftain for the
clan of Dunces. This is the critical moment for the entire cause of
Dulness; if succession fail, then its empire will fall. Hence the stress
both Dryden and Pope place on the address from the old king to his

whose 'eminence' lies in the *created* title. A man such as Sir John Barnard, held up for
admiration as a Patriot stalwart, is called 'Barnard'. To speak of 'Sir John' would draw
attention to the cit turned gentleman.

heir. To place Shadwell or Cibber in a genealogical line comprising Ogilby, Wither, Settle and the like was to hint at the permanence and durability of Dulness. For his part, Dryden enforces this point by specifying not only 'Father *Fleckno*' but also 'Uncle *Ogleby*'. And in any case, the title of his poem has already done some of the work.

The tutelary figure of Dulness herself provides the clearest example within *The Dunciad* of that imaginative merger which goes to unite the permanent and the temporary, the local and the universal, the heroic potential with the sordid actuality. The trick works just as well in a short space, however. Witness the mention of the hapless Benjamin Norton Defoe:

> Norton, from Daniel and Ostroea sprung
> Blest with his father's front, and mother's tongue,
> Hung silent down his never-blushing head...   (II, 415)

The note records (or did in earlier editions) that Benjamin was 'said to be the natural offspring of the famous *Daniel*'. Ostroea is, as Gilbert Wakefield puts it, a 'facetious name' for an oyster wench, possibly borrowed from Gay's *Trivia*. The name carries with it a mythological and vaguely classical ring. 'Daniel' has strong biblical associations, although the actual Defoe was too 'famous' (notorious?) to lie concealed in the editorial undergrowth. 'Norton' is just plain reality, boring and literal. The poetic effect is to achieve a kind of miscegenation: Ostroea, distant and latinate, submits to the embrace of mundane and familiar Daniel, like some lustful immortal in a reversal of the Leda myth. The phrasing reminds us of Benjamin's low parentage, but it also juxtaposes the commonplace with the quasi-timeless. And it is this commerce between the local and the supra-historical which the poem constantly sets in motion.[18]

Throughout the work we find an extraordinary density of proper nouns. Most refer either to persons or to places. Topographical words, which equally serve to mediate between the immediate setting and the ultimate cultural situation, must be dismissed in a summary fashion here.[19] It should be noted, however, what a high proportion of these place-names carry with them moral or legendary undertones.

---

[18] The Dunces, says Williams in a splendid phrase (p. 75), 'endure a type of historical death and imaginative transfiguration'. In the case of Norton, we might add a species of mythological rebirth.

[19] This matter is discussed at greater length in my *Grub Street* (London, 1972), pp. 18–83.

Grub Street itself is a condition as well as a real London locality;
Bridewell and Bedlam were originally particular points on the map,
but their extended applicability is shown by the fact that the words
were used of similar institutions in other surroundings. When Pope
refers to 'the neighb'ring Fleet (Haunt of the Muses)' (II, 427), he is
capitalizing on the lexical circumstances by which terms such as
'Fleet wedding' and 'humours of the Fleet' had passed into the
language. A little earlier in the poem occurs the line 'Thro' Lud's
fam'd gates, along the well known Fleet...' (II, 359). Here Pope goes
so far as to employ a form of words which, by a comic periphrasis,
replaces the expected 'Ludgate' by a piece of encapsulated myth-
cum-history. There may also be a sense that Lud's Town (Stow's
phrase, quoted in the note) is the town of the Dull – a simple phonetic
inversion.[20] Many other geographical pointers turn out to be moral
pointers, too: 'the saints of Drury-lane' (II, 30) Billingsgate, Hockey-
hold, Tyburn, the Guildhall, Lincoln's Inn, for example.

It is through persons rather than places, though, that the action of
The Dunciad is defined. At any moment in the poem, we may be
surprised by the sudden intervention of a personal name. People are
aligned with the casual freaks of English weather:

> 'Till genial Jacob, or a warm Third day,
> Call forth each mass, a Poem or a Play...   (I. 57)

where the matey Christian-name terms imply a certain amused
familiarity. Or an individual may be merged into a general category
until his, or her, identity is deeply compromised:

> (Whence hapless Monsieur much complains at Paris
> Of wrongs from Duchesses and Lady Maries)...   (II, 135)

'Monsieur' is a comprehensive mode of reference, but here it points
to the unique M. Redmond. 'Duchesses', as Aubrey Williams has
shown, conveys an idea approximating to 'all whores and cheats
under the name of ladies' – the word had a slang sense meaning 'fine
ladies of the town'.[21] Yet the last two words point unambiguously to
that lass wholly unparalleled, Mary Wortley Montagu. That there

---

[20] I owe this point to Emrys Jones, who kindly lent me the text of his British Academy lecture
on 'Pope and Dulness' in advance of publication, in *PBA*, LIV (1968), 231–63.
[21] See *TE*, V, 467.

should be more than one specimen of this creature is a whimsical fancy in itself to Pope. The plural form, attracted from the previous noun and emphasized by the rhyme, draws attention to the quiddity of *the* Lady Mary. However many fraudulent duchesses there may have been around London, there was only one Wortley.

We noted earlier the device of prefixing the indefinite article to proper nouns in one particular class, the family names of the Dunces. As well as the Heidegger case, Book I furnished a full set of such usages. The Goddess shows to her chosen king, for instance, how it is that, with suitable modifications but without any creative skill,

> A past, vamp'd, future, old, reviv'd, new piece,
> 'Twixt Plautus, Fletcher, Shakespear, and Corneille,
> Can make a Cibber, Tibbald, or Ozell.   (I, 248)

Can supply a work for Cibber and the rest, can make up a typical Cibber offering? Yet, but also there seems to be a concealed sense of 'can be the making of', 'can hatch out a Cibber...' *A* Cibber is a play by Cibber, or again a dramatist of Cibber's order. Other instances occur in the next book:

> Curl stretches after Gay, but Gay is gone,
> He grasps an empty Joseph for a John...   (II, 127)

An empty Joseph is an *ersatz* Gay; 'Joseph Gay' was a pseudonym adopted by Breval. The fictitious Gay is a swindler, as well as a pretender to a dignity as a writer (Gayhood, as it were) he can't command. At this point in the poem, the Dunces are planning a takeover campaign on the reasoning that if you can't annex talent, you can at least borrow your rival's names:

> Cook shall be Prior, and Concanen, Swift:
> So shall each hostile name become our own,
> And we too boast our Garth and Addison.   (II, 138)

This childlike wish-fulfilment has something of the character of sympathetic magic. We shall re-christen ourselves, the Goddess proclaims, and so draw the sting from our opponents – we shall be them, and so they will be unable to hurt us. The part played in this by actual nomenclature is very clear.

Later on there are references to 'the Pindars, and the Miltons of a

Curl' (III, 164), i.e. all that a man of Curll's stamp could recruit to his side: to 'a new Cibber' (III, 142); and to 'Another Durfey' (III, 146) – a reincarnated Durfey. Again, Settle's easy reference to *a* Bacon and *a* Locke suggests his inability to gauge the distinction of these men – to a Dunce they are replaceable and repeatable:

> 'Tis yours, a Bacon or a Locke to blame,
> A Newton's genius, or a Milton's fame...   (III, 215)

Similarly in Book IV Aristarchus seems to envisage a kind of distributive application for the names he cites:

> Nor could a BARROW work on ev'ry block,
> Nor has one ATTERBURY spoil'd the flock.   (IV, 245)

Close to this technique is the odd grammatical habit of appending a personal pronoun to a name: 'our Garth' has just been quoted, and there are also phrases such as 'My H[en]ley's periods, or my Blackmore's numbers' (II, 370), where the long halting line and its cumbersome feminine rhyme serve to invite sleep by themselves.[22]

A different trick, already mentioned, is the merging of the mythological with the naturalistic and contemporary. On a broad level of fable, this occurs in Book II with Smedley's account of his submarine journey – Styx is brought to the borders of the Temple. But it is found too in a closer linguistic space. We hear of a tapestry 'worth to be spread / On Codrus' old, or Dunton's modern bed' (III, 144), which is as good as an equation: ancient Codrus = modern Dunton. In the last book, the gloomy advocate of natural religion speaks of

> 'That NATURE our Society adores,
> Where Tindal dictates, and Silenus snores.'   (IV, 491)

---

[22] Other examples are 'Our Midas' (III, 324); 'my Cibber' (III, 266, 287); 'my SWIFT' (I, 26); 'other Caesars, other Homers' (IV, 360). There is something curious, too, about the locution 'On German Crouzaz, and Dutch Burgersdyck' (IV, 198). The sense appears to be 'Crousaz, representative of the German school, and Burgersdyck, a typical Dutch logician'. The names are applied as though to horses, and indeed the footnote by Scriblerus reads like a parody of Greenwood's inept examples: 'These are horses of great strength, and fit to carry any weight, as their German and Dutch extraction may manifest; and very famous we may conclude, being honour'd with *Names*, as were the horses Pegasus and Bucephalus.' The grammar is odd because we expect a definite article in such constructions; to omit 'the' further dehumanizes Crousaz and Burgersdyck.

Much the same applies in the case of an allusion to 'Curl's Corinna' (II, 70), although here the associations caught up are not classical but those of a private allegory – a literary fiction exposed in the notes, where Mrs Thomas is all but identified.[23]

Four other methods by which Pope blurs the functional distinction between the two kinds of noun may be itemized:

(1) He sometimes introduces a sort of zeugma: thus,

> But now (so ANNE and Piety ordain)
> A Church collects the saints of Drury Lane. (II, 29)

In other contexts, the coupling might imply a straightforward panegyric intent, whereby the Queen's enlightened endowment of the new churches is seen as making her the soul of piety, piety incarnate. In this case, after the lapse of years, a heavy irony obtrudes. 'Saints' in the second line refers to prostitutes, so that the honorific colouring of 'Piety' is instantly muddied. A sense emerges along the lines of 'as Anne in her do-gooding, would-be pious (but over-optimistic) way would have had it...'

A more spectacular instance occurs in the justly famous passage where the Dunces begin their cat-calling prize contest:

> 'Twas chatt'ring, grinning, mouthing, jabb'ring, all
> And Noise and Norton, Brangling and Breval,
> Dennis and Dissonance, and captious Art,
> And Snip-snap short, and interruption smart,
> And Demonstration thin, and Theses thick,
> And Major, Minor, and Conclusion quick. (II, 237)

This cacophonous roll-call merges the individual with the product, the quality with the begetter. A sort of uncompleted chiasmus works to bind in the various elements still more tightly: in the second and third lines we have abstraction/name: abstraction/name: name/abstraction. The phrasing is such that the reader is trapped for a moment into taking 'Snipsnap' as one more infelicitous name for a Dunce. 'Short' and 'smart' are both epithets that would fit persons; we read the line expectantly, looking for another minor poet. 'Thin' is both literal and metaphoric – a weak and scanty argument – while 'thick' implies, in its transferred sense, a dense and stupid work. The

---

[23] See also the juxtaposition of 'Giant Handel' with 'bold Briareus' at IV, 65.

entire passage effects a transition of striking neatness, from the
jabbering participants to the shrill illogicality which is their literary
hallmark. Alliteration is a prime means by which Pope's imagination
leaps the gap between abstract and proper nouns.[24]

(2) A favourite satiric resource, the pun, is accorded special
meaning in this context. Much of the wordplay in *The Dunciad*
activates proper nouns, which in itself gives these nouns an order of
semantic energy they would not ordinarily bear. To call the laureate,
in traditional fashion, Bays is to provide clear opportunities in this
way: thus Cibber himself alludes to 'the last honours of the Butt and
Bays' (I, 168), a mode of self-advertisement apart from anything else.
Equally, when Settle claims:

> ... long my Party built on me their hopes,
> For writing Pamphlets, and for roasting Popes...   (III, 284)

One cannot help but feel that party pamphleteering is aligned with
something more than the pope-burning processions which are
ostensibly at issue: that is, the numerous duncely attacks on the poet
himself. Sometimes the name itself suits the context. When Pope
substituted John Oldmixon for Dennis as the 'Senior' competitor in
the diving contest, this surname was admirably fitted to one who is
made to cry out, 'And am I now three-score?' (II, 285) The footnote
describes this particular Dunce as 'the most ancient Critick of our
Nation': in the text, it needs only the bare facts of nomenclature –
along with metre – to make one point:

> In naked majesty Oldmixon stands...   (II, 283)

In his earlier niche (A, II, 199, 201), the stress had been allowed to
fall naturally on the first syllable of Oldmixon's name. Now there is
at least a suggestion of stress where the regular fall of accents would
put it, on the syllable 'mix–'. Accordingly one reads, 'old *Mixon*',
not '*Old*mixon'.

(3) Pope makes great use of inharmonious names further to
blacken the Dunces' cause. Ugly formations; jagged, chiming and
undignified phonetics – these pervade the nominal roll of Dulness'
army. (Could it be that Swift and Gay are mentioned, Arbuthnot
not, because of their more elegant surnames?) An air of deformed

---

[24] Mack, p. 27, is one of the many critics to comment on this passage.

malignancy attaches to many figures in the list: Ogilby could hardly but be a founding father of the cause, with a name like that. The grating pararhyme in the verse, 'Can make a Cibber, Tibbald, or Ozell', is a reproof in its own right.[25] Contemptuous alliteration plays against crunching hiatus:

> Earless on high, stood unabash'd De Foe,
> And Tutchin flagrant from the scourge below,
> There Ridpath, Roper, cudgell'd might ye view...   (II, 147)

Note the stutter with the two unvoiced d-sounds at the end of the first line, and the almost heraldic turn of phrase in the second (a Tutchin flagrant would presumably be much like a griffin passant). Literary folly is imaged throughout the poem by horrendous-sounding words – 'Sooterkins of Wit' (I, 126), 'a Lumberhouse of books' (III, 193), 'one Rose a Gregorian, one a Gormogon' (IV, 576). It is therefore especially fitting that the devotees of Dulness should bear such unmelodious names.

A number of striking local effects depend on this circumstance. In Book I, the barbarous tomes of unread medieval scholasticism occupy Cibber's library, along with superannuated compilations of Philemon Holland:

> There Caxton slept, with Wynkyn at his side,
> One clasp'd in wood, and one in strong cow-hide;
> There, sav'd by spice, like Mummies, many a year,
> Dry Bodies of Divinity appear:
> De Lyra there a dreadful front extends,
> And here the groaning shelves Philemon bends.   (I, 149)

The library has become a mortuary; and the very names have a Gothic ring. Till we come to Philemon, that is: a preposterous braggadocio of a Christian name. The sudden switch to first-name terms carried with it an impression of genial contempt.

Another case in which an absurd given name is used to form a climax is that passage of Book II where Dulness decks out 'three

---

[25] In 'There hapless Shakespear, yet of Tibbald sore' (I, 132), Tibbald has come to resemble an illness – I am conscious, at any rate, of a subliminal meaning along the lines of 'Shakespeare, still feeling the after-effects of his bout of tibbald...' Mack, p. 28, finely characterizes the 'tumbling huddle of risible' names in the Cibber/Tibbald/Ozell coupling. Another unhappy triad are the classical scholars 'Kuste, Burman, Wasse' (IV, 237).

wicked imps, of her own Grubstreet choir' like Congreve, Addison and Prior:

> Mears, Warner, Wilkins run: delusive thought:
> Breval, Bond, Besaleel, the varlets caught.   (II, 124)

Harsh alliteration comes to the aid of the sense. The names of the admired men of letters have a dignified, even patrician air. Mears and Bond sound by contrast irredeemably low; Breval is ugly; poor Bezaleel Morrice exists largely by virtue of his wildly idiosyncratic name. Then, with the progression to the Fleet Ditch for the diving games, an even more absurd set of patronymic forms litter the text. First there is Oldmixon, which (synthetically if not etymologically) means ancient heap of excrement. A writer in Mist's *Weekly Journal* in 1718 – probably Defoe – had already had fun speculating on the origins of this name.[26] After this, the Dunces listed are in turn Smedley, Concanen (how spluttering a word beside Congreve!), Blackmore, Mother Osborne, Arnall, Milbourne. Meanwhile, there is the episode of Smedley's visit to the underworld: the full classical vowels and shapely word-forms (Lutetia, Nigrina, Alphaeus, Hylas, Arethuse) contrast joltingly with the stark Saxon phonemes which occur in the geography of modern London – Aldgate, Lud's gate, Fleet. Then there resumes the series of brutish surnames: Budgell, Toland and Tindal. Finally, a set of Frenchified or otherwise un-English styles:

> At last Centlivre felt her voice to fail,
> Motteux himself unfinish'd left his tale,
> Boyer the State, and Law the Stage gave o'er,
> Morgan and Mandevil could prate no more...   (II, 411)

Susanna Centlivre is unsexed in the process. Throughout, one notices that the habitual bare allusion to surnames tends to put all the writers on one level... The omission of 'Mr' or 'John' equates the present with the past; Quarles and Ogilby live on, in their modern avatars.

One specialized application of this principle involves Cibber himself. Contemporaries referred to him as 'Kibber' rather than

---

[26] *Weekly Journal*, 26 July 1718. P. Pinkus, *Grub Street Laid Bare* (London, 1968), p. 78, misdates the paragraph July 1716, when Oldmixon had not yet taken up office in Bridwater (his move being the occasion of the piece). Besides, Mist's paper did not begin till December 1716.

'Sibber'; hence the frequent play on words like Keyber.[27] Pope has thus got a ready-made alliteration, Kolley Kibber, suggesting much in itself. When the archduce is crowned, there are further opportunities: King Cole springs easily to mind:

> 'God save King Cibber!' mounts in ev'ry note.
> Familiar White's, 'God save King Coley!' cries;
> 'God save King Colley!' Drury Lane replies:
> To Needham's quick the voice triumphal rode,
> But pious Needham dropt the name of God;
> Back to the Devil the last echoes roll,
> And 'Coll' each Butcher roars at Hockley-hole.   (I, 320)

'Familiar' White's, because Cibber was an *habitué* of the coffee-house, because it was well known, because it was impudent enough to adopt first-name terms. Note too that Needham's, the name of a bawd, has become a place: 'the Devil' is a tavern. Much of *The Dunciad* centres on noise resounding through the city; the followers of Dulness are uniquely qualified as brayers and monkey-mimics. Significantly it is a name which echoes through the streets at this point. The last words of the book are an allusion to Ogilby's version of Aesop:

> ...Loud thunder to its bottom shook the bog,
> And the hoarse nation croak'd, 'God save King Log.'   (I, 329)

Croaking is the archetypal activity of the Dunces in this poem. Nothing could be more suitable than that the annunciation of kingship should involve a husky and unmusical jabber.

The last word I used, quite by chance, suggests the concoctions of nonsense verse. Pope was assuredly alive to the phonetic properties of his adversary's name. They are most obviously exploited in the last book, where the Goddess bestows on her progeny 'Cibberian forehead, or Cimmerian gloom' (IV, 532). This is to impute guilt by phonetic association.

(4) Pope is particularly fond of monosyllables when choosing an apposite proper noun. The clearest case is perhaps that of Curll, whose name is (in and outside this poem) declined and conjugated as though subject to the usual rules of accidence. Derivatives are formed, such as Curleus or Curlicism; the plural voice is common, often with a vaguely punning intent: '...that [seat, i.e. pillory] where on her Curls the Public pours, / All-bounteous, fragrant Grains and

---

[27] S. I. Tucker, 'A note on Colley Cibber's Name', *N&Q* (November 1959), 400.

Golden show'rs...' (II, 3). The bookseller is regularly supplied with
a seemingly honorific epithet, appropriate to epic contexts: 'daunt-
less Curl', 'shameless Curl', 'Curl's chaste press', and so on. Just as
the action shows as Curll in a quasi-heroic posture, the great
'Vaticide' who calls on Cloacina for aid and 'vindicates the race' (II,
107), so the language gestures towards ennoblement, as it besmirches.
Another significant personage designated by a brisk monosyllable is
Bays, the alternative name for the hero. The sobriquet is found twice
in two lines at one point, with the additional emphasis first of
capitals,[28] then of an extrametrical stress at the start of the verse (I,
108). The pun at I, 168, has already been noticed; later, at line 303,
we have 'the madding Bay' coupled with 'the drunken Vine'. It
requires no great displacement to link the second epithet with the first
noun, or to apply the phrase back to the laureate.

Pope delights in utilizing the actual names of real Dunces whose
pert briskness reflects something of their literary character. When
Cibber exclaims, 'To Dulness Ridpath is as dear as Mist' (I, 208) the
last word again achieves something like punning force. From the start
the 'clouded Majesty' of Dulness has been emphasized. Her cell is
located in the fenny wastes of Moorfields; her sons are beheld by 'the
cloud-compelling Queen /...thro' fogs, that magnify the scene' (I,
79). Pope was of course familiar with the continuation of Mist's
Journal under the name of Fog, beginning in October 1728. One
implication of the line is therefore, 'Dulness is drawn to a low
journalist like Ridpath as she is to her own natural habitat of murk
and fog.'

The jaunty diminutive 'Coll' exemplified a process that can be
seen more widely. Names such as Ward, Roome, Goode, Ralph are
used with mocking familiarity, as though they were small boys in a
preparatory school. Link two such names together, and one has a
limited liability company of Dunces – 'Where Brown and Mears
unbar the gates of Light...' (III, 28). The coupling is exactly similar
to that of 'Drabs and Dice' elsewhere (III, 308); it is at such a
juncture that one realizes how little it matters that the surnames, so
glibly tossed out, have no substantive referential power. It is not very

---

[28] Capitals are allotted to Swift at the outset, to Bays, to Chesterfield (IV, 43), to Wyndham,
Talbot, Murray and Pulteney (IV, 167), to James (the First) just afterwards, to Barrow and
Atterbury (IV, 245) and to Queen Caroline (IV, 409). The practice indicates a form of
compliment, sincere or ironic. In passing, it is noteworthy that the practice of italicizing
proper names is not followed in most early editions of the poem.

important even if one cannot put a face to the label 'Rich'; the surrounding language enacts his monosyllabic detachment and stability:

> Immortal Rich! how calm he sits at ease
> 'Mid snows of paper, and fierce hall of pease...   (III, 261)

A more complex effect is wrought on the introduction of the limp waxworks figure at the start of the heroic games. The entire verse-paragraph deserves attention:[29]

> With Authors, Stationers obey'd the call,
> (The field of glory is a field for all.)
> Glory, and gain, th'industrious tribe provoke;
> And gentle Dulness ever loves a joke.
> A Poet's form she plac'd before their eyes,
> And bade the nimblest racer seize the prize;
> No meagre, muse-rid mope, adjust and thin,
> In a dun night-gown of his own loose skin;
> But such a bulk as no twelve bards could raise,
> Twelve starv'ling bards of these degen'rate days.
> All as a partridge plump, full-bed, and fair,
> She form'd this image of well-body'd air;
> With pert flat eyes she window'd well its head;
> A brain of feathers, and a heart of lead;
> And empty words she gave, and sounding strain,
> But senseless, lifeless! idol void and vain!
> Never was dash'd out, as one lucky hit,
> A fool, so just a copy of a wit;
> So like, that critics said, and courtiers swore,
> A Wit it was, and call'd the phantom More.   (II, 31)

The passage reaches an almost rhapsodic note with the exclamations near the end. Pope employs a more direct technique than usual; such irony as there is brushes against the Goddess and against the critics, rather than against the ostensible subject, James Moore-Smythe. So stark a use of language, with heavy alliteration, and without the usual malicious edge, argues a peculiar distance in the attitude of the writer – if not a lack of animus (we have other evidence of Pope's feelings towards Moore-Smythe), at least a capacity to relegate the

[29] Williams has an excellent passage (*Pope's Dunciad*, pp. 68–9), confirming my findings from another angle. He appositely quotes several of Scriblerus' damaging comments, notably the attempt to prove that More 'is not the name of an actual person, but fictitious; *More* from μωρός, *stultus*, μωρία, *stultitia*, to represent the folly of a Plagiary'. As Williams says, notes like this 'put [the Dunces'] existence in jeopardy'. One additional association of this phoneme may be 'moor', i.e. fen, as in Moorfields, where the cell of Dulness is located.

personal thrust in the cause of the fictive situation. Moore-Smythe is fat, no conventional distressed poet; but his grossness is that of a Michelin man rather than that of a recognizable individual. The 'phantom', over whose nature and identity the disputes rage, has no innards – he (or rather, Pope insists, it) is void, senseless and lifeless: something like the waxworks dummy Condillac would use to illustrate the various human faculties. Its eyes were windows, its words are empty. It is 'an *image* of well-body'd air', a mere 'copy'.

This then, this sexless amorphous object, is a More. That word comes decisively last. It receives great emphasis because of the rhyme; and even more because only one rhyme word in the entire paragraph (*provoke*) is other than monosyllabic. The reader has been prepared by a succession of sharp, aggressive words – each carrying a good deal of weight, both phonetically and syntactically. When we get to the last line, the verb 'call'd' arouses our expectations. The strategically important object 'the phantom' follows. And at length the bathetic noun in apposition to that object – More, with suggestions of redundancy, dropsical growth, tedious prolongation. The effect is achieved with consummate skill: the entire strophic organization of this paragraph abets the joke.

Now it is vital to this process that the name chosen should be capable of passing itself off, on one level, as a common noun. Elsewhere, in the *Epistle to Arbuthnot*, Pope had punned on the same word:

> So humble, he [the satirist] has knock'd at *Tibbald*'s door,
> Has drunk with Cibber, nay has rym'd for *Moor*.   (372)

A few lines later in that poem, a fuller version of the name is given: 'Hear this! and spare his Family, *James More*!' In the passage from *The Dunciad*, it is essential that the ponderous formula be reduced to a bare monosyllable. James Moore-Smythe can only be James Moore-Smythe can only be James Moore-Smythe. In stripping down this grandiloquent denomination, Pope robs its bearer of his pretensions. The monosyllable ring of that word 'More' has the effect of reducing the Dunce to a dehumanized cipher.

In another place, the poet has recourse to a series of monosyllabic names for a quite different reason. Book III affords an instance of satiric contrast, where pompous tribute goes to stately fools and neglect falls on the worthy. Significantly, the fools have elaborate handles to them – they are awarded the pseudo-dignity of a classical sobriquet, or else allotted their full style. (Ambrose Philips, so as not to be confused with John Philips: the implication being that a Wren does not need a first name to identify him – 'Oh, *that* Ambrose Philips…')

> See, see, our own true Phœbus wears the bays!
> Our Midas sits Lord Chancellor of Plays!
> On Poet's Tombs see Benson's titles writ!
> Lo! Ambrose Philips is prefer'd for Wit!
> See under Ripley rise a new White-hall,
> While Jones' and Boyle's united labours fall:
> While Wren with sorrow to the grave descends,
> Gay dies unpension'd with a hundred friends,
> Hibernian Politics, O Swift! thy fate;
> And Pope's, ten years to comment and translate.   (III, 323)

Settle's vision reaches a climax in the last line but one, where the direct vocative places even more emphasis on the name invoked (just as Philips gets greater attention after the exclamation 'Lo'). The final verse is mockingly self-pitying, a calculated bathos. What we see in the passage as a whole is a kind of linguistic symbolism. Pompous idiocy is rewarded, amongst other ways, by pompous nomenclature. Forgotten merit is embodied in six short names; the very syllables have a stoic Roman air about them, when thus disposed about the verse.

III

The key fact about Dulness is that she is both goddess and quality. She stands as a personification much as does a half-dead metaphor. The word can be made to jump in either direction; in some cases, it continues to sit on the fence, with consequent ambiguity, both verbal and thematic. The word furnishes thus a special instance of the linguistic ploy under consideration: it blends the denominating (identifying, unique) function of a term with the descriptive (qualifying, characterizing, generic) usage.

Now it is true that in all allegory, personified figures tend to hover on the edge of reabsorption into that abstract realm from which they have been plucked. Allegory, that is, is deliquescent in its conformation. The basic meaning of the abstraction tends to reassert itself, in some particular idiom or construction, and the personified character drains away. We have no longer the fictive Envy but the quality envy (a distinction modern typography makes clearer than it generally is, but a real distinction all the same). The point about the Augustan satirists is that they deliberately exploit this area of ambiguity. It is part of their method to hover between the arbitrary and the necessary; and they are intrigued by the moment when a word ceases to point simply at a localized figure, with whom it has been contingently associated, and re-establishes its general applicability. Dryden anticipated Pope in going out of his way to precipitate such a linguistic breakdown. And his treatment of 'dulness' in *Mac Flecknoe*, comparatively simple as it is, prefigures the larger lexical displacements of *The Dunciad*.

'Dull' is a favourite word for Dryden, and he uses it at least sixty times in his work, often carelessly enough.[30] 'Dulness' occurs much less frequently. Half these occurrences are found in the text of *Mac Flecknoe*. Yet despite this, Dryden does not allot to the term any controlling function in the mythical or dramatic organization of his poem. It was Pope's great invention to find a role for Dulness at an early stage of his *inventio*. Or, to put the matter in more contemporary terms, to cast Dulness as a fictive character, and not just as a thematic motif. By an extension of simple prosopopoeia, the goddess is made to direct the outer course of the narrative as she does the inner drives of the horde of Dunces. An Aristotelian might say that this was because Pope had found the right fable to enact the imaginative truth he wished to convey. For the present, it is enough that Pope's feat can be seen in specifically linguistic terms. What he did was to mould the potentialities of a single word so that it has a double lexical status. He fixes Dulness among the dramatis personae *and* among the dialectical props of the work. Every time we come on the word, we are forced towards a dual response. The poem asks us at each stage (as allegory does not ordinarily do) to re-examine the basis of its central personification.

The opening sentence of Martinus Scriblerus' introduction helps to bring about this process. 'This poem,' we are solemnly told, 'as it celebrateth the most grave and antient of things, Chaos, Night, and Dulness, so is it of the most grave and antient kind.' Thus we are

---

[30] I follow Montgomery's concordance. Pope's more interesting usages include the reference to the young lord (*Horace, Ep.* I. vi. 43), who sees his Chloe '[Wed] the rich Dulness of some Son of earth'. The syntax aligns the noun with wit and worth in the previous line, but Dulness is clearly no abstraction – it refers to a rich young dullard. Put in this way, the word also suggests the accumulated store of hereditary qualities the young man possesses. 'Dulness' means dull works in the *Epistle to Arbuthnot*, line 351. Pope uses the adjective 'dull' thirty-five times in all his work.

prepared for the epic treatment; at the outset, Dulness is given a mythological location, but also what might be called a psychological identity. Scriblerus then states the action of the poem, namely, 'the Removal of the Imperial seat of Dulness from the City to the polite world'. Into this action is drawn 'the whole history of Dulness and her children'. Finally, the scholiast remarks that 'the *Machinery* is a continued chain of Allegories, setting forth the whole power, ministry, and empire of Dulness, extended thro' her subordinate instruments, in all her various operations'.[31] It will be seen that the name is invoked in many different connections. Power and ministry suggest a particular agent; empire would go well with a more abstract way of speech. Dulness is the daughter of Chaos and Night, as the poem itself tells us (I, 12); she has 'instruments' and performs 'operations'. But there is also a section in which the allegory is explained, and it is there revealed that the goddesses of poverty and dulness act in concert – Dulness being 'the mother of...plodding'. Genealogy has ceased to be a mode of *post facto* explanation; it is now consulted as a prescriptive force in the ordering of the narrative.

In the text proper, the word Dulness occurs some thirty times, in all but a very few cases bearing an initial capital. It is possible to identify these classes of usage. Two of these represent extreme polar positions, and the other an intermediary state. Actually, there is a continuous gradation, rather than a clearcut grouping of this order; but for simplicity the total register of occurrences may be divided as follows.

X pattern of usage: where the term connotes the personified figure of Queen Dulness. Here the sense is adequately covered if we simply replace the name by a phrase such as 'the goddess'. Most of these are fairly straightforward cases; examples are found at I, 11, 111, 257; II, 122, 195, 407; III, 2, 135, 300; IV, 30, 119. Ambiguity is effectively ruled out in these cases, either because of an appositional phrase ('Dulness, good Queen') or a physical reminder ('On Dulness' lap th' Anointed head reposed' – though even here there may be a vestigial sense of 'the bosom of forgetfulness'). Some of these passages were introduced in the later version, suggesting perhaps that Pope wished deliberately to emphasize Dulness' existence as a character. It is equally apparent that the queen is never addressed directly by her name, although the metre would permit this. The vocative form goes with 'Goddess, Dame, Mother, Queen, Mistress, Empress', and

[31] *Te*, V, 48–51.

even, incongruous though it seems, as spoken by the harlot figure of
Opera as '*Cara*! *Cara*'. To use Dulness as a mode of address would be
no more familiar; but it might suggest a general appeal to the hosts
of Dulness at large, in other words the Dunces.

At the other extreme stands the Z *pattern of usage*. A Z usage is one
where the predominant sense is abstract, the state or quality rather
than the personification. There are perhaps only five clearcut
instances. Alignment with other abstract nouns is one important
clue: thus, the King Dunce proclaims:

> Me Emptiness, and Dulness could inspire,
> And were my Elasticity, and Fire.   (I, 185)

In such a construction, it is surely hard to think of the Queen herself
as being present in any substantial way. Similarly in the last book:

> Ah, think not, Mistress! more true Dulness lies
> In Folly's Cap, than Wisdom's grave disguise.   (IV, 239)

Again, syntactical juxtaposition leads us to read the word much as we
do Folly and Wisdom, and not as we do Mistress. Other predomi-
nately abstract senses are found at I, 4; II, 352; and IV, 19. There are
other candidates, but I have preferred to put them in class Y, as
constituting the more ambiguous area of the taxonomy.

Y *pattern*: The intermediate category, obviously, consists of those
usages where some degree of punning obtains. A pun might be
described as a spark leaping an aperture in lexical space: it draws
attention to the difference in meaning by stressing the formal identity
of words. With Y usages, both senses of Dulness are present in greater
or lesser measure. On the whole, this class provides the most
interesting occurrences of the word from a literary standpoint. A
good example is found at III, 257, where Settle's ecstatic paean in
honour of the theatrical showman Rich includes the couplet

> Angel of Dulness, sent to scatter round
> Her magic charms o'er all unclassic ground...

Rich is a minion of the goddess, but he is also a hero of the dull, a
promoter of Dull shows – an archangel in the hierarchy of Dunces, or
an angel *in* Dulness. In the last book, again, the Queen mounts her
throne:

> ...her head a Cloud conceal'd,
> In broad Effulgence all below reveal'd,
> ('Tis thus aspiring Dulness ever shines)...   (IV, 17)

The Queen so aspires; likewise, it is a characteristic of folly at large to go around with its head in the clouds. Thirdly, there is the goddess's own cry:

> For sure, if Dulness sees a grateful Day,
> 'Tis in the shade of Arbitrary Sway. (IV, 181)

This may be in part a sort of royal we, by which the speaker refers to herself. But not entirely: the general sense is clearly present.

Other instances of category Y occur at a number of places in the revised text: I, 18, 45 (where the predominant class X implication is qualified by the abstract 'guardian Virtues', Fortitude and so on), 64, 208; II, 34; III, 120; IV, 545. Perhaps I, 165, should be added to this list: Cibber's exclamation, 'Dulness! whose good old cause I yet defend...' Aligned to these Y usages are a few cases where 'dulness' appears without a capital. One of these has already been mentioned in another context: the description of Cibber's courtiers:

> His peers shine round him with reflected grace,
> New edge their dulness, and new bronze their face. (II, 9)

The pun here is between intellectual mediocrity and physically lustreless appearance. An even better example occurs at III, 189, where the literal decay of ancient manuscripts is adumbrated along with the spiritual and human decay of the 'poring Scholiasts':

> To future ages may thy dulness last,
> As thou preserv'st the dulness of the past!

The Dunces are men whose enterprises have tarnished parts that were never shining; the works over which they labour are as dingy and sunless as their own lives.

Quite apart from the references to Dulness in the text, the word gets its own scrutiny in the notes to the Variorum and subsequent editions. Arguably, Pope confronts the nature of this entity more squarely in the notes than in the poem proper. Bentley's opening words in the revised text serve as a comment on the internecine warfare of pedants, but they also indicate Pope's sense of an omission which needs to be made good:

I wonder the learned Scriblerus has omitted to advertise the Reader, at the opening of this Poem, that Dulness here is not to be taken contractedly for mere Stupidity, but in the enlarged sense of the word, for all Slowness of Apprehension, Shortness of Sight, or imperfect Sense of things. It includes (as we see by the Poet's own words) Labour, Industry, and some degree of

Activity and Boldness: a ruling principle not inert, but turning topsy-turvy the Understanding, and inducing an Anarchy or confused State of Mind. This remark ought to be carried along with the reader throughout the work; and without this caution he will be apt to mistake the Importance of many of the Characters, as well as of the Design of the Poet. (note at I, 15)

In thus invoking the typically Augustan concept of a 'ruling principle', Pope stresses the fact that Dulness is more than a presiding spirit – she is an active agent of the fictional 'design'. Her strength has something paradoxical about it: an apparent inertia yet squashes everything that crosses its path, a hebetude which impels the Dull towards mindless activity, a confusion which results in a demented anarchy of busy futility.[32]

This 'extended sense' of Dulness may be compared with other broadly contemporary definitions. The famous eighth chapter of *Leviathan* shows us Hobbes describing wit in terms of 'celerity of imagining (that is, swift succession of one thought to another) and steady direction to some approved end'. On the other hand, 'a slow imagination maketh that Defect, or fault of the mind, which is commonly called DULNESSE, Stupidity, and sometimes by other names that signifie slownesse of motion, or difficulty to be moved'.[33] Dulness thus connotes slowness, rigidity, immobility. Pope's conscious departure from this set of associations, whereby the term retains its sense of languor, yet loses that of inactivity, is easily apparent.

Eighteenth-century dictionaries confirm the impression left by Hobbes. The primary sense is that of slowness of understanding, and the modern idea of insipidity (highly germane to *The Dunciad*) is much less in evidence. The entry for 'dull' in Nathan Bailey's *Universal Etymological English Dictionary* offers synonyms such as heavy, sluggish, stupid, blunt, obtuse, awkward and melancholy. Dunce, if you can find it amidst entries such as Dunmow, Dunstable, Dunstan, etc. (the medley of proper and common nouns once more!), is glossed 'a blockish, stupid person', with a conjectured etymology from 'dumb'.[34] Johnson's entry in the *Dictionary* is naturally much fuller, but the same general lines are discernible. 'Dull' is given ten main headings by way of definition. These cover: (1) Stupid, doltish, blockish, unapprehensive, indocile, slow of understanding. (2) Blunt,

---

[32] There are several other useful notes, e.g. I, 63 and IV, 76, where the concept of Dulness is made more precise.

[33] *Leviathan*, ed. A. R. Waller (Cambridge, 1904), pp. 42ff. (text slightly normalized here).

[34] London, 6th edn, 1733, no pagination, *s.v. dull, dulness, dunce.*

obtuse. (3) Unready, awkward. (4) Hebetated, not quick. (5) Sad, melancholy. (6) Sluggish, heavy, slow of motion. (7) Gross, cloggy, vile. (8) Not exhilarating, not delightful ('as, *to make dictionaries is* dull *work*'). (9) Not bright (of a mirror or a fire). (10) Drowsy, sleepy. For 'dulness' six principal meanings are supplied, ranging from stupidity to want of lustre and want of edge. 'Dunce' is glossed 'a dullard; a dolt; a thickskul; a stupid indocile animal'. Again the etymology is said to be uncertain, with the Dutch word 'dum' tentatively suggested as origin.[35]

It is plain that stupidity and inertia predominate over all senses in eighteenth-century usage. Equally, the word does not carry much in the way of a moral charge – it was the personal achievement of the satirists, from Dryden on, to create a set of interlocking associations which gave the notion an identity of its own. In modern English, the primary connotation of 'dull' is that of sense 7 in *OED*: not clear, obscure, muffled, insipid – along with (in England at any rate) the sense of cheerless as applied to weather. It is noticeable that Johnson gives no sense of 'inducing tedium', in the way that we may speak of a dull book, meaning one which is boring to *read*, not to put together. Similarly, though 'dulness' is said to convey drowsiness, inclination to sleep, there is nothing directly in Johnson to cover tediousness, that which *invites* slumber.[36] Clearly these modern senses were available to Pope at some mental or imaginative level. A phrase such as 'thy giddy dulness' (III, 294) beautifully renders a dense cluster of ideas in which the fundamentally boring nature of Cibber's production is assuredly one. And the last fifty lines of Book II rest on a protracted conceit by which the sleepiness of the readers implies the soporific quality of their duncely works. 'The long, heavy, painful page' (II, 388) is painful to read, but also to listen to and probably to compile. The 'drowsy God' presides over this contest in boredom-thresholds. It is obvious that the modern primary sense of 'dulness' is actively present; and one wonders how much Pope did singlehanded to bring about this shift in semantic priorities.

[35] Samuel Johnson, *A Dictionary of the English Language* (London, 1755), I, sig. 7P 2v, 7Q 1r–v.
[36] He does write in *Rambler* no. 141 of 'the dulness of a scholar', a sense not apparently covered with complete adequacy in the *Dictionary* – the implications include 'want of quick perception', but they also indicate a crushing obsession with tedious minutiae: that form of obtuseness generated by scholarly pursuits, as many of us know all too well.

IV

According to Suzanne Langer, it is lyric poetry which makes 'the fullest exploitation of language sound and rhythm':

> It is the literary form that depends most directly on pure verbal resources – the sound and evocative power of words, meter, alliteration, rhyme and other rhythm devices, associated images, repetitions, archaisms and grammatical twists. It is the most obviously linguistic creation, and therefore the readiest instance of poesis... the lyric poet uses every quality of language because he has neither plot nor fictitious characters nor, usually, any intellectual argument to give his poem continuity.[37]

The Dunciad is surely a living disproof of this theorem. I would contend that the poem is, as clearly as any lyric, a 'linguistic creation' – though what else can any poem be? In the case of Pope's poem, we have a degree of formal manipulation, of textural adjustment and of local wordplay which no lyric could surpass. Indeed, *The Dunciad* might be seen as a counter to Edgar Allan Poe's view of poetry – it *is* a long poem, in the sense that it has a plot and fictitious characters, yet it retains the verbal peculiarities of a short poem. Its surface demands the kind of minute attention we ordinarily give to lyrical poetry, but it also has a narrative and dramatic continuum demanding another kind of attention.

In the light of the issues discussed in this essay, it should be possible to meet Langer's differentiae for lyric verse purely *with reference to proper nouns* in Pope's satire. The sound and evocative power of words is exploited in the 'Noise and Norton' passage. Metre is utilized when a simple shift of accent reminds us that the name Oldmixon means 'ancient heap of dung'. Alliteration is perhaps too obvious a case to call for illustration: but the yoking of 'Morgan and Mandevil' (II, 414), Ridpath and Roper (II, 149) or Toland and Tindal (e.g. III, 212) are ready to hand. As to rhyme, there is the Corneille/Ozell half-rhyme (I, 285), and a little earlier:

> A Gothic Library! of Greece and Rome
> Well purg'd, and worthy Settle, Banks and Broome.   (I, 146)

Doubtless 'Rome' was pronounced nearer 'Roome' then; all the same, the imperfect rhyme, as with Ozell, serves to show how far the

---

[37] Quoted from *Feeling and Form* (New York, 1953), pp. 258–9, by Dell H. Hymes, 'Phonological Aspects of Style: Some English Sonnets', *Style in Language*, ed. T. A. Sebeok (Cambridge, Mass., 1960), p. 110.

moderns are from living up to the ancients whom they wish to rival. Associated images might include Mist, to go with fogs of Dulness; Bays; or indeed Grub Street, whose metaphoric and literal presence underlies all. Repetitions are too patent to enumerate. Archaisms come into play at least twice: the Gothic manuscripts are collected by one 'Wormius hight' (III, 188), whilst the library of barbaric and superannuated literature includes Wynkyn, De Lyra and Philemon, as we have seen.[38]

As for grammatical twists, there is nothing more characteristic of the methods employed in *The Dunciad* than Pope's habit of applying the rules of accidence to proper names. Articles and possessive pronouns are prefixed to such words; plurals are formed, and adjectives derived. Moreover, grammar is constantly stretched by the ambiguity surrounding the status of words such as Billingsgate, Grub Street and, of course, Dulness.

In the midst of Settle's vision, there occurs a couplet making generous use of paradox:

> Each Songster, Riddler, ev'ry nameless name,
> All crowd, who foremost shall be damn'd to Fame.   (III, 157)

The oxymoron brushes against a central resource of the poem. Pope has condemned a number of significant nobodies to a permanent notoriety: a sort of anti-fame. Their namelessness is all the greater because we still have the mere name – we read it each time we turn to the poem – but all substantiality has been lost. The Dunces survive, in the poem, because they are named; yet the very mention of their forgotten name is enough to prove their obscurity.[39]

The crucial instance of Pope's liberty with proper nouns is that of Dulness. Elsewhere the poet uses apparent individuals to convey qualities; here he takes the name of a quality to christen a single actor

---

[38] See also the list of Hun warriors and invaders, III, 90–4, where the mere names conjure up a remote and awesome past. 'Paridel' (IV, 341) is borrowed from Spenser.

[39] Pope's way of addressing Swift is interesting:

> O Thou! whatever title please thine ear,
> Dean, Draper, Dickerstaff, or Gulliver!
> Whether thou chuse Cervantes' serious air,
> Or laugh and shake in Rab'lais' easy chair...   (I, 19)

Swift will be the same, by whatever name one chooses to address him. Yet there is a deeply sceptical air about the passage: Swift's fondness for disguises *does* make it difficult to know what to call him. His eminence is perhaps guaranteed by the fact that he cannot be adequately *described* by a single name, where a Dunce can be placed as soon as named – there is not much more you can do than name him, in fact.

in his drama. The paradox is that Dulness, who literally is not real and whose title is allegorical, *exists* within the poem as More and Norton (the names of real people) do not. Aubrey Williams has some excellent things to say in this connection: 'We are faced with dunces who are neither wholly here – in the poem – nor there – in history... In the smaller compass of a single word one can often see the tension between the real and the "unreal" brought to a fine point...'[40] So it is with Dulness herself, now a literal goddess, now melting into pure abstraction. And at the climax of the work, the ominous ring of the final noun is not less because we half suspect that Darkness is yet another synonym for Dulness – συνομωνυμέω, 'to have the same name with...' (Liddell and Scott). The threat is not just metaphysical or cosmic: it has, too, the immediacy of a personal onslaught – 'And Universal Darkness buries All'.

[40] Williams, *Pope's Dunciad*, pp. 64–5. Cf. Roman Jakobson's comment: 'In poetry the internal form of a name, that is, the semantic load of its Constituents, regains its pertinence' (Sebeok, p. 376).

CHAPTER 9

Pope and the social scene

I

Pope was a parvenu and an outsider. His enemies like to say so, and they were right in a deeper sense than they can have known. What particularly angered the dunces, it has been said, was the fact that Pope had 'made a fortune by literature and [was] thus free of the captivity they [were] enslaved to'.[1] There is a massive irony here, for Pope was peculiarly disadvantaged when he started out. He did not have it made for him. In retrospect, it is easy to suppose that great writers were bound to come through – that Alfred Tennyson was always Lord Tennyson, prosperous, secure and famous. It is a misleading assumption in general, and a wild distortion in the case of Pope. He inherited one disability, Catholicism. And within a few years he had contracted another in the shape of Pott's disease, which left him a crippled dwarf. Either would have been enough to set him outside ordinary society: to limit his educational opportunities, to curtail his civic responsibilities, to blight his prospects. If we want to understand Pope's own social situation, we must give full weight to these two handicaps against which he pitted his will and his talent.

Of the two, his physical disability is the easier to allow for today. Much more strange to us is the slur involved in belonging to the Catholic faith. This was not just a matter of popular attitudes. It was an affair of the statute-book. After the heady innovations of James II, there was no likelihood that Williamite 'toleration' would extend to accepting papists as fully paid-up members of society. In Pope's lifetime Catholicism often connoted Jacobitism, which in turn spelt treason. There was a succession of attempts on William's life, real or staged; in Anne's reign the war with Catholic France was stepped up,

---

[1] J. V. Guerinot, *Pamphlet Attacks on Alexander Pope, 1711–1744* (London, 1969), p. xlii.

and the dynastic problem grew ever more acute. That the Hanoverian accession had not settled the issue in 1714 was shown by the rising of the Old Pretender the following autumn. It was not until the year after Pope's death that the second major rebellion took place, but in the interim a series of minor scares reduced England to a panicky alert, with show trials, informers and cipher-experts, intercepted letters and all the grubby paraphernalia of state intrigue.

This national insecurity bred anti-Catholic measures, which seem extraordinarily petty, as well as repressive, to modern eyes. The year after Pope was born, a measure was introduced to expel Papists from London. By this Act (I Wm & M, c. 9) the justices of London and the home counties were empowered to arrest all such persons 'as are or are reputed to be Papists'. If the suspect then refused to take an oath of allegiance, he or she would be 'esteemed and adjudged a Popish Recusant Convict'. It was then forbidden for the individual to 'remaine continue or be within the sayd City or Cityes [London and Westminster] or Ten miles distance from the same'.[2] It was probably as a result of this Act that Pope's father retired from his business as a linen merchant in Lombard Street. He moved first to Hammersmith, which, as George Sherburn says, 'if not ten miles from Hyde Park Corner, was remote enough from the City to show his good intentions'.[3] Around 1700 the family moved to Binfield in Windsor Forest. It is customary to congratulate the poet on his good luck in missing urban squalor and enjoying his upbringing amid the rural delights of this sylvan refuge. But the young Pope must have felt in his inner self a strong contrary influence. A sense, that is, that he was being shifted gradually further and further from the centre of things: a consciousness of exclusion and exile. Pope's later drive for success may be seen as an attempt to recapture an inheritance denied him. All the wry jokes in his poems and letters count for little beside the brutally stark phrasing of the statute. Whig historians have described some 'precarious' toleration for the Catholics through non-enforcement of such laws;[4] but a Popish Recusant Convict needed no persecution complex to feel he was being driven out from society.

---

[2] Statutes are quoted from *The Law and Working of the Constitution: Documents, 1660–1914*, ed. W. C. Costin and J. S. Watson, 2nd edn (London, 1961); here I, 61–2.

[3] *The Early Career of Alexander Pope.* (Oxford, 1934), p. 36.

[4] W. E. H. Lecky, *A History of England in the Eighteenth Century*, 'Cabinet edn' (London, 1892) I, 352–3. Lecky's account of the 'perpetual insecurity' of Catholics in this period remains of great value.

Other measures soon followed. By an Act of 1700 (II Wm II, c. 4), Catholics were *inter alia* forbidden to 'keepe Schoole or take upon themselves the Education or Government or Boarding of Youth'. Pope's formal education, whether by private tutors or at a mysterious establishment near Hyde Park, was thus strictly illegal. He was to a considerable extent an autodidact: an early apostle of self-help, for religious rather than economic reasons. Further, the Act laid down that Papists should be 'disabled and made incapable to inherit or take by Discent...any Lands Tenements or Hereditaments'.[5] By I Geo I, s. 2, c. 13, oaths were prescribed which effectively debarred Catholics from official posts, from the bar and other professions. In the same year, 1715, came a statute appointing commissioners 'to inquire of the estates of certain traitors', official double-talk for a scheme to compel Papists to register their estates as a prelude to jacking up the land-tax on this class. Pope's correspondence shows some anxiety on this score, for reasons his editor helps to explain: 'In anticipation of this device to increase tax on Catholics and possibly because of questionable title to the house and land at Binfield (for Catholics were not allowed to buy land, and the Popes had a sort of concealed ownership of the place at Binfield) the Popes had sold out and moved to Chiswick, there renting a new house' (*Corr*, I, 344 and n.). Once again the law had forced the family to move on like the merest vagabonds. For one so immersed in filial piety as Pope, the psychic effect must have been incalculable. Finally, we should note 9 Geo I, c. 18, by which taxes were yet further stepped up. 'If this Bill passes,' wrote Pope at the time, 'I shall lose a good part of my income...I know I wish my country well and if it undoes me, it shall not make me wish it otherwise' (*Corr*, II, 173). The Bill did pass. Later in life it seems that Pope had to vacate his house at Twickenham when the court moved to Hampton Court, and that in his final illness he was deterred from receiving medical attention in London by a royal proclamation occasioned by the first stirrings of the Forty-Five rebellion.[6]

This adds up to a long record of legal harassment. And it would not make things much better that a substantial minority of the population faced the same threats. It is true that the penal code was even harsher in Ireland. There, Catholics were excluded from positions of public trust although they made up three-quarters of the population.

[5] Costin and Watson, pp. 90–1.   [6] *TE*, IV, 168–9n.

Unregistered priests, if discovered, were to be branded on the cheek with a red-hot iron. But the state of affairs in England itself can be gauged from this anecdote related by Lecky: 'In 1729 – in the reign of George II and under the ministry of Townshend and Walpole – a Franciscan friar, named Atkinson, died in Hurst Castle, in the seventy-fourth of his life and the thirtieth of his imprisonment, having been incarcerated in 1700 for performing the functions of a Catholic priest.'[7] It was not typical but it could still happen. Such medieval implacability was commoner in the statute-book than in day-to-day life, but that can hardly have consoled Pope and his fellow-sufferers.

Of course, Pope learnt to live with his disability – as with his 'own crazie health' (*Corr*, IV, 299) – and even to laugh at it. Usually, however, there is an undertone of bitterness beneath the calm precision. As for instance in the lines on his father in *Epistle* II ii:

> But knottier Points we knew not half so well,
> Depriv'd us soon of our Paternal Cell;
> And certain Laws, by Suff'rers thought unjust,
> Deny'd all Posts of Profit or of Trust:
> Hopes after Hopes of pious Papists fail'd
> While mighty WILLIAM's thundring Arm prevail'd.
> For Right Hereditary tax'd and fin'd,
> He stuck to Poverty with Peace of Mind;
> And me, the Muses help'd to undergo it;
> Convict a Papist He, and I a Poet.   (58–67)

The quasi-legal terminology ('posts of profit', 'fin'd', 'convict' – this last the archaic form actually used in the Act) lends a quality of explicitness and reality to the complaint. We are dealing not with vague prejudices but with the letter of the law. Similarly there is an edge to Pope's voice when he writes in *To Bethel*:

> Fortune not much of humbling me can boast;
> Tho' double-tax'd, how little have I lost?   (*Satire* II, 151–2)

As a matter of fact, Pope always enjoyed guying measures of national security; he makes the Riot Act the occasion for a mildly comic gallantry (*Corr*, I, 311). But the joke covers a wound. Pope needed to succeed as a poet, to make himself independent and financially stable, for purely personal reasons. But these factors were com-

---

[7] Lecky, I, 356.

pounded by an urge to assert the power and value of his art in a society which offered him reduced citizenship. His poetry is a triumph of the spirit in an almost existentialist way. The community which blocked his chances is made the subject-matter of literature which will transcend that community. The style of a civilization which made him a 'convict' and a pariah is turned with exquisite artistry into a satiric vehicle: its language of polite acceptance is converted into an idiom of oblique criticism and ironic qualification. Society imposed its pains and penalties on Pope, and Pope took his revenge as only a great imaginative writer can. He drew up his own penal code, and found in the fictive liberties of art the personal release that the repressions of life always threatened to deny him.[8]

II

The England into which Pope was born was still predominantly rural. Indeed it was little better than scrubland over large tracts of the country. At the end of the seventeenth century, says Macaulay, 'many routes which now pass through an endless succession of orchards, hayfields, and beanfields, then ran through nothing but heath, swamp and warren'.[9] The fens had been drained, but much reclamation remained to be done. 'Huge, great and vast fens and marishes' survived even in southern England; in 1706 much of Romney Marsh was under water, and the defences had to be strengthened. As the Webbs record, 'In the interior of England nearly every county had its hundreds or its thousands of acres of "moss" or swamp.' London itself was full of foul ditches, stagnant closes, obstructed sewers: its slums wore a half-rustic air, with pigs rooting among the offal from slaughter-houses.[10] Most of the primeval forest cover had disappeared, but timber still remained basic to the economy and woodland was much less scattered than today. Enclosure had begun, but save in a few counties it was little advanced. In Enfield Chase, just outside London, there was an area of twenty-five miles' circumference which was said to contain only three houses and scarcely any enclosed fields.

Moreover, the undeveloped state of the countryside was both cause and effect of poor transport facilities. Social life in the early eighteenth

---

[8] See also Mack, *Life*, pp. 61–5, on Pope's Catholic inheritance.
[9] T. B. Macaulay, *The History of England from the Accession of James II* (London, 1909) I, 241.
[10] Sidney and Beatrice Webb, *English Local Government* (London, 1922), IV, 13, 16, 38, 88.

century was acutely affected by this circumstance, although the modern concept of 'communication', straddling geography and psychology, had not yet come into people's minds. Again Macaulay is to the point:

The chief cause which made the fusion of the different elements of society so imperfect was the extreme difficulty which our ancestors found in passing from place to place...Every improvement of the means of locomotion benefits mankind morally and intellectually as well as materially, and not only facilitates the interchange of the various productions of nature and art, but tends to remove national and provincial antipathies, and to bind together all the branches of the great human family...On the best lines of communication the ruts were deep, the descents precipitous, and the way often such as it was hardly possible to distinguish, in the dusk, from the uninclosed heath and fen which lay on both sides.[11]

So the stories of travellers losing their way on the Great North Road; the almost farcical experiences of Celia Fiennes; the complaints of the pamphleteers, and the harsh words of travellers such as Defoe; so the dreadful reputation of muddy Sussex, of Hockley in the Hole (literally), Baldock and a score of such places.

Pope cannot have missed any of this. He was a devotee of the 'ramble' and spent much of his mature life in a sustained per-egrination of the seats of the gentry, major and minor. His friends, such as Bathurst and the second Earl of Oxford, were equally incapable of staying still for long. Moreover, Pope was a great letter-writer, with a specially clear sense of what could and should be said in that medium. He was a crony of Ralph Allen, who did so much to improve the postal services. His health made riding difficult and brought home to him the dangers of the road. On one famous occasion he was catapulted into the River Crane, on his way back from a visit to Bolingbroke. As Gay told Swift, he was thrown out when the coach was overturned where a bridge had 'broken down', with the result that he was 'up to the knots of his perriwig in water' (*Corr*, II, 399). His hand was badly cut and at one time he feared that he would lose the use of two fingers of his right hand. Luckily, this did not prove to be so, and Pope contented himself with the reflection that the injury was 'a Fine paid for my life'. (*Corr*, II, 405) Soon he was talking of travelling again, scarcely abashed.

[11] Macaulay, I, 242, 287–8.

Little of Pope's poetry is directly about travel. His satire of the Grand Tour in Book IV of *The Dunciad* is not diminished in effect by the fact that he did not and could not make such a journey himself. Nor, for that matter, did he ever see Rome, which hovers behind so many of his poems. He cannot have set eyes on uplands much grander than the Cotswolds or the Yorkshire Wolds. If we are indeed to set the poet in his landscape, to borrow a phrase from Maynard Mack, we shall think first of the mellow countryside of southern England. It is estates such as John Knight's at Gosfield or Lord Harcourt's at Stanton Harcourt which fulfilled his needs best. His affinity with men such as Bathurst was first of all a community of taste, not least in the matter of landscape planning. All his days, Pope was a poet of daylight and champaign; with Swift we think of the windy downs about Letcombe Bassett or the desolate landing-stage at Holyhead. For Swift, pastoral is a gaudy fiction, to be mocked by confronting its idealities with the sordid reality of city living. For Pope, idyll and georgic can still be lived out, approximately anyway, in the sylvan retirement of Cirencester:

To say a word in praise either of your Wood or You [Bathurst], would be alike impertinent each being, in its kind, the finest I know, & the most agreeable. I can only tell you very honestly, (without a word of the high Timber of the one, or the high Qualities of the other) that I thought it the best company I ever knew, & the best Place to enjoy it in...Mr Gay is as zealously carry'd to the Bower by the force of Imagination as ever Don Quixote was to an Enchanted Castle. The Wood is to him the Cave of Montesinos: He has already planted it with Myrtles, & peopled it with Nymphs. The old Woman of the Pheasantry appears alredy an Urganda; & there wants nothing but a Christal Rivulet to purl thro the Shades, which might be large enough to allay Mr Lewis's great Thirst after water. (*Corr*, I, 476–7)

The same desire to give an imaginative grace to the diurnal, to make fancy irradiate the homely, appears in Pope's deep concern with his garden, so well chronicled by Maynard Mack.[12] And it shows, too, in *Windsor-Forest*, where the trees are at once concrete lumps of timber, ready to 'bear *Britain*'s Thunder', to sustain her trade and strengthen her fleet, and also features in the new 'Groves of Eden', pastoral machinery *and* literal treetrunks.

[12] See also Peter Martin, *Pursuing Innocent Pleasures: The Gardening World of Alexander Pope* (Hamden, Conn., 1984), supplementing *Garden and City*.

As for Pope's consciousness of what might be called psychic space, it is enough to quote the delicious poem he addressed to Teresa Blount, 'On her leaving the Town, after the Coronation'. The note is one of half-comic elegy which he made his own:

> Thus from the world fair *Zephalinda* flew,
> Saw others happy, and with sighs withdrew;
> Not that their pleasures caus'd her discontent,
> She sigh'd not that They stay'd, but that She went.
>   She went, to plain-work, and to purling brooks,
> Old-fashion'd halls, dull aunts, and croaking rooks.
> She went from Op'ra, park, assembly, play,
> To morning walks, and pray'rs three hours a day;
> To pass her time 'twixt reading and Bohea,
> To muse, and spill her solitary Tea,
> Or o'er cold coffee trifle with the spoon,
> Count the slow clock, and dine exact at noon;
> Divert her eyes with pictures in the fire,
> Hum half a tune, tell stories to the squire;
> Up to her godly garret after sev'n,
> There starve and pray, for that's the way to heav'n.

The delicacy of touch is appropriate to the subject and the recipient. But it also enables Pope to convey much in little. The flat rhyme *spoon/noon* beautifully suggests the monotony of the country round; the fact that through a transferred epithet even the tea-cup looks forlorn and bereft; the feckless stop–go enacted in the line 'Hum half a tune, tell stories to the squire'; finally the ten commonplace words creeping along to the dull conclusion – these are masterly strokes, rendering with deft economy the self-pity of the aimless girl. Pope goes on to describe the thoughts of Miss Blount as she pictures 'the fancy'd scene' of court gaiety. Once more his poetic workmanship is applied to dramatize a social situation – here, the exaggerated contrast between town liveliness and rural dumps. The theme was conventional; it is Pope's sense of poetic occasion – the neatness with which he chooses words, places rhymes, bends the metre – that brings these fashionable contrasts to life.[13]

A number of attempts have been made to tabulate the various classes in the social structure of eighteenth-century England. Unfortunately, neither the schemes of contemporaries such as Gregory King and Defoe, nor the taxonomies of later authorities, quite suit the

---

[13] For other aspects of the technique here, see pp. 15–16 above. And compare Pope's letter to Martha Blount, *Corr*, I, 375.

case. Instead I have chosen to isolate four groups with whom Pope had significant dealings and whose social identity bears on his art. A representative figure is taken for each group in turn. The categories are, first, the peer and great landowner, exemplified by Lord Bathurst; second, the country gentlemen, here Hugh Bethel; third, the professional man, the instance being William Fortescue, advocate and later judge; fourth, women, as represented by Martha Blount. The last is not a status group familiar to modern sociology, though it may be none the worse for that. The truth is that in the eighteenth century there was one class structure for men, and another – parallel but independent – for their wives and daughters.[14] To separate women in this rough scheme is therefore not to perpetrate a sexual insult, but to follow the realities of the time. In each of these cases, I shall say something of the category at large; give a brief account of the individual selected, and of the course of their relations with Pope; and finally, examine a poem dedicated to the man or woman in question, with a view to assessing the 'social' implications that lie within the poetry.

III

At the top of the social scale, then, we find Allen Bathurst (1684–1775) first Baron and later first Earl Bathurst. He was not strictly an aristocrat by origin; his father was a knight, an MP and government servant, whilst his mother was the daughter of a baronet. The son was raised to the peerage in 1712, as one of the twelve Tory nominees elevated to the Lords in order to secure the passage of the Treaty of Utrecht. Another was George Granville, Baron Lansdowne, to whom is dedicated *Windsor-Forest* – a poem celebrating the selfsame peace. Thus achieving a barony at the age of twenty-eight, Bathurst did not acquire an earldom for exactly sixty years more – which may be some kind of record. He was first elected member for Cirencester to the 1705 Parliament, which means that he spent some seventy years in public life. He survived Pope, a younger man, by four decades. This proves that he had stamina in plenty – a quality sometimes underrated, as when robustness is taken for coarseness. In some ways he was a kind of Tory version of Walpole. All this sounds unpromising material for recruitment to the select ranks of Pope's acquaintance. The case demands investigation.

[14] On class-barriers for women, see Dorothy Marshall, *English People in the Eighteenth Century* (London, 1957), pp. 268–9.

It cannot be denied that Bathurst had his limitations. He was old-fashioned in many of his attitudes. The improvements he designed for his house at Cirencester were neither architecturally pure nor, it emerged in time, structurally sound. He was a rake of the eighteenth-century kind; more like Old Q than Lord Byron, with a sensuality that was bluff and direct rather than poetic and romantic. He was certainly no vulgarian – there is a clipped bitten-off sensibility struggling to express itself in his letters to Pope – but he was no aesthete either. Along with women and (in a more lukewarm fashion) politics, landscape-gardening was the great love of his life. But he pursued it with a measure of lordly insouciance, as though he might at any time find a more suitable occupation. In this respect, as in others, he contrasts markedly with another of Pope's friends, the Earl of Burlington. Burlington was prim and punctilious where Bathurst was casual and generous. More particularly, Burlington followed *his* passion, architecture, with the stiffness of an over-coached suitor; his buildings have some of the unbending pedantry that attaches to the singleminded amateur.

Bathurst entered the purple at a fortunate moment. In the 1720s, there were only 179 English peers, of whom a third were inactive for one reason or another. A measure to restrict the creation of new peerages had been defeated in 1719; but a conservative policy prevailed until the time of George III. This meant that early in the century the upper echelons of society were a closed corporation, with the strengths and defects of that situation.[15] Moreover, it was a good time to be a landowner on a large scale. After the collapse of the South Sea Company in 1720 there was a 'panic rush for less profitable but more secure investments in land', which meant that the social (as well as the investment) value of land went up.[16] The bigger owners consolidated their position at this juncture; Pope's latter-day friend, the Duchess of Marlborough, bought up a casualty of the Bubble in 1723, and 'thereafter hardly a year passed but what she bought an estate or two, until at her death [in 1744, less than six months after Pope's] she left some thirty in all'.[17]

---

[15] J. H. Plumb, *England in the Eighteenth Century* (Harmondsworth, 1950), 34; G. D. H. Cole and Raymond Postgate, *The Common People, 1746–1946* (London, 1966), p. 143. See generally John Cannon, *Aristocratic Century* (Cambridge, 1984).

[16] W. A. Speck, 'Conflict in Society,' *Britain after the Glorious Revolution*, ed. G. Holmes (London, 1969), p. 147.

[17] A. L. Rowse, *The Early Churchills* (Harmondsworth, 2nd edn, 1969), p. 413.

In addition to this, careful planning could ensure the maintenance of family fortunes. 'The grand object of family policy', it has been said, 'was to secure the continuance and enhance the wealth and position of the family, and to this end the succession to the property and the marriage of the children, particularly the marriage of the heir or heiress were carefully regarded.'[18] So we have dynastic marriages such as those between Pope's friends the Harleys and the great Pelham-Holles line; elaborate conveyancing devices, and a series of ploys developed to strengthen the hold of one generation on its successors. These 'arrangements of immense complexity', as even H. J. Habakkuk finds them, had far-reaching social consequences. Habakkuk has shown how

the development of instruments for long-term mortgage enabled gentlemen both to survive the natural disasters of agrarian life or to undertake improvements that would otherwise have been beyond their means, and how the widespread use of stricter marriage settlements gave greater protection to estates from generation to generation; also, estates tended to grow in size and this in itself provided greater security from the follies of heirs and the disasters of time...A stable gentry obviously encouraged social cohesion...

On the whole this applies most forcibly to those who were already considerable landowners; they could employ the best lawyers, for one thing. Such men were in the most advantageous position to exploit mineral wealth, though they generally provided capital and encouragement rather than working the resources themselves. 'The mining of coal, the establishment of an ironworks or the quarrying of building stone were just as legitimate a part of estate exploitation as the letting of land to tenant-farmers...'[19] This is shown by the Duke of Chandos, with whom Pope maintained an uneasy friendship, and who dabbled in many branches of industry. But equally the self-made Ralph Allen became a leading magnate in providing building-stone for public works in London.

Bathurst was more interested in silviculture than soap-boiling. All the same, he had his own strong dynastic sense, and indeed the

---

[18] G. E. Mingay, *English Landed Society in the Eighteenth Century* (London, 1963), p. 32.
[19] H. J. Habakkuk, 'England', *The European Nobility in the Eighteenth Century*, ed. A. Goodwin (London, 1953), pp. 2–6; J. H. Plumb, *Sir Robert Walpole: The Making of a Statesman* (London, 1956), pp. 6–14; Plumb, *The Growth of Political Stability in England, 1675–1725* (London, 1967), pp. 9–10; Mingay, p. 190.

planting of woods in an offering to posterity. Pope, of course, was alive to the fact. In 1722 he wrote to a friend of his desire to conduct a Mrs Digby round the park at Cirencester:

How much I wish to be her Guide thro' that enchanted Forest, is not to be exprest: I look upon myself as the Magician appropriated to the place, without whom no mortal can penetrate into the Recesses of those sacred Shades. I could pas whole Days, in only describing to her the future, and as yet visionary Beauties, that are to rise in those Scenes: The Palace that is to be built, the Pavillions that are to glitter, the Colonnades that are to adorn them: Nay more, the meeting of the *Thames* and the *Severn*, which (when the noble Owner has finer Dreams than ordinary) are to be led into each other's Embraces thro' secret Caverns of not above twelve or fifteen Miles, till they rise and openly celebrate their Marriage in the midst of an immense Amphitheatre, which is to be the Admiration of Posterity a hundred Years hence. But till the destin'd time shall arrive that is to manifest these Wonders, Mrs. *Digby* must content herself with seeing what is at present no more than the finest wood in *England*. (*Corr*, II, 115–16)

As has been pointed out, 'Posterity did not, in fact, have to wait a hundred years, and Bathurst died a mere fourteen before the $2\frac{1}{4}$-mile Sapperton Tunnel, with its crenellated Gothic and its sober classical openings, was dug under his property and the Thames and Severn Canal formally opened by King George III in person.'[20] And it is the literal truth that we can enjoy Cirencester today, as we can Cobham's Stowe and Oxford's Wimpole, more fully than could any contemporary. More striking yet, though, is the imaginative vigour of Pope's picture. He makes the development of inland navigation sound like an Elizabethan idyll, the marriage of Isis and Thames or something of the sort. The Augustans were the last writers who could compass such a union of fancy and reality.

To us, it may have a disconcertingly literary air. But then Georgian 'improvement' was highly bookish in inspiration. All Burlington's heroes were to be found in handsome folios; none of them survived on the face of the earth. Both architecture and landscape gardening were 'essentially historical and pictorial' in quality. Sentiment determined how fabric and timber should be arranged: if the first Great Architect could not be called in personally at least his vicegerent in moral and philosophical matters, the Earl of Shaftesbury, pointed the way.[21] And of course a house was more than a stately

---

[20] James Lees-Milne, *Earls of Creation* (London, 1962), p. 44. This work provides by far the best account of Bathurst.   [21] Lees-Milne, pp. 14–16.

home or a showplace. In Habakkuk's words, 'With the family estate went the family house, the physical expression of the standing of the family and the tangible repository of its traditions.'[22] It was the focus of local life, the acme of patrician 'retirement', and a perpetual drain on its owner. But it could also be a plaything. Pope's own villa at Twickenham in a way could be regarded as a minuscule suburban country house and estate. Bathurst speaks of it with the sort of teasing affection one gives to small domestic pets. On one occasion he threatened, if Pope did not visit him, to 'send one of my wood-carts & bring away your whole house & Gardens, & stick it in the midst of Oakly-wood where it will never be heard of any more, unless some of the Children find it out in Nutting-season & take possession of it thinking I have made it for them' (*Corr*, III, 134). Patent as the humour is, there *was* a sense in which the villa, the garden and the grotto might happily have been transported to Cirencester or Stowe, to be placed alongside the Gothic follies, Temples of Virtue and other mythopoeic bric-à-brac.

It was in this area, then, that the interests of Bathurst and Pope fell most closely into line. For the rest, we have some record of the peer as a speaker in the Lords: Samuel Johnson's stint as parliamentary reporter covered speeches on the inadequacies of the Gin Act, and on the somewhat technical subject of indemnifying evidence.[23] Bathurst was an inveterate tripper, and Pope frequently makes a joke of his inaccessibility. 'I had epistolized you sooner,' he writes on one occasion, 'but that knowing you were yet in your worldly pil-grimage...I did not know how to write *at* you; and even the post, all post haste as it is, cannot shoot you flying' (*Corr*, IV, 148). A worldly pilgrim Bathurst assuredly was. 'In my late Peregrinations,' says Pope another time, 'I heard of you every where, where you *Had been*; where you *was*, no mortal cou'd tell' (*Corr*, IV, 192). As for worldliness, there are many references to Pope himself as 'one, who has out-lasted twenty, (or twenty thousand) of your Mistresses, in affection, attachment, & gratitude to you' (*Corr*, IV, 342). Sometimes Pope deals in a sort of comic insult: 'There was a Man in the Land of Twitnam, called Pope. He was a Servant of the Lord Bathurst of those days, a Patriarch of great Eminence, for getting children, at home & abroad. But his Care for his Family, and his Love for strange

---

[22] Habakkuk, p. 3.
[23] E. L. McAdam, *Dr Johnson and the English Law* (Syracuse, 1951), pp. 20–6; Dorothy George, *London Life in the Eighteenth Century* (Harmondsworth, 1966), p. 48.

women, caused the said Lord to forget all his Friends of the Male-Sex; insomuch that he knew not, nor once remembered, there was such a Man in the Land of Twitnam as aforesaid' (*Corr*, II, 292). And a more indirect version of this:

It is observd of Very Aged people, & such whose memories Long Life & much Business have worn away, that they better recollect Things long since past than those which are nearer. I therefore hope, My Lord you may have yet some glympse of remembrance, that there was at the latter End of Queen Anne's reign, a Poet of the name of Pope, to whom you sometimes afforded an hour of Conversation as well as reading (tho' indeed the former was the lesser Task of the two, for his Works were much longer than his Visits) you sometimes also, in those days, & evn to the middle or later end of the Reign of George 1st honor'd him with your Letters... I also am sensible, that many Great & Noble Works, worthy a large Mind & Fortune, have employd your cares & time; such as Enclosing a Province with Walls of Stone, planting a whole Country with Clumps of Firs, digging Wells... as deep as to the Center, erecting Palaces, raising Mounts, undermining High ways, & making Communications by Bridges. Not to enumerate those many & Various Studies which possess your Lordships mind; in which it may suffice to say Every thing has place except Polemic Divinity, but chiefly & principally Natural Philosophy, & the Art of Medicine: Witness those Instructions, which Physicians, instead of giving, Receive from You, even while you are their Patient: They come, to feel your pulse, & prescribe you physick! presumptuous Men! they return with their own pulses examind, & their own Bodies purgd, vomited, or blooded.

  Among all these Employments how can I expect to be remembered? (*Corr*, III, 130)

The air of genial insolence, with calculated exaggerations ('Enclosing a Province' – Bathurst comically seen as a kind of Roman governor for a moment) and easygoing allusions, is immediately striking. I fancy Pope was much more at home with Bathurst than with Burlington. Sterne was to meet Bathurst when the latter was eighty-five; he called the baron 'a prodigy... A disposition to be pleased, and a power to please others beyond whatever I knew: added to which, a man of learning, courtesy and feeling.'[24] A man, in fact, whom Pope needed to patronize as little as to flatter with limp obsequiousness.

  Pope came to know many of the great. For his Homer, as Leslie Stephen says, he 'received a kind of commission from the upper class to execute the translation... Every person of quality... felt himself

---

[24] Lees-Milne, p. 55.

bound to promote so laudable an undertaking.' Perhaps, as Stephen contends, Pope became 'a little too proud' of his independence and his visits from the Prince of Wales.[25] But he had earned his place the hard way. An acquaintance which included Sheffield, Harcourt, Orrery, Egmont, Marchmont, the two Earls of Oxford, Peterborough and many others was a distinguished circle for the linen merchant's son to attain. This is disregarding non-aristocrats as eminent and as *comme il faut* as the retired Secretary of State, Sir William Trumbull. However, of all these men, it was Bolingbroke, Burlington and Bathurst who counted most; and Bathurst who perhaps excited Pope's deepest affection.

In the letters we detected a note of cocky and outspoken banter. My view is that some of this quality carries over to the splendid poem Pope dedicated *To Bathurst*. Recently there has been some tendency to read this work too solemnly. It is true that there are overtones of biblical parable, as well as hints of major themes in classical myth.[26] But overall, the texture of the writing seems to me informed by a speed and a lightness of touch foreign to homiletic writing. The story of Sir Balaam at the climax is carried off with a curt, dismissive finality:

> There (so the Dev'l ordain'd) one Christmas tide
> My good old Lady catch'd a cold, and dy'd.   (383-4)

There is hardly time for the parenthesis; while 'catch'd' was already approaching a vulgarism. Pope mimics the language of the city ('a lucky Hit'; 'dull Cits'; 'chirping Pint'). And even in the more intense passages earlier, a slangy irreverence colours the diction – 'gingling' (67), 'plaister'd' (92), 'a plum' (124). Hyperbole is everywhere, as in the servant's intervention:

> A Statesman's slumbers how his speech would spoil!
> 'Sir, Spain has sent a thousand jars of oil;
> Huge bales of British cloth blockade the door;
> A hundred oxen at your levee roar.'   (43-6)

[25] Leslie Stephen, *English Literature and Society in the Eighteenth Century* (London, 1963), pp. 51, 65. Stephen remarks that the subscription list for the Homer seems 'almost a directory to the upper circle of the day'. This is a slight exaggeration. There were more aristocratic subscribers to Joseph Trapp's Virgil in 1718, though that attracted an even more overwhelmingly Tory and Oxonian clientele than Pope's translation. Bathurst subscribed to both works, Burlington and Fortescue to Pope's only. See pp. 190–227 below.

[26] See E. R. Wasserman's reading of the poem, *Pope's 'Epistle to Bathurst'* (Baltimore, 1960, especially pp. 13–33.

The same qualities are apparent at the most morally fervent junctures
of the poem. The fanciful invention of the letters is not far away when
Pope writes in this accent:

> Once, we confess, beneath the Patriot's cloak,
> From the crack'd bag the dropping Guinea spoke,
> And gingling down the back-stairs, told the crew,
> 'Old Cato is as great a Rogue as you.'
> Blest paper-credit! last and best supply!
> That lends Corruption lighter wings to fly!
> Gold imp'd by thee, can compass hardest things,
> Can pocket States, can fetch or carry Kings;
> A single leaf shall waft an Army o'er,
> Or ship of Senates to a distant Shore;
> A leaf, like Sybil's, scatter to and fro,
> Our fates and fortunes, as the winds shall blow:
> Pregnant with thousands flits the Scrap unseen,
> And silent sells a King, or buys a Queen.   (65–78)

And then Pope turns directly to Bathurst, with a plain vocative –
'What say you?' The picture is funny as much as sinister: the process
of corruption is made all too easy (note *waft, flit, ship off*, all connoting
the absence of effort). The point is not that Pope was not serious in
the *Epistle to Bathurst*. He certainly was, though I suspect he cared less
about the financial revolution than about, say, what it was to belong
to the Catholic faith in a Protestant state. The issue is the level of the
satire, or if you will the poetic temperature.

A. R. Humphreys said of the *Epistle to Burlington* that 'in lines of
complex opulence the Earl is encouraged to enrich the beauty and
bounty of his estates...'[27] Quite so; the poem is addressed to a self-
conscious aesthete, with scholarly tastes and earnest convictions.
Though even here, in passing, the portrait of Timon incorporates in
its presentation some of the subject's vulgarity – the Tritons *spew*,
light *quirks* of music are heard, two cupids *squirt*, the painted saints
sprawl like hoydens. With Bathurst it is different. Pope was addressing
a worldly, sociable, cynical nobleman, who carried his stock of
learning lightly and put on no false dignity with a man like Pope. So
the poet can sometimes adopt a jaunty carriage –

> What slaughter'd hecatombs, what floods of wind,
> Fill the capacious Squire, and deep Divine!   (203–4)

---

[27] A. R. Humphreys, *The Augustan World* (London, 1955), p. 5.

Deep suggests (1) ironically, profound; (2) deep in his cups; (3) bottomless in capacity; (4) he knows which side his bread is buttered on; (5) with unplumbed depths of depravity. And sometimes, when he chooses to be more severe, he puts the metre into its sensible shoes and darkens the imagery:

> Oh! that such bulky Bribes as all might see,
> Still, as of old, incumber'd Villainy!
> In vain may Heroes fight, and Patriots rave;
> If secret Gold saps on from knave to knave.
> Could France or Rome divert our brave designs,
> With all their brandies or with all their wines?
> What could they more than Knights and Squires confound,
> Or water all the Quorum ten miles round?   (35–42)

In each case, however, there is a note of bold defiance absent from the poem to Burlington.

It is possible to explain this difference in several ways; there are, for one thing, dissimilarities in the actual subject-matter. Nevertheless, the important factor seems to me to lie elsewhere. The *Epistle to Burlington* is built on a poetic grammar of assent. The noble peroration of this poem diffuses a basic optimism. Burlington will carry out impressive public works. However badly he does it (the implication runs) the 'falling Arts' will be no worse off; and even a projector less gifted than the Earl might hope to improve on the roadmaking and church-building of the age. There are satiric overtones to the passage, but they by no means impugn the compliment to Burlington. *Windsor-Forest* was not more confident in its yea-saying. But though Pope aligns the two lords ('Who plants like BATHURST, or who builds like BOYLE'), he underwrites Bathurst's attitudes to a greatly reduced extent. The point comes in *Epistle* II ii once more:

> All vast Possessions (just the same the case
> Whether you call them Villa, Park, or Chase)
> Alas, my BATHURST! what will they avail?
> Join *Cotswold* Hills to *Saperton's* fair Dale,
> Let rising Granaries and Temples here,
> There mingled Farms and Pyramids appear,
> Link Towns to Towns with Avenues of Oak,
> Enclose whole Downs in Walls, 'til all a joke!
> Inexorable Death shall level all,
> And Trees, and Stones, and Farms, and Farmer fall.
>   (254–63)

Burlington is to embark on a public works programme which will succeed in so far as it is judged by secular standards – in terms of immediate human benefit, or of patriotic glory, or of civic renown. Imaginatively Burlington is seen as a kind of magnified Chairman of the Town Planning and Highway Engineering Department. Bathurst is judged by the harsher standards of private conduct. His failure is an infraction of the natural order of creation. Mortality is a challenge to Burlington. His inspiration will usher in an epoch when churches will stand for centuries, unlike the present rickety collection. Bathurst encounters mortality as a defeat, for his accomplishments are viewed *sub specie aeternitatis.*

I think Pope arranged matters so for a definite reason. He is less charitable towards Bathurst's achievements – as they are poetically conceived – because he shared the hopes and dreams of his friend, as he did not quote those of Burlington. Moreover, he felt a greater intimacy with Bathurst, which allowed him to portray a less comforting outcome for his efforts. It is notable that in *Liberty*, James Thomson (who knew neither peer well) distributes the honours more evenly:

> Lo! numerous domes a Burlington confess –
> For kings and senates fit; the palace see!
> The temple breathing a religious awe;
> Even framed with elegance the plain retreat,
> The private dwelling. Certain in his aim,
> Taste, never idly working, saves expense.
>   See! Sylvan scenes, where art alone pretends
> To dress her mistress and disclose her charms –
> Such as a Pope in miniature has shown,
> A Bathurst o'er the widening forest spreads,
> And such as form a Richmond, Chiswick, Stowe. (V, 690–700)

To return from this puffy rhetoric to the racy vigour and colloquial rhythms of the *Epistle to Bathurst* is to get an inkling of Pope's close and confidential relation to his friend. Thomson writes as a humble supplicant; Pope as virtually an equal, whose easy commerce with the nobility permits him freedom of speech.

IV

The second category, that of the country gentleman, is represented by Hugh Bethel (1689–1748). The name of Bethel is familiar only to students of Pope and a few local historians. He made no impact on national life. In this, however, he is altogether typical of his breed. Bethel happened to be a Whig; this was far from universal, but it was not uncommon. Not every knight of the shire was a Roger de Coverley or a Squire Western. Bethel was better educated than many of his class, although he seems not to have attended a university. He took a keen interest in the visual arts, and stood at the centre of a group of Yorkshire connoisseurs which included the talented amateur Colonel James Moyser. Partly owing to asthma, he was a frequent visitor to the Continent, in particular Italy. This gave him a certain breadth to go with his plainer provincial virtues. It might be added that Bethel was a great-nephew of Slingsby Bethel, Dryden's 'Shimei', and that his brother – also Slingsby – was a City merchant. His home lay only a few miles from Burlington's country seat; he knew Bathurst well; and Martha Blount was also among his friends. In short, he completed a circle of intimacy, to some sectors of which – as the City – Pope stood in a marginal relation. Like Bathurst, Bethel combined rural interests with a refined taste in polite learning. Unfortunately one letter from him only survives, and that has been mislaid since Elwin and Courthope printed it. The single example indicates that Bethel, if direct in utterance ('You are too thin and weak for an issue, and it would be very painfull to you. Lord Shel[burne], who has more flesh than you, was obliged to dry them up' (*Corr*, IV, 511–2)) was thoroughly literate. Bethel was something of a valetudinarian, though this was combined with a measure of genuine invalidism. In this he contrasts sharply with Bathurst, who shrugged off illness after illness. The circumstances conditioned Pope's letters to Bethel, which broach the subject of health more often than any other topic.

If they were less well-placed than the great magnates, the prosperous gentry of Bethel's mould lost no ground in the early eighteenth century. Their political power was confirmed when they managed to get through Parliament an Act imposing property qualifications on members of the Commons in 1711. By this measure (9 Anne, c. 5), MPs had to own real property worth 'the annual Value of Six hundred Pounds above Reprizes for every Knight of a Shire [county members] and the annual Value of Three Hundred Pounds above Reprizes for every Citizen Burgess or Baron of the Cinque Ports [borough members]...'[28] The Bill was introduced by

---

[28] Costin and Watson, pp. 117–18. For the circumstances, see Speck, pp. 136–7.

Bolingbroke, but there is no doubt that it had the support of every shade of country opinion, from ardent Whig to vague Grumbletonian. This latter was a common breed, as Plumb has remarked:

The small squires tended therefore to drift into the politics of resentment. Some called themselves old whig, others tory. They had their moments of hope in the reign of Queen Anne. At times they could win an election by sheer force of numbers, particularly in the county constituencies. They remained disgruntled, crotchety, drawing consolation from the vituperation which the *Craftsman* [to which Pope may conceivably have contributed] poured on Walpole and his government. They developed a venomous hatred of place-holders, pensioners and the aristocratic world of London. They looked back with longing affection to the Stuarts, and sometimes played the Jacobite...[29]

Bethel was no Jacobite, and he was too balanced to dislike an aristocrat or a Londoner at sight. But then his brother became MP for the City of London, where even highflying Tories abjured such extreme 'politics of resentment'. Nevertheless Pope saw in Bethel an exemplar of oldfashioned 'virtue' (a term with strong political connotations at this period) and as a pillar of un-metropolitan sincerity: 'indeed for many years I have not chosen my companions for any of the qualities in fashion, but almost intirely for that which is the most out-of-fashion, sincerity' (*Corr*, II, 501).

Besides, it was not at Westminster that this class came into its own. Sometimes the squires got together to push some measure through Parliament, and there is a vestige of truth in Trevelyan's comment that Parliament 'might be called the grand national Quarter Sessions'.[30] But the petty sessions and the ordinary quarter sessions were their real homeground. It is important to remember that JPs carried out a great deal of administrative work, quite apart from their judicial functions.[31] Almost everything that could be termed welfare provision was in their hands. Until the growth of what the Webbs have cumbrously termed 'Statutory Authorities for Special Purposes', they ran sewerage, highways and the like. Indeed, when the turnpikes were first introduced, it was the county magistrates who

[29] Plumb, *Walpole*, p. 22.   [30] G. M. Trevelyan, *Blenheim* (London, 1965), p. 112.
[31] Cf. the following: 'By the eighteenth century the tradition had long been established that if anything wanted doing in the counties the justices of the peace were the obvious people to entrust with the task': Marshall, p. 120. The best modern treatment of the subject remains that of the Webbs, though there is a convenient survey in Esther Moir, *The Justice of the Peace* (Harmondsworth, 1969), pp. 77–101. See also Norma Landau, *The Justices of the Peace 1679–1760* (Berkeley and Los Angeles, Cal., 1984), especially 19–65 on 'The Justices' Influence'.

administered their affairs. When specialized turnpike trusts were evolved, the bench remained prominent as private members of the board; but from the mid-eighteenth century, they were no longer managers in their own right. In addition to the JPs, there were a number of other local offices of varying prestige and power. The most coveted were those of Lord Lieutenant for each county. The least sought after was the post of Sheriff. 'It is an interesting sidelight that the only County office which was at once compulsory and expensive, that of the High Sheriff, was always imposed, unless occasionally a County personage deigned to accept it, on one of the minor gentry.'[32] It is eloquent testimony to Bethel's status, as comfortably less than a 'county personage', that he was threatened with the office in 1739. Pope wrote to express his concern on 'being told you were in danger of being Sheriff' (*Corr*, IV, 206). It was not thus with baronets or even the old county families.

Many of Pope's rural friends were Catholics, such as the Carylls and the Englefields. This put them in a separate bracket. Others again were disguised literary men, such as Walsh, or successful entrepreneurs, such as Ralph Allen. Bethel, on the other hand, was authentic country stock; his ancestors survive today, in the same district and the same rank of unpretentious distinction. One can recognize his features in the collective portrait of the gentry supplied by G. E. Mingay: 'Rational, unsentimental, and business-like, they were at the same time jealous of their status and anxious to maintain their "port", fond of entertaining and not averse to some show and extravagance – and yet still careful to watch expenditure and keep minutely detailed accounts.'[33] Certainly Pope often writes to Bethel of bodily matters, and that includes not only health but gastronomic matters too. At first, in the 1720s, Pope tends to write in a moral vein ('I know your humanity, and allow me to say, I love and value you for it' – the agreeable impertinence of his dealings with Bathurst is gone, as 'allow me to say' indicates (*Corr*, II, 178)). But as the friendship proceeds, the relationship grows less stiff. The two men agree to exchange portraits; and indeed 'Mr Bethels Picture in a Gold Frame' hung in a place of honour in Pope's own room (the only portrait there) at Twickenham.[34] There is a gift of seeds, much in the manner of the present day. Once Pope sends Bethel a chicken for

---

[32] Webb and Webb, IV, 360; cf. Mingay, p. 118.
[33] Mingay, p. 116. Relevant to this discussion are Mingay's comments on letter-writing, p. 137.   [34] Mack, *Garden and City*, p. 255.

dinner. The poet likes to joke about the bracing Northern climate: he speaks of the 'bleaker Hills & Wolds of Yorkshire' dissipating an outbreak of fever (*Corr*, IV, 86). He recognizes, too, that Bethel's deepest involvement lay in the country life: 'My Lord Burlington goes to Yorkshire... I often wishd I could see you there, where I fancy you are most happy; for in Town you generally seem to think yourself not at home; & I would see my Friend quite at ease...' (*Corr*, IV, 113). But Pope himself felt particularly unconstrained in this relationship: ''Tis only to you, and a few such plain honest men, I like to open myself with the same freedom, and as free from all disguises, not only of sentiment, but of style, as they themselves' (*Corr*, III, 519). Hence the suitability of Bethel for his role as the modern Ofellus in *Satire* II ii.[35]

Pope had already celebrated his friend as 'blameless Bethel' in the *Essay on Man*. Now he portrays a blunt and shrewdly observant commentator, wholly bereft of Chesterfield's saving graces, but articulate and manly. In consonance with the aim of dropping rhetorical disguise, Pope adopts a direct, no-nonsense style. There are none of the large verbal gestures appropriate to Bathurst or Burlington; since the lesser gentry disdained lordly magnificence – the grand style of life – for a more cautious demeanour that one might almost call, anachronistically, bourgeois. Aptly, the vocabulary of this imitation is concrete, homely, even gross. It is replete with *objects*: 'a gilt Buffet', 'Plate to Plate', 'fish', 'plain Bread and milk', 'pheasant', 'hen', 'Carps and Mullets', 'small Turbots', 'a whole Hog', 'Rabbit', 'eggs, and herbs, and olives', and so on. These are drawn only from the first thirty-five lines. Later in the poem, to choose only the more notable instances, there occur oysters, crawfish, vinegar, cabbage, venison, sturgeon and ham-pie, bucks and much else. The characteristic note survives in Pope's rejoinder, after Bethel's own 'sermon' has ended:

> Content with little, I can piddle here
> On Broccoli and mutton, round the year;
> But ancient friends, (tho' poor, or out of play)
> That touch my Bell, I cannot turn away.
> 'Tis true, no Turbots dignify my boards,
> But gudgeons, flounders, what my Thames affords.
> To Hounslow-heath I point, and Bansted-down,
> Thence comes your mutton, and these chicks my own... (137–44)

---

[35] For Bethel's Yorkshire roots, see pp. 231–2 below.

At times the visceral emphasis grows almost nauseous; but wit and wordplay take off some of the oppressiveness:

> ... The stomach (cram'd from ev'ry dish,
> A Tomb of boil'd, and roast, and flesh, and fish,
> Where Bile, and wind, and phlegm, and acid jar,
> And all the Man is one intestine war) ... (69–72)

Whatever Matthew Arnold may have thought of the earlier passage quoted, it is not entirely representative of the mature Pope. Yet this comic diminution through ironic self-display *is* frequent in the Horatian poems. Bethel, as a man of moderate means and a social equal, is a suitable recipient for this self-dramatizing 'confession'.

As in the other cases studied here, it is clear that Pope knew exactly what he was doing in choosing Bethel as his addressee. It is not just the subject-matter, here food, which determines the character of the language or the texture of the verse. The tastes, acquirements and social standing of his friend come into it also. Bethel was practical, as Pope's choice of him as an executor makes evident. He was quite without the aristocratic breeding of Burlington, or the public importance of Bathurst. So we have a less elevated diction and a more intimate tone. Rhetorically, *Satire* II ii is as homely as its recipient. We have lost the wide historical sweep, the classical overtones and the epic implications of the *Epistle to Burlington*. Instead we are brought down to a domestic scale: 'five acres now of rented land' (line 136). In place of Rome, France, Spain, Asturian Mines, Chartreux, we have Hounslow and Banstead. The verse no longer echoes, as it did in the earlier poem, with Amphitrite, Nilus, Aldus, Milton, Laguerre, Versailles, Inigo Jones and Palladio. We are left with the glutton Oldfield, a tavern called the Bedford Head, the cosily possessive 'my Thames'. Poetry mimics social pretension, and contracts its horns appropriately.[36]

V

The third example I wish to isolate is that of a professional man.[37] The most obvious case to take might be that of a doctor. In the first place, Pope knew many members of the medical profession. There

---

[36] For Pope's admiration of Bethel as 'the soul of friendship', and as a 'male bawd' who brought friends together, see Owen Ruffhead, *The Life of Alexander Pope* (London, 1769), p. 496.

[37] For the development of the professions in this period, see Geffrey Holmes, *Augustan England: Professions, State and Society 1680–1730* (London, 1982).

were intimate friends such as Arbuthnot; literary contacts such as
Garth and Blackmore; advisers and practitioners, ranging from the
eminent Cheselden to the quack Thompson, recommended perhaps
by Bethel, whose treatment 'is said not to have delayed Pope's death'
(*Corr*, IV, 499, 512). The full list would include George Cheyne;
Richard Mead; his satiric butt John Woodward; William Oliver of
Bath; Sir Hans Sloane, virtuoso and collector; Jeremiah Pierce;
Simon Burton; and many more. Another quack to whom Pope
possibly had recourse in his final despair was Joshua Ward, famous
for his pills and effrontery. Second, the profession was at an
interesting stage of development. It was not until the year of Pope's
death that the surgeons were separated from the barbers, to whom
they had been locked like Siamese twins for centuries. However,
changes were already apparent in most branches of the profession;
obstetrics was growing slightly less primitive, whilst William Hunter
began surgical lectures in 1743. The influence of some major teachers
on the Continent, where students had to go for a serious medical
education, percolated gradually, with Herman Boerhaave of Leyden
an especially important figure. One of Samuel Johnson's most
impressive early works, indeed, is a biography of Boerhaave.
Moreover, the noisy and abrasive quarrel with the apothecaries,
which Garth turned into mock-heroic with *The Dispensary*, had spent
its force by the end of Pope's life. Since Garth's poem was closely
familiar to Pope, and in view of his own precarious health, one might
have expected to see medical imagery suffuse his works – but this is
not really the case.[38]

It is otherwise with the law, a profession which offers striking
parallels to that of medicine. If the one had its quacks ('a pretender,
basically ignorant, pretending to know when he did not. Also, he
advertised. A variety of techniques was available, including... the
carnival tactics of the mountebank'[39]) then the other had its demi-
reps in the form of attorneys. Pope makes the connection explicit in
his tribute to the Man of Ross:

> Despairing Quacks with curses fled the place,
> And vile Attornies, now an useless race.
>
> (*Epistle to Bathurst*, 273–4)

---

[38] This paragraph is based on Lester S. King, *The Medical World of the Eighteenth Century*
(Chicago, 1958); and Sir D'Arcy Power, 'Medicine', *Johnson's England*, ed. A. S. Turberville
(Oxford, 1933), II, 265–86.   [39] King, p. 47.

We must realize here that the attorney was regarded at this time as an inferior drudge, at best; a perjured rascal, at worst. Often he was the lackey of some Great Man; and Johnson was not distorting public attitudes when, in *London* (1738), he aligned 'the fell attorney' on the 'prowl' with street bullies. To see why this was so, we must look briefly at the structure of the profession.

In 1696 Gregory King had calculated that there were some ten thousand 'Persons in the Law', with an average income of £140.[40] The figure must include lesser clerks as well as scriveners, agents, and so on. Otherwise the total seems high, for as late as 1799 there were only just over 200 barristers, all based on London, plus a thousand London solicitors and attornies with twice that number in the provinces. The avocation of 'solicitor' in the modern sense had not properly evolved. Not only were attornies often ill-educated and disreputable, they were actually criminals in a number of cases. The appellation of '*Fleet* or *Wapping* solicitors' was applied to the dregs of the profession; and belatedly, attempts were made to remedy this blot on the law.

In 1725 the Legislature thought it necessary to provide that, if any person convicted of forgery of perjury or common barratry [vexatious litigation] practised as an attorney or solicitor, he should be transported for seven years; in 1739 that no attorney or solicitor who was in prison should be entitled to bring any action on behalf of a client; and in 1760 that attornies or solicitors embezzling their client's money should not be able to take the benefit of the Act passed in that year for the relief of insolvent debtors.

Shocking as this picture may appear, it is amply confirmed by other contemporary evidence.

The solicitors for the parties in the famous *Highwaymen's Case* (1725), in which one highwayman brought a suit for an account against another highwayman, were imprisoned and fined £50 each... One of the solicitors in this case, by name Wreathock, who had subsequently been transported for robbery on the highway, and who, on his return, had been readmitted as an attorney, was finally struck off the rolls.

Again, it was necessary for a court to rule that a turnkey of the King's Bench prison 'was not a fit person to be an articled clerk'; we also hear of persons who had stood in the pillory continuing to act unmolested. The Society of Gentlemen Practisers, founded some five years before Pope's death, did something to improve the situation:

[40] Dorothy George, *England in Transition* (Harmondsworth, 1953), p. 150.

but it was a slow haul upwards. Nor was education for the bar without its faults. Since Elizabethan times, 'the study of English law [had] ceased to be part of a liberal education'. The subject became esoteric, technical, crabbed. And though men such as the great Sir William Blackstone believed that 'a competent knowledge of the laws of that society in which we live is the proper accomplishment of every gentleman and scholar', the expectation grew less and less realistic. To some extent the gap was filled by popular handbooks and abridgments, such as the numerous *vade-mecum* publications of Giles Jacob, 'scourge of Grammar' and 'blunderbuss of Law' (*Dunciad*, III, 149–50). Nevertheless, the picture is increasingly one of an arid specialization, a separation from humane studies and a provinciality of outlook. In Bentham's phrase, the law had not yet been taught to speak the language of the scholar and the gentleman.[41]

It so happened that Pope was surrounded by the law all his days. His cousin married a judge, whilst his only close relative (apart from his parents) was a half-sister whose life was one long courtroom wrangle. Pope spent a good deal of time trying to sort out the affairs of Magdalen Rackett. Her husband, who had been involved with the Berkshire Blacks, died intestate; a trustee proved difficult; her annuities were not paid; one son ran into debts, one had proceedings of outlawry taken against him, and the other wanted to enter the law.[42] This was a natural choice, in so far as household conversations can have revolved around little else: unfortunately, he was a nonjuror, which effectively prohibited his entry to the profession. The later years of this saga read like a parody of *Bleak House*, with Mrs Rackett hopelessly embroiled in Chancery. Pope consulted Fortescue, Murray and others in his efforts to help her; but her affairs truly required the services of a full-time legal department.

Added to this, Pope had his own battles to fight. In 1725 he was threatened by a 'monition' from Doctors Commons, the centre of ecclesiastical law. The point at issue was the erection of a monument to Sir Godfrey Kneller in Twickenham church; the widow's ambitious proposals involved removing the monument to Pope's own father. On this matter the poet consulted his friend Viscount Harcourt (1661–1727), a former Tory attorney-general and Lord

---

[41] Based on Sir William Holdsworth, *A History of English Law*, Vol. XIII (London, 1938), *passim*; quotations from pp. 54, 58–9, 90, 96. Other information from Ronald Robson, *The Attorney in Eighteenth-Century England* (Cambridge, 1959), pp. 13, 23, 45. Robson points out (p. 58) that Warburton began as an attorney.

[42] For the Racketts, see Mack, *Life*, pp. 402–6. For the Blacking episode, see pp. 168–83 below.

Chancellor: 'My Lord, I am in Law, & in the worst Law, Spiritual Law' (*Corr*, II, 306). A year or two earlier Pope had been called before the House of Lords in the trial of Bishop Atterbury, who was accused of Jacobite conspiracy. His position had been made more difficult in advance 'by the disaffection implied in his edition of [the Duke of] Buckingham's *Works*', suppressed on ministerial authority a few months before.[43] At this juncture Pope must have felt more of an outcast than ever; the *London Journal* even reported that he 'is taken into Custody on Account of the Works of the late Duke of Buckingham'.[44] This rumour appears to have been false; but it must have had some plausibility.

In later years Pope's contacts with the lawcourts were slightly more pleasant, but still they were irritating enough. He twice had to enter chancery suits regarding piracy of his works. On a third occasion he put in a bill against his perpetual antagonist, the bookseller Curll. The phrase '*Pope* v. *Curll*' has been used in modern times as a description of a phase in literary history. It is also the exact legal reference for a suit adjudicated by Lord Chancellor Hardwicke in 1741.[45] Satire, one observes, acts out fictively the conflicts that real life assigns to the courtroom or chambers. In this light it is interesting to observe that many dunces were connected with the law; one, Thomas Burnet, actually reached the bench. Concanen, as Pope observed, was 'surprizingly promoted to administer Justice and Law in Jamaica'.[46] Budgell, Gordon, Horneck, Jacob and Popple had a close personal involvement; Theobald and Aaron Hill were the sons of attorneys. Needless to say, all the dunces lived on the periphery of legal London: Defoe holds the record for Chancery suits (at least eight), quite apart from his familiarity with Newgate, the Queen's Bench court, the Fleet and other penal institutions. But there was a *Cibber* v. *Cibber* suit, too, and innumerable Budgell proceedings (before he too landed in the debtor's gaol),[47] till one could easily see litigation as among the most characteristic duncely occupations.

Pope, then, had good cause to number lawyers among his friends. They could advise him on tangled family affairs; they could forward his own suits; and they could give him access to a leading haunt of Dulness. For criminal society proper, incidentally, Pope had another

---

[43] *Corr*, II, 306; Sherburn, p. 228. [44] *London Journal*, 2 February 1723.
[45] See pp. 184–9 below. [46] Note to *The Dunciad*, A, II, 130.
[47] Budgell's later life has been described as 'one long litigation'. He was a half-brother of Fortescue, curiously: Fortescue's mother married Budgell's father.

informant: Richard Savage, murderer, bohemian and poet, whose *Vagabond King* existence was so memorably portrayed by Johnson. At all events, Pope had at least three close friends in this province of life, disregarding the elderly aristocrat Harcourt. One of these men is relatively obscure; Nathaniel Pigott (d. 1737), Pope's own 'counsellor at Law', i.e. barrister. William Fortescue is much better known. And incomparably more eminent than either is William Murray, later Lord Mansfield (1705–93), among the greatest of all British jurists. Murray was later to become Chief Justice of the King's Bench and man of great influence in public affairs at large. At the time Pope came to know him, he was a young Scottish advocate of obvious distinction, with a rising reputation as an orator. Before Pope died, he saw Murray enter Parliament, where he soon became known as an eloquent speaker, and obtain the office of Solicitor-General. Murray was the recipient of Pope's imitation of *Epistle* I vi as early as 1738. Pope showed himself an excellent talent-spotter. Unlike a number of middle-aged men, he was capable of appreciating the younger generation without making acolytes of them. Murray was to embody in his life the same concern with humane values, the same respect for stable society and the same 'creative' disposal of a learned heritage that mark Pope's own achievement.[48]

However, a closer and longer-lasting friendship was that with William Fortescue (1687–1749). Pope and he were much of an age. His legal talents, though they took him to the office in turn of baron of the Exchequer, judge of the Common Pleas and Master of the Rolls, were more modest than those of Murray; and Pope may have liked him none the less for that.[49] The two perhaps became acquainted around 1720, though Fortescue had previously figured in the distinguished list of subscribers to the *Iliad*. Fortescue handled investments for the poet; he chased up Mrs Rackett's business, he gave advice on copyright disputes, particularly those involving Curll; and he was originally to have acted as an executor along with Bethel – Pope later relieved him of this.[50] Pope seems to have felt that his own situation bore resemblances to Fortescue's. So he compares Fortescue's circuits as a barrister to his own travels: 'What an advantageous circumstance is it...to be a grave and reputable rambler?' (*Corr*, II, 521) Or again, emphasizing the link between

[48] C. H. S. Fifoot, *Lord Mansfield* (Oxford, 1936), p. 33 and *passim*; Holdsworth, XII, 464–78.
[49] Edward Foss, *A Biographical Dictionary of the Judges of England* (London, 1870); Holdsworth, XII, 245–6. [50] *Corr*, IV, 222; for the duration of the friendship, see IV, 356.

satirist and public prosecutor which often informs Augustan criticism: 'God deliver you from Law, me from Rhime! and give us leisure to attend what is more important' (*Corr*, III, 486). More explicitly:

I for my part am willing to be old in Disposition, so far as to seek Retreat & Peace: And You, as in the Character of a Judge, are also *Vir tristis* & *gravis*. I am as content to quit the clamorous Part of a Poet, Satire, as you could be to quit that of a Pleading Lawyer...More *Quiet* cannot be in any Law-Station [than that of Master of the Rolls]; & *Quiet* is the Life of Innocence & Good nature. (*Corr*, IV, 126)

On the whole the correspondence between the two men is brief, businesslike and unexceptional. However, Fortescue must have had a vein of humour. He may well have been introduced to the Pope circle by John Gay, whose friend and fellow-Devonian he was. Fortescue is said to have helped with the composition of one Scriblerian squib, *Stradling versus Stiles*. He was also familiar with other habitués of the circle, among them Bathurst and Martha Blount. It may be added that Bathurst's son Henry became Lord Chancellor in 1771, thus further cementing the legal connections of this group of men.

The imitation of *Satire* II i was published in 1733. Pope engaged in genteel equivocation, but there is no serious room for doubt that the 'friend' representing Trebatius in the original was Fortescue. The poem is interesting because of the density of legal allusion in its text. Here Pope was enabled by the literary circumstances to develop a thread of imagery that constantly flits through his later work. It should be noted, for example, that the *Epistle to Arbuthnot* is described as 'a Sort of Bill of Complaint', the technical term for a Chancery plaintiff's submission. This fact is overlooked by all Pope's commentators: yet it provides a key to the whole method of the *Epistle*. It is to be expected that a plaintiff in stating his case will be self-justificatory, sometimes denunciatory, often allusive: he will seek to recollect material facts, and will adduce evidence of his grievances. Pope speaks of a 'truer Information' regarding his case than has hitherto been available, so that the public can 'judge' the matter. When we come to the poem itself, we find within sixty lines the following: *engross*, *apply to me*, *the Laws*, *the Mint*, *saving Counsel*, *Term*, *libell'd*, *sues*, *Commission*, *Papers*, *judge* and many other words with legal colouring more or less prominent. Throughout the poem we find mention of templars, of giving a little senate laws, Japhet in a jail, theft, libel and slander, 'Knight of the Post corrupt'. At the end comes a tribute to 'the good Man', Pope's father:

> No Courts he saw, no Suits would ever try,
> Nor dar'd an Oath, nor hazarded a Lye...   (396–7)

Virtue is directly opposed to the intricacies of the law.

In many other poems from this period, there are similar hints. A judge and a chancellor figure in the *Epistle to Cobham*, where a bequest is parodied ('I give and I devise... My lands and tenements to Ned', 256–7). In the *Epistle to Bathurst*, two successive notes allude to Chancery suits involving rapacious villains of this piece, Hopkins and Crook. We also have the bankrupt pleading his cause at court, commissions and impeachments. The poem *To Murray* had judgments, 'Senate, Rolls and Hall', 'take the Counsel', among other references. *To Augustus* employs the rare and specialized phrase, 'Courtesy of England' (62), as well as law, justice and statutes. *To Bethel* ends with a striking collocation – mortgage, lawyer, Equity, Chancery. Still denser is the frequency in other poems. The *Epilogue to the Satires* uses *law* or its derivatives six times in a short space. Neither the vocabulary nor the allusions stray far from matters judicial and criminal: Jekyll, Jonathan Wild, Newgate, Judge Page and the Treasury Solicitor, Paxton, all figure. Most directly of all, the imitation of *Epistle* II ii has *law(s)* at least six times again. Its racy style is scattered with references to legal matters, often in a carefully mounted mimicry of the appropriate jargon: 'my Cause comes on', 'My Counsel sends to execute a Deed', 'There liv'd, *in primo Georgii* (they record)...', and also

> The Laws of God, as well as of the Land,
> Abhor, a Perpetuity should stand...   (246–7)

Cowper, Talbot and Murray make a glancing appearance; precise and explicit terms are employed, such as Exchequer [the court], Rolls, Sergeants, a *Property* (231: the italics give it the accents of a land-agent).

All these hints are brought together in the poem to Fortescue. What appears elsewhere as a casual motif is here made the structural and satiric centre-piece. The literal situation envisaged is that of Pope, mockingly self-belittled once more,

> Tim'rous by Nature, of the Rich in awe,
> I come to Council learned in the Law.   (7–8)

He asks for advice from his friend 'both sage and free' and 'as you use, without a Fee'. The interlocutor replies curtly, perhaps even gruffly, 'I'd write no more.' Shortly, he justifies this desperate remedy in equally abrupt terms:

> You could not do a worse thing for your Life.
> Why, if the Nights seem tedious – take a Wife;
> Or rather truly, if your Point be Rest,
> Lettuce and Cowslip Wine; *Probatum est.*   (15–18)

The stark rhythms and sharply imperative note go along with a certain pedantry (as in the third line, with *Or rather truly* and the prim subjunctive). The friend's self-satisfied conclusion, QED, is conveyed in the clipped finality of the Latin tag. None of the emollience and high-spirited colloquy of the *Epistle to Bathurst* here.

The friend retains this sharp-tongued air throughout (as in lines 42–4, 103–4). And Pope himself takes on a certain irritation; not the highminded moral outrage of the *Epilogue*, but a captious, nervy quality:

> Not write? but then I *think*,
> And for my Soul I cannot sleep a wink.
> I nod in Company, I wake at Night,
> Fools rush into my Head, and so I write.   (11–14)

There are the familiar allusions (Judge Page, the Mint, thieves, with repetition of *the laws*). It is only at the end, however, that the drift becomes unmistakable:

> This is my Plea, on this I rest my Cause –
> What saith my Council learned in the Laws?
>   F. Your Plea is good. But still I say, beware!
> Laws are explain'd by Men – so have a care.
> It stands on record that in *Richard's* Times
> A man was hang'd for very honest Rhymes.
> Consult the Statute: *quart.* I think it is,
> *Edwardi Sext.* or *prim.* & *quint. Eliz:*
> See *Libels, Satires* – here you have it – read.
> P. *Libels* and *Satires*! lawless Things indeed!
> But grave *Epistles*, bringing Vice to light,
> Such as a *King* might read, a *Bishop* write,
> Such as Sir *Robert* would approve –
>   F. Indeed?
> The Case is alter'd – you may then proceed.

> In such a Cause the Plaintiff will be hiss'd,
> My Lords the Judges laugh, and you're dismiss'd.

(141–56)

This conclusion is a masterpiece of controlled irony. Pope dramatizes a collision of the law and good sense; the former is represented by a barbarous jargon and cumbrous precedents (beautifully emphasized by the strained rhyme *is/Eliz*), whilst the poet retorts with exaggerated deference. The joke at the end relies on the fact that Fortescue had been private secretary to Sir Robert Walpole, and remained a steady supporter of the prime minister. In many ways the poem is not wholly complimentary to Fortescue, any more than the earlier epistle was to Bathurst.[51] The overall note of jumpy petulance suggests not so much taking counsel's opinion as a cross-questioning; the dialogue proceeds in places more like a courtroom interrogation than easy conversation. Not just the diction and imagery, but the basic rhetorical mould, is conditioned by the legal setting.

This pervasive motif in the later poems could be related to a number of things: the fact, for example, that eighteenth-century culture was profoundly legalistic at its core.[52] This in turn may be connected with the desire of people at this time to discover continuities – and therefore precedents – after the constitutional upheavals of the previous age. The job of the law might almost be said to be papering over social cracks: at all events, the letter of the statute-book was held in peculiar reverence at a time when civil war was still a genuine alternative to peaceable and legitimate government. The early Hanoverians awaited the next rising or the next plot with the glum certainty with which California awaits her earthquake. More widely, however, I think that the forms of the law increasingly took on for Pope a symbolic meaning. They stood for the hocus-pocus of the administrative machine, what today might be called the system. And in imagining the law so often as arbitrary, oppressive or simply crass, Pope was adverting to something more than his own deprived role in society as a Catholic – though that assuredly came into it. He was striking against Whiggery, which is to say the politics of statutory reform, of money, of 'enlightenment' and of centralism. (Not of course that Walpole, say, aspired to or attained to all these things: I mean Whiggery as it historically evolved.) Like Burke, Pope

---

[51] See the remarks of P. Dixon, *The World of Pope's Satires* (London, 1968) pp. 32–3.
[52] Robson, p. 143, draws attention to this fact.

believed in human and moral ties, in local associations and affections, in short in the old loose-knit Toryism – a politics that could not survive the growth of central banking, the rise of institutions such as the East India Company, the floating of a huge national debt, the beginnings of industrialism. Beleaguered as he was by his religious faith, Pope must have sensed all his life that 'law makes long spokes of the short stakes of men'. He saw the judicial system, I think, increasingly as an agency of the new state machine; and lawyers as its handmaidens – deep as his personal affection for Fortescue was, their relationship lacked the social ease, the built-in intimacy, that his friendship with Bethel and Bathurst acquired. It is a classic encounter of conservative values and the new professional hierarchy.

VI

Lastly we turn to women, an order only too symbolic. Here the obvious representative is Martha Blount (1690–1763), by far the most sustained of Pope's female friendships. For a moment he may have been more infatuated with Martha's elder sister Teresa; and just as transiently it was Lady Mary Wortley Montagu who stood at the centre of his affections. But these passions died; to say nothing of the fact that Lady Mary was too individual and too gifted to be representative of anything at any time. Acutely and gloriously feminine as she was in many respects, she would have been a remarkable person had she exhibited any or none of the usual sexual attributes. Her appeal does not depend on (though it includes) her womanliness. Finally, she happened to be a writer of talent, which made a big difference to a man as single-minded in his literary ambitions as Pope was.[53]

Much more conventional, though far from dull, 'Patty' Blount exemplifies the attraction of Augustan femininity along with its tragedy. She came of an old Catholic family, and by the standards of the time she was well educated. Her personality is enigmatic. Capable of petty quarrels, she could excite lasting affection. Gossip early began to sprout around her relations with Pope, and it remains uncertain whether or not they were lovers. Fortunately this is not an essay on the Sexual Scene, and the point is of little moment; the Augustans were disposed to enjoy sex, but they unaccountably

---

[53] The most convincing treatment of the Blount sisters will be found in Valerie Rumbold, *Women's Place in Pope's Poetry* (Cambridge, 1989), especially pp. 48–82, 251–94.

thought that it had less to do with the deepest areas of the human personality than had religion, say, or even filial duty. The result is that although women were respected, admired, teased, patronized and cajoled by men, as at all times, they were not intellectualized. We have annals of lust, long before *Fanny Hill* was written (by a son of Pope's friend William Cleland). But nobody thought they were a clue to the national psyche. Such a climate meant that women had in some ways more dignity and more consequence than today, although their role in the sociocultural scheme of things was sadly un-imposing.[54]

The major disabilities of women, in fact, were more straight-forward. They had minimal rights with regard to property and the like: hence Pope's long battles on behalf of his half-sister. They had few civic opportunities, and all professions were closed to them. If they married, they could exercise a respectable and indeed honoured function in the community; their social place was secure, or as secure as their husband's, and it does not seem to have occurred to them that this was a feebly vicarious hold on status. But a woman without a husband and children had limited chances of fulfilment, even in rank which ensured her material comforts and unquestioned social privilege. There is an ominous truth behind Clarissa's words to Belinda in *The Rape of the Lock*:

> But since, alas! frail Beauty must decay,
> Curl'd or uncurl'd, since locks will turn to grey,
> Since painted, or not painted, all shall fade,
> And she who scorns a Man, must die a Maid;
> What then remains, but well our Pow'r to use,
> And keep good Humour still whate'er we lose?   (V, 25–30)

Belinda frowned, upset by the general tenor of this speech. But even she, pretty, wilful, silly little Belinda, could recognize the kernel of truth here: regardless of the tactics to be adopted, marriage was the only authentic choice of life. And the immeasurably more intelligent Martha Blount, self-willed and sprightly in wit, must have known that too. Now sexual independence as such was not the major worry, for that can always be exercised in defiance of the prevailing mores if only because sex can go on in private – if Pope or Martha engaged in physical love, we are quite in ignorance of it. But true personal

---

[54] For a representative Augustan view on the subjection of women, see *The Humourist* (3rd edn, 1724) p. 100.

independence, which comes of doing things *within* society instead of behind its back – this was what Pope, for all his civic restraints, effectively had, and Martha hadn't.

It is interesting to observe the terms in which the poet couches his moving compliment to Martha at the end of the *Epistle to a Lady*. At first sight the tone might appear condescending, with its hint of roguishness and its gentle amusement. Yet we know from the preceding passage (lines 231–47) that Pope had a profound awareness of the pathos of the lonely old woman. And gradually we see that the prettiness of the writing betokens something other than superficial 'charm', and that examples drawn from the routine of polite society need not be routine in their imaginative implications:

> Ah Friend! to dazzle let the Vain design,
> To raise the Thought and touch the Heart, be thine!
> That Charm shall grow, while what fatigues the Ring
> Flaunts and goes down, an unregarded thing.
> So when the Sun's broad beam has tir'd the sight,
> All mild ascends the Moon's more sober light,
> Serene in Virgin Modesty she shines,
> And unobserv'd the glaring Orb declines.
>   Oh! blest with Temper, whose unclouded ray
> Can make to morrow chearful as to day;
> She, who can love a Sister's charms, or hear
> Sighs for a Daughter with unwounded ear;
> She, who ne'er answers till a Husband cools,
> Or, if she rules him, never shows she rules;
> Charms by accepting, by submitting sways,
> Yet has her humour most, when she obeys;
> Lets Fops or Fortune fly which way they will;
> Disdains all loss of Tickets, or Codille;
> Spleen, Vapours, or Small-pox, above them all,
> And Mistress of herself, tho' China fall.   (249–68)

This exquisite passage is proof that Pope does not need to make the hackles of his verse rise in ugly rancour to achieve moral seriousness. Put crudely, this is how to succeed in a man's world. The way to defeat a constricting but 'polite' code, as against draconian repression, is to simulate assent. The woman seems passive but needs courage, tenacity and will. In this case the moon's 'sober light' stands for constancy of purpose, an apparent gentleness, a quality of inviolacy. Of course to accommodate oneself to the norms of society in this way involves renunciation and loss. It also can represent a feat of self-mastery and thus of moral growth. Pope doesn't so much argue this as make the poetry show it, in its delicately charted growth of confidence, its air of settled calm.

That Pope responded intensely to the feminine world, *The Rape of the Lock* is enough to illustrate. Here we have a world of gossamer. Pope has deliberately feminized the epic, by replacing the martial hero with the vain coquette Belinda; and he has transformed the stern landscapes of Homer into a pretty-pretty boudoir atmosphere.

> Loose to the Wind their airy Garments flew,
> Thin glitt'ring Textures of the filmy Dew...   (II, 63–4)

With marvellous invention he ensures that the very language of the poem shall submit to the same process. The words have a tinsel-like ring. Moreover, there is a peculiar intimacy with the objects, a close-range sensuousness which involves both sight and touch. Only a writer who was acutely sensitive to the feelings of various materials, who had observed closely the visual effects produced by domestic objects, could have achieved this. At one point (III, 105ff.) Pope has to describe the 'meal' usually consumed in epic. Of course, he reduces this to the sipping of coffee; and he contrives to give his language the same lacquered finish that the silverware displays. Again, the slightly barbarous heraldry of the playing cards is caught in the very diction of the ombre episode (III 37ff.: note *shining*, *velvet*, *sable*, *verdant*, *embroider'd*, *refulgent*, *dye*, and so on).

In short, the texture of the verse is exactly in consonance with the fundamental comic strategy of the poem. The *Rape* brings down Homer to a few inches of ivory: and the language enacts the same diminution, the same cosy familiarization, the same closeness to domestic furniture. Whether these things are of their nature 'feminine', I do not know; but they were certainly so regarded by the Augustans. So that this work, with a fashionable girl as its central character, is deliberately couched in an idiom of polished social converse. The *Epistle to a Lady* is addressed to a mature lady, although it includes much satire of less sensible women: accordingly, the verse keeps at a distance from the lofty port of *Bathurst*, the manly directness of *Bethel*, the querulous argufying of *Fortescue*. It exhibits instead a sympathetic humour, milder than that of the jokes in Pope's letters to Martha. It displays a range of moods from tenderness to scorn, from pathos to fulsome compliment; but throughout it conveys a special intimacy of tone.

Most of these qualities are seen in the correspondence, along with other attributes not present in the poem. For instance, Pope supplies Martha Blount with several evocative descriptions of romantic scenery in his letters, as of Stonor, Sherborne and the Bath region.[55] Occasionally Pope is moralistic ('This is an odd way of writing to a lady…' (*Corr*, I, 319)), more often jocular. In the early years there is a kind of comic gallantry quite often. As time goes on, however, an undercurrent of sadness approaches the surface, and Pope applies himself more to 'the extreme Sensibility which I know is in [her] Nature' (*Corr*, IV, 463). And the pictures of the social round are wearier in tone: 'But to be all day, first dressing one's body, then dragging it abroad, then stuffing the guts, then washing them with Tea, then wagging one's tongue, & so to bedd; is the life of an Animal, that may for all that I know have Reason in it… but wanted somebody to fetch it out' (*Corr*, IV, 211). Patty for her part is literate, rather less chatty than her correspondent, and innocent of self-conscious refinement. She was a woman of spirit and in her narrow circle she lived an estimable life. She made no false pretensions to intellectual attainments, unlike Queen Caroline; and if her scheme of living seems unambitious today, Pope's tribute in verse has vindicated her. It would outweigh much graver defects. To be the occasion of poetry so luminous – so assured that the recipient merits the compliment, and will accept it gracefully – so successful in adapting private communication to a public theme – this is a worthy memorial to any woman. For women in most societies have been content, rightly or wrongly, to be the private causes of public effects.

There has naturally been extensive discussion of the matters raised in the last paragraph during the last two decades, when feminism has provided the most important and revelatory new strand of Pope criticism. Felicity Nussbaum has shown that Pope's 'poetry on women resounds with themes familiar to readers of antifeminist satires', and indicates that it exhibits not only masculine attitudes (which is undeniable), but also some conventional aspects of patriarchal thinking. Ellen Pollak has extended this reading in a comparison with Swift, and other critics such as Carole Fabricant have adopted a similar approach. The most comprehensive treatment of the subject is that of Valerie Rumbold, who has made the most balanced assessment of the mixture of fascination and distaste which

[55] *Corr*, I, 429–30; II, 236; IV, 201–2. See also the letter of 11 August 1734, printed by G. S. Rousseau in *PQ*, XLV (1966), 409–18.

characterizes Pope's writing on women. This is the liveliest area of Popian studies, and the feminist readings have opened up wider areas of Pope's mind and art for our consideration.[56]

VII

This has inevitably been a highly selective account of Pope's contacts. The arbitrariness is reduced by the fact that Augustan society was a sharply graded series of plateaux, and some historians have actually detected a deepening sense of caste in this age.[57] The categories selected here may have been the wrong ones; but the categories certainly existed. None the less, some omissions should be mentioned. A group of real importance in Pope's youth was formed by a number of literary men including Walsh, Wycherley and Garth. On the edge of this circle stood the man about town and *flâneur* represented by Henry Cromwell – this at a time when Pope liked to pose as a bit of a rake. Another interesting group were the clerics, including Atterbury, Walter Harte, Joseph Spence, William Broome and Abel Evans. A major figure here at the end of Pope's life was his literary executor, William Warburton. Another member is Stephen Hales, the only scientist Pope knew at all well. Such men, according to J. H. Plumb, 'devoted themselves to everything but the administrative reform of the institution to which they belonged'.[58] But it is lucky that the country parson often had the time to function as research scholar, for Warburton, Broome and Spence all made significant contributions in their way to Pope's reputation. A thinner claim can be made for other occupations. Jervas was the only artist to have left his mark on Pope; Cobham was the lone soldier to have come at all close to the poet; whilst Samuel Buckley stood by himself as a kind of embryonic civil servant. Despite his parentage, Pope had few links with the City. He knew Alderman John Barber, a dubious character, less well than Swift, and his relations with Slingsby Bethel were far more formal than those with his brother Hugh. Pope's home at Twickenham was

[56] Felicity Nussbaum, *The Brink of All We Hate: English Satires on Women 1660–1750* (Lexington, Ky., 1984), pp. 137–58 (quotation from p. 137). See also Ellen Pollak, *The Poetics of Sexual Myth: Gender and Ideology in the Verse of Swift and Pope* (Chicago, 1985); Carole Fabricant, '"Binding and Dressing Nature's Loose Tresses": The ideology of Augustan Landscape Design', *Studies in Eighteenth-Century Culture*, VIII (1979), 109–35; and Valerie Rumbold, *Women's Place*. Other significant essays are those by Felicity Rosslyn and Penelope Wilson in *The Enduring Monument: Pope Tercentenary Essays*, ed. G. S. Rousseau and P. Rogers (Cambridge, 1988), pp. 51–76.
[57] Plumb, *Walpole*, p. 13; Moir, p. 78.   [58] Plumb, *England*, p. 49.

owned by a Turkey merchant called Vernon, but they managed landlord and tenant affairs in the best possible way – by never seeing each other from one year to the next. As for the hack writers and venal booksellers who crowd *The Dunciad*, they set quite a different problem. Pope rarely knew them personally, and though his satire has a 'social' component it is not one wholly explicable in class terms.[59]

Speaking of Pope, Leslie Stephen once wrote that 'the great author must have a people behind him; utter both what he really thinks and feels and what is thought and felt most profoundly by his contemporaries'. It was a bad instance to take. Pope did something unique. He made himself a highly respected position in the world through poetry accommodated to the social forms of the day. But, however polite and civilized the verse, Pope's vision was never softened into mild assent. Pope, it has been well said, was 'toughened by the forces of a society which could be harsh and violent';[60] his own situation as a Catholic brought that lesson home. And his friendships, even if they involved no questioning of the social structure in itself, provided the occasion for highly critical observations – on vainglory and gluttony, on feminine foibles and vexatious lawsuits. He was that most dangerous critic of society, who can ape its fashionable chat and fall in with its pointless conventions. He wrote of the social scene from within: but he was a fifth-columnist.

[59] Guerinot's comment (p. xli) that 'the duces, as a whole, belonged to the lower classes', is misleading. In origin a high proportion were middle-class; it was their writing which degraded them.

[60] Stephen, p. 129; Humphreys, p. 22. See my *Grub Street* (London, 1972), pp. 207–11.

CHAPTER 10

Blacks and poetry and Pope

In the early 1970s Mr E. P. Thompson and I independently hit on material relating to the Berkshire Blacks, who were active around 1722–3. This showed that Alexander Pope's brother-in-law, Charles Rackett, and the latter's son Michael were in some way implicated in deer-stealing in Windsor Forest. Charles was taken into custody, whilst Michael seemingly absconded. Mr Thompson planned a full-length book on the episode of history leading to the Waltham Black Act of 1723; I planned merely an article. The result was that I published my findings first, having permitted Mr Thompson to see them in advance of publication. My brief article on the Pope connection appeared in the *Times Literary Supplement* on 31 August 1973, and Mr Thompson's reply on 7 September. Subsequently my wider discussion of the Black Act appeared in the *Historical Journal* during 1974. Mr Thompson's book *Whigs and Hunters* followed in 1975: again he had seen the typescript of my article in advance. *Whigs and Hunters* was published in a paperback in 1977, with some additional material at the end.[1]

The substance of Mr Thompson's *TLS* article was reprinted as an appendix in both editions of *Whigs and Hunters*. It has therefore now reached a wide audience, including a majority of readers who in the nature of things will not have read my own contributions to the debate. I refrained from any response to this widely disseminated material, for a number of reasons. First, there is little disagreement

---

[1] See Pat Rogers, 'A Pope family scandal', *Times Literary Supplement*, 31 August 1973, p. 1005; E. P. Thompson, 'Alexander Pope and the Windsor Blacks; a reply to Pat Rogers', *TLS*, 7 September, 1973, pp. 1031–3; Pat Rogers, 'The Waltham Blacks and the Black Act', *Historical Journal*, XVII (1974), 465–86; E. P. Thompson, *Whigs and Hunters: The Origins of the Black Act* (Harmondsworth, revised edn, 1977). All quotations and references are taken from the 1977 Peregrine edition. See also Brian McCrea, 'Fielding's trial of A. P. Esq. and a problematic episode in the life of Pope', *Eighteenth Century Life*, V (1978), 30–7; and John Broad, 'Whigs and Deer-Stealers in other Guises: A Return to the Origin of the Black Act', *Past & Present*, CXIX (1988), 56–72.

between Mr Thompson and myself on the facts: his fuller enquiries yielded information I had not come across, but it would not have affected my basic judgments. Our differences lie in the area of interpretation. Second, I had hoped at one time to pursue the Racketts in other archives, notably the Chancery files: a daunting task which both of us had embarked upon, but relinquished in the face of the huge prospective labour that would be involved. As things turned out, my circumstances have not permitted this further research. Third, it seemed to me that the Pope story was a side-skirmish in a larger battle. *Whigs and Hunters* is a provocative book which rightly elicited a great deal of discussion. To isolate for special attention the single episode involving (obliquely) Pope would be to play at pitch and toss in the midst of Thermopylae. It seemed right to allow the dust to settle and the heat to subside. Lastly, I was anxious to see whether any objective mediation might be forth-coming. Mr Thompson had suggested that the questions raised ought to be considered by other Pope scholars. Apart from some correspondence in the *TLS* when the story broke, there has been no real reply to this challenge.[2]

As a result, I have come to the conclusion that some response on my part might be appropriate. E. P. Thompson has treated me with unfailing courtesy, and I shall attempt to reciprocate. I have learnt much from his book, and whilst we disagree radically on ultimates (with regard to the rights and wrongs of political action), that is beside the point when we come to look for localized truth.[3] The Pope/Rackett episode involves a finite body of agreed facts, and though it leaves room for all kinds of conjecture the common aim of historians must be to narrow down the area of speculation to its irreducible minimum. I confess that my fundamental interest in history is to discover what actually happened, and events fascinate me more than ideology. The lure is the uncovering of what was previously a mystery, not the confirmation of a theory. I would rather that someone discovered the true facts with regard to the episode

---

[2] It should be observed that Howard Erskine-Hill's important book, *The Social Milieu of Alexander Pope* (New Haven, Conn., 1975), does throw new light on Pope's relations with the Catholic gentry. See especially pp. 42–102, on the Caryll family. However, the Blacks do not figure in this account.

[3] There are other matters on which Mr Thompson and I have specific differences; for example, on the relation of the Blacks to professional crime at large. A vigorous general survey of the broader issue is Frank McLynn, *Crime and Punishment in Eighteenth-Century England* (Oxford, 1991): see pp. 202–17 for a strongly argued, if tendentious, account of game-stealing.

(whatever its implications for our view of Pope, or of Jacobitism, or of Walpole, or of Whiggery) than that we should go on speculating according to our own prejudices. I cannot pretend to have reached an objective assessment of the matter. However, it may be worth indicating the points at which Mr Thompson's conjectures (for so they confessedly are) are strained, implausible or unnecessary. The aim is not to prove his surmise wrong, something which cannot be attempted in our present state of knowledge. It is to show that very different interpretations of the facts are possible, and that a case which has now been given abundant public exposure should not be regarded as the only – or even perhaps as the most securely based – explanation of the events.

I

The background to this episode concerns the introduction of the Black Act and its attendant furore, discussed by Mr Thompson in *Whigs and Hunters*. Long before the issue absorbed the attention of modern historians, the measure known as the 'Waltham Black Act' (9 Geo. I, c. 22) had acquired a lasting notoriety. The Act was extended for five years in 1725 (12 Geo. I, c. 30), amended in 1754 (27 Geo. II, c. 15) and made permanent in 1758 (31 Geo. II, c. 42). Effectively it survived for a century, until Peel took it off the statute-book despite opposition from the *Quarterly Review*. Its main provisions were directed against 'wicked and evil-disposed Persons going armed in Disguise, and doing Injuries and Violences to the Persons and Properties of his Majesty's Subjects'. It became a felony without benefit of clergy to go abroad into woods in any form of disguise or with a blackened face. Commission of a specific act of destruction or larceny was not necessary for a prosecution to lie.

Contemporary evidence concerning the episode of the Blacks falls into three categories. First, documents in the Public Record Office, notably the State Papers. These include depositions, eye-witness accounts, memoranda of evidence, recognizances, minutes of the Lord Justices, and other papers, almost all assembled by the key government official, Charles Delafaye. The Treasury archives include a valuable schedule of activities performed by one of the royal keepers. Second, newspapers give full coverage of the prosecution and on one occasion supply a detailed history of the individual Blacks. Third, a highly circumstantial pamphlet of 1723 supplies an excellent narrative of the whole affair, even if it is a slightly establishment-orientated view, and dependent on press reports in many places. This work, *The History of The Blacks of Waltham in Hampshire: and those under the like Denomination in Berkshire*, was very possibly the work of Daniel Defoe, though it has not previously been listed in the 500-odd attributions now regarded as plausible. Defoe was an outstandingly knowledgeable student of crime, and it is certain that he knew of the Blacks (as his *Tour of Great Britain*, indeed, makes clear). But in any case, even if we cautiously treat this witness simply as an anonymous pamphleteer, his testimony makes it possible to supplant the vague and remote deponents – such as Gilbert White – who for long served as the principal source on the Blacks. There is also a second-hand account of the Blacks in Boyer's *Political State*, and some unreliable versions in popular lives of the highwaymen.

From the point of view of criminal historiography, the episode has distinct advantages. The affair was relatively brief: almost everything material happened between the autumn of 1721 and the end of 1723. Second, relatively few individuals were involved, sixty at most, and a high proportion of them are consequently traceable. This is obviously different from a town riot, as in the Sacheverell or Wilkite troubles, when a heterogeneous and unstable body of rioters was quickly lost within the swarming city. Again, the Waltham affair broke at a time of heightened public awareness. It overlapped with the Jacobite plot centring on Bishop Atterbury, and indeed witnesses of the Blacks' depredations had to fight for government attention amidst the flurry of informing, code-unravelling and general panic which attended the Jacobite scare. Moreover, in more orthodox criminal haunts, the great Jonathan Wild was then at the very summit of his power. This is of more interest than it might appear, for one particular reason. The Blacks were extortionists and protection-racketeers – as, in his more genteel and businesslike fashion, was Wild. According to Sir William Blackstone, the Waltham gang modelled themselves on the Roberdsmen or followers of Robin Hood. In fact, though there was a strong social component in their activities, their *method* was recognizably that of gangsters at large. It is therefore important to note the full provisions of the statute, which concern such matters as sending threatening letters and demanding money with violence. Wild, indeed, took a personal interest in the affair.

The affair first blew up, as indicated, around the autumn of 1721, and its main course was run by the end of 1723. In fact the deer-stealers who came to be known as 'Blacks', from the disguise they sometimes adopted, were operating during 1722–3 in two contiguous regions. One group was based in Hampshire, and drew its members chiefly from the Portsmouth area. It was active in the Woolmer Forest district, together with the Forest of Bere, one corner of which forms Waltham Chase itself. Another group surfaced around the same time in Windsor Forest, principally the Easthampstead–Bagshot portion. The first group reached as far north as Farnham, and there may well have been associations between the two areas of operation, although the evidence on this point is inconclusive. The Rackett affairs relates to the Windsor Forest sphere of activity.

The aspect of this story which I am seeking to explore is that concerned with Pope himself, especially his relations with Walpole. Mr Thompson makes some intelligent guesses with regard to the fate of various members of the Rackett family, in particular Charles' son Michael. But they are only guesses, and no subsequent research has affected their standing. It is impossible to test these hypotheses, since there is no other body of information which might bear on their plausibility. The case is quite different with Pope himself. We know an immense amount about him, even if it is never quite as much as we should wish. His public and private conduct is well documented, and the documentation is augmented in scope all the time. When speculation extends to his behaviour, consequently, there is more likelihood of reaching a balanced judgment of probabilities.

Mr Thompson's theory is that the case against the Racketts was 'not quashed but held in suspension'. He argues that Walpole may have held this charge over their heads as a hostage for 'the good behaviour of Alexander Pope'. This was useful, because Pope had seemed in early 1723 to be 'moving towards open criticism of the Walpole regime':

He had given testimony on behalf of his friend Francis Atterbury, the Jacobite Bishop of Rochester, when on trial before the House of Lords; and his correspondence with the imprisoned Bishop was well known. So also was his friendship with Bolingbroke.

While the charge was impending, it is argued, Pope was forced to 'tread very warily'. 'It is my impression', Mr Thompson adds, 'that, for several years, he did.'[4]

In support of this reading of events, Mr Thompson alludes to

---

[4] *TLS*, 7 September 1973, p. 1031: compare *Whigs and Hunters*, p. 287. McCrea, pp. 31ff., suggests that a paper by Fielding in 1740 may support the theory of 'silencing', but admits that the case is 'largely inferential'.

various passages in Pope's correspondence. One case in point is a letter to Lord Harcourt on 21 June 1723: 'You have done me many & great favours, and I have a vast deal to thank you for.'[5] Mr Thompson thinks this may relate to what he calls 'Pope's "great application" at the end of May 1723' to save his brother-in-law from immediate prosecution. It should be emphasized straight away that the phrase 'great application' comes from a press report and is there used without reference to any individual, let alone to Pope himself. The passage in Applebee's *Weekly Journal* reports in a gossipy fashion that 'great application is making to men in power in [Rackett's] favour'. The *application* to Pope of this phrase is Mr Thompson's.[6]

Also cited are a number of passages in the correspondence which show Pope in a sombre mood in the summer of 1723. These contain explicit references to the taxation of Catholics; to 'the ocean of avarice and corruption' in post-South Sea days; to Bolingbroke, Atterbury and Peterborough. What they do not mention is the Blacking episode, at least in any transparent way. Mr Thompson detects a covert allusion: an expression used to Swift around August ('all those I have most lov'd & with whom I have most liv'd, must be banish'd') might 'carry a reference to the Racketts'. In any case, the text comes from a transcript among the Cirencester papers: it might always (we are to suppose) have been doctored. A month or so later, Swift replied. His response at this point reads: 'I have often made the same remark with you of my Infelicity in being so Strongly attached to Traytors (as they call them) and Exiles, and State Criminalls.' This passage was excised when Pope printed the letters, and the source is again a transcript: but, Mr Thompson assures us, a 'more reliable' one.[7]

The conclusion reached, in what is conceded to be 'a matter of speculation', is this: the Blacking affair turned Pope 'decisively' from the pastoral mode, and 'directed him more urgently towards satire'. Of course, the shock was postponed:

yet, though evidently working inside him, the satire was delayed expression for several years. It is customary to attribute this to his preoccupation with the work on his Homer. But if we recall the earlier suggestion that – at least until Charles Rackett's death – Pope remained in some way a hostage to Walpole's favour, one may see his predicament in a different way.[8]

[5] *Corr*, II, 175.
[6] *TLS*, 7 September 1973, p. 1032; Applebee's *Weekly Journal*, 25 May 1723.
[7] *Whigs and Hunters*, pp. 292–3; *Corr*, II, 184, 198.   [8] *Whigs and Hunters*, pp. 287, 293.

Thus does Mr Thompson dispose of the most sustained labour of Pope's life, and explain by a single obscure incident a creative process which Popian scholars have been gestating over many troubled years.

II

Before turning to these arguments in detail, I should like to mention two incidental stages of Mr Thompson's argument. One concerns the insertion of two new lines in *Windsor-Forest* on its publication in 1713:

> Fair *Liberty, Britannia's* Goddess rears
> Her cheerful Head, and leads the golden Years.   (91–2)

The copy of the poem Pope made in 1712 had four different lines at this point, alluding to the wrongs endured under 'a foreign Master's Rage' – formally, anyway, relating to the treatment of New Forest by William I. These four lines were printed in a note when Pope revised the text for editions from 1736 onwards.[9] It is quite clear that the revised version is more discreet: we should, however, note that this discretion was exercised before the Hanoverians came to the throne, and may well have to do with its offensiveness concerning William III – *not* the future George I. Secondly, Mr Thompson calls the revised a 'more gummy' couplet than the material it replaces. It is also poetically superior, surely; more economical, more apt to the stylistic decorum of the work as a whole, more resonant for the total allegory. The mention of Britannia cements a theme later developed. One phrase introduced ('the golden Years') has often been quoted as a key image,[10] central to the imaginative design of *Windsor–Forest*. Such aesthetic concerns plainly occupied a large part of Pope's attention when he revised the manuscript for publication. They do not enter at any point into Mr Thompson's calculations.[11]

A second indicative phase in the argument is this:

One need not propose that the poet had any active sympathy with Blacking. But one does note that several men who were Black targets or actors in the

---

[9] See Robert M. Schmitz, *Pope's Windsor Forest 1712: A Study of the Washington University Holograph* (St Louis, MO., 1952), pp. 23–4.

[10] In all innocence I have done this myself: see 'Time and space in *Windsor Forest*', *The Art of Alexander Pope*, ed. H. Erskine-Hill and A. Smith (London, 1979), p. 46. But, in case this should appear tainted evidence, compare E. R. Wasserman, *The Subtler Language* (Baltimore, Md., 1959), pp. 165–6.

[11] *Whigs and Hunters*, p. 292. For a detailed analysis of the alterations, amply documenting the aesthetic concerns paramount in Pope's mind, see Schmitz, pp. 50–68.

prosecution of the Blacks turn up as subsequent targets for Pope's satire; these include Cadogan, Governor Thomas Pitt, Sir Francis Page and Paxton. Pope kept on friendly terms with only one of the prosecuting cast, Lord Cobham; but Cobham was replaced as Governor of Windsor Castle in June 1723, and throughout the earlier months of the year Colonel Negus, his deputy, appears to have performed his duties.[12]

Detailed scrutiny of what Mr Thompson terms 'only indirect, inconclusive evidence' shows it to be less than that. Cadogan was notoriously unpopular, and it may reasonably be assumed that Pope shared the general opinion;[13] but the one supposed example of 'satire' against him in Pope's poetry is highly conjectural. 'Narses' in the *Epistle to Bathurst*, line 91, has been associated with Cadogan only because a manuscript reading (never published in Pope's lifetime, or for long afterwards) points that way. Satire so impenetrable and casual scarcely constitutes strong evidence of compulsive hated. Thomas Pitt is made the object of fun, if he is made such, as a miser and a cit turned gentleman, not as a rapacious landlord. The entire portrait of Sir Balaam contains nothing that could be turned so as to make it directly relevant to Blacking. And the idea that Pitt is Sir Balaam was first proposed as late as 1869: F. W. Bateson reached the considered view that the portrait 'was modelled on Pitt in the first instance and later generalised'.[14] Other scholars have regarded Sir Balaam as pure invention – the kind of reading that Mr Thompson stigmatizes as offering 'extravaganzas' rather than 'a shaft of solid information'. Either way, the good temper of the satire gives no warrant for discerning concealed ferocity against Pitt in Pope's breast.

As for Judge Page, it is hardly necessary to expatiate upon his reputation for brutality. Mr Thompson himself remarks, earlier in his book, that Page 'was already known to contemporaries as "the hanging judge" and he went down in literary tradition with a reputation only a little more salubrious than that of Jeffreys'.[15] So he

---

[12] *Whigs and Hunters*, p. 291.

[13] See *TE*, III, ii, 181, and the passages from Spence cited there. The reference here is in the unpublished 'Master key to Popery', and again it is oblique. The fullest expression of Pope's views comes in a letter of 9 August 1726 (*Corr*, II, 386). As Sherburn says there, 'Cadogan's attitude towards Atterbury probably prejudiced Pope.'

[14] *TE*, III, ii, 118. Since 1951 the weight of scholarly enquiry has tilted our view of Sir Balaam *against* a narrow personal identification, with Pitt or with anyone else. However, Erskine-Hill, pp. 263–5, suggests that Pope's 'artfully ambiguous portraiture' is based as much on Sir John Blunt as on Pitt.   [15] *Whigs and Hunters*, p. 211.

did: Johnson refers to 'his usual Insolence and Severity' in the conduct of Savage's trial,[16] whilst Fielding's Man of the Hill presents him in colours only a little softer.[17] But that very fact works *against* the supposition that Pope cherished a special and personal hostility towards him. The *Dunciad* note, again quoted by Mr Thompson, speaks of the 'hundred miserable examples during a long life' which bespoke Page's cruelty.[18] Pope said more graphically what many others said: there is nothing to indicate a private pique grounded in the Blacking episode.

This is also true of Paxton, but here the evidence is more interesting. Nicholas Paxton was less of a general villain, though his work for Walpole in the 1730s brought him the dislike of writers and journalists whose work he censored. After the fall of Walpole he was accused of exercising corruption by a Secret Committee of Parliament, but when interrogated he remained silent. However, in 1723 the important fact lay elsewhere. Paxton was only Assistant Solicitor to the Treasury, but it was he rather than Anthony Cracherode who supervised much of the day-to-day business of investigation and law-maintenance, as the State Papers reveal. In some respects he acted in the capacity of a Director of Public Prosecutions. He came into special prominence at the time of the Jacobite scares in the aftermath of the 1715 Rising. More than once he was instrumental in measures taken against the high-flying printer Nathaniel Mist. And he gained the lasting enmity of Stuart sympathizers for the apparent relish with which he conducted the prosecution of Atterbury. He was thought to be the controller of the battery of informers and suborned witnesses whom the government were alleged to employ, and it was suggested he tried to bring in false evidence during the hearings. Another 'martyr' of the period was the Duke of Wharton, whose lines on the subject have been preserved in *The New Foundling Hospital for Wit*:

> And bid his old tool, Delafaye,
> Keep Lynch and Mason in full pay,
> Paxton should teach them what to say.
> For hatching plots, and coining treason,
> Paxton's esteem'd, with mighty reason.[19]

---

[16] Samuel Johnson, *Life of Savage*, ed. C. Tracy (Oxford, 1971), p. 34: see also pp. 40–1, where a satire by Savage on Page is quoted.

[17] *The History of Tom Jones*, ed. M. C. Battestin (Oxford, 1974), I, 459.

[18] Note to *Dunciad* IV, 30 (*TE*, V, 343).

[19] *The New Foundling Hospital for Wit* (London, 1784), I, 227. For the prosecution of Atterbury, see G. V. Bennett, *The Tory Crisis in Church and State 1688–1730* (Oxford, 1975). 'Mason' was

It was the vastly publicized trial of Atterbury, in which Pope took his faltering but altogether visible part, that long established the reputation of men like Paxton. Pope's only surviving references in prose and verse date from the late 1730s; they clearly relate to Paxton as he was operating in the Walpole regime at that later period. It was not until 1739 that Pope thought of giving Paxton a niche in *The Dunciad*, and even this reference was eliminated when the new passage appeared in the 1743 text.[20] Mr Thompson repeats as fact a story that Paxton hired Whig hooligans to break Pope's windows while he was dining with Bolingbroke and Bathurst.[21] The tale was retailed much later by Joseph Warton; it may or may not be true (though there is no contemporary corroboration), but it serves Mr Thompson in his desire to read the texts in a more 'literal' way – here *Epilogue to the Satires*, II, 140–5.

In each case it emerges that Pope's contact with these men was slight, inconsequential, distant or non-existent. The references are sometimes dubious, sometimes exceedingly oblique, sometimes belated, always brief. They can be paralleled in writers with no involvement in the Blacking episode. They can always be explained by obvious facts quite outside Mr Thompson's area of concern – I do not say quite outside the subject, because there *were* links between the Atterbury affair and the hue and cry over the Waltham Blacks. But it is important to keep separate allusions which could just fit the episode and references that unarguably bear on it.

What, then, of Lord Cobham, about whom Mr Thompson might have felt more embarrassment than he evidently does? It is admitted that Pope 'kept on friendly terms' with Cobham; but this is grossly to understate the case. Pope cultivated the man's acquaintance for a number of years; their friendship seems indeed to have begun just about the time of the Blacks affair, or a little after. The first mention of a visit to Cobham's home comes in September 1724; thereafter Pope regularly directed the course of his rambles towards Stowe, and in the next few years he acted as a sort of landscape consultant. Long before Cobham had gone into the opposition to Walpole and become a Patriot leader, Pope lauded his achievements. In the *Epistle to Burlington*, as Morris R. Brownell puts it, he 'propagated the fame of

---

a woman, and a key witness in the trial. For an allegation against Paxton, see *The Parliamentary Diary of Sir Edward Knatchbull 1722–1730*, ed. A. N. Newman (London, 1963), p. 19. For Knatchbull on the Blacks, see p. 21.

[20] See *Corr*, IV, 179.   [21] *Whigs and Hunters*, p. 213.

Stowe ... [as] the epitome of landscape garden design'.[22] Then, three years later, came the *Epistle to Cobham*, and this of course was set conspicuously at the head of the collected 'Epistles' in the *Works*. By this time Pope had unambiguously identified himself with Cobham's political stance. He was proud to advertise his connection with the peer, before and after Cobham's break with Walpole. There could not be a more open tribute than the reference in the opening line of *Horace, Epistle* II. ii, or a more adroitly flattering irony than that in the *Epilogue to the Satires*, II, 130. It is in fact the precise inverse of the situation obtaining in the cases just reviewed: the contact was long, eagerly maintained by Pope, and loudly proclaimed.

Mr Thompson would have it that Cobham played little part in Forest affairs during 1723. Some acts he did continue to perform, however, with a significant relation to the Blacking episode. For example, it was on his recommendation that the keeper Baptist Nunn, almost the arch-villain of *Whigs and Hunters*, was appointed as a Porter of Windsor Castle on 25 June.[23] His personal interviews with Cobham went on at least until January 1723; during the summer of 1722 it was Cobham above all who spurred Nunn on to action, which led in due course to the arrest of Charles Rackett and the apparent flight of his son Michael. It also emerges that Cobham had got the ministry to defend Nunn in a suit which was brought against him in 1718; Mr Thompson does not mention this, although he does give us titbits concerning the keeper's earlier career, and speculates on a 'pre-history' to the running battles of 1722–3.[24] If Cobham felt any misgivings over his conduct as Constable of Windsor Castle, he did not make them public. There is even a story that, as an old man, he returned two deer-stealers to their wives (having been implored to do so) – but as dead bodies strung on a cart. Mr Thompson defends the veracity of this 'firm local tradition' against Professor John Cannon in the new edition of *Whigs and Hunters*.[25] If it *is* true, then the argument that Cobham had washed his hands of the campaign against Blacks grows more dubious. If Cobham genuinely was capable of such acts into his last days, this casts doubt on the assertion that he can be used in evidence to show that 'the general run of

[22] Morris R. Brownell, *Alexander Pope and the Arts of Georgian England* (Oxford, 1978), pp. 195–207, charts Pope's connections with Stowe; quotation from p. 195.
[23] Public Record Office, SP 44/290/21: see also 'The Waltham Blacks and the Black Act', p. 476. Mr Thompson mentions Nunn's later promotions (*Whigs and Hunters*, p. 220), but does not mention that Nunn was a client of Cobham.
[24] *Whigs and Hunters*, pp. 64–6.   [25] *Whigs and Hunters*, pp. 223, 308–9.

Pope's values would have been against the courtiers, the fashionable and moneyed settlers in the forest, the judges and prosecutors'.[26] Pope certainly was opposed to many such people, and nothing in my own account of the matter is incompatible with that fact. But that he wished in every way to be associated with Cobham's values, as enshrined at Stowe during the 1720s and 1730s, is scarcely controvertible. If he wished to repudiate Cobham, he assuredly went a peculiar way about it.

Mr Thompson's citation of names puts great emphasis on a sprinkling of badly supported references alleged to be 'satiric'. It blithely disregards a volume of conspicuous evidence to show that Cobham – who was by far the most centrally involved in the Blacking affair, of all those named – received homage and affection from the poet. It conveniently assumes that Cobham repented of his hard line in 1722, though no facts have been brought to support this.

III

I now return to the passages in Pope's correspondence which Mr Thompson quoted. From them he made his own reconstruction of events, and reached the conclusion that Pope found himself impelled to moralize his song as a result of his experiences over the Rackett episode. However, Walpole exercised a continuing hold over him, through Charles Rackett's tactically delayed prosecution, and this satiric urge was held in check until Rackett's death in 1728.

There are things that could be said on the side: that delayed prosecution was generally a sign of difficulty in pressing the charges, rather than a cold-blooded policy of blackmail;[27] or that Pope actually was engaged in translating the *Odyssey* and editing Shakespeare at the relevant dates, which would have been more than sufficient impediment to the creation of major satiric poems. Pope himself regularly testifies to the crushing labour and expense of nervous energy. But let us turn directly to the central issues raised.

First, there is Pope's alleged 'wariness' in the 1720s. One of the precipitating factors in Walpole's suspicious attitude, we are told,

[26] *Whigs and Hunters*, p. 291.
[27] It was common for charges to be held over from one session to the next, as the authorities struggled to obtain evidence and witnesses: in the end charges were often dropped or a pardon granted. This last seems to have happened with Nathaniel Mist in 1721 (see successive reports in the *Daily Journal*).

was Pope's friendship with Bolingbroke. In fact this only became fully manifest after Bolingbroke was allowed to return from exile: the first surviving letter between the two men dates from February 1724. Their most prolonged and open relations belong to the very years when, as Mr Thompson describes it, Pope had to lie low on account of such embarrassing friendships. Something of the same reasoning applies to Peterborough, admittedly a less embarrassing friend from the point of view of Walpole's surveillance. The first letter here dates from July 1723, though earlier correspondence may well be lost. The fact is that Pope's friendship with both men flourished and expanded at the period in question. The open alliance of both with the Scriblerian Group at the time of Swift's two visits to England – in 1726 and 1727 – falls squarely into the years when Rackett is supposed to have been 'on ice'.

Consider now the letter to Harcourt of 21 June 1723. Pope compares the public gratitude Harcourt has incurred by his part in Bolingbroke's restoration with the private gratitude Pope owes him for many favours. Mr Thompson suggests this could refer to efforts going on at this time to stop the prosecution of Rackett. It *could*: but it could just as easily refer to much else. Pope's next sentence is 'But I shall now go near to forget all that is past',[28] since these previous deeds have been overtopped by Harcourt's present act of nobility, that is, in respect of the pardon to Bolingbroke. The favours that lay in the past might be recent, and if so they could include help over Pope's appearance before the Lords a month earlier or advice given about Buckingham's *Works*.[29] But they could well be more distant, and extend back to the many kindnesses that had been shown during the lifetime of Pope's beloved friend Simon Harcourt (d. 1720), for whom Pope wrote an epitaph warmly expressive of their mutual regard. Lord Harcourt gave the tribute to his son most careful vetting, and Pope must have regarded this as a favour. Again, in 1718 Pope passed a long period as a guest of the family at Stanton Harcourt, where he made considerable progress on the *Iliad*. There are many such memorials to a well-established friendship. Mr Thompson's theory requires us to fix on a single, unsupported 'favour', the presumed intervention in favour of Rackett. Such

---

[28] *Corr*, II, 175.

[29] We know that Harcourt did help Pope on both these matters: see *Corr*, II, 146, 156, 161, 171–2. All these references are clearly prior to the Rackett arrest, and it is wholly unnecessary to invent a new antecedent for Pope's letter to Harcourt on 21 June: we already have abundant expressions of gratitude in the earlier letters.

selective application to a complex body of evidence makes anything possible. We *know* the areas in which Harcourt did assist Pope: the rest is pure surmise.

Next, the letters written in 1723 reflecting Pope's sombre mood. As I have remarked, none actually mentions the affair of the Blacks. The phrase concerning those whom Pope had 'loved...and lived with' is directly followed by an explanatory sentence, making direct mention of Atterbury's banishment. Pope goes on to say that he fears lest Peterborough, too, may incur this fate. Mr Thompson would like the phrase to carry over also to the Racketts; but there is no evidence to show that the poet ever lived with his relatives, unless the expression is taken to include neighbourly intercourse (the families lived seven miles apart in Pope's youth). As for the allegation that the transcript may have been tampered with: it is true that Pope himself excluded certain portions of the text when he reprinted it, but Curll naturally did not. We must therefore assume that the copy from which Curll printed contained the same tactical omissions as that followed by Sherburn; if the allegation is to be sustained, that is.[30] The tampering theory has no serious palaeographic or bibliographic support. It is required only if we wish to suppose that certain dark thoughts have been surreptitiously excised. Mr Thompson does wish to suppose that.

Swift's reply is dated 20 September. His phrase concerning 'Traytors...and Exiles, and State Criminalls' has already been quoted. Swift himself, as an exile, was often drawn to such rhetorical conjunctions. The reputed traitors he would have in mind can be determined with fair confidence: Ormonde (whom he much admired), Mar, Bolingbroke and Atterbury. State criminals would include Oxford. There is no reason to suppose that anything is missing in Pope's letter to prompt the reflection from Swift; the reply makes perfectly good sense at this point, with Pope's text just as we have it. Swift had taken a close interest in the Atterbury affair, and refers to it more than once in his work (including *Gulliver's Travels*).[31]

[30] See *Corr*, II, 183–6, 198–200. There are no grounds known to me for regarding the transcript among the Bathurst papers as unreliable, or for presuming the Harley transcripts of Swift's letter to be either a more or a less reconstructed text. (For Sherburn's doubts concerning other Harley transcripts at Longleat, see *Corr*, II, 324). It should be added that Sherburn's dating of Pope's letter to Charles Rackett (*Corr*, II, 181) is too conjectural for much weight to be placed on it. It could easily belong to an earlier year.

[31] See Edward W. Rosenheim, 'Swift and the Atterbury case', *The Augustan Milieu*, ed. H. K. Miller *et al.* (Oxford, 1970), pp. 174–204.

Already he had composed a bitter verse dialogue, *Upon the Horrid Plot*, whose subliminal message might be paraphrased by, 'Walpole and his gang are the real dirty dogs.' More recently still, in January 1723, he had produced a birthday poem for Charles Ford. One passage runs:

> Observe where bloody Townshend stands
> With Informations in his Hands,
> Hear him blaspheme; and Swear, and Rayl,
> Threatening the Pillory and Jayl.[32]

This was before the Blacks became well known, and some months before Rackett's arrest. Again it is evident that the animus is generated by Atterbury's fate.[33] Of course, it is conceivable that what was a public issue for other writers had a special private meaning for Pope; it could be that he writes indecipherable messages to Swift, in which the recipient will decode 'Atterbury' where the personal meaning reserved to the sender is 'Rackett'. But that is surely to invent complexity where none exists.

From such passages Mr Thompson reaches his view that Pope's malaise in 1723 was occasioned, not by Atterbury or by the troubles over the edition of Buckingham, but by the Rackett episode. He further suggests that Pope's switch to satire has a direct basis in biographic events, indeed specifically in the clash with Walpole over the Blacks. He pleads for a more literal approach to early Hanoverian satire, involving the need for critics to 'review the assumption of hyperbole'.[34] The general conclusion may be sound, but it is not well supported by the localized instance. No doubt some Jacobite rhetoric has some definable relation to actual events and to an actual view of the world. Whether it is best to regard Swift's onslaughts on the Hanoverian court ('Swarms of Bugs and Hanoverians', he writes to Ford) as 'straight' political comment is another matter. Hyperbole, which Mr Thompson seems to think of as something that gets in the way of true personal expression, can often be a major instrument for conveying a vision of the world. Swift's most fantastic 'extravaganzas', that is, contain some of his most heartfelt writing. For the

---

[32] *The Poems of Jonathan Swift*, ed. H. Williams (Oxford, 1968), I, 297–301, 312–13.
[33] Later on Swift did come to hear of the Blacks, when Thomas Power (the *agent provocateur* used by the ministry) was awarded an Irish benefice. There is not the faintest sign that Pope had alerted him to a personal interest in the affair. See *The Correspondence of Jonathan Swift*, ed. H. Williams (Oxford, 1963–65), III, 116. The letter is quoted in *Whigs and Hunters*, p. 221, from Ball's text, which erroneously prints 'Walsh Black' for 'Waltham Black'.
[34] *Whigs and Hunters*, pp. 293–4.

critic to read them as literary fictions, works of creative *invention*, is not to assert or deny anything about the real world outside. It is simply to accept the facts concerning what goes on in literature, and the reasons why certain writers command a special expressive power.

The evidence assembled here indicates a number of things. It shows that the effects attributed by Mr Thompson to Pope's involvement with Blacking can always be explained (and usually more simply explained) by other known causes. It suggests that far more evidence is needed before we can confidently speak of a new wariness in Pope's conduct in the mid 1720s. It shows how much of Mr Thompson's case is built on supposition, guesswork and the neglect of contrary evidence. It illustrates the difficulty of applying 'solid information'[35] to poetry, however solid that information might be, unless we have some concrete evidence of how the poet did or did not receive the appropriate data. All Mr Thompson's theorizing is built upon an assumption of how Pope reacted to the Blacking episode – something history does not reveal, so far anyway. My original account of the episode was based on one set of assumptions; Mr Thompson's account rests on a quite different set, but it does not do more than supplant my guesswork with another guesswork, more generous in the latitude it allows to neglect of the established biographic data. It is of course permissible for speculation to go on, when the facts are insufficient to produce any degree of certainty. But it would be grievously wrong to suppose that any of the 'solid information' we now have concerning the Blacks, rehearsed so fully in *Whigs and Hunters*, has yet clarified Pope's position. On that issue we are as much in the dark as we were in 1973.

[35] *Whigs and Hunters*, p. 294. It is curious that Mr Thompson does not consider the later history of Pope's dealings with Walpole, on which quite a lot of 'information' exists. Their relations were at their most affable in the very period when (according to the Thompson theory) Pope should have been in awe of the prime minister, and resentful of his blackmail. They dined together quite regularly from about 1726 (*Corr*, II, 368). Pope's kindest comments, to Fortescue, come in a letter Sherburn originally dated 1725 but later placed in 1728 (*Corr*, II, 294; V, 2). In case Mr Thompson should wonder whether the transcript might have been tampered with, it might be added that the original letter, once in the possession of Samuel Rogers, has now turned up and is deposited in the Library of University College, London. See *Scriblerian*, VIII (1975), 57. For the best account of Pope and Walpole, see Mack, *Garden and City*, especially pp. 121–3. Finally, it should be remembered that Pope's first openly political anti-court poem was *The Dunciad*, which was written and, I think, published before Charles Rackett died.

CHAPTER II

The case of Pope *v.* Curll

All students of Pope are familiar with his lengthy battles in print with the notorious bookseller Edmund Curll (1683–1747). The brash advertising methods of Curll helped to make him one of the key figures in what I have called elsewhere 'the invention of publicity'.[1] But Curll and Pope also tangled in the courts, and one could say that their skirmishes in print were no more than the extension of legal disputes by other means.

The Chancery suit of *Pope* v. *Curll* (1741) is significant on a number of different levels. It remains a leading case in English law as the first important test regarding copyright in personal letters.[2] In fact, Lord Hardwicke's judgment constituted one of the first major interpretations in court of the celebrated Copyright Act of 1709. Additionally, the suit provides evidence of Pope's increasing willingness to go to the law in his final years[3] – a development which may be associated with his friendship with Murray (the future Lord Mansfield),[4] his counsel in this instance. It affords yet another chapter in the continuing battle with Curll. As it happens, the struggle of Pope versus Curll had gone on outside the courts for twenty-five years. On one occasion Curll had threatened to have recourse to 'a Legal Remedy' against Pope or his agents. And Curll himself had been obliged to appear before the House of Lords for allegedly contravening its standing orders.[5] But it was only at this late stage that Pope deigned to apply to the courts for redress. The episode throws a little light on the

---

[1] See *Literature and Popular Culture in Eighteenth-Century England* (Brighton, 1985), pp. 18–28.

[2] For citation of this case, see for example Sir William Holdsworth, *A History of English Law*, (London, 1922–38). XII, 283; *Copinger and Skone James on Copyright* (London, 10th edn, 1965), p. 33; *Goodeve's Modern Law of Personal Property* (London, 8th edn, 1937), p. 398; and *Mews Digest of English Case Law* (London, 1925), V, 1251.

[3] See Howard P. Vincent, 'Some *Dunciad* Litigation', *PQ*, XVIII (1939), 285–9.

[4] For Mansfield's connection with the case, see C. H. S. Fifoot, *Lord Mansfield* (Oxford, 1936), p. 222.   [5] *Corr*, III, 476; 464–5.

complex publishing history of the letters of Pope and Swift,[6] and it offers a number of bibliographical clues, e.g. hints regarding Curll's methods and scale of operation.

Surprisingly, the case has never been examined in detail. It is not mentioned in Ralph Straus' life of Curll[7] (nor in the extensive collections of W. J. Thoms), and none of the standard biographies of Pope alludes to it. The Lord Chancellor's judgment is found in Atkins' reports (1781)[8] and has been abstracted by biographers of Hardwicke.[9] More recently, Harry Ransom has used the report in his valuable article, 'The Personal Letter as Literary Property', and assessed the importance of this judgment in the history of copyright.[10] Ransom's coverage of the matter is admirable, but it rests wholly on the printed version of the decision by Hardwicke. However, Pope's original bill of complaint, drawn up by Murray, survives, as does Curll's reply.[11] These give a more detailed picture of the issues at stake.

The only reference I have found to these documents is that of George Sherburn, in his annotation of a letter from Pope to Ralph Allen dated 14 May 1741:

> Pope perhaps foresees the probability of a suit in Chancery against Curll for pirating the Swift–Pope letters. The suit was entered on 4 June, Curll's answer was sworn on the 14th; and the Chancellor on the 17th laid down the revolutionary decision (made for the first time in the *Pope* v. *Curll* suit) 'that a letter is not a gift to the receiver, and that he has no right to publish it.' See George Harris, *Life of Hardwicke* (1913), ii, 464. Since Curll's piracy is not now a really rare book, one assumes that its sale went on.

A few pages later, Sherburn offers a number of reasons for dating a letter to Allen (headed by Pope 14 June) '[14 July 1741]'. One of these concerns Pope's observation in the letter:

---

[6] On this subject see *Corr*, I, xi–xxv, as well as Maynard Mack, 'The First Printing of the Letters of Swift and Pope', *The Library*, IV, xix (1939), 465–85; and V. A. Dearing, 'New Light on the First Printing of the Letters of Pope and Swift', *The Library*, IV, xxiii (1943), 74–86.

[7] Although Straus has three chapters entitled 'Curll v. Pope', in *The Unspeakable Curll*, (London, 1927).

[8] John Tracy Atkins, *Reports of Cases Argued and Determined in the High Court of Chancery*, (London, 1781), II, 356–7.

[9] See for example P. C. Yorke, *The Life and Correspondence of Philip Yorke Earl of Hardwicke*, (Cambridge, 1913), II, 464.

[10] Harry Ransom, 'The Personal Letter as Literary Property', *Studies in English*, XXX (1951), 116–31. The other case discussed by Ransom is *Thompson* v. *Stanhope* (1774).

[11] Quoted by permission from the Public Record Office, C 11/1569/29.

That Rascal Curl has pyrated the Letters, which would have ruin'd half my Edition, but we have got an Injunction from my Lord Chancellor to prohibit his selling them for the future, tho doubtless he'l do it clandestinely.

Sherburn comments that Pope's Chancery suit 'was decided 17 June, and the injunction mentioned could not antedate 14 June'.[12] In fact this is inaccurate in two particulars, though Sherburn's dating of the letter may none the less be correct.

Actually, Curll's reply was sworn on 13 June, and not 14 June. Moreover, it is clear from what he says that an injunction *had* already been obtained before this time. He was indeed concerned to make his plea to the court to have the injunction lifted. Hardwicke's decision on 17 June simply embodied a refusal to dissolve the injunction, as requested by the defendant. In effect, it was renewed as the plaintiff wished. Curll's plea makes it apparent that, ostensibly anyway, he had bowed to the terms of the injunction. He had been 'stayed in the sale' after disposing of only sixteen copies out of 500 printed. Perhaps, as Pope surmised, he went on distributing the edition by clandestine means. But Sherburn's argument from the present-day situation is not wholly clinching: no order was made for the physical destruction or impounding of the books (something Pope envisaged at a similar juncture in 1735).[13] Curll did not go on advertising the edition, to the best of my knowledge. It may be that the books survived because they were left safely in a warehouse and sold off, months or years later, as remaindered stock.

The background to the suit is reasonably simple, as Pope/Curll dealings go. The offending edition was published as *Dean Swift's Literary Correspondence, for Twenty-Four Years*. It is Griffiths 534, Sherburn's '1741 Lb.' According to Straus, it appeared on 30 May 1741.[14] As regards it content: 'Curll announced this as a reprint of the Dublin edition [by Faulkner], but actually he reprinted the London quarto [by Knapton, Bathurst and Dodsley].'[15] Strangely, this subterfuge formed no part of the ensuing legal wrangle. Curll indeed proclaimed his title in the preface:

... It is well known, that the Dublin Edition of these Letters is Lawful-Prize here, and whatever we print is the same there. The safe hand to whom Dean

---

[12] *Corr*, IV, 343, 349–50. Incidentally Pope was intending to visit Murray on 28 May (IV, 345); this may indicate that Curll's piracy was already before the public and that the bill of complaint was drawn up on that day.

[13] *Corr*, 472 (Pope to Fortescue, ? 13 July 1735).   [14] Straus, p. 310.

[15] *Corr*, I, xxiv.

Swift delivered them, conveyed them safely to Us; so that all the Pretences of sending a Young Peer to go in Search of them, or the Attempts by an old Woman to suppress them, was arrant Trifling.

Unfortunately, the major contention is false.[16] But in any case the decision in Chancery was to show that the supposed common law right was a myth; and Curll's reference in his bill to 'the Practice of Booksellers in both Kingdoms' availed him nothing. It seems odd that Pope did not seek to demonstrate that the material was reprinted from the London edition, but presumably he had not realised this. In the event it was of no consequence.

One other small anomaly may be noticed. The dates of the letters, as laboriously cited in the bills, are of course those given by Pope, whether imperfectly remembered or concocted or inaccurate or not. Thus, to take a single example among many, the letter dated in his bill of complaint 14 April 1730 was so located in the printed editions; but, as Sherburn shows, it must date from around 4 March of that year.[17] In an age when the law was particularly literal-minded, it seems probable that Curll would have greatly strengthened his case if in his reply he had been able to point out these inaccuracies; but of course he could not. Such technicalities then carried a lot of weight.[18]

It remains only to summarize the main contentions on either side. Pope's bill of complaint alludes to the provisions of the Copyright Act (8 Anne, c. 19) and specifically to the first section. He claims protection not only for his own letters but also for those addressed to him by Swift. Further, he contends that Curll was well aware of the true ownership of the title. He claims that he has no redress through common law and must consequently appeal to the court of equity. He asks for Curll and his unknown associates to be interrogated as to what arrangements they have made and what profits have accrued. Pope's bill also requests that Curll should reveal how many copies of the book remain unsold in his possession. Specific penalties are not sought, other than a restraint on further distribution. Finally, Pope asks through his advocate that Curll be summoned by writ to answer the charges. There is no mention of the Irish printing.

---

[16] See Straus, p. 193: *Dean Swift's Literary Correspondence* (London, 1741), sig. 4ʳ.

[17] *Corr*, III, 95.

[18] 'The rules of pleading and of procedure were applied with rigorous precision; there was no power to allow the amendment of the most venial error. If a plaintiff spelled the defendant's name incorrectly in his process, he was non-suited', Sir F. D. MacKinnon, 'The Law and the Lawyers', *Johnson's England*, ed. A. S. Turberville (Oxford, 1933), II, 294. Pope's bill has it both ways: *Curll* and *Curl* were equally common, so Pope uses each form in turn.

Curll's reply is a mixture of bluster, injured innocence, and shrewd calculation – rather like his work at large. Much of the time he simply pleads ignorance: he does not know whether Pope has sold his copyright to anyone, and so on. He argues that the letters sent to Pope were 'not to be Considered' as the recipient's property. And he contends that such letters were not 'a work of that Nature' for which protection had been afforded by the Copyright Act. Whilst he never had any express licence to print the letters in dispute, he is advised that it was legal for him to do so, as they had been first printed in Dublin by Faulkner. Further, he points out that one third of the book consists of material written by other authors (Atterbury, Arbuthnot, *et al.*), the rights to which he had obtained through gift or purchase. He denies unlawful confederacy, as charged by Pope, and refuses to supply details of publishing arrangements or profits. He reveals only that he had 500 copies printed, of which he claims a mere sixteen had been sold. Finally, Curll asks to have the suit dismissed and to be allowed to continue the sale of the book. It is a somewhat confused defence, but not in every respect an insubstantial one.[19]

The Lord Chancellor's judgment has been cited by Ransom and need not be dwelt on here. In outline, he rejected one ground of Curll's defence totally, whilst he declined to accept another, though with some qualification. Hardwicke observed that it would be mischievous if letters passing between the learned should have no protection whatsoever from an Act designed 'for the encouragement of learning', and instanced sermons as a possibly analogous case. He considered the view that a letter is to be regarded as a gift to the receiver; but concluded that sending conferred partial ownership at most. The actual paper on which the missive was written might be looked on as an outright gift; but this did not carry with it freedom to publish the letter. The Lord Chancellor reviewed Curll's assertion that it was lawful to reprint material which had appeared in Ireland. He decided against this, too, on the grounds that an unscrupulous pirate could simply arrange for material to be published in Ireland, and would then be free to bring it out in England, with no redress

---

[19] Curll's attorney was J. Browning, possibly John Browning of Hatton Garden, gent., who was admitted to Lincoln's Inn on 24 June 1724: *Records of the Honourable Society of Lincoln's Inn* (London, 1896), I, 386. For another defence by Curll against a copyright claim, see *Knaplock v. Curll*, PRO, C 11/690/5. Curll's assertion that a third of the book consisted of material 'not before published' is demonstrably false in respect of the contributions by Arbuthnot and Wotton (pp. 229–82). See L. M. Beattie, *John Arbuthnot Mathematician and Satirist* (Cambridge, Mass., 1935), p. 194.

possible.[20] Finally, he met the objection that letters on familiar subjects are not strictly 'learned works' with the assertion that such works may none the less be of great service and value to the world. He even ventured into something like literary criticism: 'For I must confess, for my own part, that letters which are very elaborately written, and originally intended for the press, are generally the most insignificant, and very little worth any person's reading.' Ransom calls this 'paradoxical';[21] some might see the whole argument as sophistical, especially in view of Pope's careful doctoring of his correspondence. But Pope got most of what he wanted. The Lord Chancellor accepted Curll's plea that Pope had no title to the letters addressed to him. For the rest, the injunction was continued, and the edition as it stood effectively prohibited.[22]

Pope, then, obtained more satisfaction from this legal encounter than he did from many bouts with Curll, in life and in books. An important legal principle was laid down, but more than that Pope (who had earlier abjured the law) found that even so slippery a customer as Curll could be brought to order with its aid. It was all part of the professionalized way of life to which Pope committed himself in his later career.[23]

---

[20] Samuel Richardson ran into the same trouble with *Sir Charles Grandison* a decade later; the Irish printers strongly asserted their right to bring out the work in spite of the author's opposition. See Eaves and Kimpel, *Samuel Richardson: A Biography* (Oxford, 1971), pp. 378–83.

[21] Ransom, p. 121.

[22] This paragraph is based on Atkins, II, 356–7.

[23] For Pope's self-fashioning in his professional life, see David Foxon, *Pope and the Early Eighteenth-Century Book Trade* (Oxford, 1991).

CHAPTER 12

Pope and his subscribers

It is the unchallenged verdict of history that Alexander Pope achieved
a major coup for the literary profession, as well as a personal triumph,
with his ventures into the subscription market. J. W. Saunders calls
the Homer translation 'the success of the age'; while Pope's
biographer, George Sherburn, refers in the course of a few lines to the
Iliad as a 'an astonishingly successful subscription' and 'so phenomenally successful subscription' and 'so phenomenally successful an
undertaking'. Alexandre Beljame saw the Homer as a crucial
watershed in the status of authorship. Not only is the dedication to
the *Iliad* 'a very important landmark in the history of English
literature... nothing less than revolutionary'; the work itself is
interesting 'because of its brilliant financial success' and the change
of attitudes which it reflects; 'the aristocracy of birth at last paid
homage without reserve to the aristocracy of genius'. Similarly Leslie
Stephen asserted that Pope 'received a kind of commission from the
upper class to execute the translation. The list of his subscribers seems
to be almost a directory to the upper circle of the day; every person
of quality has felt himself bound to promote so laudable an
undertaking; the patron has been superseded by a kind of joint-stock
body of collective patronage.' For Stephen (and this is an important
stage in his overall argument) Pope may be seen as 'the authorized
interpreter of the upper circle, which then took itself to embody the
highest cultivation of the nation'.[1]

I do not seek to set aside this verdict. That Pope attained in a few

---

[1] J. W. Saunders, *The Profession of English Letters* (London, 1964), p. 136 (an inaccurate
account); G. Sherburn, *The Early Career of Alexander Pope* (Oxford, 1934), p. 129; A.
Beljame, *Man of Letters and the English Public in the Eighteenth Century* translated by E. O.
Lorimer (London, 1948), pp. 366–81; L. Stephen, *English Literature and Society* (London,
1904), pp. 51, 65. Sherburn provides much the fullest and most reliable information, though
his narrative is spaced out through the biography. I should like to thank Michael Treadwell
and David Foxon for useful comments on a draft of this chapter.

190

years financial independence and a different social rank, permitting intimacy with the great, is unquestionable. However, the impression left by these and other commentators is misleading in several respects. The received account exaggerates the certainty with which Pope was able to define his audience, and the ease with which he could reach his market. It overlooks important differences in the composition of his public as between the *Iliad* and the *Odyssey*, and it quite fails to reckon with the Shakespeare venture, which called out a miserably disappointing response. To describe the nature of Pope's 'success' more accurately, we need to examine much more carefully the mounting of all three subscriptions, and to analyse in detail the identity of the subscribing public.[2]

In this chapter I shall be concerned with these three ventures: that is, the *Iliad* (1715–20), the *Odyssey* (1725–6) – both published by Bernard Lintot – and the edition of Shakespeare (1725), published by Jacob Tonson. I ignore the Dublin reprint of *The Works of Shakespeare* (1726), which elicited a small and unimpressive band of subscribers,[3] and Faulkner's duodecimo edition of Pope's *Works* (Dublin, 1736).[4] Pope does not seem to have taken any active part in their mounting – no doubt a factor in their relative failure, though not a sufficient cause in itself. It is the three London productions which engaged Pope's personal interest (though the Shakespeare to a markedly lesser extent as it was undertaken for Tonson's benefit) and which serve to illuminate his relations with an identifiable audience.

The examination is conducted along two lines. First, I shall review the circumstances in which the various subscriptions were set in hand. From Pope's correspondence and other evidence, I shall consider the means utilized, the persons employed and the aims expressed, with a view to assessing Pope's own notion of his 'success'.

---

[2] Our knowledge of subscribing habits has increased in recent years, chiefly as a result of the work of the Book Subscriptions List Project at the University of Newcastle, headed by P. J. Wallis and F. J. G. Robinson. See, for a valuable summary of present knowledge, P. J. Wallis, 'Book Subscription Lists', *The Library*, XXIX (1974), 255–86. It is interesting to observe that no more than 2 per cent of the near-400 subscribers to the *Encylopédie* can be identified, which limits our knowledge of its diffusion and influence; see John Lough, *The Encyclopédie in Eighteenth-Century England* (Newcastle, 1970), pp. 105–20.

[3] This is item 163 in R. H. Griffith, *Alexander Pope: a Biography* (Austin, Tex. 1922–7), where it is misdated '1725–26' and incompletely described. The 150 subscribers included only four entered for multiple copies and there is a low correlation with other lists, even Trapp and Prior. The proportion of women is 9 per cent.

[4] This is Griffith's item 433, with 230 subscribers. As Griffith notes, Swift's name is absent from this wholly Irish list.

Secondly, I shall analyse the composition of the subscribers, according to such matters as social rank, political complexion, age, sex, and so on. The degree of overlap between the three subscription lists will be discussed. And in order to set Pope's ventures in their context, they will be compared with four other subscription books of the period: that is, volumes by Joseph Trapp, Prior, Gay and Addison, all issued between the original appearance of the *Iliad* and that of the *Odyssey*.

I

The six volumes of the *Iliad* came out in five instalments between June 1715 and May 1720. Naturally it was the lead-up to the first volume which involved the principal effort as far as subscription was concerned. This is when money had to be put down, in advance of publication. All the evidence shows that the operation was laborious, time-consuming, fraught with anxiety. Contrary to Stephen's implication, subscribers to the Homer did not fall out of heaven; for the most part, Pope had to go and get them. Or someone had to do so on his behalf. Lintot had no particular interest in assembling a large corps, other than his desire to see the book talked about; since he was to make his profits out of the separate trade edition, he might have preferred the work a *succès d'estime* which was yet poorly subscribed for. The only direct beneficiary from a long list was Pope himself. (Lintot's own editions were large ones in the event; Bowyer's ledgers show that quantities of the order of 2500 were regularly needed for both octavo and duodecimo editions, even with the competition of T. Johnson's piracies.) The case is different with the Shakespeare, but even here subscribers had to be attracted if the whole venture was not to fall flat.

Pope contracted to translate the *Iliad* on 5 October 1713; it is possible that proposals were privately circulated around this time, and by the end of the month Lord Lansdowne and Joseph Addison were writing to support the venture. On 2 November Bishop Kennett observed Swift instructing everyone in the antechamber at Windsor to subscribe, and promising that Pope should not publish until he had 'a thousand guinea for him'.[5] In fact Pope had been encouraged to

[5] *The Correspondence of Jonathan Swift*, ed. H. Williams (Oxford, 1963–5), V, 229. The major source for the narrative which follows is *Corr*, supplemented by G. Sherburn, 'Letters of Alexander Pope', *RES*, IX (1958), 388–406. References are supplied, in the form *Corr* or 'Letters', only where direct quotation is made in the text; otherwise letters mentioned can be located by their date. For the proposals, see Griffith item 22, and his correction at II, 539.

embark on the work as far back as 1708 by his elderly mentor Sir William Trumbull. The plan had borne concrete fruit in the shape of one episode, if not more, by 11 March of that year; and on 9 April – if Pope's dating can be relied on – Trumbull was urging the poet to make a complete translation of Homer, in order 'to make him speak good English'.[6] However, Pope appears not to have done any serious work on the text until the proposals were issued four years later; consequently, he had to go in quest of subscriptions at the same time as he was actually assembling his translation. The early auguries were good: by 19 November 1713 he could write to Trumbull, 'I can honestly say, Sir William Trumbull was not only the first that put this into my Thoughts, but the principal encourager I had in it, and tho' now almost all the distinguished names of Quality or Learning in the nation have subscribed to it, there is not one of which I am so proud of as of Yours. Even if I should not succeed in my Undertaking, it were honour enough to me that Such Persons were of opinion I was equal to it, or at least not less equal to it than others.' There follows a significant passage:

My Friends here have pushd this matter with so much Earnestness, that Proposals in writing have been deliverd into all the chief hands even before I cou'd inform you I had ingaged. For they sett the matter upon this foot, that unless They raise me such a certain number of Subscriptions, as may make so great & laborious a Work absolutely worth my while, I shall not be obliged to undertake it. Nor am I to begin till this is performed, nor any Proposals made publick, so as to depend upon the Town in generall, till then. I am to make it my Request to your Good nature that you'll please engage what number of your Acquaintance you can best make to this Subscription. and I believe I do not flatter my self in thinking the number very great of those who wou'd make it their Vanity or pleasure to gratify Sir William Trumbull.[7]

It is not known what the 'certain number' or cut-off point of subscriptions was. However, the private list ultimately seems to have been inadequate, for Pope emphatically did need to 'depend upon the Town in generall' to fill out his list. Pope's uncertainty as to whether it will even be worth his while to start at all suggests that Stephen and others have overstated the urgency of the 'commission'. Trumbull wrote back on 21 November, assuring Pope of his 'Zeal to promote his Interest' and readiness to pass on proposals to his

[6] *Corr*, I, 45.   [7] 'Letters', 398.

friends.[8] In that quarter at least Pope could count on firm support, dispensed as it was in the accents of traditional patronage.

A lighter tone prevails in Pope's letter to Swift, written from Binfield on 8 December and announcing *inter alia* completion of the revised *Rape of the Lock*. Swift had jokingly offered Pope twenty guineas to renounce his Catholicism; the letter refers to Pope's success in gaining the support of Lord Halifax and other Whigs for his Homeric venture. He then compiles a witty mock subscription list for the redemption of other heretics and free-thinkers, from Dryden and L'Estrange to Gay and Jervas. Through the badinage one senses Pope's anxiety to achieve a spectacularly successful body of patrons for his translation. A week later he reminds John Caryll, who was to be his principal agent in promoting the scheme, how important it is to proceed with expedition:

> I say nothing to you of the affair of my subscriptions for Homer, since I am sure in my dependence on the utmost of your interest. I would recommend the promoting it with what speed is convenient, since I know the danger there is of letting an affair of this nature cool too much. As to the task it self I am about to undertake, I confess I begin to tremble at it; it is really so great an one, that a disappointment in the subscription will not occasion me any great mortification, considering how much of life I am to sacrifice if it succeeds.[9]

Sherburn annotates this passage perceptively: 'Pope seems not to have begun intensive work on the translation until the success of the subscription was assured.' The poet was wary of committing himself finally until his list began to take shape. In other words, he was uncertain of his audience right up to the time he began composition.

As the New Year of 1714 set in, Pope's energies remained in the promotional side of his work. On 9 January he thanked Caryll for help as a 'solictour', adding the further request that

> you will send me the subscriptions by the first sitting of the parliament 18 February at which time it will be necessary to know exactly what number we have secure, – there being then to be printed a list of those who have already subscribed or shall to that time: upon the Credit and figure of which persons a great part of the success with the town will inevitably depend.[10]

However, things were looking more 'secure' by now, for Pope could finish by saying, 'I now think it is pretty certain, that I shall be warmly supported on all sides in this undertaking.' For this he had to

---

[8] 'Letters', 399.   [9] *Corr*, I, 204.   [10] *Corr*, I, 207.

thank as well as Caryll his original patron, Trumbull. A letter of 12 January testifies to Pope's continuing obligation, and mentions Pope's hopes of gaining valuable new contacts – Lord Weymouth, who was not to subscribe, and Richard Hill, a retired diplomat who was a friend and neighbour of Charles Jervas and duly took an *Iliad* set.[11] By 26 February Pope had been introduced to Hill, and this was one of many favours in connection with the project which Pope acknowledged to Trumbull. In the same letter he described the way of life his venture was imposing upon him: 'This Subscription having forced me upon many Appointments, Visits, & Tavern-Conversation, which as little agree with my Nature & Inclination, as with my Constitution.'[12] In his reply Trumbull, always solicitous regarding Pope's health, begged him to 'get out of all Tavern-company, and fly away *tanquam ex incendio*'. The old man had heard that as regards Homer, Pope's 'business was done', and he could therefore afford a holiday.[13] But the truth was that Pope was still actively engaged in preparing his list of certainties in order to woo the indecisive. On 25 February he asked Caryll to send him

a list of every person who has actually paid you his subscription, or whom you can engage for, on his promise to pay you; for I must print a catalogue of all who have already subscribed in a very *short time*, and it would be of equal ill consequence either to omit any that have paid, or add any that have not. I wait only for these names to send the catalogue to the press.[14]

The passage indicates how chancy an affair the whole subscribing business was. Names were entered on vague promises or casual report, at least in certain cases, and it was by no means unknown for one individual to put down the name of a friend without the other's knowledge – this happened with Pope and Swift in the matter of posthumous John Hughes collection of 1735.[15] Caryll did not immediately comply with the request made on 25 February, and Pope had to repeat it on 12 March. This must have achieved the desired effect, for a week later Pope thanked Caryll for his diligence: 'I think you have been very successful in procuring so many, and too kind in listing so many out of your own family.' The letter goes on:

I must own, many of the names in the catalogue I shall exhibit, are of so great figure, that I should not be much mortified even if I failed in my

[11] For Hill, see A. Coyle Lunn, 'A New Pope Letter', *RES*, XXIV (1973), 310–15.
[12] 'Letters', 4.   [13] *Corr*, I, 212.   [14] *Corr*, I, 210.
[15] *Correspondence of Swift*, IV, 382–3, 400. For a subscription by Swift on behalf of an unknowing acquaintance, this time to Prior's volume, see his *Correspondence*, II, 274–5.

attempt; while posterity would see at least, if I was no good poet, I was the happiest poet that ever appeared upon record, in the good opinion of such a number of such persons.[16]

The tone is significantly different from that of his letter to Caryll on 15 December previously. His confidence is growing, and he sees the eminence of his patrons as a support or even a challenge, rather than as a burden of impossible expectations. Around the same time he was thanking Trumbull for supplying another useful contact (Sir Clement Cottrell, later a close friend of the poet, and more relevantly here an inveterate book-subscriber). Other certainties are recorded, and further chasing-up narrated.

By now all the signs were favourable. On 23 March Pope and Lintot signed their agreement; as Sherburn remarks, the terms were exceptionally favourable to the poet, and this suggests that the success of the venture looked secure – so much so that Lintot could offer unprecedented rewards, and Tickell and Tonson could imagine that there was enough demand for a rival version. On 19 April Pope wrote to enlist further support, this time for the poet and musician John Hughes; he enclosed proposals for the learned woollen draper William Pate, but unlike Prior and Addison he failed to get a subscription from Pate. On the same day he composed a jaunty letter to Caryll, mentioning his new facility as a writer of receipts, and once more thanking Caryll for his contribution – according to Elwin, thirty-eight names were drummed up by this agency, whilst Dr Erskine-Hill's more recent estimate is twenty.[17] But if there were helpers, there were also – so Pope believes – persons deliberately blocking his venture: in a letter dated 8 June 1714, probably to Caryll, he accused Ambrose Philips of keeping a hold on subscriptions paid to him (Philips) as secretary of the Hanover Club, by members of that Whig organization. There seems to be no evidence to establish the truth of this accusation. However, it is certain that at least twelve members of the club did subscribe, including Addison and Steele but not Philips; against this, seven or eight names are missing which do appear on the *Odyssey* list. It was not to be expected that Pope should achieve the blanket Hanoverian coverage that Addison could look for.[18]

[16] *Corr*, I, 215.
[17] *Corr*, I, 219: H. Erskine-Hill, *The Social Milieu of Alexander Pope* (New Haven, Conn., 1975), p. 78.
[18] *Corr*, I, 229. After the publication of the first volume, Jervas wrote to Pope, 'Philips sent me a Note for Receipts to be conveyed to the 11 Members of the late Hanover Club', apparently

The new proposals, garnished with subscribers to date, came out in the middle of May.[19] It is a pity that no copy is known to be extant, for it would be exceedingly interesting to know how many (and which) of the ultimate list were already safely in the bag. A tiny minority can be identified as bound to be present, in that they died before May 1714 and can hardly have been added at any subsequent date. Otherwise we have no clue as to the scale of the subscription by this date, a year before the first volume was published. There are signs that an effort may have been mounted at this point to widen the geographical basis of the list, previous efforts having concentrated on the metropolis. Jervas, we know, spoke to the Whig magnate, the Duke of Devonshire, 'to join Lord Wharton's interest & move your affair, that we may set 'em agoing About the Counties'.[20] Not for the first time, the language suggests electioneering and headcounting at the polls, rather than a literary enterprise. In the end there was a good sprinkling of knights of the shire and provincial gentry on the *Illiad* – rather more indeed than on the later lists.

With the project well mounted, Pope could take a more relaxed attitude towards it. He wrote to Caryll on 29 June that it was not the least of his designs

in proposing this subscription, to make some trial of my friends on all sides. I vow to you, I am very happy in the search (contrary to most people who make trials), for I find I have at least six Tory friends, three Whig friends and two Roman Catholic friends; with many others of each who at least will do me no harm. I have discovered two dangerous enemies whom I must have trusted; besides innumerable malevoli, whom I will not honour so far as to suppose they can hurt any body. They say, 'tis in the conduct of life as in that of picquette, one shows most skill in the discarding part of the game.[21]

It is not hard to discern beneath the persiflage an element of serious self-inquiry: the editor of Pope's correspondence actually surmises on the identity of those mentioned. More generally, one perceives that the young poet really was able to use the *Iliad* subscription to take stock of his career: to estimate how far he had arrived, to sort our varying reactions in his audience, to get a line on his own ambiguous situation in politics and religion. To that extent it is fair to see the

those Philips had held up (*Corr*, I, 296). Evidently one of those on my count of members had subscribed directly or through some agency other than the club. See also Spence, I, 71.
[19] A copy of the proposals was also attached to the third edition of *The Rape of the Lock* – see Griffith item 35. According to the *Monthly Catalogue* this edition came out in May 1714.
[20] *Corr*, I, 226. In the final outcome perhaps 350–400 *Iliad* subscribers lived in London (including those who had a separate establishment elsewhere).   [21] *Corr*, I, 233.

attempt to win subscribers as an effort partly to *define* an audience, so as to create one, it is not a question of Pope's simply reaching out for an existing, foreknown public.

As the summer progressed, Pope found himself 'wholly employed upon Homer', and for the first time translation rather than subscription-seeking was the activity commonly so designated. After the Queen's death in August he paid a short visit from Binfield to Oxford, and doubtless put out feelers among the resident members. In a letter to Jervas at this time, Pope singles out among the services performed for him by Swift those done 'in relation to the subscription for *Homer*'.[22] How successful were the efforts to browbeat the court into subscription, as witnessed by Bishop Kennett the previous November, it is difficult to be sure. According to Kennett's account, on the same occasion Swift had buttonholed the Earl of Arran to speak to the Duke of Ormonde about a place for Richard Fiddes – Arran and Ormonde were on the list in 1715 but Fiddes (who subscribed to the Addison volume) was not. Again, Swift intercepted Francis Gwynne, who figures in the *Odyssey* subscribers, as in those of Gay and Prior, but not in the *Iliad*. His most officious act, as reported by Kennett, concerned Henry Davenant; and here there was more direct success, since Davenant took a set of both Homeric translations in due course. One gets the impression that Swift's enthusiasm for the cause was short-lived, but it is likely that his forceful promotion had something to do with the strong representation of the Harley family, amongst others, in Pope's list.[23]

At this politically sensitive time, the most significant item of assistance was provided by another Scriblerian colleague, John Gay. In June Gay had gone out to Hanover with a mission led by the Earl of Clarendon, and had made the acquaintance of the electoral Prince and Princess (later George II and Queen Caroline). His own works had gone down well at Herrenhausen, and he took the opportunity to push Pope's subscription. The results are chronicled in a letter to Charles Ford on 7 August (as New Style dates were current in

---

[22] *Corr*, I, 245.

[23] Much later Swift wrote to Pope that he had told the second Earl of Oxford he 'had no credit to get one Subscriber for Mr Samuel Wesley', except for himself. Pope had written supporting Oxford's plea on behalf of Wesley's *Dissertationes in librum Jobi*, for which proposals went out in 1729 and which appeared posthumously in 1736. See *Corr*, I, 504. At what date Swift began to doubt his capacities as a subscription-monger is not clear; by February 1731 he was again speaking confidently of extracting 'obedience' – Swift, *Correspondence*, III, 440.

Europe, this would be four days before Queen Anne's death): 'the Princess and Countess of Picbourg have both subscrib'd to Pope's Homer, and her Highness did me the Honour to say, she did not doubt it would be well done, since I recommended it'.[24] It is significant that Pope obtained this intensely coveted name – the only royal subscription to the *Iliad* – not on his own merits but on those of Gay. He had, quite simply, no contacts with the incoming regime, and it would be quite wrong to deduce from the presence of Prince Caroline any positive Hanoverian coloration to his public.

For the next few months we are able to catch only fleeting hints as to how the subscription was progressing. At the beginning of October Pope wrote to Ford of a certain Dr Elwood, and asked that Swift should 'do that business'.[25] Swift knew Elwood, a Fellow of Trinity College, Dublin, and Pope was hoping to widen his clientele in Dublin through this agency. In the event, his hopes were largely unrealized: the Irish presence is anything but strong in the *Iliad* list, as will appear later. Another possible promoter, so Pope may have hoped, was Addison; but again there is little concrete evidence to suggest help was forthcoming. William Broome managed to prevail on 'Sir Robert [? Cotton]' to enter his name, and this induced Pope to ask Broome if he could 'procure me any of the Cambridge colleges to subscribe for their libraries'.[26] Yet again the result was a failure. Oxford colleges were to supply ten subscriptions to the *Iliad*, its sister university none. In general Cambridge proved stickier to those touting subscriptions; even Matthew Prior, who obtained a large number of Cambridge men as individual subscribers, could do virtually nothing with the college libraries. Nevertheless, Pope must have been disappointed to draw a complete blank, and made renewed efforts when the *Odyssey* was being mounted. Broome continued to turn up the odd name for the list, most valuably Lord Cornwallis, and for this Pope returned mild gratitude.

By the end of 1714 the first volume was seemingly ready for the press, if not indeed printed. A newspaper advertisement on Christmas Day promised that the date of publication, scheduled for May 1715, would be advanced by two months. In the event this did not happen, but the announcement does indicate that the volume was well forward. Moreover, a letter to Halifax on 3 December 1714 can be taken to mean that an advance copy had been sent to the peer, whilst

[24] *The Letters of John Gay*, ed. C. F. Burgess (Oxford, 1966), p. 12.   [25] *Corr*, I, 259.
[26] *Corr*, I, 266.

the Duke of Chandos acknowledged such a copy on 9 January 1715. This last was a 'present' from Simon Harcourt, one of those most active among Pope's friends in pushing the subscription, and was surely meant as reminder to Chandos. If so, the ploy worked. Chandos promptly asked to be put down for ten copies; in the printed list he is actually credited with twelve. A munificent patron of all forms of art and – until his later years – an almost ubiquitous name on subscription lists, Chandos was to be entered for no fewer than fifty copies of Gay's poems in 1720. Such flamboyant gestures often represented an outright gift to the author, and at the same time they constituted blows in a battle of competing patronage (the Earl of Burlington also scored fifty for Gay). It is therefore important not to misinterpret or overvalue multiple subscriptions: they commonly tell us more about the subscriber than about the subscribed for. The absence of Chandos would certainly have been conspicuous when the *Iliad* came out, and Harcourt's 'present' may be written off against the expenses of promotion. One advantage to Chandos was that it gave him a handy stock of gifts to be used as political *douceurs*: a copy of the fourth volume of the *Iliad* (1718) was presented to the King's mistress, Madam Kielmansegg, as part of the campaign to gain a dukedom. It is a warning against ascribing motives too undistractedly literary to the persons we encounter on a list of subscribers.[27]

Eventually copies of Volume I of the *Iliad* went out on 6 June. Lintot undertook most of the actual distribution,[28] although subscribers who had a complaint were likely to contact Pope himself. Such an individual was Edward Young, who had evidently agreed to circulate the copies due to Oxford libraries, and found himself allotted one too few. Gift copies were still being presented – the Duke of Rutland got at least one more than his published entitlement, Lord (Carr) Hervey was given one apparently without subscribing, and other notable figures received the volume while still in default on their payment. A number of discrepancies had to be cleared up between Lintot and Pope, and overall it is apparent that Pope was not always clear who had subscribed and who had not. Those who had paid were sometimes left off the list by inadvertence: this happened with Richard Hill's nephew Samuel. It emerges from the

---

[27] For Chandos as patron, see C. H. Collins Baker and Muriel I. Baker, *The Life and Circumstances of James Brydges First Duke of Chandos* (Oxford, 1949), especially pp. 68–9, 112; and Samuel Johnson, *Life of Savage*, ed. C. Tracy (Oxford 1971), p. 103.

[28] This is clear from Lintot's letter of 10 June (*Corr*, I, 295), though it conflicts with statements sometimes made on the point.

surrounding correspondence that Pope's dealings with much of his 'audience' had been vague, fitful and slight.[29]

With the publication of Volume I, Pope's labours as translator had scarcely begun; but his activities as a promoter were now very much reduced. His original task had been to identify and capture an audience. This had been achieved, and although it would be going too far to say that the subscription could be left to look after itself, Pope certainly put the best of his mind elsewhere. Of course, subscribers had been required to put down only two guineas, and could in theory renege on their further commitment of four guineas. But few seem to have done this. As the successive volumes came out (in March 1716, June 1717, June 1718, the last two together in May 1720), each attended after a short interval by Lintot's trade edition, a fresh bout of controversy arose concerning Pope's qualifications and performance as a translator. If Pope's project had been carefully mounted, so the opposition campaign betrays signs of deliberate orchestration. Not only the content of the *Iliad*, but even Pope's advertisements, were burlesqued; what J. V. Guerinot calls 'the first collective attempt to discredit Pope' began 'well before Pope had even published his translation'.[30] It was commonly argued that Lintot had burnt his hands through his involvement in the Homer, but no one dared to suggest that Pope had not done very well out of the subscription money.

Whilst this noisy campaign was in progress, the patrons themselves remained silent but loyal. Very occasionally we hear of a defaulter. Around 1717 Pope was asking for the return of copies of Volume I which had not been paid for; these were 'wanted for some new subscribers, no more having been printed than were Subscribed for at first'.[31] Presumably the printing of subscribers' copies for future volumes took account of this new demand. At the same period Pope forwarded Volume III through Jervas to twelve Irish subscribers obtained by Dr Elwood; these represented the core of Pope's very disappointing Irish contingent. In Oxford his agent was now Dr Abel

---

[29] Copies shipped to Ireland were likely to be tardy in arriving. Swift reported that 'some people complain for want of Mr Pope's 2 last Volumes of Homer' (Swift, *Correspondence*, II, 381) – and this in April 1721, eleven months after the publication of the fifth and sixth volumes. Pope sent Broome a complimentary copy of the first volume apparently in November 1715, five months after publication – Elizabeth Arlidge, 'A New Pope Letter', *RES*, XII (1961), 398–402.

[30] J. V. Guerinot, *Pamphlet Attacks on Alexander Pope* (London, 1969), p. xxii.

[31] *Corr*, I, 420.

Evans, who apparently had to supply individual subscribers as well as the ten college libraries, and who found Lintot reluctant to forward copies where money was outstanding. Another problem was posed by the exiled Bolingbroke: his neglected wife used the printer John Barber as an intermediary in an attempt to obtain Volume III despite (almost certainly) a lapse in the subscription.[32] Nevertheless, there are few such difficulties reported, and the second and third 'calls' passed off in a surprisingly smooth manner. Once men and women were visibly committed, in conspicuous print at the head of a famous volume, they were reluctant to withdraw their support.

A new subscription was, however, a different matter; and when Pope embarked on his translation of the *Odyssey* in 1723 he was forced, in many respects, to start all over again. It is true that he was now much more famous than he had been a decade earlier. The appearance of his collected poems in 1717 had marked the culmination of his early career; the non-stop hum of comment and criticism upon his *Iliad* had ensured everything he wrote from this time onwards attracted maximum publicity. Long before the war with the dunces, Pope's fame had extended well beyond the narrow circle of polite literature. Not all this exposure was to his advantage: his involvement in publishing the works of Buckingham (1723) was soon followed by his appearance on behalf of Atterbury in the House of Lords. Both these were potential embarrassments from the point of view of those soliciting *Odyssey* subscriptions. In any case, as I shall document in due course, the *Iliad* audience was beginning to fragment through the onset of old age and death, not to mention the dispersal of Jacobite sympathizers following fresh reversals almost every year. Perhaps the factors pro and con roughly balanced one another. In the end Pope was probably glad to increase his subscribers by more than thirty, as compared with the *Iliad*, while the number of copies subscribed for went up by almost 200 – the larger sprinkling of multiple copies is a marked feature of the *Odyssey* list.[33] The more concentrated publishing programme may have been an asset here.

---

[32] In fact Lady Bolingbroke had herself been listed separately among the original subscribers. She died not long afterwards, on 25 October 1718 – an event hastened, Swift apparently thought, by her husband's association with the Marquise de Villette (Swift, *Correspondence*, II, 308). The Marquise in 1720 became Bolingbroke's second wife and appears under her own name in the *Odyssey* list.

[33] There were some 55 multiple subscriptions to the *Odyssey*, ranging from 2 to 10 copies. 15 multiple subscribers to the *Iliad* yielded only 78 additional copies among them. By contrast Gay's 43 multiple subscribers (out of 365) were responsible for around 240 extra copies.

Pope had at first intended to issue proposals around Michaelmas 1722, so as to have the opening batch of six books published in a single volume about March 1723. As the year elapsed Pope's thinking changed, and by 22 November 1723 he was informing his collaborator Broome that it was not a 'ripe' time to put the proposals to the public. In a world 'much heated by politics and plots' Pope's connection with Jacobite scandals prompted understandable caution. According to Sherburn, 'The public campaign for subscribers was exasperatingly postponed', and the same editor cites a newspaper item of 9 March 1723, twenty-two months before the proposals were actually appeared on 25 January 1725.[34] Again an interim list of subscribers seems to have been compiled to accompany the proposals, and again it is lost. What does survive is the agreement between Pope and Lintot, signed on 18 February 1724, and once more permitting Lintot his own edition a week after the 750 copies for Pope's benefit had been delivered.[35] This time there was a complication in the shape of the collaborating team, Fenton and Broome; but the agreement does not acknowledge them. In the event, one of the many disagreements occasioned by the collaboration centred on subscription volumes. Lintot seems to have resented supplying a free copy to subscribers obtained by Broome, and indeed on one interpretation of the agreement only Pope was entitled to such copies. But Pope, confident in his case, had Fortescue to advise him, and the fourteen subscribers Broome is known to have obtained[36] (as against Fenton's none) doubtless qualified for the official set. Further trouble arose when Lintot advertised his own edition as a cheaper subscription venture. Moreover Lintot would allow *his* subscribers to pay for the second instalment (Volumes IV and V) on delivery, where Pope again required a sort of running hire purchase in advance. As Sherburn says, 'Of course Lintot's "subscription" was merely an unscrupulous advertisement of his trade edition', and so it has nothing properly to do with the subscription proper.[37] The terms in which Lintot couches his announcement do nevertheless give some indication of the standing which this mode of publication had acquired.

We know little of the way in which Pope managed to augment his

---

[34] *Corr*, II, 164.   [35] Reproduced by Sherburn, *Early Career*, pp. 313–16.

[36] *Corr*, II, 293.

[37] Sherburn, *Early Career*, p. 257, where the most reliable survey of the *Odyssey* subscription is to be found.

list. At the outset he wrote to Lord Harley of his determination 'to push the subscription', requesting his lordship 'to do me all the good you can... with the Town, particularly to take the enclosed paper with you to the House of Commons' (the paper may or may not be the formal proposals).[38] He soon enlisted the help of Mrs Caesar, wife of the amiable Jacobite, and to good effect too: by 10 September 1723 she had evidently fixed on twelve subscribers, and by the following April five more. As well as members of the Caesar family this group may well have contained several Cowpers – five are listed, not counting Mrs Caesar's friend Judith, who married Martin Madan at the end of 1723. After his experiences with the *Iliad*, Pope was looking for someone with a strong interest in Cambridge. With affected unconcern he tried out on Broome the name of Dr Andrew Snape, Provost of King's. This does not seem to have yielded results, though Snape himself was to subscribe, and in November 1724 Pope took a more direct tack when writing to Broome:

I received the names of your subscribers, and wish you could have procured more of the colleges in Cambridge, for the honour of the matter, since those of Oxford are much forwarder in this affair.[39]

In the end four Cambridge colleges obliged (St John's, King's, Clare Hall and Trinity Hall), with the Oxford battalion now up to thirteen. Only a handful of Cambridge senior members joined Snape on the list. Pope never properly penetrated Cambridge; his lack of influence with the Duke of Somerset, Chancellor of the University virtually all his lifetime, cannot have helped.[40]

On this occasion Pope had no cause to fear defaulting on the part of his subscribers. Again the price was one guinea a volume, but three guineas were to be put down at the time of subscription and the remaining two on delivery of Volumes I–III – that is, before any dissatisfaction with the performance could make itself felt. The first three volumes duly appeared in the middle of April 1725 (Pope's first advertisement occurs on 13 April), with an edition on sale to the general public at the end of the month. There are 572 names listed, two fewer than the *Iliad* had captured, but 37 more were added when

---

[38] *Corr*, II, 156–7: the extent of Pope's obligations to the second Earl of Oxford (as he had then become) emerges from a letter written in December 1724 (*Corr*, II, 275–6), together with the Earl's reply (II, 277). Oxford was puzzled by Pope's unusual procedure in printing the subscribers to hand with his proposals.   [39] *Corr*, II, 271.

[40] It is fair to add that Somerset – Chancellor from 1689 to 1748 – did subscribe to both Homers, as well as to Prior; but Pope never came at all close to this aloof Whig grandee.

Volumes IV and V went out in mid-June 1726. These were presented as inadvertent omissions, and must have included such cases along with a few late entrants.[41] At the head of the 1725 list stood the King and the Prince and Princess of Wales. The King in particular was not a regular subscriber to works of any kind (whether or not from a hatred of books and painting), and it was a real *coup* to have enlisted his support. This was a prelude to the grant of £200 from the Civil List on 29 April 1725, 'as his Matys Encouragement to the Work... of Translating the Odysses of Homer into English Verse'. Carteret may have been instrumental in obtaining this 'encouragement', as Sherburn indicates; but Walpole, as ultimate Treasury paymaster, must have approved. A record of the transaction survives among the Prime Minister's papers.

Otherwise the most interesting feature of the catalogue is the special star awarded to Mrs Caesar, whose name is printed in capitals for further prominence. As Pope put it, he had 'made a Star of Mrs Caesar, as well as Mrs Fermor',[42] a usage which unwittingly anticipates the modern vernacular sense of 'star', identified in *OED* as a nineteenth-century theatrical coinage. Sherburn reports that a receipt survives, signed by Pope on 20 February 1725, covering no less than seventy subscriptions obtained by Mrs Caesar. Between April 1724 and that date she had evidently secured a total of more than fifty, an outstanding feat of promotion conducted, one may suppose, entirely amongst influential sections of society. Lord Harcourt, whose personal commitment ran to ten copies, seems to have played some part in pushing the affair, as his son (now dead) had done with the *Iliad*. Chandos, whose wings had been somewhat clipped by the South Sea Bubble, restricted himself to a modest ten on this occasion. Another multiple subscriber was Lord Townshend, whose town-house in Cleveland Court stood immediately adjacent to that of Jervas, the distribution-centre for subscription copies. (Pope would advertise the availability of his book and those entitled to sets would then make their own arrangements for collection, normally by sending a footman; highly favoured persons only, it seems, had their copies sent unbidden.) Gift copies were again presented, in some cases to individuals who were listed in the subscription – presumably they were simply let off payment. How many such 'free' sets were allowed it is impossible to be certain, as is the extent of Pope's

[41] See Pope's comment to Caryll, *Corr*, II, 299.
[42] *Corr*, II, 293, where Sherburn's comment is found (n. 2).

occasional rigging of the books (as undoubtedly happened in the case of Caryll).[43]

At the same time Pope was engaged in a separate enterprise, the edition of Shakespeare. This was carried out in a more half-hearted way, for the obvious reason that Pope this time received an outright fee ($£217$) for his editorial labours. Press advertisements indicated that the subscription was for Jacob Tonson's own benefit. Therefore, in Sherburn's words, 'it was not expected that Pope and his friends would solicit subscribers, and consequently the list is somewhat less distinguished than that prefixed to the *Iliad* or to the *Odyssey*'.[44] (Though Pope did once write to Tonson of 'putting you down as a Receiver of the Subscriptions for me',[45] and it has been suspected that some at least of the subscription money came to Pope.) The official version was certainly not calculated to entice the public or to gain the goodwill of the trade, for Tonson's claim to perpetual copyright in Shakespeare aroused a good deal of resentment. Mist's *Weekly Journal* for 20 March 1725 alludes to the arrangement, and manages to insert a sly reference to Pope's collaborators on the *Odyssey*:

I am very well inform'd, that the Benefits of this extravagant Subscription are not design'd for the ingenious Gentleman who revises the Work; nay, he has himself publickly declar'd it, and, indeed, he had Merit of his own to support him; and, I believe, would scorn to take in Subscriptions for the Labours of another. – As to the Bookseller, if he should be pleas'd to give us a more correct Edition of *Shakespear* than has yet been printed, we should be oblig'd to him, provided it was at a reasonable Price; and tho' he should pay handsomely for revising it, the Thing it self would reward him in the Sale.[46]

The price of this edition (five guineas for the six volumes, with a down payment of three guineas) seemed high to many observers, and this must have been one of the factors against it success.

Pope began work on Shakespeare during the latter part of 1720 or the first half of 1721. He was busy with the task intermittently

---

[43] *Corr*, II, 299; see also Buckley (II, 286) and Aikman (II, 294). Townshend, like Walpole, may have been credited with the ten volumes in return for the Treasury grant of £200.

[44] *Early Career*, p. 240. As with the other undertaking. Sherburn is particularly good on the financial side; he does not concern himself with the recruitment drive itself.

[45] *Corr*, II, 286. In this letter Pope may well be referring to his statement in the *Odyssey* proposals that the Shakespeare subscription 'belongs wholly to Mr Tonson' ('Testimonies of Authors' in *The Dunciad*, in *TE*, V, 31). The implication is that Tonson was trying to make the public believe that Pope was to share in the profit of the Shakespeare venture. I owe this point to Mr David Foxon, who further suggests that an active campaign *against* the Tonson subscription may have been mounted by the promoter of the *Odyssey*.

[46] Quoted by Sherburn, *Early Career*, p. 242.

throughout 1722 and 1723. On 31 October 1724 he could report, 'Shakespeare is finished. I have just written the preface, and in less than three weeks it will be public.'[47] But the delays attendant on book-making were predictably to follow. Advance copies (or proofs?) of the preface were circulated to noble friends at the end of the year. On 18 November Tonson advertised the edition as 'very near finish'd', and named 16 December as the cut-off date for subscriptions, after which the price would be raised by a guinea. A list of subscribers to date was printed, but it was disappointing enough for Tonson on 18 January 1725 to extend the deadline to 10 February. Delivery was now scheduled for the end of February, but it was 12 March before the promise was fulfilled. George Sewell's supplementary volume containing the poems was issued concurrently, but had to be bought separately.

Sherburn summarizes the fortunes of this edition as follows: 'Ultimately 411 subscribers took 417 copies of the six volumes. According to Dr Johnson 750 sets were printed, and of these 140 remained unsold in 1767 when they brought only 16s. each instead of five guineas. These statements (if authentic) hardly indicate the low regard for Pope's editing that Johnson asserts; they rather indicate a preference for the octavo and duodecimo editions which followed the quarto during the years 1728–35.'[48] This argument is less than fully convincing. We do not have detailed sales figures for the octavo or duodecimo sets. One thing we do know is that Sir Thomas Hanmer's six-volume edition of 1744 in quarto succeeded remarkably well. Six hundred sets were printed, sixteen of these were given away as presents, and the remaining 584 quickly disposed of – almost all within the year. 'The selling out of an edition in so short a time as three years is without precedent in the history of the Delegates' publishing.' Hanmer and nine heads of houses had taken unequal quotas and obtained their own subscribers (not listed in the volumes).[49] Tonson undoubtedly had far more trouble to get his quarto set off his hands, and the dubious critical reception enjoyed by Pope's Shakespeare was matched by an indifferent public response. The subscription is lower in quality as well as quantity; there are far

---

[47] *Corr*, II, 270.   [48] *Early Career*, pp. 240–1.

[49] Harry Carter, *A History of the Oxford University Press: Volume 1, to the Year 1780* (Oxford, 1975), pp. 301–5. Note also: 'Hanmer's Shakespeare was much to the taste of the age. The price of a second-hand copy had risen by 1763 to £10, while Pope's edition was sold off in 1767 for 16s' (p. 304).

fewer multiple subscriptions, even Chandos for once sinking to a bare two,[50] and the social register is inferior in every respect. Not only did Pope's previously loyal subscribers abstain in large numbers (only about 7·5 per cent of the original *Iliad* list survive), he lost the support of regular names who grace almost every serious subscription in this period. Hanmer, curiously, was one such absentee; so was Edward Young, who appears on most of the big literary subscriptions at the time. (Both appear, for example, in the undistinguished list for Savage's *Miscellaneous Poems and Translations* in 1726.) The clientele was younger than that for the Homer, which may again suggest that Pope had lost some of his established audience. Whilst not a total flop, the Shakespeare promotion can only be considered deeply disappointing in view of the editor's fame and his earlier success in these ventures. Theobald, one might add, attracted 428 subscribers for his Shakespeare, eight years later, with almost 500 copies entered for.

The interim conclusions prompted by this narrative can now be stated. In my view Pope started out with a hazy sense of whom he might be reaching with the *Iliad*, and embarked on his venture with many doubts as to its feasibility. Of course, we must not confuse subscribers with readers; nevertheless, if Pope had been aware of an established reading public, he would surely have mounted the subscription with entire confidence. As it was, he had to work hard to achieve the kind of list he wanted. Again with the *Odyssey* he had to set up a long and energetic campaign to get his subscribers, often from a wholly new quarter. He was glad to utilize the help of friends where he could. Moreover, he made every effort to use his most distinguished and best-placed acquaintances to secure further subscribers: it was not the bare name of Lord Harley he wanted on the list, but that nobleman's active promotion. Even when Pope himself became famous, he could not rely on his own prominence to swing everything his way. The work advertised by Tonson as 'Mr Pope's Edition of Shakespear' fared really quite badly; the subscription was left to take care of itself, as far as Pope went, and the outcome was a relative failure. In short, the evidence assembled thus far points to the view that Pope's audience was initially ill-defined, not wholly dependable, dissimilar in the case of different works, and required very much to be wooed. This is not the traditional picture.

[50] Several habitual multiple subscribers, where they were present at all, entered their name for a single set only. No one took more than three sets (George Bubb Dodington among them): even Trapp did better than this.

II

In order to set Pope's ventures in context, as stated earlier, I have used four 'controls', that is well-known subscriptions mounted for prominent literary men during the same period. The results of these comparisons are tabulated in various ways, though it should be emphasized that their aim is to produce suggestive facts rather than strict statistical findings. The total for each list is rounded off, which produces exactly 5000 subscriptions for all seven lists. The most popular item with the subscribing public among these controls was Matthew Prior's folio *Poems on Several Occasions* ('1718' for 1719). Indeed, with 1446 names on the list it ranks among the top seven pre-1801 subscriptions recorded by P. J. Wallis.[51] Joseph Trapp's translation of the *Aeneid of Virgil*, Volumes I (1718) and II (1720), runs to 620, including a separate list of 68 Irish subscribers.[52] John Gay's *Poems on Several Occasions* (1720), a joint production of Tonson and Lintot, contains only 365 names, but as will appear they constitute a distinguished list. Finally, Thomas Tickell's posthumous collection of *The Works of Joseph Addison* (1721) has 980 subscribers. These were all larger than average ventures (the median is around 250) and the books attracted wide publicity. Gay's biographer says that 'his list of subscribers rivals any of the famous successes of the time',[53] while Prior's list has been stated to include 'the names of most of those who were celebrated in the social, political and literary life of the time'.[54] Pope, incidentally, subscribed himself to three of the controls but not to Trapp. The books concerned went out to subscribers about the following dates: Prior, by 17 March 1719; Gay, 14 July 1720; Addison, by 3 October 1721 (Trapp not determined).[55]

[51] Wallis, 'Book Subscription Lists', p. 5.
[52] I discussed Trapp's ventures in 'Book Subscriptions among the Augustans', *TLS*, 15 December 1972, pp. 1539–40, but on that occasion omitted the Irish list from the discussion. For the purposes of this chapter I have included the Irish contingent.
[53] W. H. Irving, *John Gay Favourite of the Wits* (Durham, NC, 1940), pp. 177–8.
[54] Francis Bickley, *The Life of Matthew Prior* (London, 1914), p. 250. For Swift's efforts to get Prior subscriptions in Ireland, see his *Correspondence*, especially II, 290: 'I have sent Mr Prior all the Money which this hedge Country would afford, which for want of a better Sollicitor is under 200 pounds', that is approximately 90 subscribers. B. H. Bronson uses Prior's volume to argue that 'the reading public of Milton, Cowley, Waller, Dryden, Prior – and even, to a degree... of Pope himself – was probably roughly commensurate with their social world as a whole' ('The Writer', *Man versus Society in Eighteenth-Century Britain*, ed. J. L. Clifford (Cambridge, 1968), p. 107.) The argument is not sustained.
[55] Some light on Tickell's management of the Addison subscription is cast by R. E. Tickell, *Thomas Tickell and the Eighteenth Century Poets* (London 1931).

Table 1. *Common subscriptions*

	I	O	S	M	A	G	T	Total
I		166	44	189	94	103	81	575
O	166		90	227	124	148	79	610
S	44	90		76	91	54	22	410
M	189	227	76		164	131	167	1440
A	94	124	91	164		92	50	980
G	103	148	54	131	92		31	365
T	81	79	22	167	50	31		620
								5000

The first mode of comparison attempted was to ascertain the number of common subscriptions between the various books. Table 1 shows the results. If anything, the figure may represent a very slight understatement, in cases where a given individual has not been identified under a different style. Abbreviations used throughout are: *I* Iliad, *O* Odyssey, *S* Shakespeare, *M* Prior, *A* Addison, *T* Trapp, *G* Gay.[56] These figures are of course raw returns, not percentages, and approximations at that. But they are sufficiently revealing for my purposes. They immediately show such things as the low correlation between *Iliad* and Shakespeare subscribers, already mentioned in the text; the high correlation between Gay and both Homeric versions (especially the *Odyssey*: 41 % of all *G* names appear in *O*); the fact that only a trivial proportion of Prior subscribers, just 5 % indeed, were listed for Shakespeare; the fairly good representation of Trapp subscribers in both *Iliad* and *Odyssey* lists, higher than anywhere except for Prior's large Trapp contingent. The size of that contingent is partly explained by Irish subscribers common to Prior and Trapp, but it is also connected with the Tory complexion of both lists. Politically the lists can be spaced out on a curve ranging from Trapp (the most emphatically Tory) to Addison (the least). On such a curve, in terms of descending degrees of Tory sentiment, the order would be *TMIOGSA*, though the middle positions (especially *G*) are the hardest to locate with certainty. It is noticeable that Trapp's extreme position causes his list to correlate less highly in general, with

[56] Higher numbers are regularly rounded off: thus Gay's 367 names are listed as 365. For technical reasons it has been convenient to adopt a regular order for tabulating the findings, that is *IOSMAGT*.

Table 2. *Age of subscribers*

	I	O	S	M	A	G	T	all
70+	2	1	1	1	1	1	1	1
60–69	8	12	5	8	7	5	7	8
50–59	15	18	15	16	12	12	14	15
40–49	24	29	15	27	29	21	40	26
30–39	26	23	22	27	27	34	30	27
20–29	21	13	27	16	21	24	22	19
20	3	3	6	4	2	2	3	3
% under age of 40	50	39	55	47	50	60	55	50

only 3·5 % on Shakespeare and 8 % on the large Addison list, but this is not true to quite the same extent of Addison at the Whig end. Of course, factors other than those of political allegiance have their effect, but there are grounds for believing that Pope's success in holding the middle ground, especially on *O*, enabled him to reach a broader public. Gay did nearly as well in finding both Prior and Addison audiences, but he largely missed Trapp's clientele (the *I/T* correlation is 14 % and the *O/T* correlation, as a proportion of Pope subscribers, is 13 %; for *G/T* is 8 % of *G* subscribers).

As regards Pope's own volumes, it emerges that 29 % of *Iliad* subscribers went on to enrol for the *Odyssey*, but less than 8 % for the Shakespeare. It is true that a good number of the original subscribers from 1714 must have been dead within the decade. In fact I know of 93 individuals on *I* (16 % of the total list) who had died by 1725, although the actual total must be at least 100. This should have operated against *O* as strongly as against *S*, in any case.[57] Looking at the matter from the *Odyssey* list, 27 % were found among *I* names and 15 % occur in *S*. This last is an extraordinarily low correlation for two subscriptions mounted simultaneously, though hardly in a synchronized manner. The point can be enforced if we consider that 18 % of *Iliad* subscribers had been named, five years earlier, on Gay's list,

[57] A far from negligible proportion of *M* subscribers would be dead by the time *O* came before the public: I know of 136 in this category, and by projection we can infer perhaps as many as 250. Nevertheless 37 % of *O* listees had been on *M*, as against 18 % of *S* subscribers. The position is different in only one case, that is the correlation with Addison's list. Here *S* for once took a larger share (22 %) as against the 20 % of *O* subscribers on *A*, and the mere 16 % of *I* subscribers. By every test *A* and *S* are, in that order, the most strongly Whig lists.

which is smaller by some way than the Shakespeare clientele; and 24% of the *Odyssey* subscribers had been enrolled by Gay. The data here illustrate the fact that Shakespeare evoked in some measure a new public, less 'literary' perhaps and certainly less attuned to the subscription habit.

Table 2 concerns the age of subscribers. I have established reliable birth-dates, to within a year either way, for more than half the subscribers; in the case of *O* this information is forthcoming for more than two thirds of the list, for *I* for three fifths. Individuals have been ranged in cohorts according to their age at the time of publication. Thus for the *Iliad* I have taken those born between 1685 and 1694, 1704 and 1714, etc. The figures are in percentages. The figures in Table 2 may be read alongside Table 3, which gives the 'average' age of each list, variously calculated. The figures are in years. There is enough consistency in these figures to suggest that they may be taken as dependable. On every major test we find that Pope's two versions of Homer took with them an ageing public, with a heavy concentration of subscribers around the poet's age or a little older. Perhaps, unknown to us, writers have always carried their audience along with them in this fashion. The *Odyssey*, in fact, brought the average age overall up into the forties. However, the Shakespeare list was markedly younger, a fact which seems to square with the lesser eminence, in worldly terms, of its members. Curiously, Gay's youthful group, with its strong cohort of those in their thirties, does display high eminence, which challenges this assumption concerning the Shakespeare public.[58] Prior was the oldest among this group of authors, both absolutely and at publication date, and his list has a slightly middle-aged appearance, but even he is outdone by the *Odyssey* group. Pope's oldest subscriber among those I have traced, nevertheless, was for the *Iliad*: Sir Christopher Wren, no less.[59] Exactly 10 per cent of those on all lists were over sixty years of age.

It is worth looking briefly at the survival rate of the subscribers to

[58] It may be relevant that one of the oldest subscription publics which I have encountered, and a distinctly uninfluential one for all its 655 names, was that for John Oldmixon's *History of England* ('1730' for 1729). Here the mean age, for those whose birth-date is recoverable, is as high as 48. A third of those identified were dead within ten years and 82·2 per cent within thirty years – a steeper rate of loss even than Trapp's. I suspect that historical, theological and moral works often elicited a more elderly audience, but the evidence is incomplete.

[59] Sir Stephen Fox would have attained the age of 91 if he had survived to see *T* published. In fact he died on 28 October 1716. James Johnston, on Oldmixon's list, was about 86. Significantly this Twickenham neighbour of Pope's declined *I*, *O* and *S*, though he did take *M*, *A* and *G*.

Table 3. *Average age of subscribers*

	I	O	S	M	A	G	T	all
Arithmetic mean	40	44	37	42	42	38	39	41
Median	39	43	37	41	39	36	39	40
Mode (commonest single age)	28	40, 45	30	34	33	36	39	45
age range	14–83	9–77	16–77	4–81	14–81	11–77	13–89	4–89

Table 4. *Term of subscribers*

died within xxx	I	O	S	M	A	G	T	all
died within 10 years	21·8	27·4	18·3	31·9	27·6	25·5	34·2	27·5
20 years	52·3	55·3	44·7	57·2	53·1	43·8	60·7	53·9
30 years	72·3	73·0	62·0	74·6	74·4	65·2	79·5	72·7
40 years	87·1	86·6	85·4	90·4	89·1	85·0	89·3	88·3
50 years	93·2	95·2	93·7	97·3	95·9	93·2	96·6	95·7
60 years	98·3	98·9	99·0	99·6	100·0	99·2	99·6	99·6
70 years	99·8	100·0	100·0	99·9	100·0	100·0	100·0	99·9
50% dead by	1732	1743	1747	1736	1740	1742	1734	1738

each volume. A number of individuals lived on for sixty years or more; on Pope's three lists the longest survivors include William Rollison (d. 1774), Lord Bathurst (d. 1775), the Duke and Duchess of Queensberry (d. 1778 and 1777), the Duke of Rutland (d. 1779), Thomas Townshend (d. 1780), Judith Madan (d. 1781), Daniel Wray (d. 1783), Lady (Catherine) Petre, Lady Margaret Harley and the Countess of Harrold (all d. 1785). Outliving even these was the Countess of Albermarle, who died as late as 1789. It is a piquant thought that some *Iliad* subscribers witnessed the American Revolution, whilst two individuals on other lists lived to see the French. The broad picture is provided by Table 4. The percentages relate to those whose deaths have been located, rather more than half the total number. These figures indicate that Pope's younger Shakespearian clientele survived better than any other group – even the youthful Gay list. On the other hand Prior and Trapp (whose lists have a slightly lower average age than that of the *Odyssey*) were to display less power of survival than any Pope list. It would be rash to build too much upon these statistics, which are complicated by differing publication dates, but there is a clear departure from purely random distribution. Perceptibly more Shakespeare subscribers than Trapp listees, for example, lived on to spread the word in the 1740s and 1750s: half of the former group were still alive in 1747. The proportion alive in 1750 (of those identified) was: I 18%, O 35%, S 44%, M 24%, A 26%, G 35%, T 18%, all 27%. The same calculation applied to the year 1770 yields the following results: I 3·5%, O 7%, S 9%, M 2·5%, A 4·5%, G 7%, T 3%, all 4·5%. It is the youth of S and G clients at the time of subscription which accounts for their high scores, for in absolute terms they were more short-lived than I or O; the average life-span runs: I 65·8 years and O 65·2, as against S 62·4 years and G 62·3.

Another simple demographic test concerns the sexual distribution of subscribers. The proportion of women is as follows: I 8%, O 13%, S 4%, M 10%, A 7%, G 15%, T 4%, all 9%. The score for G is one of the highest I have noted for any subscription of the period.[60] The low percentage for T might be thought at first sight to indicate feminine disinclination for the classics, even in translation, until one notes that S scores far below either Homeric version. The average age of women subscribers is consistently around the general norm – occasionally a little lower (as with O and S) but not to a significant extent.

Matters such as age and sex are not ordinarily in dispute. In turning to levels of achievement, we obviously enter a more contentious field. It seems useful therefore to begin with comparatively objective tests, even if the value they possess is correspondingly narrow. A simple model is furnished by inclusions in the *Dictionary of National Biography*. This work notoriously possesses its own peculiar strengths and weaknesses, among which might be put its low tally of women and poor coverage of the mercantile interest,

---

[60] The nearest I have seen is the 14% for Henry Carey's *Poems on Several Occasions* (1729), a remarkably similar subscription to Gay's in many respects. The total number of subscribers is almost identical, though Carey has fewer multiple copies; Handel is again present, as is Pope. A particularly low ratio of women is Oldmixon's 1%, which seems again to indicate an inferior social catchment. Michael Treadwell points out to me that Eliza Haywood's *Letters from a Lady of Quality to a Chevalier* (1721) attracted 125 women out of 310 subscribers, a staggering 40%. (For marginally different figures see G. F. Whicher, *The Life and Romances of Mrs Eliza Haywood* (New York, 1915), p. 11.) The largest absolute number I have seen is 278, for *The Works of the late Aaron Hill* (1753), making 20% of the list. The volumes were issued for the benefit of Hill's daughters.

at least as far as the eighteenth century goes. However, it is still instructive to see the relative score between the seven lists. Again my count may be a little on the conservative side.[61] The numbers are: *I* 159 (27%), *O* 158 (26%), *S* 68 (17%), *M* 183 (13%), *A* 149 (15%), *G* 96 (26%), *T* 72 (12%). Again this leaves the broad pattern clear, with *G* joining *I* and *O* at the top and *T* well to the rear. Such approximations forbid too precise analysis, but in my view the crude figures do point to a certain massive distinction in *I* which was never quite matched at the very top. The *Iliad* list contains three men of unmistakable genius: Wren, Newton and Marlborough. None of these occurs elsewhere, except Newton on Prior's list; and perhaps only Handel, on Gay's, can be put in the same category. Swift, Walpole, Somers, Chesterfield, Bolingbroke, Congreve, Sloane, Stanhope and others are considerable historical figures, but their stature is surely a little less than Olympian. On several tests *I* is outdone by *O*, but not in my judgment on this one.[62]

The aristocratic and official element in *H* has been analysed by R. H. Griffith, who observes, 'The subscription list is one of fashionabilities. H. R. H. the Princess leads. There are 17 dukes, 3 marquises, 49 earls; and 7 duchesses, 1 marchioness, and 8 countesses. Names of women number 47. The army is well represented – by not less than 9 generals, 10 colonels and 2 captains; the church perhaps relatively not quite so well – by a bishop (an Irish one at that) and 19 reverends.'[63] My own count differs slightly in one or two particulars – there are for instance two Irish bishops – but the main analysis stands. The low count of clergy is indicative, since the list normally designates churchmen by their ecclesiastical title. Trapp does not do this, otherwise the number of reverends in *T* would be far ahead of *I*. (The true number of clergy in *I* is about 27.) If we go behind the figures in another way, it emerges that something like 30 soldiers on *I* held at some time in their life the rank of general or field-marshal. The list gives 12 (not 9) of these holding such a rank. In terms of the categories mentioned by Griffith, the *Iliad* list is comparatively weak

---

[61] For example, I have omitted 'Mr Gibbs' on *G*, though this is almost certainly the artist James Gibbs; along with other dubious cases. The overall average of *DNB* inclusions is 17%. This of course is not allowing for the same name occurring in several lists (from two to seven).

[62] No significant presence in the *Dictionary of American Biography* is found, though many lists have one or two inclusions.

[63] Griffith, I, 41. It should be noted that Griffith's score for *Odyssey* copies, 1057 sets (I, 121), is about 200 in excess of the real total; it has, none the less, been repeated by Sherburn, *Early Career*, p. 255, and by J. P. Hardy, ed., *Johnson's Lives of the Poets* (Oxford, 1971), p. 361).

on bishops (*M*, *A* and *T* all stand out here), as well as on lesser clergy. On all other tests *I* offers a high score, and the tally of around 50 baronets is particularly remarkable.

The *Odyssey* subscription leaps ahead in one particular respect: dukes and duchesses have shot up to 23 and 7 respectively.[64] The remainder of the peerage has increased a little, but a noticeable change involves a reduction of baronets and an increase in the knightage. The army is less well represented, medicine a little better. There is an ampler presence of clergymen, especially doctors of divinity. In some of these categories Gay matches the Homer lists, but in general the traditional view that Pope did well among the upper echelons of society is endorsed by comparison with the controls. As for Shakespeare, that sees the ducal contingent remarkably well maintained (nine dukes, two duchesses), but in all other respects the count is down. The list is particularly weak on the lower ranks of the peerage and on knights, as compared with the *Odyssey*. The clergy are thinly in evidence, as though Shakespeare appeared a more pagan and improper author than Homer.

A more interesting criterion is perhaps the parliamentary connection of subscribers, particularly in view of Pope's known attempts to lobby for support at the House of Commons. Members of Parliament are not normally signalized as such in these lists, but it is possible to identify a larger number of past, present and future Members in each subscription. Once again, it is the two Homer lists which stand out. Something like 75 (probably rather more) of those on *I* were elected to the 1715 Parliament, and it must be recalled that a number of Pope's friends had lately lost their seats with the demise of the Tories after the Hanoverian accession. A number of these were among the *I* subscribers, despite the high total which was reached for current members. A still more striking result emerges for the *Odyssey*. A matter of 120 among those listed were sitting in the House in the year 1725, quite apart from former members and a not negligible segment – twenty or more – who were later to enter Parliament. These 120 represent a fifth of the subscribers and (what is truly astonishing) 22 per cent of the sitting Members, who numbered 558. It is an extraordinary penetration into the legislative body and must of course be seen along with the comparable figure of members of the

---

[64] Comparable figures are *S*, 9–2; *M*, 15–7; *A*, 8–5; *G*, 10–3; *T*, 4–4. I omit Addison's foreign dukedoms and enter the titular 'Duke' (more correctly Marquis) of Powys. The Duke of Buccleuch on *S* should presumably be Duchess, but I have left the tally as it appears.

Lords (about 130). In my judgment this is the single most impressive feature of this group of subscriptions. It points to what might be called the meritocratic aspect of the list, despite the survival of Tory and Country interests. More than anything else it demonstrates the success Pope attained in the bustling practical world of the nation: by no means all his 1725 MPs were knights of the shire, any more than court placemen. He could almost be said to have a broad power base. Administration supporters, Grumbletonians, disappointed Jacobites, ur-Patriots, unrepentant opportunists – there are members of every age and party hue. One could write much of the parliamentary history of the 1720s without straying far beyond these men.[65]

The Shakespeare list is yet again far less imposing, with MPs down to just over forty. Proportionately Gay is stronger than any other non-Homeric subscription, a finding we have seen repeated on other tests. Prior includes a rather higher ratio of former MPs to current or future Members, indicating a superannuated quality in his field. None of the other lists matches the density of coverage for major statesmen which Pope achieved on his *Iliad* and *Odyssey* ventures. Between them these two subscriptions account for nine men who became Lord Treasurer or its equivalent (Harley, Newcastle, Pelham, Carlisle (nominally) Shrewsbury, Sunderland, Stanhope, Compton and Walpole). Several others achieved senior government posts such as Lord President of the Council or Secretary of State, and these include one or two who effectively led administrations (Addison, Bolingbroke, Bromley, Buckingham, Carleton, Carteret, Craggs, Halifax, Methuen, Pulteney, Roxburgh, Townshend, Trumbull and Wharton). Lord Chancellors or Lord Keepers named are Cowper, Harcourt, Parker, Somers and Yorke. The higher echelons of the army are represented by Argyll, Cadogan, Cobham, Ligonier, Marlborough, Ormonde, Peterborough, Stair and Wade (plus Stanhope again). Variously distinguished men and women who subscribed for one or other Homer were Chesterfield, Coke of Norfolk, George Bubb Dodington, Sampson Gideon, Mrs Howard,

---

[65] This is of course a slight exaggeration, but in view of the presence on *O* of Walpole, Townshend, Pulteney, Carteret, Newcastle, Henry Pelham, Lord Stanhope (later Chesterfield), Sir William Wyndham, Spencer Compton, Hervey and many more, some licence may be permissible. Unlike Pope, Gay secured Colonel William Stanhope, later Harrington. Though excluded from the Lords, Bolingbroke was a significant influence upon affairs. By way of comparison, the posthumous collection of *The Works of Aaron Hill* (1753), in which Bubb Dodington clearly played a large part as promoter, attracted 144 members of the 1754 Parliament among its 1410 subscribers. Another 60 of those listed sat in the Commons at an earlier or later date.

the Duchess of Marlborough, Lady Pomfret and Archbishop Dawes. Artistic patronage is represented by Chandos, Burlington and Edward Harley; performers and composers by Barton Booth, Anastasia Robinson, Colley Cibber and Dr Pepusch.[66] Painters are led by Dahl, Jervas, Kent, Thornhill and John Wootton. Pope attracted more of his fellow-writers than any of the controls: Addison, Arbuthnot, Berkeley, Blackmore, Anthony Collins, Congreve, Fenton, Gay, Lady Mary Wortley Montagu, Parnell, Prior, Rowe, Steele, Swift, Tickell, Lady Winchilsea and Young head this group. He is weak on science (only Newton and John Keill) but comparatively strong on medicine with John Freind, Sir David Hamilton, Mead, Ratcliffe, Shadwell and Sloane amongst others. The weakest aspect of all, particularly compared with Addison's lists, is commerce: the few prominent members of the mercantile profession include Sir Theodore Janssen, Sir Richard Hoare and John Barnard. On every one of these headings the Shakespeare subscription shows a distinct falling-off. Only the book-trade improved its representation, and that to a lesser degree than would have been seen except for the copyright dispute.[67]

Earlier on, mention was made of the broad political characteristics of each list. Though the overall shift towards a more Whiggish list in the *Odyssey* is not really pronounced, some movement in this direction can certainly be detected. Inevitably the more prominent Jacobites are more conspicuous in 1715, just before the rising, than in 1725: only Derwentwater actually lost his life among *Iliad* subscribers, but others were exiled or suffered attainder. It is interesting, however, to see how evenly Jacobites (declared or strongly suspected) are spread across the two lists. Among leaders there are Berwick (*I*), Bolingbroke (*I O*), Derwentwater (*I*), Dr Friend (*O*), Kinnoul (*O*), Lansdowne (*I O*), Mar (*I*), Norfolk (*I O*), North and Grey (*I O*), Ormonde (*I*), Orrery (*O*), Powis (*I*), Scarsdale (*I O*), Strafford (*I O*), Wharton (*O*), Wyndham (*I O*). Less prominent supporters of the cause include Robert Arbuthnot (*O*), Bagot (*O*), Barrymore (*I*), Bruce (*I*), Charles Caesar (*I O*), Cotton (*I O*), Downes (*O*), Echlyn (*I*), Eden (*O*), Everard (*I*), Fownes (*I*), Grosvenor (*I O*), Levinz (*O*), Masters (*O*),

---

[66] The impresario Heidegger figures on *S*.

[67] Thirty-five booksellers are listed, mostly members of the London trade, but also representing Bath, York and Bristol. Even this is not an outstandingly high tally, though it is the best in the group studied here. For a more impressive spread, see W. B. Todd and P. J. Wallis, 'Provincial Booksellers c. 1744: the *Harleian Miscellany* Subscription List', *The Library*, XXIX (1974), 422–40.

Montacute (*I*), Packer (*O*), Pole (*I*), Rashleigh (*I*), Seaforth (*I*), Slingsby (*O*), Snell (*O*), Father Southcote (*I*). A high proportion of these men subscribed to Prior, but virtually none of them to Shakespeare. Tonson's Kit-Cat associations seem to have ensured that the latter came to be regarded as a Whig undertaking. The High Tory element in the Homer lists can be gauged by reference to the presence of October Club members. I have noted Abdy (*I O*), Bampfield (*I*), Peter Bathurst (*I O*), Beaumont (*I O*), Henry Bertie (*I*), Campion (*I*), Cartwright (*O*, also *S*), Cholmondley (*S* only), Kay (*I*), Gulston (*O*), Lutwyche (*O*), Morice (*I*), Nicholas (*I O*), Shuttleworth (*I*), Strangeways (*O*), Trevanion (*I*), Warburton (*O*).[68] Several of these appear on *G*, where the outright Jacobite element is thinner. A relevant factor in this connection might be the proportion of Roman Catholics, but I have found it impossible to make an estimate with any true accuracy. At least twenty-five Catholics subscribed to each Homer set, but that is certain to be lower than the actual total. This is likely to indicate the highest ratio among the groups examined, with Prior next in line, but the figures are too imprecise to be sure.

One peculiarity of the lists which may be mentioned here concerns the Stuart legacy in a more direct form than political or sentimental allegiance. Royal progeny and their consorts scatter Pope's clientele, with natural sons of Charles II (Northumberland, St Albans) and a grandson in Richmond. There is a daughter of James II (Duchess of Buckingham), together with his natural son Berwick. Monmouth's widow (Duchess of Buccleuch) is there along with his son (Deloraine). The relatively feeble contribution of the house of Nassau lies in the Countess of Orkney, who had been mistress to William III. Pope also managed to obtain for *I* the name of the Countess of Darlington, the mistress of George I.

Pope's success in building up family loyalties is an interesting feature in his success. He managed to achieve extensive penetration into a number of the ruling dynasties, including the Churchill-Spencer-Godolphin nexus; the Pelhams, together with a number of families into which they married (Harley of course, but also Castlecomber, Lincoln, Stanley); the Harcourts; and the wide

---

[68] Perhaps we should add Archibald Hutcheson (*O*), who was bold enough to take Atterbury's side at the time of his trial. Pope missed William Shippen (though he has his brother), Sir Robert Davers and Sir John Chichester, among the Highest of Tories, who are all on Trapp's list, along with Count Gyllenborg. Prior's most interesting inclusions here are Dennis Kelly, arrested at the time of the Layer plot in 1722, and Sir Henry Goring.

Harley connection, which brings in Foley, Dupplin, Carmarthen, etc. Gay achieved something of the sort with the Hyde and Boyle families; Prior with Finch, Bathurst and again Harley linkages. Pope also achieved at least twelve pairs of brothers; again Gay and Prior are his nearest rivals. One feature of Pope's lists is the way in which the relatives of a deceased subscriber will claim a reversionary interest in the later undertaking. Several women appearing on the *Odyssey* list, including the Duchess of Marlborough, were the widows of men found on the *Iliad* subscription; similarly Trumbull's son took his place, as did Wharton's. These family subscriptions did not in general extend to Shakespeare. Complicated genealogical patterns occasionally lie beneath the surface. Thus Mrs Newsham, *née* Anne Craggs, listed in *O*, had a father and brother in *I* (both now dead), and her future second husband also in *O*. One sister, Mrs Elliot, occurs in *OA*; another sister, Mrs Trefusis, appears in *AG*, and then crops up in *O* as Lady Cotton. Her third husband is blessedly absent. A simpler case, representative of many, concerns Lady Mary Wortley (*O*); she has a husband (*O*), father (*IOS*) and brother-in-law (*I*) as well as more distant relatives. Her sister is in *M* and *G* but in none of the Pope lists.[69]

The school and college connection of subscribers is hard to establish with complete accuracy, but at least we can provide minimum figures. For Westminster School, the numbers discovered are *I*, 12; *O*, 26; *S*, 11. Prior almost equals the *Odyssey* tally with 25. The score for Eton is *I*, 4; *O*, 9; *S*, 5. These are certainly underestimates. A count was also made for Charterhouse, Merchant Taylor's, St Paul's and Winchester, but the figures proved too low to be of value. Rather more positive results were achieved with college affiliations. To the data provided in Table 4 should be added institutional subscriptions. Oxford, excluding the gift copy Pope apparently earmarked for the Bodleian, entered library subscriptions as follows: *I*, 10; *O*, 13; *S*, 1. The respective Cambridge figures are 0; 4; 2. Gay was another to draw a blank here, and Trapp's 12 Oxford entries stand out. Addison scored 6. In reading Table 5, it is worth noting that Prior achieved 25 for his own college, St John's, Cambridge; while Trapp reached around 50 for Christ Church and 25 for Magdalen. Over 100 of the

---

[69] Similarly Lady Catherine Hyde (*IG*) has a niece, her namesake who became the Duchess of Queensberry, on *OGA*; a brother, the Earl of Rochester, on *MGT*; a sister Lady Dalkeith on *IMG*; a nephew Lord Dalkeith on *G*; and another niece, the Countess of Essex, on *O*. Her sister-in-law the Countess of Rochester appears on *IM*. There are further ramifications.

Table 5. *College affiliation of subscribers*

OXFORD	I	O	S	CAMBRIDGE	I	O	S
All Souls	7	2	2	Caius	0	2	0
Balliol	3	6	2	Christ's	2	1	0
Brasenose	2	3	1	Clare	1	4	1
Christ Church	30	38	8	Corpus Christi	2	0	1
Exeter	5	2	2	Jesus	2	3	1
Jesus	2	1	0	King's	4	5	3
Lincoln	3	0	0	Magdalene	1	1	0
Magdalen	10	1	3	Pembroke	0	1	2
New	5	10	5	Queens'	2	4	1
Merton	7	0	2	Peterhouse	1	6	1
Oriel	1	0	3	St Catharine's	1	3	1
Pembroke	2	3	1	St John's	1	7	3
Queen's	2	0	2	Sidney Sussex	0	0	2
St Edmund Hall	2	0	0	Trinity	12	10	10
St John's	6	6	2	Trinity Hall	2	2	3
Trinity	14	12	6				
University	3	2	4		I	O	S
Wadham	3	2	3				
Worcester	1	0	2	all Cambridge (% of list)	5	8	8
Hart Hall	2	3	1	all Oxford			
St Mary's	0	1	0	(% of list)	19	15	12

198 Oxford men noted in *Oppian's Halineuticks* (1722) were for Balliol. It should be emphasized that the data relate to past and present (but not future) members of the colleges; thus they reveal a failure on Pope's part to secure subscribers from older Cambridge alumni, not just among resident members at this date. This is strikingly apparent in the case of the *Iliad*. The figures in Table 5 are perhaps more eloquent in showing where the eighteenth-century ruling class came from, than in locating Pope's exact bases of support. Nevertheless, it is apparent that the Oxford spread for *I* is patterned very much like that of *T*; but that he lost favour among Magdalen men. In absolute, though not in relative, terms his Cambridge showing is poorer than that of the Oxonian, Addison, whose subscription was mounted by another Oxford man, Tickell. Nor did Pope pick up more than a handful of Trinity College, Dublin, men; as one would expect,

Addison, Prior and (thanks to his Irish list) Trapp all do much better. There is a thin scattering from the Scottish universities.

Whom did Pope *not* get, then, individually? Not Handel, whom Gay did; not Oglethorpe, whom Trapp did;[70] not John Law, whom Addison did. Surprisingly he did not pick up Atterbury (*MT*), or William Cleland (*M*) although it is possible they asked for their names to be omitted. He would not mind that he missed Colonel Charteris and Dennis Bond (both *M*), and could have lived philosophically with the loss of Sir Gilbert Heathcote (*A*) and the South Sea cashier Knight (*MAG*): he had John Blunt to live down.[71] Where he conspicuously failed, by the side of Addison, was coverage of foreign dignitaries. Addison clearly profited from his experience as Secretary of State, and his list has the air of a diplomatic handbook. There is the Queen of Sweden, Prince Eugene, the Regent of France; a whole clutch of Italian princes and grand dukes, doges and cardinals. There are Florentine scholars, Portugese savants and imperial ambassadors. France is particularly well represented, with the statesman Cardinal Dubois and writers such as Madam Dacier (the French translator of Homer), the Abbé du Bos, Fontenelle, and Houdart de la Motte. When we add the Princess of Wales, Prince Frederick and the Duke of York, it is evident that conventional tests of eminence – such as the *DNB* check – may overrate Pope's lists, so far as contemporaries would have judged the matter. In a different quarter – the navy and admiralty personnel – Addison far outstrips all his rivals. Oddly, Addison also attracted an obscure young man from Newark, William Warburton, absent from Pope's subscriptions. Outstanding in most respects, the coverage of both *Iliad* and *Odyssey* could not be called total saturation of the upper end of the market. There were areas of national life (not to touch on Addison's European range) where Pope fell down. He was weak on the business community; very unequal on the universities; poor on Ireland, despite Dr Elwood and – potentially – Swift; nor did he draw heavily on the Hanoverian entourage who surrounded the royal family, where Addison prospered once more. His episcopal showing was

---

[70] Gay secured Theophilus Oglethorpe, the philanthropist's brother. Handel subscribed, incidentally, to the humdrum collection of Aaron Hill's *Works*.

[71] A particularly strong South Sea element is apparent in *G*, with Sir George Caswall, Robert Chester, Francis Hawes, Sir John Lambert, as well as Secretary Craggs and Knight's brother-in-law John Page. These were more embarrassing names than Blunt had been for Pope in 1715. Even on *O* and *S* Pope had his share of venal men, with MPs such as Bowater Vernon not noted for financial purity.

feebler than that of everyone except Gay.[72] Whether he liked it or not, these were significant parts of the nation's elite, and his failure to penetrate them is pointed up by the greater success achieved by the controls.

Finally, it is worth considering shortly the subscribing habits of individuals. Only three men are found on all seven lists, that is the spread of *IOSMAGT*. They were Spencer Compton, Sir Clement Cottrell and Edward Harley, second Earl of Oxford. Pope had close ties of friendship with the last two, much less so with Compton. Twenty subscribers occur on six lists. Ten of these drop only Trapp (*IOSMAG*). The next most common omission, significantly, is Shakespeare (*IOMAGT*), with five such cases. Two drop Addison and two drop Gay; only one individual dropped Prior, and this was the Duke of Chandos, under special circumstances apparently.[73] No one at all in this group drops either Homer: there is no occurrence of either *ISMAGT* or *OSMAGT*. Thirty-seven subscribers are found in five lists in various permutations. These include two women, the Duchess of Hamilton and Pope's friend Lady Scudamore. None of this group dropped both Homers: the commonest pattern is *IOMAG*, that is omitting Shakespeare and Trapp.[74] Thirty-five men subscribed to all three Pope sets;[75] only nine confined themselves within Pope to *I* and *S*. There were by contrast 131 *IO* subscribers who omitted *S*. These included Arbuthnot, Gay and Swift. *OS* alone, despite their joint appearance ten years after *I*, totalled only 54. All these groupings indicate that regular subscribers were far more likely to miss out Shakespeare; however, none of the 60 most regular omitted the *Odyssey*, and none dropped both the *Iliad* and Shakespeare.

[72] Pope secured 2 bishops for *I*, one for *O* (plus the Archbishop of York), none for *S*. *T* has 8, a notably High Church selection for that era; *A* has 5, a less striking bunch, together with the same Archbishop; *M* has Dawes yet again and 8 bishops, 6 of them identical with *T*'s. The ranks of deans and archdeacons are especially strong in *M*. It should be added that Dr Sacheverell subscribed to *IMT*; he was dead by the time *O* and *S* appeared. As for medical men, the proportion of recognizable physicians and surgeons seems to vary (*S* excepted) with the degree of Toryism in the list: it runs *I* 1·7%, *O* 0·8%, *S* 1·2%, *M* 1·8%, *A* 0·7%, *G* 0·8%, *T* 1·9%.

[73] See Baker and Baker, p. 68, for Hearne's story that Carnarvon (as he then was) had withdrawn a subscription originally made. The two dropping Addison were Pope's friends Bathurst and Harcourt.

[74] The scores for five-time subscribers are: *IOSMA* 3, *IOMAG* 11, *IOMAT* 2, *IOSMG* 4, *IOSMT* 1, *IOSAG* 2, *IOMGT* 4, *IOAGT* 1, *OSMAG* 5, *OSMAT* 2, *OSMGT* 2. The group includes one corporate body, the library of All Souls (*IOMAT*).

[75] Among all subscribers, that is; the combination *IOG* (with or without additional items) occurs by contrast 60 times and *IOM* just short of 100 times.

Table 6. *Items dropped by regular subscribers*

n = total number of items dropped by this group

Subscriptions entered	n	I	O	S	M	A	G	T	t
				Items dropped					
7	3	—	—	—	—	—	—	—	—
6	20	—	—	5	1	2	2	10	20
5	37	9	—	18	3	11	8	25	74
4	82	23	17	62	17	49	30	48	246
Total	142	32	17	85	21	62	40	83	340

n = number of subscribers in the given group
t = total number of items dropped by this group

Equally, analysis of the 82 names found on four subscriptions shows the same pattern of support and withdrawal. (See Appendix 2.) There are 23 combinations, of which the commonest are *IOMG* (17), *IOMT* (11), *OMAG* (8) and *IMGT* (7) – all involve dropping Shakespeare. In fact 62 in this group of 82 failed to take up the Shakespeare proposals. Only two omitted both *Iliad* and *Odyssey*, one returning *SMAG* and the other (alone among the 142 most regular subscribers) dropped all three Pope editions (*MAGT*): as it happens, he was dead by the time *O* and *S* appeared.[76] The numbers dropped by four-time subscribers were as follows: *S*, 62; *A*, 49; *T*, 48; *G*, 30; *I*, 23; *O* and *M*, both 17. It is noteworthy that Gay is omitted far less frequently than Addison, whose total subscription was almost three times as large. Prior's low rejection rate is of course in some measure a function of the size of his list, but he does seem to have commanded the loyalty of regular subscribers. In this respect Pope's two Homer translations are again outstanding, the *Odyssey* most of all. Table 6 summarizes the habits of the most eager members of the subscribing public. These negative returns amply confirm the earlier findings. Looked at purely from Pope's point of view, they exhibit clearly the loss of a regular clientele which he suffered with Shakespeare.

[76] This was the Jacobite suspect, Hon. Robert Mansell. He was only twenty when the *Iliad* began to appear, and he died in 1723, so his defection cannot be regarded as serious. The *SMAG* formula belongs to Walter Cary, MP, a placeman and friend of Edward Young. An exact contemporary of Tickell, he was at Oxford at the same time and followed him to Dublin Castle; it seems possible that his abstention from the Homer subscriptions is pointed. In 1725 he was living in Hanover Square, as was Pope's enemy Ambrose Philips.

III

It would not in my judgment be overestimating the evidential value of these statistics to assert that they put Pope's subscriptions in a truer perspective. Table 1 shows very obviously that he did not have a single homogeneous market for each production and that (for instance) there was only a tiny carry-over from the *Iliad* to Shakespeare. Tables 2 and 3 show the markedly older public for the later Homer translation as compared with the earlier. Table 4 illustrates the differential survival rate as between Shakespeare subscribers and the rest. Table 5 indicates Pope's unequal penetration of the universities, and is supplemented by other evidence in the text regarding his poor coverage of some sections of the nation's elite. Table 6 illustrates something of a flight from Shakespeare even by habitual book-subscribers. With this edition Pope simply failed to reach the traditional (and no doubt anticipated) audience.

The two examinations I have conducted suggest that mounting a subscription was an exceedingly tricky and uncertain business, even for a distinguished writer at the height of his fame.[77] The narrative brought out the amount of labour and anxiety that were entailed for Pope. The statistical analysis showed that the results were imperfect, despite all the effort. True, the *Iliad* and *Odyssey* are confirmed as highly successful subscriptions by most tests,[78] though not by all. But even these ventures were by no means that which Stephen implies, automatic homing on to a simple target. As with the far less propitious Shakespeare, they were risk issues, aimed at a fluctuating and capricious public. The easy 'commission' is a myth: there was only the struggle to find, and to keep, an audience interested enough to subscribe.

Pope's 'triumph' was largely financial rather than social. The

[77] A few years later James Thomson, who had shot to fame with *Winter, Summer and Spring*, put a great deal of effort into his subscription edition of *The Seasons*. According to William Aikman, 'Thomson is so strong about his Subscription, that he minds nothing else', quoted by Douglas Grant, *James Thomson: Poet of the Seasons* (London, 1951), p. 80. Thomson had the help of Edward Young and also of Joseph Spence; see *The Correspondence of Edward Young*, ed. H. Pettit (Oxford, 1971), p. 66. Yet on publication in June 1730, after two years' effort, his 390 subscribers were not fantastically impressive, though they did include Caroline, now Queen, as well as Pope. Grant's conclusion (pp. 93–4) is a little generous: 'There were few subscription lists in which so many men of birth or genius were brought together. Thomson's conscientious canvassing had clearly proved successful.' As with Pope, Thomson hit some targets and missed others.

[78] For example: eight of the nine residents in fashionable Arlington Street, in 1725, were enlisted for *O*; the one exception was the Earl of Cholmondeley.

terms he extracted from Lintot meant that he took all the subscription money, without the deductions for printing, paper, distribution etc. which normally came off the author's share. In addition he was paid £200 per volume, terms that Lintot soon began to find onerous in view of the pirate competition. To earn £5320, as Pope is supposed to have done from the *Iliad* alone, he would normally have had to recruit not 650 subscriptions (including multiple copies) but more like 900 to 1000.[79] Fortunately, in the end Lintot did well enough out of his own edition not to regret his generosity. But publishers in the future would be more cagey. Subscription ventures went on unabated, but few – if any – authors could demand Pope's terms. The whole episode was less typical than historians of literature and of the book trade have chosen to believe.[80]

APPENDIX I

Subscription pattern of Pope's friends

John Arbuthnot	*IOAGT*	William Congreve	*IOSMG*
Lord Bathurst	*IOSMGT*	William Fortescue	*IOSG*
Hugh Bethel	*OG*	John Gay	*IOM*
Martha Blount	*OG*	2nd Earl of Oxford	*IOSMAGT*
Teresa Blount	*G*	Lord Peterborough	*IOG*
Lord Bolingbroke	*IO*	Matthew Prior	*IGT* (d. 1721)
Lord Burlington	*IOMG*	Jonathan Swift	*IOMT*

Addison scored *IT* (d. 1719), and Trapp scored *M*.

[79] Fielding, for instance, probably made not much more than £800 for his *Miscellanies* in 1743, although he had a high proportion of royal paper subscribers and a good array of multiple copies (see the edition by Henry Knight Miller Oxford, 1972), p. xlvii). The list of 427 names collected by Fielding is reasonably impressive, but not outstanding; *DNB* inclusions are about average, for a major venture, at 17%. Women also score around the norm at 9%.

[80] For a parallel enquiry to this, reaching broadly similar conclusions, see Matthew Hodgart, 'The Subscription List for Pope's *Iliad*, 1715', in *The Dress of Words*, ed. R. B. White (Lawrence, Kan., 1978), pp. 25–34. For the general context in which the subscription campaigns were mounted, see David Foxon, *Pope and the Early Eighteenth-Century Book Trade*, ed. J. McLaverty (Oxford, 1991). Useful background is supplied by W. A. Speck, 'Politicians, Peers, and Publishing', *Books and their Readers in Eighteenth-Century England*, ed. I. Rivers (Leicester, 1982), pp. 47–68.

APPENDIX 2

Four-time subscribers

IOSM 2	*IOAG* 2	*OSMA* 2	*MSAG* 1
IOSA 1	*IOAT* 4	*OSMG* 1	*MAGT* 1
IOSG 4	*IOGT* 1	*OSMT* 2	
IOMA 2	*ISMA* 1	*OSAG* 5	
IOMG 17	*ISMG* 1	*OMAG* 8	
IOMT 11	*IMAG* 1	*OMGT* 3	
	IMAT 5		
	IMGT 7		

The lone individual to drop all three Pope items was Robert Mansell (d. 1723), a Jacobite MP.

CHAPTER 13

The Burlington circle in the provinces: Pope's Yorkshire friends

Friendship was an important concept for Pope and a major element in his versions of the desirable self. Eighteenth-century schoolboys learnt from Cicero of the moral strength which radiated out from a properly maintained friendship, and as adults many, like Pope, put great energy into preserving ties with some kindred spirit. The best known and most intimate of these relationships, in the case of Pope, were his dealings with the Scriblerus group, headed by Swift, Arbuthnot and Gay. But earlier on there were mentors such as Trumbull, Garth and Wycherley; whilst in his later life Pope developed close friendships with men such as Bolingbroke, Orrery and Lyttelton. (His relations with women have been studied by Valerie Rumbold, and as seen above, pp. 161–6, involve slightly different issues.) However, Pope also enjoyed links with less celebrated individuals, and it is one such subset in his friendship – previously unexplored – which is the theme of this chapter.

I

Recently there have been a number of signs that the contributions of the third Earl of Burlington to English culture has been more widely recognized. An index of this growing appreciation of Burlington came in the exhibition mounted by the University of Nottingham in January 1973. The exhibition catalogue, entitled 'Apollo of the Arts: Lord Burlington and his Circle', constituted in itself an important advance in our understanding of early eighteenth-century taste. Essays by John Wilton-Ely, Peter Willis, Stanley Boorman and Clive Probyn took as their respective themes Burlington's connections with architecture, landscape design, music and literature. In showing Burlington's centrality, however, the catalogue perhaps did something to conceal one pertinent fact about Burlington's influence. This lies in the group of followers which arose in districts remote from the capital – most especially in the North of England and North Midlands, where Burlington had strong roots. His marriage into the Savile family brought him Nottinghamshire links, although it was not until late in his life that the marriage of his daughter (and sole heiress) Charlotte established a connection with the great dynasty of Chatsworth. More important, Burlington's estate at Londesborough lay close enough to York to give him a significant sphere of influence in that part of the country. Burlington's own architectural skill is commemorated in York by the Assembly Rooms, which Rudolph Wittkower and others have brought fully to our attention.

However, it has not previously been remarked that Burlington's Yorkshire 'interest' extended rather further. There is evidence, in fact, that a group of devotees with a base in East Yorkshire spread the Burlington doctrine through the second quarter of the eighteenth century. As amateur architects, connoisseurs of painting, landscape improvers and followers of contemporary literature, they shared many family and personal ties. All of them had close connections with Beverley, which lies about fifteen miles from Burlington's former country seat (now demolished.[1] Most seem to have attended the local Grammar School, and several proceeded to St John's College, Cambridge. This common background drew them together and may also explain to some degree their allegiance to Burlington, the local magnate.

But at the same time they were equally attached to a different cultural eminence – one who had no Yorkshire associations in his own right and who had been debarred by his religion from the universities. This was the poet Alexander Pope, who enjoyed Burlington's friendship and patronage. Pope maintained a warm friendship over a number of years with this Yorkshire cell of the Burlington connection, and it is thanks to references in his letters that we can reconstruct some of their doings and their attitudes. Pope may once have visited Londesborough (if so, it was the furthest north his 'rambles' ever took him); and he certainly used one member of the group as an embodiment of sane country living in his imitation of Horace's second satire of the second book.

[1] See Canon Wilton, 'Historic Londesborough', *Transactions of the East Riding Antiquarian Society*, III (1895), 1–12; and Rev. R. C. Wilton, 'The Cliffords and Boyles of Londesborough', *ibid.*, XIV (1907), 18–44. For Burlington's own alterations to Londesborough Hall, see James Lees-Milne, *Earls of Creation* (London, 1962), p. 161.

At the centre of this group stood two non-University men – the Bethel brothers, in particular the elder, Hugh, Pope's Ofellus. It might be observed, however, that Hugh remained a Yorkshire country gentleman all his days. Apart from a visit to Italy, occasioned by poor health, he was living near Beverley during the whole period of his surviving correspondence with Pope. And though he died in London, it is certainly misleading to regard him (as Miss Rachel Trickett seems to do) as primarily a City man.[2] The group, indeed, was in no sense a metropolitan one. Its members were united by ties of blood, intermarriage, shared interests and, to a large extent, common origins. The proximity of Burlington's seat at Londesborough is a further indication of the geographic basis to their association. In one way or another, they were in contact with many of Pope's acquaintances, from the Codringtons to William Cleland (father of *Fanny Hill's* creator) and the lawyer Fortescue.[3] Hugh Bethel also knew that polymath of the decorative arts, William Kent – yet one more East Yorkshireman, and yet another client of Burlington. And the Cambridge thread which joined a number of them supplied another bonding element.

As I have said, much of the relevant evidence is to be found in

[2] Miss Trickett writes: 'Pope's friendship with men like the Bethels, the one brother a City merchant, the other a Whig landed gentleman, and both descended from Dryden's Shimei, would have prevented him making any glib personal association between the City and bad taste' (*The Honest Muse* (Oxford, 1967), p. 177). It is true that the Bethels were great-nephews of the republican Slingsby Bethel; but Hugh's City interests appear to have been comparatively slight. He normally spent the winters in town and the summer in Yorkshire (see George Sherburn's note in *Corr*, III, 287). It appears that his asthma was often better in the country; and Pope once observed to him, 'My Lord Burlington goes to Yorkshire... I have often wished I could see you there [Beswick], where I fancy you are most happy; for in Town you generally seem to think yourself not at home' (*Corr*, IV, 113). Italy, of course, was the proper nation for any Burlingtonian to visit.
  The best source for Slingsby Bethel is John Brooke's article in *The House of Commons 1754–1790*, ed. L. B. Namier, J. Brooke (London, 1964), II, 90. Note however that Slingsby succeeded his brother not, as there stated, in February 1747 but a year later – for Hugh's death in Ealing, see *Gentleman's Magazine* (1748), VIII, 92. On the Bethels, see also *EC*, IX, 147ff. The best account of the wider influence of Burlington is to be found in *Apollo of the Arts: Lord Burlington and his Circle* (Nottingham, 1973).
[3] See for example *Corr*, IV, 40. Later members of the Codrington family inherited a Beverley interest, and Hugh's nephew was indeed MP for the borough from 1747 to 1761. See G. E. C[okayne], *The Complete Baronetage* (Exeter, 1906), V, 54–7; V. T. Harlow, *Christopher Codrington 1668–1710* (Oxford, 1928), pp. 9–10; Robson Lowe (ed.), *The Codrington Correspondence* (London, 1951), pp. 1–4. Members of the Moyser, Gee, Bethel and Hotham families were all representatives of the borough in Parliament around this period. Pope was also well acquainted with Burlington's uncle, Lord Carleton, whose seat at Middleton lay only five miles from Londesborough, and who was actually buried in the vault of Londesborough church – as was his nephew almost thirty years later.

Pope's correspondence. It is therefore a cause for regret that only a single letter from either Bethel has come down to us; and that has been mislaid since the nineteenth-century editor printed it. The Bethel papers which were deposited at the East Riding County Record Office contain no information on this branch of the family.[4] Previous editors have supplied some detail on the Bethels themselves, but virtually nothing on the rest of the group. George Sherburn offers only a bare gloss or none at all for the other members of the group considered here. I hope to show in this chapter that Pope in his last years enjoyed the friendship of a tight knot of Yorkshire gentlemen, for the most part Johnians and Beverlonians, whose interests lay very much in the fields Burlington had cultivated.

The poet, indeed, avouches as much. More than once he mentions two or three of the group by name in a direct collocation. And on one such occasion his phrasing indicates that neither the strong local piety of these men, nor their readiness to stand together, had escaped his attention. The letter is that to Hugh Bethel on 2 November, 1736:

I beg you will remember me among your friends, Mr. Moyzer, Col. Gee, &c. No Yorkshire Hearts can bear you more good wishes, than ours do here.[5]

It is possible from other sources to guess at the identity of those covered by Pope's '&c.'. They would include Colonel Richard Pierson, son of an East Yorkshire knight; Dr John Kay, Bethel's York physician; and certain others, including members of the Draper and Strickland families.

The principal members of the group can be identified as follows:

(1) Hugh Bethel (1689–1748). A Whig country gentleman, resident at Beswick near Beverley. Not to be confused with his distant relative Hugh Bethel of Rise and Watton Abbey (d. 1752), through whom the main Bethel line has descended. (Henceforth 'Hugh Bethel' refers to the friend of Pope.) His mother, née Elizabeth Brooke, was a cousin of General Cadogan, the coadjutor of Marlborough, for whom Pope expressed a total lack of esteem. Two of Hugh's sisters married Sir William Codrington and Sir Charles

---

[4] There is however a useful MS genealogy, compiled by B. G. Bouwhins, and dated 1926 (DDRI/45/7). I am grateful to the former East Riding County Archivist for allowing me to use these papers. Most of the material deposited concerns Hugh Bethel of Rise (d. 1752); a number of links with the Gee family are documented. For the mislaid letter, see *Corr*, IV, 511.   [5] *Corr*, IV, 40.

Cox (or Cocks). A third, who seems to have remained unmarried, was, like her sisters, known to Pope.[6]

Pope refers in a letter to Hugh in 1736 to a 'Mr. Draper'. Sherburn conjectures that this was a friend of Lady Strickland, a Yorkshire neighbour of Bethel who 'would carry letters' to him. All this is correct, but it leaves out the main fact. Draper was probably Hugh's father-in-law, for the latter married Dorothy, daughter of William Draper. The Drapers were prominent in the village of Beswick and it may have been through the marriage that Bethel obtained his residence, later known as Beswick Hall.[7]

Like other members of the group, Hugh took a keen interest in the visual arts. He and Pope agreed to exchange portraits at one time (see above, p. 149): but only the picture of Bethel was executed. It hung 'in a Gold Frame' in Pope's own room at Twickenham. Kent was apparently to paint the poet for Bethel, but for unknown reasons this fell through.[8] The Yorkshireman was something of a traveller, with a fondness for Italy; and, like Pope, he seems to have combined genuine invalidism with a certain measure of valetudinarianism. He was certainly the most intimate friend of Pope among all the members of the Beverley group.

(2) Colonel James Moyser (*c*. 1693–1753). Only one letter to Moyser survives, dating from 1743; but he is frequently mentioned in Pope's correspondence with Hugh Bethel. Pope regularly sent 'hearty Compliments' to Moyser, who also suffered from bad health. He was Bethel's travelling companion in Italy in 1741. Additionally, Moyser moved in Bath circles, and it is evident that Ralph Allen was in personal contact with him at the end of 1742.[9]

The Colonel came from a well-established family whose estate lay

---

[6] *Corr*, II, 386 and n., 513 and n. Hugh's birth is given as 4 September, 1689, by Bouwhins, *loc. cit.*

[7] *Corr*, IV, 21 and n. Some of the Strickland papers are included in the Everingham MSS, formerly deposited at Beverley, but I have been unable to find any reference to substantiate the personal acquaintance of Lady Strickland and Pope. For Hugh's marriage, see Bouwhins, *loc. cit.* A certain Daniel Draper of Beswick is listed among the subscribers to John Oldmixon's *History of England* ('1730', i.e. 1729), p. xviii – a fact arguing strong Whig attachments in Draper. Few but zealots subscribed for this work. A Daniel Draper was Registrar of Beverley in 1729 and 1746 – George Poulson, *Beverlac; or, The Antiquities and History of the Town of Beverley*... (London, 1829), I, 425. 'Dan Draper' was one of a number of uninvited visitors who came to Londesborough one Sunday in 1735; Colonel Moyser was another, along with two Stricklands. Burlington writes to his wife of having 'all the joys of the East Riding'. See Lees-Milne, p. 163.

[8] *Corr*, IV, 500, 509, 512. Mack, *Garden and City*, p. 225, and W. K. Wimsatt, *The Portraits of Alexander Pope* (New Haven, Conn., 1965), p. 114, shed some light on the matter.

[9] *Corr*, IV, 460–1. Cf. III, 197, 228, 427; IV, 40, 207, 225, 255, 433–4.

originally at Lockington, a matter of two miles from Beswick and six from Beverley. His grandfather had been at Trinity, whilst his father followed a common pattern by proceeding from Beverley School to St John's College, Cambridge.[10] The father, John, was MP for Beverley in the middle of the reign of Anne; he has achieved more prominence, however, as an amateur architect of some distinction. He occupied himself with some timely repairs to Beverley Minster in 1706. According to an early historian of Beverley, Hawksmoor was employed to survey the fabric, but in the restoration it was the plans of John Moyser ('an adept in the science of architecture') which were implemented.[11] Whether this is so or not, it is certain that Moyser took a good deal of interest in the undertaking; a letter from him to Robert Harley on the subject has been preserved among the Portland papers.[12] According to a recent authority, John Moyser was 'on friendly terms with Lord Burlington, seems to have counted architecture among his polite accomplishments and there is reason to think he may have provided the plan for Nostell Priory, Yorkshire (1733)'. The same writer observes that James, the son, 'dabbled in architecture' too.[13] This is perhaps understating the matter. The younger Moyser provided plans for a block of almshouses in Keldgate, near the Minster, known as Anne Routh's Hospital. These were erected in 1748/49 to the proposed design.[14] James Moyser was in addition a subscriber to the building fund for the York Assembly Rooms, which were almost certainly Burlington's own work.[15] An account of Moyser's architectural activities has been given by Howard Colvin.[16]

Pope usually referred to him as 'the Colonel'. He had been a

---

[10] J. Venn and J. A. Venn (eds.), *Alumni Cantabrigienses* (Cambridge, 1922), Part I, III, 225.

[11] George Oliver, *The History and Antiquities of the Town and Minster of Beverley* (Beverley, 1839), p. 239.

[12] *Historical Manuscripts Commission* 29 (London, 1897), IV, 305. Cf. K. A. MacMahon (ed.), *Beverley Corporation Minute Books (1707–1835)* (London and Hull, 1958), p. xiii.

[13] G. W. Beard, *Georgian Craftsmen and their Work* (London, 1967), p. 25. Moyser senior appears to have lived in North Bar Within, Beverley; whilst the Gee family around the same time (1723) had a house in Toll Gavel – J. J. Sheahan and T. Whelan, *History and Topography of the City of York…and the East Riding of Yorkshire* (Beverley, 1856), II, 227. Pope expressed himself 'truly a Condoler of Mr. Moyser', that is the son, when John Moyser died in 1738 (*Corr*, IV, 113).   [14] MacMahon, p. 30; Poulson, II, 798.

[15] Beard, p. 55. For the subscribers' list, see item 38 in *Apollo of the Arts* (Nottingham, 1973), p. 39. For the Assembly Rooms, see Rudolf Wittkower, 'Burlington and his Work in York', *Studies in Architectural History*, ed. W. A. Singleton (London and York, 1954), pp. 47–66.

[16] Information in a personal letter from Mr John Harris, Curator of the Drawings Collection, RIBA Library. See Howard Colvin, *A Biographical Dictionary of British Architects 1600–1840* (London, 1978), pp. 565–6.

professional soldier in his youth (consequently he did not follow other members of his family to Cambridge); his promotion to a captaincy in the First Regiment of Foot Guards (the Grenadiers) is recorded in December 1709.[17] Another military member of the group, Colonel Gee, was a relative by marriage, possibly a brother-in-law. The coupling of these two names by Pope (see the letter of November 1736, already quoted) appears in this light even more natural. The pair had in common not only 'Yorkshire hearts' and an Army background; they had also family alliance.

(3) Colonel Gee. There is only one other reference to this figure in Pope's correspondence. It occurs in a letter to Hugh Bethel of 14 April 1741. Pope had been enquiring as to the state of Bethel's health. From the latter's sister, Lady Codrington, he heard that the patient was on the mend 'as Col. Gee had also acquainted Lord Burlington and Mr. Cleland'.[18] Thus, lost within a parenthesis, a name so far quite unexplained – Sherburn has no note at this point.

There are two candidates, both members of a family long settled at Bishop Burton, three miles west of Beverley. The less likely is James Gee (1686–1751), educated at Queens' College, Cambridge, and the Inner Temple.[19] James was appointed Receiver-General for Yorkshire in 1734,[20] and one might have imagined that he devoted his life to a legal career. But we know that at the time of the Jacobite rebellion he enlisted in Sir Charles Hotham's Regiment, and that in June 1715 he was appointed Captain and Lieutenant-Colonel in the Third Foot Guards.[21] The allegiance to Hotham, the head of the most prominent local family and Whig MP for the borough of Beverley, is easy to account for. Gee's father married as his second wife a Hotham, daughter of an earlier baronet; whilst his own half-sister Bridget became Sir Charles Hotham's wife until her untimely death in 1707.[22] To complicate matters further, it was this James Gee who married Constantia Moyser in 1727, and thus became brother-

---

[17] Charles Dalton, *George the First's Army* (London, 1910), I, 125. A 'John Moyser' who became an ensign in Sir Charles Hotham's Regiment of Foot in 1715 seems unlikely to have been Moyser senior; perhaps it was another son. See Dalton, I, 172, 201. For references to a petition by Colonel James Moyser in January 1716, see Secretary of State Stanhope's letter-book, Public Record Office, SP 44/117/387.

[18] *Corr*, IV, 338. [19] Venn and Venn, II, 204.

[20] *Gentleman's Magazine*, XXI, 427. [21] Dalton, I, 172, 173n., 201.

[22] There is a family tree in Poulson, opp. I, 398; and in Oliver, p. 496. Neither is wholly accurate but Poulson is on the whole more reliable. See also the pedigree of the Hothams, in Poulson, opp. I, 315, in Oliver, opp. p. 508 – the same provisos apply. See also A. M. W. Stirling, *The Hothams* (London, 1918), I, 126–38.

in-law of James Moyser – the previous member of the group we have considered.

But there is a second, and more plausible candidate. This is William Gee (1698/9–1745), son of James Gee's half-brother Thomas. To clear away at the start a further genealogical involution, it may be recorded that William Gee married Philippa, the beautiful second daughter of Sir Charles Hotham and Bridget Gee.[23] (There were further intermarriages in succeeding generations.) William Gee's military career is more to the present purpose. He, too, became a captain in 1715, in Colonel Handesyde's regiment. He had reached the rank of Lieutenant-Colonel in the 20th Foot when he was killed at Fontenoy in 1745.[24] He seems to have remained a full-time serving officer for the whole of his adult life, though he too (unusually) had been at Cambridge. The familiar pattern turns up once more: he had been at school at Beverley and proceeded to St John's, Cambridge, in 1715.[25]

It is unlikely that a positive identification of 'Colonel Gee' can be made at this date, so bald are Pope's references. In favour of James may be mentioned the close tie with Moyser through marriage, and the rather greater likelihood that he would be in England at any one moment and thus able to frequent the society of Bath or London. But these are tenuous claims. In the case of William, we can urge the school and family connection, plus the fact that as a serving soldier he would be more probably styled 'the Colonel'. But we do not know enough of the tastes or character of either men to come to a definite conclusion.

The point is not entirely academic. Preserved in the library of the Royal Institute of British Architects is a drawing (possibly by Flitcroft) of a house at Bishop Burton.[26] This is described as 'Colonel Gee's house'. All the indications are that this was one of Burlington's few achieved works of architecture; more the pity, then, that the house has long been demolished. It would be pleasant to know which of the two Lieutenant-Colonels was in fact the privileged owner. From Pope's letter in 1741, it is apparent that Colonel Gee and Lord Burlington were then in personal contact, and that the poet himself

---

[23] Stirling, I, 126ff.   [24] Dalton, I, 306; II, 219.
[25] Venn and Venn, II, 205. If the facts supplied by various authorities are correct, it can only be assumed that Gee left Cambridge very speedily after matriculation in order to go and help quell the rising.
[26] Reproduced in Fiske Kemball's article, 'Burlington Architectus', *JRIBA*, 15 October 1927, p. 683.

may well have enjoyed Gee's company. Clearly Gee – whoever he was – can be numbered amongst Hugh Bethel's close friends, and among the leading spirits of the group.

(4) Dr Kay (or Key). There are half a dozen references here, scattered about the later years of Pope's correspondence.[27] Sherburn hazards no guess respecting the doctor's identity. However, I believe that he can be named as Dr John Kay (b. 1679/80), the son of a West Riding druggist, who attended Beverley School under Mr Lambert and went up to St John's in 1698. In 1703 he took his MB.[28] On Pope's own testimony Kay 'wrote [him] letters' concerning Bethel, but these are lost.[29] From the surviving references he appears to have been a good friend to Bethel, whose Yorkshire physician he was, and a man of catholic tastes; Pope's bees and lead urns alike aroused his interest. In 1742 Pope writes that Key 'is now gone for Flanders', which perhaps suggests that he served in the British forces during the war of the Austrian Succession.[30] But I can find no trace of his name in the extant Army lists.

(5) Colonel Pierson. There are only two brief references here. In both cases Pierson is mentioned as passing on to Pope news of Hugh Bethel's health, a task in which he is joined by Dr Kay. Sherburn offers the conjecture, 'Possibly the Col. Richard Pearson who died at York, 3rd January, 1742/3. *Gent. Mag.* xiii (1743), 51'.[31] I believe this guess to be a happy one. Sherburn was presumably working purely on the basis of the York connection; but another clue has recently emerged. In a unique file of the *York Gazetteer* now in Beverley Public Library, I came on the final issue for the year 1742, that for 28 December.[32] This records the event to which Sherburn alludes, but puts it a week or so earlier: 'Last week died in this City

---

[27] *Corr*, III, 114; IV, 375, 395, 473–74, 512. There is an assumption that Kay was a physician, as most of the references suggest. But there are other possible candidates, including John Kay, another Johnian who became deacon and then a prebendary of York. Other Yorkshiremen at St John's at this period were Richard Kay and William Kay, both of whom held livings in the North Riding (Venn and Venn, III, 13–14). For the suggestion that Pope's acquaintance was a cleric – 'the Reverend Doctor *Key*', who sent fossils from Knaresborough – see Mack, *Garden and City*, p. 259. See also *Admissions to the College of St John the Evangelist* (Cambridge, 1893), II, 147, 160.   [28] Venn and Venn, III, 13.

[29] *Corr*, IV, 375.   [30] *Corr*, IV, 395.

[31] *Corr*, IV, 375–6, 395. Sherburn's conjecture is at IV, 375n.

[32] Misdated '21 December', which is taken over from the headline of the previous week's issue. The file, complete for 1742 apart from the first and one subsequent issue, was formerly in the possession of my father and was presented to Beverley Public Library by my mother following his death in 1964. I would like to thank the then Assistant Borough Librarian, Mr G. P. Brown, for his help in facilitating my work.

the Honourable Colonel Pearson, who was a younger son of Sir Matthew Pearson, of Lowthorpe in this County, Knight.' Now Matthew Pearson (1650/1–1711/2) had been educated at Bridlington School and then entered St John's as a fellow-commoner in 1666. Three years later he was knighted, for what service to the crown does not appear.[33] Lowthorpe is between Driffield and Bridlington, some fifteen miles north-east of Beverley (where the name Pearson was none the less very common at this time).[34] We are surely justified in concluding that Sir Matthew's son was the Colonel Pierson we are pursuing.

If that is a fair conclusion, then a distinctly sprightly individual is added to a roster of Pope's acquaintances. Pierson's last, possibly quixotic, gesture was to order that his body should lie in state for forty days.[35] Earlier than that, however, we find references to injuries in a duel.[36] A Richard Pierson became an ensign in the Grenadier Guards (Moyser's regiment) in 1702, and in the course of time was promoted captain with the rank of Lieutenant-Colonel. He retired in 1742.[37] It seems highly plausible that this high-spirited Guards officer, well known in York and the East Riding, was a friend of Moyser, Gee and Kay.

Cementing this slightly disparate membership were a number of factors personal and genealogical. A single connective agent, never mentioned in Pope's letters, would be Rev. Joseph Lambert, Master of Beverley School from 1674 to 1716.[38] Lambert was born in Hull, and proceeded from Hull Grammar School to St John's in 1667. During his period as Master, several members of the group, or their close relatives, attended Beverley School. A contemporary of many of them was Robert Lambert (1676/7–1735), who, after studying under his father, went on to become Master of St John's, as well as Vice-Chancellor of the University, Lady Margaret preacher and a Doctor of Divinity.[39] Robert, unlike most members of the group – from Burlington downwards, if we may count him – was a Tory. Indeed this election to the Mastership in 1727 was made along

---

[33] Venn and Venn, III, 331; W. A. Shaw (ed.), *The Knights of England* (London, 1906), II, 243.

[34] It is also interesting to reflect that in the will of William Kent, who came from nearby Bridlington in all probability, his sister is named as Esther Pearson. See Margaret Jourdain, *The Work of William Kent* (London, 1948), p. 89.

[35] *Gentleman's Magazine*, XIII (1743), 51.   [36] *Gentleman's Magazine*, II (1731), 721.

[37] Dalton, I, 289.

[38] The resolution of the Borough Council to appoint him is printed in full in A. F. Leach, *Early Yorkshire Schools* (Yorkshire Archaeological Society, Record Series, XXVII) n.p., 1899, I, 138.   [39] Venn and Venn, III, 38.

distinctly political lines, and there are signs he may have been a somewhat unwilling candidate.[40] His entire career was spent in Cambridge, and we may suppose that the worldly but cultivated circle attached to Pope would have found him a boorish pedant.

Joseph Lambert, however, is another matter. We know that his reputation was high as a schoolmaster. 'He produced many great scholars', a later Beverlonian wrote;[41] and that is the kind of boast which even the least academically inclined will make if it ministers to local piety. It is noteworthy that every member of the group was either himself, or had a close relative, at St John's in the late seventeenth century – this applies even in the case of the Bethels, whose connection with the College was more slender.[42] In addition, it can be shown that other notabilities alluded to in the Pope–Bethel correspondence were likewise Johnians. Dr Pelham Johnston (1680/1–1765), whom Pope recommended to Bethel, is described by Sherburn as 'a London Practitioner, who came of a Yorkshire family'. That is true enough; it might be added that Johnston had gone up to St John's in 1700.[43] It almost comes as a surprise to find Pope writing to his Yorkshire friend of someone who did *not* belong to the college.

II

It should emerge that the 'group' is not a complete fiction on my part. A fairly tight knot of friends can be discerned, though inevitably their day-to-day dealings with one another are not now recoverable. Several features stand out with particular clarity. The partly military character of this fraternity may be a chance contingency; but their interest in *virtù*, their genial concern with their own health and that of their fellows, their adherence to Burlington, their devotion to Pope and, not least, their sturdy allegiance to their provincial background – these are no accident. They are the bonds of a union which Pope perceived, with amusement but with kindly sympathy too.[44] I have

[40] J. B. Mullinger, *St John's College* (London, 1901), pp. 219–21.
[41] [J. R. Witty], notes in a commemorative booklet for Beverley Grammar School Old Boys' Association Jubilee Dinner, 22 June 1957.   [42] See Venn and Venn, I, 145.
[43] *Corr*, IV, 338 and n.; Venn and Venn, II, 480. Another Johnian familiar to Pope, of course, was Matthew Prior, who in 1689 wrote an epistle 'To Dr: F[uller?]' in a Letter to Beverley'. See *The Literary Works of Matthew Prior*, ed. H. B. Wright, M. K. Spears (Oxford, 1959), pp. 93, 856–7.
[44] Pope notes Bethel's concern for such friends as Moyser in a letter of 1740; and ten years earlier he had hinted at Yorkshire pride (*Corr*, IV, 269; III, 113). Many other examples along these lines could be quoted.

argued that Hugh Bethel's 'tastes, acquirements and social standing' made him a particularly apt exemplar and dedicatee for Pope's 'Sermon' on rural living, just as Burlington's made him an admirable recipient for the noble epistle 'Of the Use of Riches'.[45] It is interesting that when Pope shifted his attention to 'the middle state' (*Sat.*, II, ii, 61), he picked on Bethel as his spokesman in a poem concerned with such topics as hospitality, property and country life. For Bethel, with his friends, had shown Pope that taste could be transmitted to outlying regions, and be the proper study of the professional classes, the business community and the lesser squirarchy. There was a Burlington set at St James' and Chiswick; but there was another one much nearer Londesborough, where the Earl's estate lay and where his remains now rest.

[45] See pp. 146–51 above. I should like to thank Peter Dixon for reading an earlier draft of this chapter and offering useful comments upon it.

CHAPTER 14

Pope and the antiquarians

We all know that Pope, like his fellow members of the Scriblerian group, was against the antiquarians.[1] He *must* have been. Were not antiquarians the sort of people who, in the manner of Scott's Jonathan Oldbuck, mistook commonplace domestic objects for ancient relics? Did they not invent absurd explanations for Stonehenge, dream up fanciful Trojan origins for the British, fantasize about the wanderings of the peoples, and track down Hyperborean sources in every rivulet of European history? Were they not regularly misled by ingenious but totally unfounded etymological reasoning? Did they not reconstruct Babel by their preposterous ethnologies of the tribes of Noah? Were they not literal-minded to the point that they accepted any ancient gnomic statement as Holy Writ? Did they not convince themselves that modern men and women were puny descendants of a once Titanic race? Cannot we see them as shading into the much derided virtuosi who collected things for their oddity value, rather than for their real historic worth? And were they not linked to the equally suspect class of dilettanti, who looted the archeological sites of Greece, Rome and the Middle East, as well as Britain itself? Were not many in the eighteenth century actually members of the Dilettanti Society, of whom Horace Walpole famously said that the nominal qualification was to have studied *virtù* in Rome, but the real mark was to have got drunk there? In short, are they not at best a collection of amiable enthusiasts?[2]

The answer to all these questions is a qualified yes. Each description fits some of the antiquarians some of the time, but none applies to all

---

[1] This chapter is based on a paper delivered at a conference to commemorate the tercentenary of Pope's birth, held at the Center for British Studies, Yale University, in April 1988.
[2] For a general overview of the subject, see T. D. Kendrick, *British Antiquity* (London, 1950); David C. Douglas, *English Scholars 1660–1730* (London, 1951); and Joseph M. Levine, *Humanism and History* (Ithaca, 1987).

of the antiquarians all of the time. The other side of the picture can be filled in if we ask further questions, as the Latin grammars used to say, expecting the answer 'yes'. First, was not Dr Arbuthnot, Pope's Scriblerian colleague, much preoccupied by the study of ancient measurements and coins, and did he not get involved in a controversy over the geology of the Flood with that prime antiquarian Dr John Woodward? Second, do not many of the minor Scriblerian satires deal directly with this same Woodward, and operate freely through a parody of antiquarian methods, forms and styles, sufficient to show close familiarity with this area of enquiry? Third, were not many friends and allies of the Scriblerian group given to antiquarian pursuits – notably the first and second Earls of Oxford, building up the wonderful Harley library with the help of a leading paleographic scholar, Humfrey Wanley?[3] Not to mention collectors such as Dr Richard Mead, and Swift's friend the numismatist Sir Andrew Fountaine. Fourth, did not Pope perform the 'dull duty' of an editor in sober earnest, and go through 'due gradations of dulness' from a creative writer, to a translator, to an editor? Fifth, did not Pope support the first translation of Geoffrey of Monmouth,[4] and return to the study of Trojan myth for his unfinished epic *Brutus*? And finally, did not Pope make extensive use of the Anglo-Saxon chronicles, Camden, and John Selden's notes to *Poly Olbion*, in writing *Windsor-Forest*? Did not he not employ Nordic scholars for *The Temple of Fame*, and allude to Olaus Wormius, about whom Gibbon produced some scathing sentences in the *Decline and Fall*, in Book III of *The Dunciad*? And did he not know Thomas Hearne's laborious editions of early works well enough to cite them at length in the *Dunciad* notes?

These questions hinge on matters of fact and we need not stay long for an answer. But a further, more contentious, question could be put; or rather a series of linked questions. Does not much of Scriblerian satire deal directly in antiquarian currency? Does not *The Memoirs of Martinus Scriblerus* enter immediately into the very discourse of antiquarianism? And, above all, is not *The Dunciad* itself, particularly *The New Dunciad* which became Book IV, a kind of antiquarian document or artefact? Here some readers might be inclined to offer a defiant 'no' to break the monotony of assent. This

---

[3] Wanley's involvement with the Pope circle, and his part in the creation of the Harleian library, can be traced in James Lees-Milne, *Earls of Creation* (London, 1962), pp. 173–85.

[4] *Corr*, I, 425.

chapter is designed to enforce that final 'yes', and aims to convince the presumed sceptic.

I

The orthodox view is well represented in the comments of Charles Kerby-Miller, in his fine edition of *Martinus Scriblerus*:

Though aimed primarily at Woodward, the satire touches all excessive antiquarianism and zeal for collecting. Interest in antiquities had become widespread in the early eighteenth century, and not only wealthy noblemen and improvident scholars collected ancient objects, but professional men such as Dr Mead, Dr Sloane, and Dr Woodward devoted considerable portions of their earnings to the purchase of ancient as well as modern rarities. The Scriblerians themselves were not exempt from the current taste. The Earl of Oxford and his son built up a large collection; Pope, though he confined his collecting to objects for his garden and grotto, told Spence he had once developed enough interest in antiquities to write a treatise in Latin on the old buildings in Rome; Swift showed in occasional references in his letters and in his purchase of books that he was attracted by the ancient and curious; and Arbuthnot displayed in his *Tables of Ancient Coins* and other writings a strong interest in various aspects of ancient life and learning. We may safely assume, therefore, that the intention here, as in other cases in the *Memoirs*, is not to ridicule the subject itself but to satirize those who carried their enthusiasm for all things connected with the ancients to the point of folly.[5]

That is all well said, but in practice it is not always so easy to isolate the 'subject' itself from the attendant follies. The satirist can rarely attack abuses in learning without some blurring at the edges, whereby learning itself is exposed to a measure of ridicule. As Joseph M. Levine has shown in his superbly illuminating book, *Dr Woodward's Shield* (1977), even though Woodward could be mistaken, fallacious and absurd in his work as geologist, medical adviser, Egyptologist and much else, he was at the same time creative, innovative and ahead of his time. As Levine states in his conclusion: 'So it was with Dr Woodward's shield. The method of the antiquaries had been right; only their comparisons were too circumscribed. The evidence was not yet in, at least in sufficient order and quantity to demonstrate the truth.'[6]

---

[5] *The Memoirs of Martinus Scriblerus*, ed. C. Kerby-Miller (New Haven, Conn., 1950), p. 203. Kerby-Miller's introduction supplies valuable background in assessing Pope's relation to antiquarian studies; see especially pp. 68–77.

[6] Joseph M. Levine, *Dr Woodward's Shield: History, Science, and Satire in Augustan England* (Berkeley and Los Angeles, Ca., 1977), p. 279.

What Levine's study shows us is something critical to the understanding of Scriblerian art, and the art of Pope generally – that the antiquarians were in effect the moderns, and the Augustan humanists who derided them were the ancients, in all the disputes they entered upon. In different ways men such as Woodward, John Wood, William Whiston, John Toland and William Stukeley – the kind of figure indigenous to Augustan satire – were pioneering, however crudely, the procedures, methods, concerns, concepts and vocabulary of later scientific enquiry, in subjects such as archaeology, physical anthropology and paleobotany. And they knew some things which the Scriblerians needed to know, to do *their* business.

For example, Levine observes at one point, 'The unresolved problem of the Ancients was how to achieve knowledge without losing the polish of gentleman [as Woodward and his kind tended to do], how to employ philology without becoming a philologist.'[7] One can see this anxiety to maintain amateur status in such remarks as that of Lord Chesterfield, 'You are likely to hear of it as a virtuoso; and if so, I should be glad to profit by it as an humble dilettante.'[8] But Levine's comment is surely most directly applicable to *The Dunciad*, a work which employs pedantry as well as just parodying it. Pope's poem satirizes minute attention to words rather than things, yet it deploys the most minute and fastidious care in refinements of poetic language.

In a later essay, Levine has described the progress of the 'antiquarian enterprise' in Britain.[9] Again he seeks to show that the old-guard humanists, with their classical background and preconceptions, were instrumental in retarding the new scientific archaeology. In this context it is the Scriblerian group who represent the traditional humanist outlook. As for the new inquirers, they might range from students of innovative subjects like epigraphy to grammarians and editors. In the latter class, a typical figure is Thomas Hearne, who was the object of Pope's satire earlier in *The Dunciad*, as 'our own Antiquary Mr *Thomas Hearne*, who had no way aggrieved our Poet, but on the contrary published many curious tracts which he hath to his great contentment perused' (note to III, 188). The text is less kindly:

> 'But who is he, in close y-pent,
> Of sober face, with learned dust besprent?'

[7] Levine, *Shield*, p. 242.   [8] Letter of 1748, quoted in *OED*, s.v. *dilettante*, 1.
[9] Levine, 'The Antiquarian Enterprise, 1500–1800', in *Humanism and History*, pp. 73–106.

Right well mine eyes arede the myster wight,
On parchment scraps y-fed, and Wormius hight.
To future ages may they dulness last,
As thou preserv'st the dulness of the past!   (III, 185–90)

Hearne, as a medievalist, had perpetuated in his editions 'The
Classics of an Age that heard of none' (I, 147). He had achieved
further notoriety in an episode Levine has described, involving the
discovery of a Roman pavement near Oxford: Hearne had confidently identified the subject of the design as Apollo, but was
comprehensively outgunned in the ensuing debate, which showed
that the subject was actually Bacchus.[10] It was the kind of 'blunder'
to which the new disciplines were inevitably subject, and which made
their practitioners an easy target for conservative wit. None the less
Pope apparently did read Hearne's laborious compilations, notably
editions of early English chronicles, and his poetry reflects a degree of
absorption in the materials of antiquarian study even as it rejects the
pedantry, uncontrolled speculation and bizarre use of time that
seemed to accompany this study.

    The essence of the problem, from the point of view of someone with
a mind so differently constituted as Pope's appears to be, lay in the
disjunction between raw empirical data and intellectual inference.
The word 'curious' which is used of Hearne's tracts points to this
issue. Antiquarians were much taken up by *curiosa*, curious things,
curiosities. From the humanist standpoint, this deflected attention
from deep cultural implications and especially from moral consider-
ations. It is for this reason that the Scriblerian attack is often ranged
against the activity of collectors, since they appear to have divorced
the act of assemblage from the act of interpretation. Today we can see
that both undertakings were necessary if the modern sciences were to
get off the ground. This was not so obvious in the early Hanoverian
period. We may note the history of the word 'collector' as set out in
the first definition under this heading in *OED*:

One who collects or gathers together; *spec.* one who gathers separate literary
compositions, etc., into one book, a compiler (now *rare* or *obs.*), one who
collects scientific specimens, works of art, curiosities, etc.

Scriblerians would prefer the older meaning, now 'rare or obsolete',
to have prevailed, and for the mere assembler of 'curiosities' to
occupy a lower rung in the cultural hierarchy. What seemed to be

[10] Levine, 'The Stonesfield Pavement: Archaeology in Augustan England', in *Humanism and
History*, pp. 107–22.

happening in Pope's day was that the simple act of gathering together disparate objects had supplanted serious thought about the life behind such objects. The riposte Pope made was characteristic: he put together *The Dunciad*, which is at once a cento of literary fragments (and thus the work of a strangely transformed 'compiler'), and an assemblage of bric-à-brac. It is a collection in the old and the new sense.

In the educated society of Pope's day there were antiquaries everywhere one looked. They were the representative students of mankind before the evolution of human sciences; they were consulted whenever a constitution needed to be drafted, and they were put on the board of hospital trustees. Their findings were to inspire art, as with Piranesi, and to underpin architecture, as with John Wood and Robert Adam. In these circumstances Pope could hardly have avoided some friendly contacts in this varied group, which ranged from editors and philologists such as Hearne and pioneer Saxonists to the constitutional historians, the diggers-up of Avebury, the Celtic fabulists and proto-musicologists. Moreover, the contribution to political debate made by men such as Dugdale is fully apparent from studies such as J. G. A. Pocock's seminal book *The Ancient Constitution and the Feudal Law*.[11] Pope would have had to be far narrower in his intellectual interests and in his human allegiances than he actually was to dismiss everyone in this group.

None the less it is surely significant that the very first sentence of *The Memoirs of Scriblerus* refers to the hero's father Cornelius as 'by Profession an Antiquary'.[12] This is a joke in itself, since there were scarcely any professional antiquaries as such. It was Montfaucon in his monastery, or the English clergymen, doctors and wealthy amateurs who prosecuted the study. Art history as a regular discipline had to wait for such figures as Winckelmann to arrive a generation after *The Dunciad*. Yet one can surely argue that the poem, especially its fourth book, is already replete with not just the materials, but also the attitudes, of these branches of enquiry. The texture of the verse is invaded by the detritus of early archaeological investigation. The entire work consists of 'a Lumberhouse of books... never to be read' (III, 193–4). Throughout the poem we are assailed by toads, fungi, cockle-shells, mosses, dried butterflies and other faintly disagreeable

---

[11] J. G. A. Pocock, *The Ancient Constitution and the Feudal Law* (Cambridge, 2nd edn, 1987), pp. 182–228. Cf. Christopher Hill, 'The Norman Yoke', in *Puritanism and Revolution* (1958).
[12] *Memoirs of Scriblerus*, p. 95.

collectibles. The verse thus textualizes the concerns of virtuosi, but it also lovingly denominates the trophies of antiquarian study, such as the coins and gems which underlay their fantastic theories about the progress of humanity.

This element in the design becomes clear if we look at the major passage dealing with the mania for collection, which occurs towards the end of Book IV:

> But Annius, crafty seer, with ebon wand,
> And well dissembled em'rald on his hand,
> False as his Gems, and canker'd as his Coins,
> Came, cramm'd with capon, from where Pollio dines.
> Soft, as the wily Fox is seen to creep,
> Where bask on sunny banks the simple sheep,
> Walk round and round, now prying here, now there;
> So he; but pious, whisper'd first his pray'r.
>   Grant, gracious Goddess! grant me still to cheat,
> O may thy cloud still cover the deceit!
> Thy choicer mists on this assembly shed,
> But pour them thickest on the noble head.
> So shall each youth, assisted by our eyes,
> See other Caesars, other Homers rise;
> Thro' twilight ages hunt th' Athenian fowl,
> Which Chalcis gods, and mortals call an Owl,
> Now see an Attys, now a Cecrops clear,
> Nay, Mahomet! the Pigeon at thine ear;
> Be rich in ancient brass, tho' not in gold,
> And keep his Lares, tho' his house be sold;
> To headless Phoebe his fair bride postpone,
> Honour a Syrian Prince above his own;
> Lord of an Otho, if I vouch it true;
> Blest in one Niger, till he knows of two.
>   Mummius o'erheard him; Mummius, Fool-renown'd,
> Who like his Cheops stinks above the ground,
> Fierce as a startled Adder, swell'd, and said,
> Rattling an ancient Sistrum at his head.
>   Speak'st thou of Syrian Princes? Traitor base!
> Mine, goddess! mine is all the horned race.
> True, he had wit, to make the value rise;
> From foolish Greeks to steal them, was as wise;
> More glorious yet, from barb'rous hands to keep,
> When Sallee Rovers chac'd him on the deep.
> Then taught by Hermes, and divinely bold,
> Down his own throat he risqu'd the Grecian gold;
> Receiv'd each Demi-God, with pious care,

Deep in his Entrails – I rever'd them there,
I bought them, shrouded in that living shrine,
And, at their second birth, they issue mine.
  Witness great Ammon! by whose horns I swore,
(Reply'd soft Annius) this our paunch before
Still bears them, faithful; and that thus I eat,
Is to refund the medals with the meat.
To prove me, Goddess! clear of all design,
Bid me with Pollio sup, as well as dine:
There all the Learn'd shall at the labour stand,
And Douglas lend his soft, obstetric hand.
  The Goddess smiling seem'd to give consent;
So back to Pollio, hand in hand, they went.   (IV, 347–96)

Then come the specialist collectors, headed by the tulip-fancier and the lepidopterist:

Then thick as Locusts black'ning all the ground,
A tribe, with weeds and shells fantastic crown'd,
Each with some wond'rous gift approach'd the Pow'r,
A Nest, a Toad, a Fungus, or a Flow'r.   (IV, 397–400)

Of course not all antiquarians were collectors, and vice versa; but the general sense of their interchangeability is reinforced here by the direct succession of Egyptologist and numismatist by the fungus and bug brigade.[13]

Annius has been identified with fair plausibility as Andrew Fountaine. Mummius may well be Woodward himself, though Joseph Warton suggested that this was Richard Mead, someone with whom Pope had good relations (not, in this context, any sort of argument against the ascription). The Twickenham editor believes that the likeliest candidate is the Earl of Sandwich, who was President of the Egyptian Club and a well-known virtuoso.[14] This is the very same Sandwich who was later a prominent politician, an alleged Medmenham 'monk' and crony of Wilkes, the patron of Cook's voyages of discovery and the supposed inventor of the sandwich. In 1743 he was just back from his Grand Tour and flexing his muscles as a cultural potentate. Marjorie Nicolson and G. S. Rousseau have reintroduced the candidacy of Woodward, in my

---

[13] One of the features which marks out these contemptible objects of enquiry is their smallness – an odd fact, since (as many commentators have observed) Pope was himself drawn to the miniature. On the concept of miniaturization, see Susan Stewart, *On Longing: Narratives of the Miniature, the Gigantic, the Souvenir, the Collection* (Baltimore, Md., 1984), pp. 37–69.

[14] *TE*, V, 449–50.

view with fuller warrant;[15] and Levine's study tends to support the attribution, not least in showing just how visible this man was in the intellectual scene of his day. The crucial issue is not the precise identity of Mummius, however; it is rather the obsession with things Egyptian, a trait Pope would have been likely to latch on to quicker than most with his own awareness of the hermetic lore of ancient Egypt.[16]

It would be possible to go through the roster of other antiquarians who could have made some contribution to Pope's portrait of the species. There was for example John Anstis, a herald who wrote a history of the Order of the Garter, an institution with a significant though partly concealed role in *Windsor-Forest*. Anstis also collected seals and studied Cornish antiquities, a field in which Pope's close friend William Borlase specialized. There is Sir Hans Sloane, whose collections made up the foundation of the British Museum. But two representative figures who illustrate different aspects of the anti-quarian movement, Woodward and Stukeley, will serve to make the point most shortly.

II

John Woodward can be seen as merely daft – cantankerous and misguided, but if we utilize the frame of reference supplied by Levine, it is clear that there are obvious ways in which he could have *mattered* to Pope and ministered to his creative needs. We might consider, for example, the hope he expressed when taking up a controversy on Egyptology, that he might 'set forth the first appearance of science in the world and trace her through all ages and climates'.[17] This points directly to the Scriblerian squib 'On the Origin of Sciences', but also to *The Dunciad*, with its review of the progress of learning from ancient to modern times. Woodward's central intellectual aim was sum-marized in the title of one of his books: *Fossils of all Kinds Digested into a Method*.[18] This kind of methodization was something which called out the scorn of both Swift and Pope, but it was of course to underlie

---

[15] Marjorie H. Nicolson and G. S. Rousseau, '*This Long Disease, My Life*': *Alexander Pope and the Natural Sciences* (Princeton, NJ, 1968), pp. 125–9.

[16] See Douglas Brooks-Davies, *Pope's 'Dunciad' and the Queen of the Night* (Manchester, 1984), pp. 121–39, where the author relates Pope's increasing knowledge of Egyptian matters to his friendship with Warburton, who had developed a special interest in this field. For Woodward's obsession with ancient Egypt, see Levine, *Shield*, pp. 75–9.

[17] Levine, *Shield*, p. 76.

[18] See Levine, *Shield*, pp. 104–06. The title would make it all the more applicable that Annius should 'digest' the coins he collects (IV, 387–94).

the rise of modern science. In so far as Woodward sought to construct a regular map of knowledge from the objects he collected and described (as opposed to merely sticking them up on the wall, as Pope did with his geological specimens in the grotto), we are confronting an epistemological gap as well as a mere discrepancy in taste and habit. Yet, paradoxically, such regularization was exactly what Pope was about in his own work. As he anatomized dulness, he codified its activities in orderly lines and neatly tagged footnotes, and then displayed its manifestations in the capacious exhibition gallery of *The Dunciad*. Woodward had given a lot of thought to the best way of housing and storing his collections – just as Pope did on how to set out his long-hoarded collections, in the preliminaries, the appendices and other parerga attached to *The Dunciad*.

There are several descriptions of the Woodwardian museum. One is by the noted antiquarian Ralph Thoresby, who had first visited Sloane's ample collection of books, manuscripts, coins and gems. He then went to see Woodward's home, where he found another 'fine and representative museum':

It was 'most curious in natural curiosities, fossils, gems, minerals, ores, shells, stones, etc., of which he made me a noble present.' It was the beginning of an exchange that brought to Thoresby a startling number of new accessions. But Dr Woodward's museum was not lacking in books, either, and 'a curious collection of Roman antiquities, not only of urns, but gems, signets, rings, keys, "stylus Scriptoriis, res turpiculae," ivory pins, brass "fibulae," etc.' The Doctor had obviously more than the ordinary credentials of an antiquary. Thoresby thought it only a pity that 'so ingenious a person should not have more friends.'[19]

This was reported by Thoresby to his friend Archdeacon William Nicolson, who came to London a few years later and made his own tour of the great collections kept in the capital. Woodward, however, was the star turn, and (as Levine explains) a friendship developed:

On Nicolson's visit to London in 1704, the two men dined together and Woodward showed his visitor a reputed Celtic coin. He was very angry at the Archbishop of York for renouncing once and for all what Nicolson continued to describe (in his Diary anyway) as 'the hasty-pudding doctrine of his Theory of the Earth.' He showed Nicolson his method of arranging his fossils, also a 'Northern monument' with inscription, and other curiosities both natural and human. On another visit to Gresham College, Woodward would hardly let the bishop view the College collection but

---

[19] Levine, *Shield*, p. 120.

hastened him to his own, 'as he thinks it, richer Museum.' Still, Nicolson was impressed by the Doctor's immense collections, and found agreeable conversation there with Mr Harris, Mr Hutchinson, and others in Woodward's entourage. Among the vegetable remains that the bishop viewed there were some mosses which Woodward insisted were an 'infallible Argument that the deluge happened in May.' Woodward was obsessed by the subject. When it got dark, 'just as we came to the first Drawer of his "Cornue Ammonis,"' they withdrew to dinner. Afterward they returned to the Library and were shown several of Woodward's manuscripts, especially his *Catalogue of the Rarities of the Museum,* 'with discourses on the chief of 'em in a good Method.' (This was the work published, still incomplete, twenty-five years later.) There was also a *History of Metals* in two parts, a work that was ready for the press. (It was recopied again in 1724, but never published.) Most interesting was his *History of America.* Here Woodward tried to prove that at a very early time America was populated by Europeans who had brought with them their culture and implements. (He argued from the similarity of their remains.) While discoursing, Woodward enlarged on a favorite theme, running down the Egyptians 'as mistaken Masters of ancient Learning.' (As we have seen, Woodward left a manuscript on this subject, but the American History seems to have perished.)[20]

Two detailed comments may be interjected. The first is that the foolish virtuosi who follow hot on the heels of the antiquarians in *The Dunciad* have the same heterogeneous set of interests and objects of concern (IV, 397–402); slightly later Queen Dulness tells them that every maggot has a collector stupid enough to appreciate it:

> Yet by some object ev'ry brain is stirr'd;
> The dull may waken to a Humming-bird;
> The most recluse, discreetly open'd, find
> Congenial matter in the Cockle-kind;
> The mind, in Metaphysics at a loss,
> May wander in a wilderness of Moss;
> The head that turns at super-lunar things,
> Poiz'd with a tail, may steer on Wilkins' wings. (IV, 445–52)

The second observation is the statement of a simple fact: Pope's own garden contained many varieties of moss.[21] It could be argued that it is one thing to place such items in their allotted place in a garden designed to show off specimens from all over the world, and another thing to elaborate grotesque theories about the date of the Flood on the basis of these items. Nevertheless, Pope can scarcely have written

[20] Levine, *Shield,* p. 121.
[21] 'Moss of Many Sorts' is included in the inventory of the grotto; see Mack, *Garden and City,* p. 259.

the last passage without some sense of this own possible complicity: a poet as self-aware as he was could not have escaped a glancing recognition that some of the activities under satiric attack lay not too many miles from his own construction of a private shrine at Twickenham. The difference is that Woodward's collectanea fed wild ideas about scriptural and secular history; Pope's ministered to a complex local piety and the invention of a personal myth surrounding his garden and his grotto.

Another visitor who was able to compare the respective collections of Sloane and Woodward was the German savant Zacharias von Uffenbach. He had enjoyed a pleasant meeting with Sloane when he came to London in 1710, when the two men looked at weapons, gems and insects amongst other objects of virtuoso interest. When Uffenbach called on Woodward, he had much more trouble gaining admission, and then finally when he did obtain access to the collection there were further affectations on the owner's part. 'Nevertheless', Levine tells us, Uffenbach 'was impressed by the collection. Besides the natural curiosities, there were all sorts of ancient urns and vases. Woodward showed them his manuscripts, the future works have so often promised. He wanted to show them he had not been "idle".'[22] This is the true duncely posture, with a demented would-be author surrounded by his fantastic dream-children:

> Round him much Embryo, much Abortion lay,
> Much future Ode, and abdicated Play...
> All that on Folly Frenzy could beget,
> Fruits of dull Heat, and Sooterkins of Wit. (IV, 121–6)

Woodward, much more than Sloane, was addicted to the ancient *per se*; the antiquity of his objects was a guarantee of their importance and value, and also the prop of many of his controversial theories.

Levine also quotes a standard character sketch of the virtuoso at large, written in 1696:

The 'virtuoso,' it began, was one who had 'abandoned the Acquaintance and Society of Man for that of Insects, Worms, Grubbs, Maggots, Fleas... he is ravish'd at finding an uncommon shell or an odd shap'd stone... he trafficks to all places and has Correspondents in ev'ry part of the World... He visits Mines, Colepits and Quarries frequently, not for... gain but for the sake of the fossile Shells and Teeth that are sometimes found there.' With the accretion of each detail, the portrait of Woodward was gradually drawn. 'He is a smatterer of botany... he is the embalmer of diseas'd Vermin, and

[22] Levine, *Shield*, pp. 123–4.

dresses his Mummyes with as much care, as the Ancient Egyptians did their Kings. His cash consists much in old Coins, and he thinks the Face of Alexander is one of 'em worth more than all his conquests.' At last the Doctor was unmistakable. 'His collection of Garden Snails, Cockle Shells and Vermine completed ... he sets up for a Philosopher and nothing less than universal Nature will serve for a Subject ... hence forward he struts and swells, and despises all those little insignificant Fellows, that can make no better use of those noble incontestable Evidences of the Universal Deluge, Scallop and Oyster Shells, than to stew Oysters or melt brimstone for Matches.' At that point, the sketch continues, he gives the world and *Essay*, defends Moses, and shakes the World to Atoms, pumping out even its center and clearing it of all imaginary loopholes in order to 'Make his Hypothesis hold Water.' Finally, the portrait concludes, 'he is a Passionate Admirer of his own Works without a Rival and superciliously contemms all Ansers, yet the least Objection throws him into Vapours.' The stock character and the real Doctor had become one, and the ironic portrait in this obscure but popular work was alarmingly close to the real one.[23]

Some of the hints offered by this passage had already been used by the Scriblerians, either in their history of the pedant from whom they took their name, or in the intellectual farces they had produced at the start of the Hanoverian era. Woodward's interest in Egyptian mummies had been utilized, for example, in *Three Hours after Marriage* (1717). But the portrait of Mummius is at once more detailed and less personal; for the satire is extended by the notes, which contain references to the historiography and mythography of the Orient. At IV, 375, a long note introduces well-known figures in French antiquarian study, Jean Francois Foy-Vaillant and Philippe Sylvestre Dufour. By this time Mummius has overtaken the single individual Woodward, but it is still safe to regard the main lineaments of the portrait as deriving from Woodward's own remarkable personality and career.

But we need to pause a moment at this stage. Do not the shells and the other objects dredged up from mines, as well as the correspondence with fellow-collectors, remind us of something? Pope's laborious efforts to fill out his own grotto have been dignified in recent criticism as a heroic quest of self-definition, and the grotto – as a sanctuary of dedicated to opposition virtue – has become almost an abstract entity.[24] Yet we should remind ourselves that it was

[23] Levine, *Shield*, pp. 125–6.
[24] See Mack, *Garden and City*, pp. 3–115. Mack prints in an appendix (pp. 259–62) an 'Account of the Materials' contained in the grotto. Borlase sent up 'giant shipments of *rare* minerals and fossils' to Twickenham (Mack, *Life*, p. 763; my emphasis).

equally a collection of rarities, that is of rare *things*, as well as an embodiment of retirement. Pope ransacked the world for mineralogical specimens, and he used William Borlase, a prime specimen himself of the antiquarian tribe, to find the choicest samples. It is a short step from this realization to move to a sense that *The Dunciad*, as set out on the page, represents a direct translation of the collector's habits into graphic terms, defined by print and white space. The poem, with its apparatus, textualizes tasteless antiquarian praxis. Indeed, the entire *Dunciad* has become a sort of cabinet of curiosities. The printed work ranges one odd specimen after another; it sorts and classifies them in verse just as Woodward tried to do in his boxes and cases; it displays the counterfeit along with the real, much as the Earl of Pembroke's coin collection did;[25] it lumps together the beautiful, the exotic, the crude and the mis-shapen, the truly ancient and the modern, all in one capacious gallery. The rhetoric serves to impale Pope's victims to allow us clearer observation of them, just as the trophy-hunters pinned up their butterflies and grubs. The footnotes label these specimens still more neatly. Together with the surrounding apparatus of prefaces, 'testimonies', royal warrants and appendices, the volume parodies a kind of crazed over-documentation which is found among the antiquarian disputes of the age.

III

Apart from Woodward, the most representative figure in the movement is perhaps William Stukeley, and he deserves some attention even though there is less evidence to connect him directly with Pope's satiric intentions.[26] Stukeley was another medical man, in fact a pupil of Dr Mead; he became a Fellow of the Royal Society in 1718 on Mead's recommendation. Isaac Newton was then President and Stukeley came to know Newton well, discussing with

---

[25] For Pembroke's coin collection, see Levine, *Shield*, pp. 284–7. Pope's scornful reference comes in the *Epistle to Burlington*:

> He buys for Topham, Drawings and Designs,
> For Pembroke Statues, dirty Gods, and Coins;
> Rare monkish Manuscripts for Hearne alone,
> And Books for Mead, and Butterflies for Sloane. (6–10)

Plainly Pope did not understand the way in which the study of material remains (including the coins and *objets d'art* which found their way into Pembroke's collection) could illuminate past civilizations.

[26] Information on Stukeley is drawn chiefly from Stuart Piggott, *William Stukeley: An Eighteenth-Century Antiquary* (London, 2nd edn, 1985).

him such matters as the dimensions of the Temple of Solomon. The next President was Sloane, for whom Stukeley made drawings of an elephant in the course of dissection (1720). Other scientific contacts in the earlier part of Stukeley's career included Halley and Wren. With more immediate relevance to Pope, he was – like the poet – a freemason. Again like Pope, he was interested in architecture, and carried out a certain amount of amateur practice in this area: he designed a Gothic bridge for the Duke of Montague (famous as an eccentric animal-lover, as Grand Master of the English freemasons, and as a leading figure in the Egyptian Society) and he devised a scheme to support a sinking pier on Westminster Bridge. He knew, and was disliked by, Thomas Hearne; he saw in manuscript John Aubrey's important collections, many of which have only reached print in very recent years. Stukeley came into contact with the egregious John Toland on the subject of Druids, which was to evolve into his own great specialism. Like Newton and Woodward, he worked out elaborate chronologies of earlier history, especially the periods described in Scripture. After his ordination in the Church of England in 1729, he came to believe that the doctrine of the Trinity had already been correctly apprehended by the ancient Egyptians, by Plato, and of course by his favourite Druids. His idea that the British Druids had migrated from Phoenicia, as soon as Tyre was founded and 'during the life of Abraham, or very soon after',[27] has significant parallels with the legend of Brutus and Troynovant – a myth at the centre of Pope's projected *Brutiad* and obliquely present in *The Dunciad*.

During his varied antiquarian career Stukeley offered up many sitting targets for Pope's satiric art. He helped to found the Society of Antiquaries in 1717 and acted as its Secretary. Early on, a major part of his reputation derived from his collection and knowledge in the field of British coins. Like Dr Arbuthnot, he became interested in ancient measurements, and invented what he called the 'cubit of the ancients' or Druidic cubit. He planned a medallic history of Britain, and kept a coin cabinet, a fact which would not be lost on the author of the verses 'To Mr Addison, Occasioned by his Dialogue on Medals'. He was a member of the Gentleman's Society of Spalding,

---

[27] Piggott, p. 99. The entire section in Piggott (pp. 79–109) shows Stukeley darting back and forth among figures who made their own contribution to Pope's work. For a possible link between Stukeley's description of Chatsworth in *Itineranium Curiosum* (1724) and Pope's picture of Timon's villa, see pp. 85–92 above.

to which Pope and Gay were likewise elected, though they took no active part in the group's doings. Stukeley also had some contact with the second Earl of Oxford and worked on a project with Humfrey Wanley, another figure well known to Pope. It might be added that in later life one of his friends was a young clergyman named William Warburton, who lived fairly close at hand. After his death, Warburton was to write a character sketch of his friend, telling Richard Hurd that 'there was in him such a mixture of simplicity, drollery, absurdity, ingenuity, superstition and antiquarianism, that he afforded me that kind of well-seasoned repast which the French call an *Ambigu*, I suppose from a compound of things never meant to meet together'.[28] It is natural to wonder whether Warburton could have given Pope some hints of this character in 1742, so well does it fit the woolliness of the collector which surround the collector figure in *The Dunciad*.

The range and daring of Stukeley's ideas are breathtaking; like others in his era he wrote on earthquakes, gout and the spleen, but he also was able to prove (*pace* Woodward) that the flood took place in autumn, and to find out 'the nature of Solomon's Temple'.[29] He discovered remains of the Druids in almost everything, including Stonehenge and the Robin Hood ballads. He made notes on the origins of letters and on Adam's pectoral; he thought there was a Roman camp at St Pancras, just as Woodward had placed a Temple of Diana under St Paul's. Yet in some ways he was a pioneer of serious modern archaeology. He was the first person to survey Stonehenge and Avebury accurately. And behind the strange quirks was a deep sense of history, and a set of lofty aims summarized in a statement he made in 1723 to the Society of Roman Knights, one of the many bodies floating on the edge of antiquarianism which proliferated in this period:

With what grief have these eyes seen the havoc, the desolation, the fate of Roman works, owing to the delusion and abominable superstition of cloyster'd nuns and fryers, what the fury of wars could not demolish, their inglorious hands have destroyed... Whilst others therefore are busying themselves to restore their Gothic Remnants, the glory is reserved for you to adorn and preserve the truly noble monuments of the romans in Britain... The business of this Society is to search for and illustrate the Roman monuments in the Brittanic Isles. The name of Knights (equites) dictates to us that travelling is part of our province and we are so far to answer our title

---

[28] Piggott, p. 152.   [29] Piggott, p. 147.

of Roman, as never to return home without conquests. We are to encounter time, Goths and barbarians...we are to fight, pro ara et focis, to save citys and citysens, camps, temples, walls, ampitheatres, monuments, roads, inscriptions, coyns, buildings, and whatever has a Roman stamp on them...The motto is Temporis utriusque vindex, which intimates to us that we are able to be the Secretarys, the interpreters and preservers of the memorials of our ancestors.[30]

This sense of the fragility of civilizations, and the need perpetually to renew ancient heritage, was not far from Pope's own. He was the sort of man Pope often found himself satirizing precisely because, with a small shift of emphasis, the attitudes Stukeley displayed might almost have been Pope's.

It might be noted in this regard that Stukeley was passionately fond of gardening, which he found as restorative as did Pope himself.

Throughout his lifetime his enthusiasm for gardening came second only to that for his antiquarian studies – he tells Gale, 'I have worked so hard in my garden as to sweat out all the London fog, am become vastly athletic...my ancient country complexion is returned to my cheeks...my lips recover their pristin red, and my own locks, moderately curled, resemble the Egyptian picture of Orus Apollo, or the emblem of rejuvenescence.'[31]

He laid out his garden as a Druidic grove and performed a ceremony there after his wife had suffered a miscarriage:

The embrio, about as big as a fillberd, I buryd under the high altar in the chapel of my hermitage vineyeard; for there I built a niche in a ragged wall oregrown with ivy, in which I placed my roman altar, a brick from Verulam, and a waterpipe sent me by my Lord Colrain from Marshland. Underneath is a camomile bed for greater ease of the bended knee, and there we enterred it, present my wifes mother, and aunt, with cermonys proper to the occasion.[32]

Bizarre though this ceremony may be, there are again obvious links with the design of Pope's garden, with its primary aim of commemorating his mother in a quasi-mythological complex of ornaments and horticultural gestures. In 1738 Stukeley built a hermitage in his garden, just as Pope was busy grottifying at Twickenham; again there is some connection with the allegories of opposition which had multiplied in Pope's circle:

A drawing survives of this charmingly whimsical structure, with niches, pointed windows and a fountain, and surmounted by a very rustic stone

---

[30] Piggott, p. 55.   [31] Piggott, p. 75.   [32] Piggott, p. 77.

arch insecurely carrying a pillar and globe, and we see it must have been very similar to the contemporary Hermitage at Richmond 'the Architecture of which is…very Gothique, being a Heap of Stones thrown into a very artful Disorder, and curiously embellished with Moss, and Shrubs, to represent *rude Nature*'.[33]

It might be objected that all this is the obverse of the inward and philosophically far richer meanings enshrined in Pope's garden, but in its simpler way Stukeley's garden fantasy represents a similar current of feeling. Pope's vision of his own philosophic retreat would not have been the same unless he had been surrounded by people with these antiquarian obsessions. He borrowed from them, and he satirized them – his usual combination of poetic deeds.

Finally, it is worth returning to the friendship with Warburton. He and Stukeley corresponded for some forty years. Even though Warburton did not make Pope's acquaintance until long after he knew Stukeley, he did so in time to serve as a possible informant for the *New Dunciad*. There could well be a very direct link, since when the Duke of Montague was admitted in 1742 to the Egyptian Society (his kinsman Sandwich, as already noted, was then President), he asked Stukeley the meaning of the sistrum which was used as an emblem of office by the Society. Stukeley was apparently able to give an account of 'the so famous Egyptian rattle', garnishing his discourse 'with an appropriate reference to Abraham and Genesis XV, which was later written out and sent to his Grace'.[34] This was the very juncture when Pope was getting ready the new book of *The Dunciad*, published two months later. It is perhaps a coincidence that the relevant passage attaches the very same verb to the sistrum:

> [Mummius,]
> Fierce as a startl'd Adder, swell'd, and said,
> Rattling an ancient Sistrum at his head.   ((IV, 373–4)

But perhaps it is not a coincidence, and perhaps Pope had an informant within the Egyptian Society.

[33] Piggott, p. 115.
[34] Piggott, p. 118. Pope's possible knowledge of the doings at the Egyptian Society deserves further investigation.

IV

It is hard to be sure how closely Pope would have identified with Stukeley's doings, even the admirable and respectable ones (as they might seem today). But he can hardly have failed to be aware of the many spheres of Stukeley's activity, especially as his own friend and neighbour Stephen Hales was another correspondent of the eccentric clergyman. As with Woodward, there are some strange convergences; and the explanation for these is that all three men pursued interests rooted in the lore of the antique. Pope indeed *could* have been an antiquarian, as Swift or Gay could not. He was far from believing, with Thomas Gray, that 'if a thing cannot be understood without notes, it had better not be understood at all'.[35] *The Dunciad* is among much else his splendid tribute to the buried scholar within him. It ravages dull scholiasts, but it incorporates the most arresting scholiastic literature of the age, along with that of Bentley and (fitfully) Theobald. It is not a very paradoxical observation that the matters about which Pope made most fun in his poetry were often very close to the subjects about which he cared most deeply.

There is anyway in much Scriblerian satire a quality of palinode. Amidst the savage onslaughts, a note of tenderness creeps in – a sense of roads that could once have been taken, but are now sealed off for ever. In Pope especially we encounter what might be termed Parthian satire, that is, a mode of attack which implies a previous renunciation of the attitudes now under assault. Few would quarrel with the view that *The Dunciad*, more than the Homer or the Shakespeare, shows Pope as potentially one of the greatest editors of his time. In the light of the material discussed here, it seems possible that the poem also constitutes a rhetorical gesture of solidarity with the goals and methods of antiquarian study, even as it assails the foolish extremes to which acolytes of the subject might go. The poem cleaves to the culture of antiquarianism, even while it makes sport of people such as Woodward and antiquarianism. Beneath its surface lies Pope's awareness that, given the slightest tilt, his grotto might have ended up infested with the insignia of Druids, like Stukeley's hermitage, or piled up with fossils, like Woodward's treasure-house of historically

---

[35] The *Correspondence of Thomas Gray*, ed. L. Whibley and P. Toynbee, revised by H. W. Starr (Oxford, 1971). Since this essay was written, Joseph M. Levine has published a new book, *The Battle of the Books: History and Literature in the Augustan Age* (Ithaca, 1991). He discusses Pope's satire of historians and grammarians in *The Dunciad*, pp. 218–44.

charged trivia. By exposing such absurdities in *The Dunciad* – both in his localized satire of the collectors, and in his wider mimicry of the collector's mind-set – Pope got these things out of his system, and was able to cleanse his own doings at Twickenham of any imputation of antiquarian foolery. The imputations might have come from his enemies, but probably they would have arisen in Pope's own heart.

In her book *On Longing*, Susan Stewart has written suggestively, if elusively, on the subject of collecting. She argues that 'the collection replaces history with *classification*, with order beyond the realm of temporality. In the collection, time is not something to be restored to an origin; rather, all time is made simultaneous or synchronous within the collection's world.' This may be true of the doings of a virtuoso and to some extent of Pope's own grottification; it does not really apply to the activities of a Woodward or a Stukeley. Stewart goes on to contend that 'the spatial organization of the collection, left to right, front to back, behind and before, depends upon the creation of an individual perceiving and apprehending the collection with eye and hand.' In the case of *The Dunciad*, it is the reader who thus perceives and thus apprehends; the 'collection' of duncely products is anatomized, not just as a series, but as a totality of concerted folly. Steward proceeds, 'In acquiring objects, the collector replaces production with consumption; objects are naturalized into the landscape of the collection itself. Therefore, stones and butterflies are made cultural by classification.' What happens in the text of *The Dunciad* is that stones and butterflies become metonyms for the illicit dreams (of knowledge, or of intellectual power) of their collectors. In addition Stewart distinguishes between the taste for souvenirs and the mania for collection: 'The souvenir magically transports us to the scene of origin, but the collection is magically and serially transported to the scene of acquisition, its proper destination.' Pope's grotto was a site for personal association and cultural souvenir; the aims of a man like Woodward were closer to those of the programmatic and *interested* collector, whose would-be classification of the world is mirrored in the over-determined form of *The Dunciad*.[36]

All these matters can be related more directly still to the sphere of antiquarianism, the enterprise which made most purposive use of the

---

[36] Stewart, pp. 151, 154–5, 156, 165. Stewart's book is sometimes confused and obscure, and its historical narratives dubious (e.g. the evolution of antiquarianism into folklore, which was just one of the streams flowing from older antiquarian study); but it contains many important insights relevant to my enquiry here.

trophies of collecting. For Stewart, 'in antiquarianism we see a theory of history informed by the aesthetics of the souvenir...In contrast to the historian, who looks for design and causality, the antiquarian searches for material evidence of the past.' She writes too of the antiquarian theme of the childhood of the nation/race: it is 'a collage made of presents rather than a reawakening of the past'.[37] Pope, I think, saw the matter a little differently. His own sense of the history of the race was a strong one, but it served largely private and literary needs, rather than those of (in modern terms) a serious historiography. He lovingly assembled fragments of history at Twickenham, and just as lovingly assembled fragments of anti-quarian zeal in the cabinet of *The Dunciad*. His collage is, pointedly and poignantly, made up of the bits and pieces of the lives of others. *The Dunciad* takes the *disjecta membra* of a study which its devotees wished to raise into a science, and reclassifies the specimens as an inventory of collective monomania. The past is restored to its private, myth-making function, that is the role it played in Pope's own career as writer, virtuoso and gardener; the general systems and large-scale theories of history called out in the fecund imagination of Woodward and Stukeley are consigned to the realm of fantasy, along with the other creations of Dulness.

[37] Stewart, pp. 140, 143, 145.

Index

Figures or topics mentioned glancingly on a single occasion are omitted. Matters relating to Pope (his works, interests, opinions etc.) are grouped under his name.